Diary of a
Jack the Kid
<u>Minecraft LitRPG</u>

An Unofficial Minecraft Series

FULL SEASON ONE!

Books 1-6

NOT OFFICIAL MINECRAFT PRODUCT.

NOT APPROVED BY OR ASSOCIATED WITH MOJANG.

Skeleton Steve

<u>www.SkeletonSteve.com</u>

Copyright

"Diary of Jack the Kid – Season ONE Box Set"

"Diary of Jack the Kid, s1e1 (Book 1)

"Diary of Jack the Kid, s1e2 (Book 2)

"Diary of Jack the Kid, s1e3 (Book 3)

"Diary of Jack the Kid, s1e4 (Book 4)

"Diary of Jack the Kid, s1e5 (Book 5)

"Diary of Jack the Kid, s1e6 (Book 6)

Published in the United States of America by Lightbringer Media LLC, 2019

To join Skeleton Steve's free mailing list, for updates about new Minecraft Fanfiction titles:

www.SkeletonSteve.com

Table of Contents

Contents

Book Introduction by Skeleton Steve

Love MINECRAFT? ****Over 156,000 words** *of kid-friendly fun!***

This high-quality fan fiction fantasy diary book is for kids, teens, and nerdy grown-ups who love to read epic stories about their favorite game!

All Six Episodes from "Jack the Kid" Season ONE in a single book!!

This Minecraft LitRPG Series will directly involve <u>YOU</u> the Reader!***

Every new episode of 'Jack the Kid' will involve a reader's suggestion coming to life, chosen from the reviews of the last book! If you'd like to see something happen to Jack, Alex, and Steve, make sure to let me know in the review comments! If you'd like to see a new character or mob or anything else, tell me in the reviews! Describe their name, stats, skin, etc., and I might put it in the next episode!

Thank you to <u>all</u> of you who are buying and reading my books and helping me grow as a writer. I put many hours into writing and preparing this for you. I *love* Minecraft, and writing about it is almost as much fun as playing it. It's because of *you*, reader, that I'm able to keep writing these books for you and others to enjoy.

This book is dedicated to *you*. Enjoy!!

After you read this book, please take a minute to leave a simple review. I really appreciate the feedback from my readers, and love to read your reactions to my stories, good or bad. If you ever want to see your name/handle featured in one of my stories, leave a review and *tell me about it* in there! And if you ever want to ask me any questions, or tell me your idea for a cool Minecraft story, you can email me at steve@skeletonsteve.com.

Are you on my **Amazing Reader List**? Find out at the end of the book!

August the 15th, 2019

For those of you who love my Jack the Kid Series, and like a good deal, enjoy this Full Season ONE Box Set! If you'd like to see me continue the adventures of Jack, Alex, Steve, and their other friends, please let me know in the review comments!

- Skeleton Steve

P.S. - Have you joined the Skeleton Steve Club and my Mailing List?? (www.SkeletonSteve.com)

P.P.S. – I've recently updated my website with the covers of the books that are *coming up!* Make sure to check it out!

You found one of my diaries!!

Well—it's not a diary of *mine*, per say, but instead something completely wacky from a different Minecraft world—a mysterious server called Vortexia. This is a mildly-modded world where Steve and Alex are living their normal Minecraftian lives until one day they're visited by the *Weird Walker*—a real, live boy stuck in the game named Jack! What would you do if *you* became stuck in Minecraft; not as a pixelated avatar of yourself, but the *real you*, body and all...?

This is the continuing LitRPG story of Jack the Kid, Steve, and Alex, and their adventures in Vortexia as Jack learns to survive in a video game. This is an adventure that includes *YOU*, and you're encouraged to participate in the review comments!

Be warned—this is an *epic book!* You're going to *care* about these characters. You'll be scared for them, feel good for them, and feel bad for them! It's my hope that you'll be *sucked up* into the story, and the adventure and danger will be so intense, you'll forget we started this journey with a *video game!*

So with that, dear reader, I present to you the tale of **Jack the Kid**, Full Season ONE...

S1E1 – "The *Weird Walker* Arrives..."

S1E2 – "One Block at a Time"

S1E3 – *"Save the Village!"*

S1E4 – "Shifting Sands"

S1E5 – "The Quest for Iron"

S1E6 – "Unwanted Guests" *Season Finale!*

Season 1, Episode 1:
The *Weird Walker* Arrives...

The Weird Walker Arrives

Jack Walker is a kid in the real world, and he's obsessed with gaming. When he finds that his school's computer lab has just installed a brand new Virtual Reality System, he can't resist sneaking a peek at it while all of the other kids are outside watching a rare solar eclipse. But when Jack finds himself suddenly transported INTO his familiar Minecraft world--real life body and all--the boy finds that he's gotten into a VR gaming experience that is a little TOO real!

Minecraftians Steve and Alex live a pretty peaceful life in their mountain home that Alex built around a mysterious anomaly she called 'the Divining Pool'. One day while repairing some creeper damage to their animal pens from the night before, Alex is perplexed when the sky suddenly darkens and a shadow passes over the sun. The Divining Pool offers cryptic words about the arrival of the Weird Walker, and when she and Steve go looking for their missing sheep, they find a strange creature like nothing they've ever seen in their blocky world before...

S1E1 - Chapter 1 - Jack

Running to the edge of the bedrock Divining Pool, Alex wiped her eyes and stared into the blue waters within. The torchlight on the water's surface shimmered...

Then, hazy white words gradually formed inside, which Alex slowly read aloud...

"The time of the Weird Walker has begun..."

"Okay, you two get ready!" Mom said suddenly.

Jack looked up from his Minecraft book, pulling out of the adventures of the *Skull Kids*. The Minecraftian characters were fighting off a bunch of zombies that had invaded their home while they were away.

Pff. Zombies, Jack thought. *How hard could it be to fight zombies?*

Normally, Jack would rather *play* Minecraft than read about Minecraft any day of the week, but he didn't have his *computer* in the family van, so...

He did have his *game pendant* around under his shirt around his neck. Closing the book and setting it aside, Jack felt at the little USB flash drive on the necklace against his chest with a smile. He would be playing Minecraft in the school's computer lab soon enough...

The boy looked ahead into the rear-view mirror to see Mom's eyes looking back at him and his little brother as she slowed the van down, pulling over to the side of the school. All of the little kids from the elementary grades were already running toward their classroom doors. Jack's sixth-grade classroom would be all the way around the corner of the building, but Mom always dropped him off next to Dexter's class door so that Jack could make sure that his little brother got to his classroom first.

"Ready!" Dexter exclaimed from his booster seat. Jack didn't have to ride in one of those boosters anymore. He was too big. He hadn't used a booster seat in a long time now, but Dexter was still small. Jack was pretty small himself for a twelve-year-old—shorter than most other kids in his class—but at least he didn't need a *booster*...

The van glided to a stop next to the curve.

"Hey, Mom, what about the permission slips?" Jack asked, suddenly remembering the forms were still sitting up in the front seat.

"Oh yeah!" his mom said, making the lever behind the steering wheel go *ca-chunk* as they stopped. She reached over and grabbed two papers. They would need those sheets to be able to watch the solar eclipse today.

Jack unbuckled his seatbelt and jumped to his feet, grabbing his *Avengers* backpack. Squeezing between the seats, he rushed up to where Mom's hand held both forms for him and his brother. Taking them both from her grip, he kept the one with his name on it and gave Dexter the other.

"Mom, we're gonna make *box things* to look at the sun with!" Dexter exclaimed with a broad grin. "There's a solar eclipse!"

"It's kinda cool, I guess..." Jack added.

"I know, baby. Have fun and listen to your teacher," she replied with a warm smile.

Smirking, Jack hugged his mom and backed away to let Dex get a hug, too. He opened the sliding side door of the van, making it lock back.

"Love you, Jack!" Mom said, calling out while hugging Dex. "Dexter, don't look at the sun without your teacher's help, okay? I don't want you to go blind."

"Okay!" Dex said, pulling away from the hug and slipping his backpack on over his narrow shoulders.

Jack looked out over the playground. Part of him wanted to go nuts out there and climb and swing—if there was still time—but he also knew that he was getting too big for that now. His school had both elementary grades and middle grades in the same place. All of the sixth, seventh, and eighth graders hung out on the other side of the building during breaks. Just last year—in fifth grade—Jack was still playing on the huge playground full of cool equipment in front of him with the younger kids. But now, he was *too old*. He was almost a teenager!

"You too, Jack!" Mom added. "Don't look at the sun without protection! You can go blind!"

"Alright, Mom," Jack said, rolling his eyes. *Duh.* He adjusted his glasses, which were slipping down his nose a little.

"Oh, and *hey*, you too, make sure you're standing here right after school today, okay? I'm gonna pick you up right after the bell. Joel has a soccer game. "

"Alright, mom," both boys muttered.

"Seriously, Jack," Mom said. "No playing in the computer lab after school! Be *here*—got it?"

"Okay, Mom!" Jack said.

"Love you, boys!"

"Love you too!"

Jack and Dexter jumped down from the van onto the sidewalk. Jack adjusted his glasses and his backpack, then closed the door. With one last wave, Mom drove away, and the two boys turned to face the playground. Most of the kids were already waiting in line at their doors.

"I wanted to *play*," Dexter whined.

Jack shrugged and gave his little brother a shove. When Dex looked up at him confused, Jack grinned, making the smaller boy smile too.

"Let's go, Dex."

The two of them ran down the mound from the sidewalk, across the corner of the playground, and joined the hordes of other little kids lining up at the doors. Just like they did every day, the two boys found Dexter's classroom, and Jack's little brother got in line after a quick hug from the older boy.

"See ya, Jack!" Dex exclaimed with a big smile, then immediately turned to his friend Melody in line. "Hey, don't look at the sun without the box-thing or you'll go *blind!*"

"Pff—*I know that!*" the little girl replied, crossing her arms over her chest.

"Bye," Jack said, putting his hand on his brother's shoulder for an instant, then he took off, running as fast as he could past the playground, then around the edge of the field and the building to the opposite side where the big kids would be.

Jack was fast. He loved how fast he was. He was shorter than most other kids in his class—even though he was older than some of them—but he could run like the wind!

On the other side of the building, a lot of the older kids were taking their time getting to class—especially the eighth graders—but the big kids didn't line up like the little ones did. Jack ran for the door to the hall that would lead to his classroom from the inside. He knew a quicker way to get to class, but he always went this way because it let him pass by the computer lab. Today Mom had been running late getting them to school, but normally whenever they'd get here with a little time to spare, while Dex played on the playground with the little kids, Jack would plug his *game pendant* into his favorite computer in the computer lab and play five or ten minutes of Minecraft before class...

Now, as he approached the computer lab, he saw several older kids lingering around the outside, chatting excitedly.

"Why does there have to be just *one* of them?" one guy said. "They need at least two to play multiplayer games. It's *stupid*..."

"Cause it's not for games, dummy," another replied. "You don't play games in school."

"I do," the other kid muttered, staring through the windows of the lab.

I do too, Jack thought with a smile. He approached the door, pushing through a crowd of kids, then reached down and pulled it open just like most mornings. The latch stuck a little but popped open. What Jack saw inside made him *gasp*...

The computer lab was empty, save for Mr. Hayes. The normal rows of computers on long tables were there like any other day, but there was something *new* on one corner that took up a lot of space! It reminded Jack of something from the arcade at the mall—kind of like that *dance* game—but also not. It was more complicated than an arcade game. There was a thick pad on the floor—likely for standing on—and a half-enclosure with a single wide computer monitor built into a curved wall. Jack saw a bunch of cables. There were also two joystick-type-things on the table next to the keyboard as well as some kind of *virtual reality headset* hanging from a hook near the monitor. The entire system was black and dark grey with bright blue and yellow lettering on one curved wall:

Vortex Wave Virtual Reality System 1.0.

"Virtual reality??" Jack said to himself, standing half-inside the room as the other kids chatted and pressed in around and behind him. "Whoa...!"

"What are you doing in here?" Mr. Hayes said suddenly, standing and frowning down at Jack. "The door was locked! The computer lab is closed until later today!"

"It was locked?" Jack asked, looking down at the door handle still in his hand. He looked up again as Mr. Hayes approached. Mr. Hayes was his friend. Jack spent a lot of time in here. "Sorry, sir..."

"Come in here, Jack," Mr. Hayes said. "Close the door behind you."

"Hey I wanna come in and see it too!" an older boy cried from behind Jack.

"*Nobody's* gonna see it until later!" Mr. Hayes replied. "Now come in, Jack."

Jack obliged, closing the door behind him. Immediately, the noise of the kids in the hall quieted down. The computer lab teacher smiled down at the boy and fiddled with the door's lock a little.

"What's that for?" Jack asked. "It's virtual reality—I can see that."

"Dang sticky lock," Mr. Hayes muttered, then he looked back at Jack, then the VR system. "Oh, for *science*," he exclaimed. "We have programs in there that'll let students experience what it would be like to be on a space station, or to travel to Egypt or Europe, and some other good stuff."

14

"Neat," Jack said. He eyed the impressive piece of equipment. His *game pendant* around his neck seemed to almost *burn* on his chest; he wanted to plug it into there so badly. "Are there any actual *games* on there?"

"No way!" Mr. Hayes said with a laugh.

"Would games be *able* to run on there?"

The teacher shrugged. "Probably. It's just a computer like any other. It just has a fancier monitor, basically, and other kinds of controllers ... and sensors. It's actually *really cool*." Mr. Hayes sighed and smiled at the new Vortex Wave for a moment, then shook his head and looked down at Jack again. "Now—it's time for class, Jack," Mr. Hayes said. "You'd better get to first period."

"Can't I try it out?"

"Not now," the teacher replied with a chuckle. "Of *course* not. That wouldn't be fair to all of them out there..." Mr. Hayes pointed at the many faces in the windows glaring at them and drooling over the VR system. "I'm going to open up the lab after the solar eclipse. The eighth grade classes are going to experience the Vortex first, so it'll be a while, but ... I bet I can find a turn for you sometime today," he said with a smirk. "Now get to class."

"Yes sir."

With that, Jack took one last long look at the new VR system, then opened the door and plunged back into the loud chaos and crowds of kids getting to class.

He wondered what playing *Minecraft* would be like on a fancy virtual reality rig like that...

Jack sat at his desk looking up at the clock.

It was almost lunchtime.

The boy was hungry, but he didn't care. All he wanted to do was play with that new virtual reality system. It was too bad that all of the older kids would be playing with it after the eclipse. Heck—there was only one for the whole school! That thing had to be the coolest thing ever, and he would hardly ever get to touch it; especially *today*, since he couldn't stay after school because of his older brother's stupid *soccer game*...

Jack looked back to his desk and stared at the lame *pinhole projector* he'd made for himself for viewing the solar eclipse. What a jip. It was just a cardboard box with foil and white paper. He wouldn't even be looking at the sun. They were all just going to look into their boxes and watch the solar eclipse project light onto the white paper inside...

Ugh. He wanted to play Minecraft on the Vortex Wave...

"Okay, let's go!" his teacher exclaimed to the class, snapping Jack out of his sour thoughts.

"Are we going to lunch now?" one of the girls asked. "Should we leave our projectors here?"

The teacher, Ms. Sanderson, put her hands on her hips and smiled broadly at the class. "Everyone take your projectors and *follow me*. All classes are going outside to see the solar eclipse. *Then* we're going to go to lunch, okay?"

The entire class stood and the room was filled with sounds of murmuring students and shoved chairs. Jack stood and picked up his projector to take with him.

"Now—all of the classes in the *whole school* will be heading outside, so everyone follow me *single file* through the hall," she added. "And remember—don't look directly at the sun! The eclipse will be starting very soon and it will be dangerous to look

16

at! When we get to our spot outside, we'll all stand with our backs to the sun and look through the projectors, okay? Everyone understand?"

The students all murmured in agreement.

"Yes, Ms. Sanderson," Jack said automatically. This was boring. Science was cool, and knowledge about astronomy and planets and stars and the universe was all really great stuff, but watching the sun move slowly on a piece of paper was going to be *really boring...*

Jack sighed and gradually joined the group of students that were all crowding around the door as Ms. Sanderson waited to open the way to the hall. When she did, Jack saw one of the seventh grade classes walking past. He looked down at his cardboard box in his hands then back up again as they waited...

Eventually, Ms. Sanderson led them out into the hall. The class started toward the outer doors.

Jack was so bored and wished that he could just go to lunch instead, scarf some food down super-fast, then spend the rest of his free time playing Minecraft until next period.

He sighed, remembering that the lab would be closed anyway...

As bored and disappointed as he was, Jack found himself following his class, trailing along at the back of his class's line. He followed Ms. Sanderson and his class down the turning halls until they were walking down the long one toward the outer door where he'd come in that morning. Craning his neck, Jack saw a line of eighth graders up ahead of them, almost at the door. Looking back, he saw that the halls behind him were mostly-abandoned. It was strange to see the school so *empty...*

When his class passed the computer lab, Jack lingered for a moment to peer through the window. He saw the Vortex Wave Virtual Reality System 1.0 standing there in all of its glory, all alone and all by itself at the end of a table lined with the school's normal, old computers. Stretching to see around the corner of the window, Jack didn't see Mr. Hayes at his desk. The computer lab's lights were off.

The briefest fantasy of playing Minecraft on that system—feeling like he was *inside the game*—invited Jack to linger a little longer. He stared at the Vortex Wave with a broad grin...

Then Jack suddenly snapped back to reality when he realized that he was seriously lagging behind his class! With a gasp, he looked to the back of the line and saw that they were all walking along without him. He had to catch up, or he'd be left behind...

The boy looked down at the cardboard projector in his hands.

Looking back down the hall deeper into the school, Jack saw that—aside from his class way ahead of him—he was *alone*...

The *craziest* idea suddenly came over him...

Reaching out, feeling a thrill sweep through him like cold water, Jack reached out to the door handle of the closed computer lab. He turned the latch. The lock stuck a little, then *popped* open...

He gasped again, looking once more at his disappearing class...

Could I? he thought with a grin. *Could I really??*

He was terrified. And excited as heck!

So bad! Jack thought. *So much trouble!*

Jack stared through the window at the VR system. The *game pendant* in his shirt felt like it was burning on his chest...

He looked back at his class—they hadn't noticed him lagging behind. He looked down the hall the other way...

Then Jack did the crazy-bad thing.

He slipped into the computer lab and closed the door behind him.

With his heart hammering in his chest, Jack rushed up to the VR system, tossing his cardboard box projector down onto a nearby desk, forgotten. With reverence, the boy stepped onto the dark-grey platform with wide eyes and looked around at all of the pieces...

Jack knew his way around computers and tech.

Yes, there was the monitor. It was probably for navigating the operating system into whatever program the lab was trying to run. It would probably also double as a 'mirrored' monitor showing whatever the person wearing the headset was seeing, right? He looked down at the keyboard. Jack picked up the two controllers. They were both wireless, handheld joysticks that would let him navigate through programs inside the VR.

Jack looked around for the CPU and he found it near the floor. It was off.

Reaching down, Jack pressed the computer's power button. The monitor lit up and went through a normal computer's boot-up procedure, eventually loading the operating system. Jack saw a variety of educational VR programs on the desktop.

Looking down at the computer's tower again, the boy searched for some USB ports and quickly found them.

He smiled, pulling his *game pendant* off from around his neck. His necklace was a unique flash drive permanently loaded with a copy of Minecraft. There was storage on the device set up in a way that Jack could save games, and he'd modded his *game pendant's* Minecraft slightly with some basic things: letting torches cast light without having to be stuck in a wall, putting a health bar over the heads of mobs, showing how much damage he did when he hit a mob—little things. Jack liked to keep his game pretty *vanilla*. He only added mods that made the game more convenient. The *most important thing* about his pendant, however, was that it could *autoplay* and run *itself* on any computer he plugged it into...

Jack regularly played Minecraft in the computer lab on whatever computer was available. He had his favorite computer of course, but it didn't really matter. His necklace was *plug and play*.

Joel, his sixteen-year-old brother, had given Jack the *game pendant* two years ago for his birthday. It was Jack's favorite thing. It was a *great* birthday present...

Smiling, Jack held the flash drive portion of his necklace and looked down at the USB ports on top of the Vortex Wave's CPU. He gave one last frightful glance out of the computer lab windows and saw the halls empty. The building was *very* quiet and Jack could hear students making noise and chatting and laughing outside. He looked through the outer windows and saw classes standing around together in the grass out there, far away.

It was strangely dark outside, like on a really stormy day.

Looking back at the Vortex Wave Virtual Reality System 1.0, Jack bent down and plugged his *game pendant* into an open USB port. Just like on all other computers, Jack watched the operating system recognize his drive and eventually run the program. And just like on other computers, Jack logged into the game with his handle *Weirdwalker000* and navigated Minecraft's menu to where he could play.

"A new game," the boy said to himself, "for a *new* experience..."

Jack didn't put in a game seed or anything. He let the program create the new world randomly. He typed in ... *Vortexia* ... naming the new game after the Vortex Wave.

"Is that a little lame?" he said to himself. "Vortexia?"

Then Jack shrugged and clicked 'create world'. He quickly (but carefully) pulled the VR headset off of its hook as the game started working to parse and put together a new world. Jack slipped the headset over his head, immediately covering his eyes with a dark screen and feeling headphones rest against his ears. The rig was a little loose, but he quickly found the adjustment areas and tightened it down.

Now blind, the boy reached out to where he remembered the joysticks sitting. He found them and—feeling at the various buttons—he held the things in his hands in the way they felt like they were supposed to be.

With his heart pounding and his face feeling stretched by a massive smile, Jack waited, holding the controls, staring at the black screen...

He wondered if he'd missed something about turning on the headset, but then heard the soft, peaceful Minecraft music playing in his ears.

As he waited, he heard kids' voices outside exclaiming sounds of surprise and wonder...

Was he missing something cool? How could looking at a solar eclipse on a piece of paper be that cool...?

He heard a teacher's voice say from outside, "Here it comes!"

Nothing was happening.

Then, as soon as Jack was about to take the headset off to check the monitor, the screen in front of Jack's eyes suddenly *lit up*, almost blinding him with the light of day! There was a bright blue sky and bold, green grass! Jack appeared in Minecraft in a mountain valley—it looked like a *wooded forest* biome—with no mobs or animals around him. He turned his head to look to the right and watched the Minecraft world move around him. He saw the sun rising in what had to be the east.

Jack laughed. As his head shook from it, his vision moved around.

"Awesome!" he exclaimed, suddenly hushing himself, remembering that he was sneaking into the computer lab and could get into *serious trouble*. "How do I ... move?" he said, playing with the controllers in his hands. He found a control stick under his left thumb that let him suddenly *surge* forward. "Whoa!"

Stopping, Jack took a moment to look around again. This was awesome! The resolution was great, and he didn't feel dizzy or anything—it was like *really* being in the game!

He heard a little *crunch* sound on his left and quickly spun to seek out its source. He saw a rabbit hopping around in the distance. Trying to walk toward the animal—not too fast on the stick!—Jack smiled at the sound of his own footsteps. He lifted the controllers in his hands and saw his blocky *Minecraftian* hands moving around where his real hands were in reality. The digital hands were coated in Jack's custom skin: something he'd created on *Skindex* that looked like a dark ninja with hi-tech armor and glowing red trim and a demonic face. He watched his black and red hands and arms move as he whirled the controllers around...

"So cool!"

Then something odd happened.

Without warning, the sky suddenly grew dark. Jack had seen time pass in this game in fast-forward before, and this wasn't that. He looked back to the sun—still amazed at how cool it was to look around—and saw that the brilliant block of light in the sky was covered by a *shadow*. The shadow was also square, and by the time Jack looked up, he was that it was mostly covering the sun. A moment later, the eclipse was complete!

"What the...?!" Jack muttered to himself, staring at the Minecraft sun in a full solar eclipse. He'd never seen *that* before. Was it a mod that he didn't remember installing?

As the boy stared at the blocky sun covered in blocky shadow, the brilliant lines of light shining around the gloom increased in intensity until it *flared*, suddenly blinding Jack and hurting his eyes!

He looked away, down at the green, pixelated grass. Jack's eyes burned. He saw a huge, black block in the way of his vision, which grew until he couldn't see a thing! Then the ground under Jack seemed to fall away, making his stomach *flip-flop* and his whole body shudder in terror!

The boy felt himself drop the controllers.

Jack reached up for the headset, his heart pounding with fear, his head swimming and feeling like it was swirling over and over—like he was tumbling; falling! The boy lost track of what he was doing and gasped, unable to hear himself because of a roar in his ears! Jack was falling! His stomach flipped around and he was choked with terror just like that time he went on the *Tower of Doom* ride at the carnival; that grownup ride that carried people to the top of a tall column and *dropped* them back down to the bottom! Jack felt for the headset over his eyes and ears. He couldn't see—everything was black—but he could *feel* his head, his hair, and ... his glasses...

Where was the headset?!

Then Jack fell down.

He assumed that in his freak-out—in the malfunction of the headset—he'd fallen down to the grey platform where he was standing, but the floor felt *weird* under his hands. It felt spongy and like he was touching a rippled blanket covered with bits of cellophane...

Jack could still hear—even after that terrifying falling sensation—and he noticed that his surroundings were quiet again. Jack heard the *crunch* of the same rabbit hopping around on his left.

Gradually, the pitch-black blockage in front of his eyes faded. Slowly, the color came back into the world, and Jack found himself still in Minecraft.

Was he still wearing the headset?! Reaching up, he couldn't feel it. Jack felt his hair. His glasses were slipping, so he reached up and pushed them up the bridge of his nose.

Then he realized that he was staring at his hands...

His *real* hands.

"What?!" Jack exclaimed, jumping to his feet.

He looked down and realized that he was standing on his own *real* feet and legs. His shoes were planted on a *Minecraft* ground—one foot in pixelated grass, the other on a black block that looked like *obsidian*.

"What the heck?!"

The boy looked up at the sun—ready to shield his eyes if it still hurt him—and saw the bright, square sun low in the sky. There was still a sliver of shadow slipping away from it, as if there had also been a solar eclipse in his Minecraft world and it was now passing...

A moment later, the eclipsing shadow completely vanished and Jack was left looking up at a typical Minecraft blocky sun.

The sky was bright and blue and huge, blocky transparent clouds lazily crossed over far above. Low mountains rolled all around Jack, built of blocks as high as his family's kitchen table back home and covered in vivid green grass with thin, pixelated clusters waving in the wind. Jack recognized Spruce and Oak trees around him. He recognized them, of course, because he played a lot of Minecraft and knew the game backwards and forwards.

But now, he was *in it*...

Jack looked down at his hands again. He looked over his whole body—his black 'gamer' t-shirt, his favorite pants, his new shoes that he loved—he was *really in here!* He wasn't a Minecraftian or a blocky *Steve*-type character. He was a real boy of flesh and blood! He had glasses, for goodness sake! Jack was hungry—it was time for lunch! And he was stuck in ... *oh gosh* ... was he trapped in a video game?!

Suddenly too terrified to move, Jack looked all around him. He peered down at the obsidian block next to him, squinting his eyes. Why was *that* there?! *That* wasn't normal...

Normal! Jack thought with a startling laugh. He heard his voice echo across the blocky hills. Had he gone crazy?! Looking to his left, the boy saw the little, brown blocky rabbit hop away from him. It had heard his laugh and fled.

Oh gosh—what was he going to do?!

Jack was stuck *inside* Minecraft...

Fear flushed through the boy. His heart pounded and he looked at his familiar paradise with wide, frightened eyes.

25

Suddenly something deep inside Jack calmed his heart and reminded him of how much he *loved* this world. He knew everything about it!

Then Jack smiled. He was ... stuck inside Minecraft!

S1E1 - Chapter 2 - Alex

"What a beautiful morning," Alex said.

Putting her hands on her hips, the Minecraftian stood tall and stretched, tilting her face up at the bright, blue sky. She smiled at the warmth of daylight. A soft breeze blew through the gulch of Alex and Steve's homestead, tossing the woman's orange-red hair back from her shoulders. She smiled then turned and frowned again at the huge hole in the fence. Alex picked up the iron hoe again.

"*Moo,*" one of the cows said from nearby.

Alex smiled over at the cow—a big white cow with deep brown spots—who looked dumbly back at her from behind the wooden rails of its pen. Then she looked back again to the gaping hole in the sheep enclosure and the big crater in the dirt and grass under it.

She scowled.

Oh, Steve, Alex thought. Now all of their sheep were missing. *Why is he always screwing around and breaking things?!*

So far this morning, she'd spent her time collecting what she could salvage from their farm's rows of wheat when Steve ran off to find the missing sheep. Fortunately, some of the grain was still on the ground, scattered around and somehow uneaten by the sheep that had escaped.

There was tons of work to do and where was Steve?! Was he *really* looking for the sheep? Or was he off getting sidetracked and running around on some fool adventure, soon to get himself killed and lose more of their gear?!

Now Alex was left to fix the damage caused by *Steve's* recklessness...

The woman growled as she tilled the fresh dirt, trying to get their wheat rows back to the way they were before the creeper blew up last night. Heck—that creeper would have never blown up if Steve didn't feel the need to run outside and try to kill it! If he'd just stayed in bed instead of rushing out into the night to challenge the mob, the creature would have just wandered off eventually.

At least when Steve blew himself up they didn't lose any of their stuff this time, being right outside the house. The only problem was that the creeper also took out part of their farm and destroyed a whole section of fencing that had been holding in their *sheep*.

Now the sheep were gone.

And sure—Steve regenerated like he always did and was more than happy to run right outside and grab the stuff he'd dropped, but did he stick around to help repair the damage in the morning?

"Nope!" Alex muttered, striking the dirt extra-hard with her hoe.

The senseless jerk left *her* to do the work. Her friend went running off into the woods to find the sheep himself.

That was hours ago...

Alex sighed. They should have stayed together; fixed the farm and the fence together, then gone looking for the sheep together. Alex was much better at dealing with the animals than Steve was. What was he thinking?!

"He *wasn't* thinking..." Alex said to herself.

"Moo," another cow added.

Looking up with a smile, Alex wiped her face with a dirty hand and considered all of the farm animals. With the exception of a few chickens, they were all watching her work. Alex laughed. It was probably the wheat in her bag and the seeds in her pouch that captured the animals' attention. Every time she prepared and tilled a new block of dirt where the broken wheat row used to be, she stopped to plant new seeds.

Pausing again, Alex looked out over the surrounding countryside. She'd built this house and farm—what they call *the homestead*—in a moderate-sized gulch in between a mountain ridge and some forested hills. The mountains extended for quite a ways in all directions except for one side—Alex could never remember *which* side—and the forest was dense and thick. They were fairly close to a village. It was on the other side of that ridge, although—looking up and down the long mountain ridge—she wasn't sure exactly *where*. She and Steve were also fortunate enough to have a nice mountain stream passing through the gulch on the other side of the farm which they used for water. Back when the two of them had been looking for a place to build on, the stream was part of why she'd chosen this gulch. It wasn't the *main* reason, but it was a definite perk of the area...

It was a nice place.

Feeling the morning sun warm on her face again, Alex sighed and smiled.

Steve. Jeez...

Alex looked around the wooded areas she could see from where she stood in the farm and saw no sign of her Minecraftian friend. He'd probably be distracted from finding the sheep by now, and was off exploring a cave or something instead...

Still, Steve had his good points. He was one *heck* of a warrior. He was also good at bringing Alex whatever resources she needed—assuming he could keep on task and not go running off on some sidetracked adventure. Steve could fight—boy, could he fight! When he was around, Alex was never afraid of zombies or skeletons or other mobs sneaking up on them and causing trouble.

She frowned down at the crater again.

Well—except for that creeper, she thought. As awesome of a swordsman Steve was, he didn't always win *all* of the fights. When he went charging outside to kill that creeper last night, he must have missed at a critical time or something, because that weird, green mob blew Steve to smithereens...

"Six sheep gone," she said. "No more wool."

"*Moo*," a cow said.

Alex worked at the wheat row and soon finished the last block, tilling and seeding. Then—since she didn't like the look of the repaired area being empty and seeded while the rest of the field flowed with waving and tall, golden wheat—Alex took the time to harvest the entire crop and re-seed the other rows, too.

A short time later, she brought the hoe back to the chest at the farm-side door of the house, where she kept the gardening and animal-tending tools. Opening the chest with a *creak*, she carefully placed the iron hoe into the container next to her shovel, sheep shears, and a good collection of seeds and animal feed. The chest was out of fencing material. It looked like the last time they extended the cow pen, they never replaced the fence poles and rails with more.

She'd have to make more fencing.

In the meantime, Alex figured that she may as well feed the animals. Pulling out the salvaged wheat from her pack and the seeds she had left over, she grabbed whatever additional food she needed from the chest—as well as a couple of bright orange carrots—and put it all into her pack.

Closing the chest, Alex clapped the dirt off of her hands, sighed, and looked at her finished work. The wheat field was repaired and the newly-seeded rows looked totally back to normal. She still needed to fill in the holes left where the fence had been blown up and repair the fence itself, but if she hurried, she'd probably be done by lunchtime—maybe a little bit afterwards.

"Who's hungry?" Alex exclaimed, walking up to the animal pens that hadn't been damaged in the explosion.

Cows, chickens, and a pair of pigs all came stamping and scurrying up to the oak fence rails closest to her. They were all excited and hungry and pushed and shoved each other, trying to be the closest to Alex when the food came out.

Pulling out handfuls of wheat, Alex smiled at the cows.

"Moo!" they said, plodding around on their heavy hooves. The little calf that had been born recently crowded around the fence rails with the adults. It called out to Alex with a smaller, higher-pitched sound that always made her laugh.

"No need to shove!" she said, giving a handful of wheat to the first mouth closest to her. "There's plenty for everyone!"

After feeding the cows, Alex moved on to the next pen, casting grass seed out over the bustling crowd of loud, clucking chickens as they hopped and pushed through each other, scratching at the dirt and pecking at the seeds that landed.

Finally, Alex moved on to the pig pen and gave a carrot to each of the big, pink pigs that snorted and stamped around inside. She and Steve had harvested some of the pigs recently, and she hoped that the two remaining would breed more soon.

When the animals were all fed and she'd filled their water troughs, Alex brought the remaining seeds and wheat back to the gardening chest. She put all of the seeds and half of the wheat in there. The other half she'd put in the kitchen. Before this morning, Alex hadn't been planning on grinding the wheat to make bread any time soon, but that was okay—they were low on bread anyway.

Letting herself in through the small spruce-wood door on the farm-side of the house, Alex stomped the dirt off of feet to keep from tracking it in. Heading into the kitchen, she smiled, looking at all of her handiwork. She'd built this house out of oak and pine with a stone foundation. It took days of her crafting and building, and Steve ranged out from the gulch time and time again to collect more wood and stone and fight off all of the native mobs in the area to keep them safe.

Walking into the kitchen, Alex put the rest of the wheat harvest into the dry goods chest, then headed out through the farm door again, grabbing an axe on the way from the gear room.

Looking out across the woods and the ridge again, she wondered what Steve was doing.

Probably out looking for creepers, she thought, *or exploring a cave, of wrestling giant spiders or something...*

She was hungry.

Lunch soon, she thought. She had to finish the fence. In case Steve actually *was* out there looking for the six lost sheep, they'd need a complete pen whenever—*if* ever—he brought them back home.

Alex looked across the farm along the ridge. She had no idea which direction she was looking, but chances were pretty good that the woods up ahead would just lead to more and more rolling, low mountains and lots of trees.

Where are those sheep? she thought.

She should be the one out looking for them. The animals listened to her much better than they listened to Steve. Alex tended to them every day and—even though they rarely bothered to *name* the animals—she knew each of those six sheep well.

Movement suddenly caught Alex's eye and she looked up to the big ridge behind the house to see the fleeting form of Steve running by far away in the distance. Yep—that was him, alright. The sunlight glinted on his iron armor and she saw the shadows his helmet and of the sword in his hand.

What was he doing...?

"Looking for sheep, I hope..." she said to herself.

Then Alex heard a *ba-ah-ah-ah* from the woods somewhere nearby. She looked toward the sound, into the forest on her left.

That had to be one of their sheep! It was somewhere below the ridge, *that way* off of the homestead...

The animal was somewhere past the edge of the gulch— maybe along the stream. Were the sheep just inside the woods near the water? That would make sense. Alex could imagine them just standing around eating grass, drinking from the stream deep inside the trees...

The woman looked down at the axe in her hand.

"I need to get some wood *anyway*," she said.

Running back to the gardening chest, Alex pulled out several sheaves of wheat. If she found the sheep, she would need some food to help her bring them home. She closed the chest with a *creak* then looked past the animal pens at the dark woods.

Alex instantly felt nervous and put her free hand on the hilt of the iron sword on her belt...

With that, trying to ignore her fear, Alex ran across the farm to the stream at the other end and followed the water around the edge of the crops and animal pens toward where she'd heard the sheep's call. At the edge of their property, Alex paused, looking back at the house she'd built, her farm, and the fences full of cows, pigs, and chickens.

She turned and peered into the distant woods.

From the darkness ahead, she heard another *ba-ah-ah-ah*.

Alex sighed and shook her head trying to clear the rising fear from her mind...

"It's okay," she said, looking down at the creek. "You've got the stream. If you get lost, just follow the stream back home."

That could work, she thought in response, *or it might take you the other direction, deeper and deeper into the mountains*...

A cold dread boiled up inside Alex. Steve *always* found his way home. He must know this whole area backwards and forwards, but Alex didn't know anything about the woods outside of their house and farm. It wasn't like she didn't try to keep track of things. She just couldn't ever remember what was what or where was where.

"Might get lost..." she muttered, looking into the dark woods full of oak and thick with dark spruce trees.

You always get lost, she thought.

Then she heard the sound of the sheep again. Yep. It was definitely somewhere up ahead in the woods...

Looking up at the ridge again, Alex wished that Steve was there. She hoped for him to suddenly appear looking down at her so that she could wave at him and call him down to join her. She really needed him to go in there with her...

But he didn't appear.

With a big *sigh*, Alex tried to shake the fear from her heart and mind and stepped into the shadows of the forest.

The ground was thick with tall grasses and crunched under her feet. In the shade of the trees, Alex felt the chill of the mountains sweep through her and shuddered. Gripping her axe tightly and feeling the hilt of her sword again to make herself feel better, she slowly walked deeper into the woods, following the trickling stream. The water was deep blue in the dark of the forest.

There were so many shadows everywhere!

Alex looked back and saw that she'd only stepped about ten feet into the forest, out of the sunshine.

Up ahead, she could see the ground rise and fall, covered with trees all over. The forest was a painting of sunshine and shadow, green and dark with areas here and there of daylight cutting through as brightly as it did on her farm.

"There could be mobs here," she said quietly, listening for the sheep and staring ahead, searching for movement. She hoped to see something white moving up ahead—one of her missing animals—but only saw more trees...

The stream wound into the woods, curving around the bottom of the ridge's slope until disappearing around a bend far ahead.

Steeling her nerves and trying to ignore her pounding heart, Alex suddenly ran forward along the side of the stream, finally stopping at an open area full of sunshine.

At least in the sun, zombies wouldn't be able to reach her without catching on fire...

Skeletons can still shoot you from the shadows, she thought, then grimaced.

Staring ahead, Alex hoped to see the sheep. She didn't.

Reaching into her pack, the woman took out a handful of wheat. The sheep *had* to be around here somewhere! She'd heard it! It couldn't have gone far—it had to be next to the water, right?

Alex gasped when she realized how far she had run into the woods. She looked backwards, suddenly terrified that her farmlands would be out of sight. She could still see the house and the farm, just *barely* in the brilliant daylight outside of the forest.

"That's the way," she said. "That's the way home. Don't get lost. Don't get—"

Suddenly the sky darkened.

It darkened *fast*. Alex had never seen something like this happen before and looked up into the sky with a gasp...

"What the heck?!" she said.

From where she was standing in a small clearing, the sun was barely peeking at her through the tops of a bunch of spruce trees. Now, the sun was quickly being covered by a strange, moving *shadow* that blotted out its light.

Alex felt a cold chill run up her spine. She wondered for a moment if the woods this direction from her house were *haunted* or something—if this darkness had been waiting for her to finally leave home without Steve to help her...

No, she thought. *That's stupid.*

But the fear was real. Looking back at the homestead, she saw that the entire world around her was darkening as if it was suddenly *nighttime*. The bright, sunny farmlands disappeared and she could only barely see the yellow, flickering light of their torches on the fence posts and outside the side door.

Looking up at the sun again, Alex gasped when blazing slivers of light—almost blinding to look at—made her turn away. Her eyes hurt.

Then, just as suddenly as the sky had darkened, it began to lighten again, going from black to dark blue like just the night just before dawn. Then everything finally back to normal.

Alex heard the *clunk* of a skeleton's bones from somewhere in the woods.

"Dang!" she cried, fear sweeping through her like a cold wind.

She dropped the wheat to the ground, turned, and ran as fast as she could through the shadowy forest. Alex followed the stream and popped back out into the sunshine a moment later at the edge of their property.

Running until near the gardening chest again—those skeletons could shoot their arrows pretty far—she finally stopped near the cows and looked up at the sky and the sun.

"Moo," a cow said.

The sun was normal again. All traces of that weird shadow-thing were gone...

"What the heck *was* that?!" Alex said to herself.

The sky was normal. Clouds floated by far overhead...

Alex turned to the house, her mouth hanging open as she thought about...

"The Divining Pool!" she said, then threw open the spruce door and ran inside.

Back when she and Steve had passed through this gulch looking for a place to build a new home, they'd chosen this location for a number of reasons. For one, it was rich in resources and not too cold. There was the stream of course—a constant source of clean water—and the village nearby on the other side of the big ridge. The gulch was special because of its wide open space that Alex could make into farmlands and pens for animals. But it was special for another reason, too: *the Divining Pool*.

On the day that they'd hiked through this gulch for the first time, Steve—running up ahead with his sword out like usual—found something strange that Alex had never seen before. There was a weird *mountain spring* of some kind in the middle of the gulch; a sort of *fountain*. It was a small and bizarre structure and neither Alex nor Steve had any idea who had crafted the thing.

What they eventually called 'the Divining Pool' had been sitting in the middle of a grassy clearing surrounded by yellow and red flowers. The fountain was small—just large enough to hold a small amount of water like the troughs they used to provide water for their animals—and it was seemingly *indestructible*. Made of the tough black and grey *bedrock* stone that Alex had only ever seen deep, deep underground, the Divining Pool was completely untouched by weather and natural erosion.

The strangest thing about it was that, sometimes, peering into the water, Alex would *see things*...

Usually, those things were really weird indeed, like the time Steve's friend KittyPaws30 had mysteriously appeared living in the nearby village. That day, strange words appeared in the pool, shimmering and hard to read, but Alex stared at them until she understood:

"Could you like add a character in one of your books? :) Can you name it KittyPaws30? Thank you thank you THANK YOU!!!!!! my character strangely acts like a tamed cat and she is shy and adventurous and loves CATS!! She also has a white hoodie and blue eyes and a kind, sweet voice... but she can be VERY protective of her CATS!!"

"What's it mean?" Steve had said with his arms crossed over his chest.

Back then, Alex had only shrugged, but the next day, they *met* KittyPaws30. The strange Minecraftian still lived in the village nearby today ... with all of her cats.

Even though both she and Steve had felt really weird about the mysterious Divining Pool, they went ahead and built the house around it. Ever since ... sometimes ... strange things happened.

Usually, the Divining Pool had some kind of *hint* about it.

Alex now stormed through the house, down the hall past the bedrooms, then threw open the door to the large room that was kind of like a *shrine* to the bizarre pool. She'd built the room around the Divining Pool entirely out of spruce wood then lined it with torches so that there was always plenty of light. Whenever the pool did have a message, the torchlight made it easier to read. The room held nothing else. It was just a big, well-lit room of spruce with the bedrock Divining Pool in its center.

She'd built the house around the Divining Pool, which could not be broken or moved. Alex was certain that if a catastrophe ever happened to her and Steve and the entire house fell down or burned up until nothing was left ... the Divining Pool would still stand.

Running to the edge of the bedrock Divining Pool, Alex wiped her eyes and stared into the blue waters within. The torchlight on the water's surface shimmered...

Then, hazy white words gradually formed inside, which Alex slowly read aloud...

"The time of the *Weird Walker* has begun..."

S1E1 - Chapter 3 – Steve

"Come back here!!" Steve shouted, chasing after the sounds of panicked hooves.

Running after the fleeing sheep, the armored Minecraftian ran up the ridge, leaping from rock to rock, then got himself stuck trying to get up an area that was too steep for him. He saw the white wool of the animal's back disappear over the other side.

Dang, he thought. *These are like ... mountain-climbing sheep!*

Steve growled in frustration and leaped and scrambled, trying to find a ledge low enough that he could climb up and catch up to the escaping animal. Finally, he saw a chunk of grassy dirt that extended from the cliff's edge, jumped over to it with great athletic skill, then continued huffing up the mountainside.

As the warrior ran along the wooded ridge, he saw the dumb eyes of the sheep stare back at him in horror. It bleated loudly, then ran off down the ridge toward the stream again, stumbling and half-falling most of the way.

"Grr ... stupid sheep!" Steve exclaimed, pulling himself up onto a huge rock.

Dummy! he thought to himself. *Don't be mad at the sheep!*

"My fault," he muttered, kicking a stick. Steve swung his iron sword at a tree as he passed, chopping off a large chunk of its bark.

He looked down at the sheaf of wheat in his left hand. It was becoming crushed and all tangled up as he climbed around the mountains chasing the dumb animals.

Steve shook his head, feeling the sunshine warm on the lower half of his face that was exposed from beneath his iron helmet.

How many sheep were there again? He was pretty sure that Alex had said *six*. Six sheep scattered all over these darned hills.

It was his fault—*sort of*.

Steve chuckled to himself a little, scanning the woods below his vantage for the white sheep that had been running away from him for the last several minutes. Alex had been *so angry* with him. Hey—he *had* to take out that creeper, right? When they heard that mob padding around outside in the wheat fields, it was almost morning!

"Creepers don't burn up like zombies do, Alex," he'd said. "It'll just hang around outside all day!"

"Then let's mine today instead. We need more iron anyway. It'll go away eventually..."

"I'm not afraid of a silly *creeper!*" Steve had said, staring at the weird green creature wandering around near the sheep pen through the window. The mob frowned with a big, black mouth and glared around with sad-looking, deep black eyes. "Besides—I wanted to go to the village today!"

Alex had sighed, crossed her arms over her chest, and stared at him.

She always thought the worst. Expected the worst.

"Just be careful," she'd said. "Don't make that thing blow up and hurt the house or the farm..."

Steve had smiled and drawn his iron sword. The sword was starting to get beat up already, and he'd only crafted it three days ago. He still had his armor. If anything *really* bad happened, he'd be okay. Probably.

"Don't worry!" he'd replied with a grin. "What's the *worst* that can happen??"

Just before dawn, Steve hadn't been able to wait any longer. He opened the farm door of their house and charged out to kill the creeper in the wheat field. As expected, the mob had started to sputter and hiss and freak out the instant he'd slashed into its weird, leafy body with his blade as Alex gasped and closed the door.

Maybe it *was* too close to the house. Maybe Alex was right. Perhaps Steve should have waited *just a little longer* to attack the thing—at least until after the sun was out...

Alex had been afraid because the creeper was about to blow right next to the house, but Steve knew better. As soon as he'd hacked into the thing, he ran away from the farm door, drawing the mob away as it pursued him. Once it calmed down again, he dashed in, stabbed it good, then immediately backed off again before it became too excited and blew itself up...

That's where things had gone wrong.

Since Steve had attacked the creeper outside their home during the end of the night, the undead mobs were still roaming around outside. He ran right into a big, stinking zombie that he hadn't noticed, and in the excitement of trying to get away from the undead brute—trying to stay away from the sputtering, advancing creeper at the same time—Steve had zigged when he should have zagged, and the creeper exploded!

By the time Steve had regenerated in his bedroom—empty-handed and dressed in nothing but his blue clothes—the sun had started to rise and the undead in the gulch around the house were on fire.

"Dang it, Steve!" Alex had said.

"What?!" he'd replied, running past her angry form in the hall and heading to the farm door again. He had to get his stuff! "It was away from the house! No big deal!"

"It blew up two rows of wheat and the sheep pen, you *blockhead!*"

"That's no big deal. Let's go get the sheep and repair the stuff!"

"It *is* a big deal! Our sheep all *ran off!* The last one just disappeared into the woods!"

Yeah—so Alex was mad. Again.

Honestly, Steve felt bad. He'd made a dumb decision, and now Alex was back home fixing his mess. Taking a deep breath, the Minecraftian looked down from his high spot over the woods. This forest extended far in all directions except to the east. If he were to climb the *big ridge* on his left—the landmark he could always see from home—he'd see the desert and the village on the other side.

Looking up at the sun, Steve figured that it was late morning.

He had six sheep to find and hadn't caught a single one of them yet.

Stupid, he thought.

He should have waited until morning to kill the creeper like Alex had said. Then he wouldn't have run into that zombie and gotten himself blown up. Alex would be happy, working on her mine or cooking a cake or something instead of working in the dirt and repairing the stuff Steve had destroyed with his carelessness...

Steve sighed.

He had to be more *careful*. He had to take his time and try to think first instead of just charging off and doing whatever he felt like doing in the moment! Alex said stuff like that all of the time. But he couldn't help it! Steve just ... tended to get ... sidetracked...

Something small and bright blue flying through the sky caught Steve's eye. It looked like ... a bird? Was that a *parrot?!*

Rushing and jumping down the smaller ridge back into the trees, Steve ran east after the strange bird. He sprinted toward the big ridge. When he crossed the small valley in between, he rushed up the incline, leaping from flat spot to flat spot, eventually climbing up the stone formations when the ground became too steep. When he realized that he was still crushing the wheat in his left hand—even more than it was already—Steve shoved it into his pack and continued his climb. He watched for the blue bird...

Finally cresting the big ridge, Steve scanned the sky for the blue bird.

He saw nothing.

The sky was partly clear and bright blue with thick, blocky clouds lazily passing by far overhead. It was a beautiful day.

Looking east away from the gulch, Steve stared out across the shimmering desert. On the east side of the ridge, the forest continued downhill for a little while until quickly transforming into a dry grassland without trees, then transitioning into nothing but sand. The desert was vast and full of dunes and sandy plateaus cut by the wind and erosion, decorated by nothing more than spiky bramble bushes and the occasional cactus or two. Not far from the grassland at the base of the ridge was the village. Sunlight glimmered on the sandstone roofs and the glass windows of the many small huts and handful of larger buildings down there.

Even from up on the big ridge, Steve could see the bustling villagers moving around on their morning business pretty clearly.

He'd always had great eyesight—Steve could see really far. His eyes were very sharp, so it was kind of funny that he mostly fought with a sword and left the bow and arrow stuff to Alex. She preferred to fight from a distance anyway.

Alex, he thought, immediately feeling bad again. *Oh yeah...*

How long would she be mad at him this time? It felt like he was screwing up more and more and she was mad at him most days. But what could he do? Steve was a *warrior*. He was an adventurer! An explorer! He wanted to fight—he needed it like a yearning deep in his soul!—and Alex was ... well ... *boring*. All she ever wanted to do was stay home and farm and mine all of the time. Heck—if it wasn't for them coming across that weird *Divining Pool* that she watches so much, they'd probably still be on the road, visiting new places and biomes, meeting new people, trading and looting dungeons deep underground...

Honestly, Steve couldn't believe that he'd ever convinced Alex to hit the road and leave their last house in the first place: a tiny wooden shack on a boring prairie surrounded by flowers and boring horses...

Heck—Steve still had to find a jungle temple! And a desert temple! And ... ooh ... a *Stronghold*. Steve knew all of the lore of the world. He'd learned everything he could about the dangerous places of Vortexia from all of the village libraries they'd visited and the other adventurers he chatted with from time to time.

But here they were, Steve and Alex, putting down roots again.

The Minecraftian sighed.

Looking down at the desert, Steve saw many villagers rushing around in the sun doing *villager stuff*. He also saw his new friend, KittyPaws30 running through one sandstone street, followed by the tiny, fleeting forms of a few of her cats. KittyPaws30 was easy to see wearing that bright white hoodie jacket of hers—especially down in the desert.

Today Steve was supposed to help KittyPaws30 build a swimming pool; a very nice thing to have in the desert, he reckoned.

Now he was stuck looking for sheep.

He'd been thinking about the best way to build the swimming pool in the desert. It would be best to build a little bit of a roof over it—at least part of it—to give shade, right? He'd have to dig about ten feet into the sand and sandstone. Steve wondered if there were any caves under the town. A lot of villages had old tunnels and caves underneath. Wouldn't that be crazy if they started digging the big hole for the swimming pool and broke into a cave system under the desert instead? Maybe a deep, dry cavern full of those weird, desert 'husk' zombies, or perhaps something that he'd never even *seen* before?!

Looking into his pack, Steve recalled that he had nothing on him.

That's right, he thought. *I died.*

All he had was his armor and his sword and some ratty wheat.

He would need a shovel. He could make a wooden one at least. And he'd have to make a crafting table real quick to do that...

Running over to the nearest tree, Steve sheathed his sword and gave the trunk a hearty *punch*.

Then he stopped.

"Oh yeah," he said. "Stupid *sheep*..."

Steve looked down the big ridge to the west; back down to the homestead. He saw Alex down there messing around near the chest outside the farm door. It looked like she'd fixed the broken crop rows and harvested and replanted the wheat, but the sheep fence was still broken.

"Probably feeding the animals," he said to himself, then started running along the top of the big ridge to the north, hopping from rock to rock.

He knew that the white sheep he'd lost was somewhere west of him and north of the house. Descending the big ridge on the forest side, Steve delved back into the shadowy trees, pulling his sword again. He searched for several minutes.

"Sheep!" he called. "Hey—stupid sheep! Where *are* you?!"

Eventually, Steve growled in frustration again and found a nice little clearing where he could sit in the sunshine. His stomach complained, so he ran up to an oak tree and started cutting into its branches until an apple fell to the ground.

Picking up the shiny, red apple, Steve sat down under the tree and took a bite.

As he chewed, watching the woods around and below him for sheep, Steve looked down at the house again. He could barely see the crops and animal pens from his vantage point—they were almost covered-up by the trees around him—but he knew that the house was there. He could see the roof and its wooden shingles.

This gulch was actually a pretty simple place, logistics-wise. Their property and the Divining Pool were surrounded by a low-mountainous forest on all sides. A creek ran north and south past the eastern edge of their farm up into the woods that were below him now. Steve knew that if he were to follow the creek north and keep going—way past where the six sheep were hiding—it would eventually lead him to a big mountain lake at higher elevation. If he were to follow the creek south past their property, however, it would go through more woods, lower and lower, until eventually escaping into an open floodplain far away. Running along going north and south to the *east* of their house was the *big ridge*, and on the other side of that was the vast desert and the village.

"Easy peasy," Steve said, chomping on the apple. He didn't know why Alex had such a hard time with the layout of the land. That girl had *no* sense of direction...

Suddenly, the sky darkened.

Steve looked up.

He couldn't see the sun from where he was sitting, but he was still eating his apple, so he didn't bother standing. It was the strangest thing: the bright late morning sky turned ... murky ... and within about a minute, the world was suddenly as dark as night!

"What the heck?" Steve asked, chewing on a bite of apple.

Looking down at the house again, Steve scanned for Alex but it was too dark to see her.

Then, just as suddenly as the sky had darkened, it became light again and everything was totally back to normal. Steve looked down at his apple, took his last bite, and threw the core down to the ground. He chewed and listened to the forest around him. He looked up at the sky.

Everything seemed the same as before. It was once again a normal day.

"Huh..." Steve said with a shrug that made his armor shift.

Then he stood, clapped the apple bits off of his armored gloves, and continued north, veering down the slope into the dark forest.

As Steve pressed on, uphill from the trickling stream but thick within the shadows of the oak and spruce pine trees, he clenched the hilt of his sword and narrowed his eyes, searching for any signs of the sheep. He stayed wary for hostile mobs hiding in the darkness...

Then he suddenly heard one of the sheep—a faint 'ba-ah-ah-ah' sound up ahead, deeper in the woods.

"Ha!" Steve exclaimed, reaching into his pack and grabbing a handful of wheat. "I've got you now!"

Running up ahead, Steve charged toward the sound, dashing through the shadows of tall trees and leaping over boulders and around pine trunks. He paused to listen...

"Ba-ah-ah-ah..."

Looking toward the sound, Steve grinned and continued. There had to be mobs hiding here and there in the forest—he had to be on his guard. Maybe a skeleton archer would shoot at him from under a tree, then he'd have to dodge its shot and sprint up while sidestepping the monster's follow-up arrow. He could already imagine his iron blade crunching through the mob's ribs and felt the excitement that he always felt during battle light up his blood like fire...

Steve stopped.

Up ahead was the small mouth of a cave. Well—maybe it wasn't a cave. It was more like a long tunnel going through a crevice of the mountain, very shallow in the side of the ridge. Steve approached, holding his sword before him. When he crouched to look inside, he saw that the tunnel went on for a while through darkness then there was a bright spot of blue sky in the distance where it emerged into the sunlit forest again.

There, standing in the sunshine at the end of the long, dark tunnel, was one of the sheep!

"Hey!" Steve shouted with a grin. It was the grey one. What the heck was it doing across the stream and way up on the big ridge?!

Scrunching up his armored body, Steve slipped into the hole and started through the long, dark tunnel toward the sheep that waited in the sun on the other side...

It wasn't long before he realized how freaking *dark* it was in the tunnel. Steve checked his pack for torches, already knowing that he had none.

"Dang!" he said to himself. The long, narrow corridor was apparently tight all over, because his voice didn't echo at all. He should have brought some torches with him from home when he'd left earlier...

Always have torches! Alex's voice said in his mind. His best friend was always prepared—annoyingly so.

Feeling ahead with one gloved hand and his sword, Steve proceeded carefully, blind except for the bright daylight ahead and the light behind him where he'd come from.

Jeez—it was so dark!

Grunting and huffing as he struggled against the rocky walls in the dark tunnel, Steve watched the grey sheep standing in the sunshine ahead. It turned and looked at him with dumb eyes, then plodded away out of sight.

"No—hey!" Steve shouted, his voice very big in the tight space. "Wait!"

Squirming to hustle through the tunnel, Steve hurried after the animal. He had to catch *this one* at least—Alex would be so mad at him if he didn't have at least—

Suddenly the ground dropped out under his boots.

Steve fell.

"Whoa!" he cried. One second, stone and earth was pressing in at him from all sides. The next second, he was flailing in open air with his stomach leaping up into his throat and—*dang*, he was falling!

As the wind and the darkness rushed past Steve's face, he reached out all around him for something to grab onto, but found nothing. He tumbled through empty space, and when he pitched down in a full freefall, the inky black underworld was suddenly glowing with red and orange light of lava far below!

He was falling into a ravine!

There was a freaking *ravine* under that tunnel!

Steve tumbled end over end, reaching out to catch himself but grabbing nothing. The wind of his own fall roared in his ears, and he watched the ravine floor far below rushing up to meet him...

Before Steve smashed into the ancient stone deep, deep underground, he found himself marveling at the sight of two lava falls nearby. He could feel their heat, even while falling. Bright, blazing magma poured slowly from fissures in the rocky cavern walls and descended steadily—burning and glowing brightly—until hissing violently against a vast underground pool of glittering water near where he—

S1E1 - Chapter 4 – Jack

It was real!!

Oh, gosh—it was real! *Was it real?!*

Jack spun around on the strange ground looking all around him with wide eyes. His long, brown hair flopped in his face and he reached up to pull it out of the way as he stared at the pixelated trees and leaves and pine boughs and huge, semi-transparent clouds and otherwise empty bright blue sky with a sun that—the sun was square! It was square!!

"No, it can't be real!" he shouted, suddenly surprised at how weird his voice felt in his ears, surrounded by this Minecraft world but not within a headset like he normally wore while playing. Normally when Jack played games, he wore headphones with a mic sticking out of one ear. He was used to hearing his voice amplified through his computer and played back to him through the speakers in his headset, but now it was only ... *his voice!*

This can't be real! he thought, suddenly looking at his very real hands, feeling his face stretch in wide surprise and thrilling terror. Jack opened and closed his hands, watching his normal fingers flex in and out of fists in front of bright green pixelated grass.

"Oh gosh!" he said, rapidly crouching down to touch the ground.

The boy looked at his shoes for a moment. *They* were real. His shoes were worn and dirty and his laces were messy because he always tied lazy bows that frequently came undone. There were his shoes, standing on freaking *grass blocks*, squishing the pixelated grass under his feet! Clusters of more grass as tall as

Jack's knees—looking as thin as paper—popped up here and there, repeating forever into the hills and short mountains around him that rose and fell as blocks; stairs of dirt with thin green grass on top and plain, grey stone...

"Wow!!"

Jack recognized the trees around him. They were a mix of the normal oak trees that had been in Minecraft since the beginning, and the spruce pines—in the game since version 1.2—that reached high above him with their dark boughs. Still—these trees weren't like normal trees. Normal trees in the real world would *tower* over him as tall as houses! These trees were—Jack laughed; this was *crazy!*—maybe as tall as house ... he couldn't tell! This was *so weird!*

Looking back down at the ground, Jack touched the grass around his feet.

The ground—bright green pixels that were supposed to be grass on top of dirt—felt bumpy in a way that the boy couldn't quite understand. It was like the grass was there and *not there* at the same time, but the ground itself was a little ... *spongy*.

He stomped once, feeling his foot hit the ground like...

Jack thought of playgrounds. Sometimes the playgrounds in his city had areas of soft, rubbery ground. It wasn't soft like a pillow or a bed mattress or foam—it was harder than that; denser than that—but the playground floor was still soft enough to help it not hurt so bad when kids fell down. Jack's big brother's school had a race track going around the football field that was made of the same stuff.

That's what this was like. The ground was like that springy, rubbery playground stuff. Or, at least the *grass* was. Jack

54

wondered if stone would be the same way. Was bedrock the same way??

"What the heck?!" he exclaimed suddenly, laughing like a crazy person. It seemed totally *bonkers* to be wondering what one block or another would feel like. This *couldn't* be real, could it?

Jack had to be *passed out* or something still back in the computer lab and hooked into the *Vortex Wave*. Maybe ... maybe something weird had happened and there was an electricity surge! Maybe he was knocked out somehow, or fell down with the headset on and hit his head really hard—yeah! He was probably lying half in and half out of that plastic platform in front of the monitor, mouth gaping open and drooling with the headset still covering his eyes and ears. He was probably just having a crazy, wacky *dream* about being in Minecraft—yeah—any second now, he would wake up! He'd be in a lot of trouble if Mr. Hayes came back to the lab while Jack was still sleeping in front of the virtual reality machine, but at least he'd be awake...

"Any moment now," Jack said, passing one hand through a long sprig of grass sticking up out of the green ground. The grass didn't wave. It didn't do anything in his fingers, as if he didn't touch it at all. When Jack touched the grass, it felt like weird, stiff ribbons against his normal hand. "Any moment now, I'll wake up..."

He waited.

Jack thought about the actual game and recalled that punching the grass would make *seeds*.

"Come on," he said to himself, looking around. "Wake up. Wake up ... now. Riiiiight ... *now*."

He heard the crunching sound of that rabbit hopping nearby and looked off into the woods. Jack didn't see the animal.

Why wasn't he waking up?!

He looked back down at the waist-high cluster of tall grass next to him. Feeling a rush of fear—not sure whether or not he wanted to know the truth—Jack swung his fist out and tried to hit the pixel-wide fan of grass.

The boy's hand slashed through the grass with a threshing sound, and the bunch of grass exploded into tiny bits of green. It almost immediately dissipated and left nothing more than a handful of tiny, green and yellow seeds bunched together. The seeds bounced once as a group, then settled into a hover a few inches above the ground. A small, circular shadow appeared under them as it slowly hovered up and down ... up and down...

"Holy cow!" Jack exclaimed, standing straight up. "Holy cows and horses—I'm *in Minecraft!!*"

He'd already thought it a million times, but seeing his real, actual hand cut through the grass and leave behind *seeds* hit Jack like a ton of bricks.

It was real. Oh gosh—it was real!

Jack felt all over his body. It was really him—not some sort of avatar. Not his handle, *Weirdwalker000*; not his blocky body with his custom skin of a black-suited armored ninja with glowing red trim and a demonic face. This was actually *him*. Twelve-year-old Jack Walker was *in the game*, real-life body and all!

Reaching up to his face, Jack checked to see if his glasses were still there. They were. He took them off for a second and saw the entire bright and colorful world become blurry, then put them back on.

So he came through with his clothes, shoes, and glasses...

Jack checked for his *game pendant* around his neck and found that it was gone.

"Of course," he said. "It's back in the *Vortex Wave*..."

How in the world was he *in* the game?! That didn't make any sense! That couldn't happen—not in the real world. Maybe this could happen in the movies, or in stories—places with *magic*—but this didn't *really* happen, ever! Not really!

If Jack's game pendant was gone, still stuck in the Vortex Wave's computer back in the lab, then where was he? Was Jack sleeping or something in front of the VR machine? Or had he *vanished*—teleported into the game somehow—leaving the headset and the joysticks abandoned on the floor?

Was he *sucked* into the computer, living in the hard-drive and *RAM?* Was he now just *data* saved on his game pendant's storage? What would happen when Mr. Hayes got back into the computer lab and turned the computer off? What would happen if someone found his game pendent plugged into the USB port of the VR machine and pulled it out...?

"Oh man..." Jack said, suddenly feeling afraid again.

The boy looked around and took some steps. The ground was soft. Jack passed through more bunches of grass harmlessly.

Reaching up to his head, Jack closed his eyes and tried to imagine the VR headset still over his eyes and ears. He tried to *feel* it; to take it off...

All he felt was air and hair and the temples of his glasses.

"Dang!"

Looking back to where he'd first appeared, Jack saw a single black block in the ground, standing out among the grass. It looked a little like Minecraft's *obsidian* blocks, but it wasn't pixelated or showing any other colors. It was simply *black*. Jet-black.

"Huh," Jack said, scratching his head. "Haven't seen *that* before..."

He looked up at the sky again, suddenly realizing that there was no wind; no breeze at all. Way up at the top of the world, Jack saw the huge, blocky clouds lazily drifting by, but there was no wind at all—not even the barest bit of air flow—down on the ground. The sun was a little higher in the sky.

Would time pass just as quickly for Jack now as it did when he was playing the game? How long was a day? Ten minutes?

A chill suddenly ran up Jack's spine. He looked around the forest for any movement.

All was peaceful, quiet, and very, very green ... for now.

What would he do at nighttime? Did he have ten minutes—less than that now—to build a shelter before the mobs came with the darkness?!

"Oh, snap..." he muttered, watching the sun some more. The bright, square sun inched upward in the sky before his eyes...

Looking around for the nearest tree, Jack ran over to a taller oak about fifteen feet away. Stepping into its shadow, Jack felt the same mild temperature. The sun was warm on his skin, and Jack didn't feel the warmth while in the shadow of the oak tree's blocks of pixelated leaves, but he wasn't too hot or too cold. The air was very nice.

When he focused closely, Jack could distinctly see where the blocks separated. He touched the middle of a block of tree trunk. He felt its bark. The sensation was kind of like touching rough plastic. It was somewhat soft, just like the grass...

"Is this *entire world* soft like a playground?" he asked no one.

Feeling a little afraid of hurting his hand, Jack reared back, formed a fist, and laughed.

This is crazy, he thought.

Jack punched the tree.

It was like punching dense foam, but with a hard surface that flexed a little under his blow. Pulling his hand back, Jack saw a single dark pixel where he'd struck the tree, which promptly disappeared.

Of course, Jack thought. Blocks heal themselves almost instantly. He looked at his fist. There was no damage to his skin and his hand felt fine.

He hit the tree again. He hit it a third time, hard.

A small crack appeared in the middle of the oak block, then quickly reversed.

"Okay," Jack said. "Let's punch a tree..."

He hit the tree again and again, over and over, rearing back and punching it as hard as he could until his arm started to burn. The block showed a spot, then a crack, then the crack grew larger and larger—just like in the normal game—until it looked like the entire block would break at any moment. Jack's shoulders started to burn but he kept at it...

Pop.

The big block of oak tree trunk suddenly disappeared, leaving a smaller, miniaturized version of itself that fell onto the top of the oak tree trunk block below it, hovering a few inches in the air, drifting slowly up and down...

"Sixteen punches," Jack said. "Sixteen freaking punches..."

The boy had never thought of it back when he was just *playing the game* at his computer, but he needed to punch that tree block sixteen times before it broke into a collectable form. Now, his arm burned from the exercise but his fist felt okay. At least it didn't feel like punching a real tree!

Jack picked up the small block of oak. It was about the size of a small soccer ball. It felt a lot like it looked, though a little spongy and almost weightless.

Now what? he thought.

"Now's where it goes into my inventory," Jack said to himself, looking down at the block in his hands. He looked over his body; looked up into the sky. He had no 'E' key. He had no keyboard. How would he access his inventory?

Jack moved the big wooden cube down near his pockets. He didn't know what to expect, but he hoped that it would somehow suddenly *disappear* and go into some sort of inventory that he didn't understand. When nothing happened, Jack tried to shove the wooden block into his pocket, but—of course—it was just too big to fit.

"What am I supposed to do with this?!" he said, staring at the miniature block of raw oak wood.

Not coming up with any new ideas, Jack dropped it to the ground and put his hands into his pockets. When the little cube of wood hit the ground, it bounced once then settled into a wavering hover once again with a little, circular shadow under it.

Scrounging through the pockets of his pants, Jack came up with nothing more than the two dollars he always carried on him in case he ever ran into an ice cream truck. He shoved one dollar back into his pocket, then looked at the other. His eyes flashed over to the wooden block.

"I wonder..." Jack said, then dropped the dollar to the ground next to the hovering oak block.

The dollar bill fell flat onto the green grass and just sat there, real and lifeless. It didn't hover. It didn't change.

"Weird," Jack said, scooping the dollar up again and shoving it back into his pocket.

How would he survive in this world if he didn't have an inventory? He needed his 'inventory window' to be able to craft things, too!

Jack looked and saw that the sun had risen to the top of the sky.

"Dang!" he exclaimed. How was he going to survive the night?! What would happen if he *died?*

Jack sat down on the grass.

He put his hands into his lap, closed his eyes, and tried to relax.

"E..." he said. "Open inventory..." Taking a peek at the sunny clearing he was in, Jack noticed nothing different. He closed his eyes again. The boy imagined a keyboard hanging in midair in front of him, and visualized pressing a gigantic 'E' key. "Eeeee..." he said loudly, then opened his eyes again.

Nothing.

Jack growled in frustration. "Open crafting window!" he announced to the world. He heard the rabbit behind him hopping around again. "Computer! Open inventory screen!"

Nothing happened.

The boy stood.

He sighed.

"What am I gonna do without an inventory or crafting window?!" he shouted at the sky. Then, suddenly worried about hostile mobs hearing him from the woods, Jack felt a jolt of fright and looked around.

The forest was quiet.

With another sigh, Jack bent down and picked up the hovering cube of oak. Picking a random direction, he started walking.

The pixelated grass crunched softly under his shoes. When Jack came to a small rise, he climbed the grass blocks to the next level—the blocks were individually about as tall as his chest—then kept walking. It occurred to Jack suddenly that he'd always played this game as a character that was basically an *adult*. Real-life Jack was a kid. He was short and he could tell that the Minecraft world around him was a little *bigger* than he expected. Jack figured that if he was standing next to a zombie or a skeleton or a Minecraftian, it would be like standing next to an adult in real life! Jack was *too small* for this pixelated world. The idea gave him a fright, thinking of what zombies and other hostile mobs would be like when he finally saw them...

"I'll see them tonight," Jack said to himself. "If I don't find a place to stay for the night, this will be over real quick..."

Just then, Jack's heart leapt into his throat when he heard an animal sound. It was the *ba-ah-ah-ah* of a sheep.

"Holy beetles!"

The boy spun to the sound and his heart started pounding when he heard the soft *thud* of a footstep in the dark forest up ahead...

Jack froze, holding his cube of oak as if it was a big rock he could throw at something.

Peering into the dark, shadowy woods, Jack searched for motion. He looked for a sheep.

"Ba-ah-ah-ah..."

He heard the animal again and his eyes landed on a faint white shape in the shadows.

"Are you a sheep?" Jack asked, trying to keep his voice from shaking. He was *terrified.* "If you're not a sheep, tell me now! I'm ... um ... I'm an *admin*, and you have to tell me if you're not a sheep! It's the rules of this server!"

Pff—stupid, he thought.

Whatever.

Jack listened to the clomping steps up ahead and he eventually felt comfortable enough that it was just a sheep when it let out another *ba-ah-ah-ah*.

Taking careful, quiet steps forward—his shoes making softer *crunching* sounds in the grass—Jack stepped out of the sunlight and into the shadows of the spruce trees. He saw the big, white shape of the sheep up ahead. Whenever it moved, he heard its hooves *clomping* around.

Definitely a sheep.

Trying to calm his pounding heart, Jack slowly approached the animal. When he was closer, the sheep turned its head and Jack saw the typical pixelated face he expected. It looked at him with dumb eyes that pointed in different directions.

"Ba-ah-ah-ah," the sheep said.

Jack's fear slowly faded away. He approached the sheep holding his open hand in front of him like he would approach a horse or something in real life, though if this was truly the game, Jack knew that he had nothing to worry about. This was a *passive* mob. It wouldn't ever try to hurt him. Even if he decided to attack it, all it would do was try to run away.

As soon as Jack stepped within a few feet of the wandering, white sheep, he saw a display suddenly appear above it, hovering in the air. There was a small, semi-transparent window that was easy for him to read showing a little profile picture of a sheep on the left. On the right, there were two bars. One simply said 'Sheep' in white letters and the other had a green *health bar*, showing eight out of eight hit points.

It was Jack's 'Damage Indicator' mod.

He was indeed in his own game, somehow connected to his *game pendant*. That must mean that he'd see numbers appear whenever any mobs were damaged, and he'd also be able to illuminate the area around him by merely *holding* a torch instead of attaching it to a wall or floor...

"If it works that way," he said. "Gosh—this is crazy!"

Reaching for the sheep, Jack wasn't quite sure what to expect. He touched its fluffy-yet-blocky white back—almost as high as his face—and gasped. The wool of the sheep's back felt soft and ... maybe like a fuzzy blanket? But at the same time, it felt completely different in a way that Jack didn't understand...

"So weird!" he exclaimed, petting the sheep.

"Ba-ah-ah-ah..." it said, randomly looking away from him.

Jack reached up to touch the Damage Indicator window and found that his hand passed right through it. The semi-transparent window with the sheep's information didn't feel like anything.

"So there are sheep in these woods, huh?" Jack said. "I hope there aren't any wolves..."

Jack suddenly heard more footsteps behind him—a little quieter than the sheep's clumsy hooves. He turned, smiling, expecting to see another sheep approaching from farther away or—

Ten feet away from Jack and closing fast was the bizarre and quiet form of a *creeper*. He knew exactly what it was when he saw it. The mob was taller than Jack. Looking into that alien face with empty, sad eyes and a deep, frowning mouth instantly filled Jack with freezing terror! The creature was scuttling toward him on stubby little legs with small, pixelated claws that padded quietly on the grass...

Jack opened his mouth to scream, but only gasped.

The creeper suddenly loomed, rushing in at him—much quicker than it looked—and Jack stared in horror as the thing began sizzling, sputtering; a *hiss* that filled his ears and made his knees feel like jelly.

As the creeper closed in on him, its Damage Indicator window appeared over its head: a little picture of the mob, the title 'Creeper', and a green bar showing 20/20 hit points...

He had to run!

Jack had to run away as fast as he could, but instead he stood, frozen in fear as the violent hissing filled his ears...

S1E1 - Chapter 5 – Alex

"The time of the *Weird Walker* has begun...?" The words in the Divining Pool shimmered and shifted. They were hard to read, but Alex peered intently at the blue surface and read the mysterious message aloud again. "What in the world does *that* mean?"

It sounded like an ominous warning about a traveler of some kind...

What in the world was that with the sun?

What was going on in Vortexia?!

Alex had been around for a long time, and she and Steve had wandered this world far and wide. Sometimes they stayed in one place for a while. She loved stopping to build a house and have a quiet life for months at a time, but Steve would always inevitably get itchy feet and want to move on to see more; to journey and seek adventure and riches...

Of course, their riches came and went. Heck, Steve *died* so frequently in his reckless running around that it was a huge job just to keep them in enough iron and supplies and food to live in comfort and safety from day to day!

She suddenly heard his voice.

"Lava!" Steve shouted from the bedroom. "I found lava!"

Alex pulled her gaze away from the Divining Pool with a scoff. The words shimmered and dissolved into the blue water. She rolled her eyes. Had he *really* died again?!

She heard Steve's rapid footsteps in the hall.

"Alex!" he shouted, excited and riled up like he always was after regenerating. "Alex! Are you in here?!"

She sighed. "I'm here!" she called out to him. "I'm in the Divining Pool room!"

A few seconds later, Steve burst through the doorway grinning from ear to ear. He was dressed in his blue shirt and pants. His armor was gone and his hands were empty for once.

Yep. He'd died again.

"OMG, Alex, you're not gonna believe it!" he exclaimed, his blue eyes wide and full of exhilaration. "It's a ravine! There are *lava falls!*"

"Did you *die* again?!"

"Oh, Alex, I was in a dark tunnel—not very far from here—and I fell! I fell down and down forever—almost to the bedrock—and I saw lava falls! It's a ravine, right next to our—"

"What about the *sheep*, Steve?" Alex said, grimacing. "Dang it, Steve—you were wearing full iron armor, weren't you? Do you have any idea how much work it takes to make a full suit of armor?!"

He was practically panting as if he'd run all the way home, but she knew that he'd just worked himself up from only down the hall, appearing in his bed.

"Yeah—the sheep. But it's ... a ravine! Do you have any idea what that *means* for us? We can find all sorts of ore down there—iron, gold, redstone, even emeralds to trade with down in the village! Heck—we can even find some *diamonds* down there! We've got to go back! I'll show you—come on!"

"What about the sheep, Steve?" she repeated. "You were supposed to be looking for the sheep!"

The Minecraftian in blue clapped both of his hands over his face as if surprised, then calmed himself down.

"The sheep! I ... was following one. One of our sheep—the grey one—is up near this little cave tunnel where I fell into the ravine but ... I didn't have any torches. I couldn't see! Let's go there *right now* and find the sheep. Maybe I can still get my stuff! Bring torches!"

Alex groaned, standing from where she'd been crouched next to the Divining Pool.

She checked her pack, making sure that she had her bow and plenty of arrows. Of course she did. She also had lots of torches, some food, dirt, stone, sticks, wood, coal, and everything else that she might need. Her supply of wood and sticks was low, which was why she'd gone off with her axe in the first place before the weird sun-shadow thing...

Alex paused.

"Steve, did you see that weird thing with the sun?"

"The sun?" Steve replied, idly punching the wall. He hit the spruce planks with his bare fist several times, making it crack up, then watched it repair itself back to normal. Then he did it again. "I didn't see anything with the sun. Wait—*oh yeah!*" He looked at her and smiled. "There was a weird thing where the sky went dark for a minute. It was right before I found the sheep."

So he didn't see it...

"How many sheep?" Alex asked.

"Eh ... just one," he replied.

"You only found one sheep?" she said, putting her hands on her hips. "What have you been doing? I've been fixing the farm all morning and I still need to repair the sheep's fence."

"Oh, you know," he replied with a shrug. "Stuff. But I *have* been looking for the sheep. I saw the one sheep next to the cave where I fell. I bet the others are nearby, don't you think?"

Alex sighed and pushed past him into the hall.

"Well let's hurry then before they get any farther." She paused at the crafting table. "Actually, hang on a sec. Let's fix the fence first so there's a pen for the sheep to come back to..."

"Eh, okay."

"Stay with me, okay? I need to get more wood."

"Alrighty. Let's hurry. I can probably still get my armor and sword back if we hurry."

"Okay."

The two of them headed out into the sun. Looking up, Alex saw that it was already mid-day. They headed to some trees at the edge of the gulch. With Steve with her—even unarmed as he was—Alex felt a lot better than when she was alone.

"Watch my back, okay?" Alex said, pulling out her iron axe.

"Sure."

She started cutting down a tree, harvesting block after block of oak. When Alex paused at one point to look at Steve, she saw him punching a tree of his own. After he collected a few blocks— far slower by hand than she was with her axe—Steve quickly put together a crafting table then made some sticks. Before long, he was holding a wooden sword.

Alex took down a few more trees as quickly as she could then rushed over to Steve's hastily-made crafting table. They really needed to hurry. She started making sticks and planks, then fence rails and a gate for the sheep pen.

Looking up from her work, she watched Steve as he leaped and milled around the area cutting down grass for some reason.

Alex sighed.

"Steve," she said. "You know that every time you die, it—"

"Sorry, what?" he exclaimed, stopping to watch her.

"Every time you die, it costs us resources. We're pretty much out of iron. We're low on wood. We'll have to go back down into the mines to—"

"Eh—that's okay," he said. "We can always mine more. Now there's a ravine we can explore, too, and find all sorts of ore down there!"

"Yeah but *still!*" Alex replied. "Maybe you should be more *careful*, huh?"

Steve scoffed. "Alex, we can always make more stuff. This world is ours for the taking! We can do anything we want!"

She sighed and glared down at the rail she was crafting.

When Alex was finished, she put away all of her rails and the new gate, looking around the forest near them. There was no sign of the sheep. She looked back at Steve, who was dashing around randomly.

"Hey," she said. "I saw something strange in the Divining Pool after the sun-shadow and the dark sky..."

"What?"

"There was a message: *The time of the Weird Walker has begun.*"

Steve paused and looked up at the sun, filling his pack with grass seeds. He ate an apple that he'd cut down from an oak tree.

"Weird Walker, huh?" he said. "That's cool..."

"Any idea what that might mean?"

Steve shrugged. "Eh. Let's finish that fence and get back to the ravine, okay?"

He didn't care.

Whatever.

"Do you want this crafting table you made?" Alex asked.

"Nah. Just leave it. I can make another."

Alex stared at Steve, then the crafting table. She was tempted to take it herself. She tried not to care, but the woman didn't want to see random crafting tables and stuff strewn all around in the wilderness surrounding their homestead. Pulling out her axe, she broke it down and stashed the pieces.

They headed back to the farm, where Alex replaced the fence rails and broken gate as quickly as she could. It had been ... perhaps an hour since Steve regenerated? His stuff should still be there...

"Okay, let's go," Alex said, drawing a broad smile from Steve. "But hey—make sure to grab some wheat from the gardening chest. You'll need it to help get the sheep back."

"Ugh ... okay," Steve said, then he did.

With that, they walked across the crop fields, and Steve led Alex across the stream toward the big ridge. Up the steep slope, around pine trees, and occasionally climbing from boulder to boulder, they headed up the ridge. All the while, Alex kept looking behind her to make sure that the homestead was still in sight.

"You remember the way?" she asked.

"Oh sure," Steve said with a grin. He pointed in a direction away from the house with his wooden sword. "It's kind of ... up north along the ridge for a while until we can see the village, then down the west side heading north into the trees, then I went down toward the creek a little ways, then back up again, and we should be able to find the cave ... I hope."

Alex sighed, taking a fearful glance back at the house and farmlands again.

She followed Steve up the ridge until they crested the top.

When Alex looked out over the vast desert on the other side and the faraway village in the sand, she instantly felt nervous.

Vortexia was a *huge* world, and seeing so much of it from such a high view made Alex feel very small.

As Steve ran on along the ridge, hopping from rock to rock like a madman, Alex looked back at the homestead again, suddenly terrified that soon she wouldn't be able to see their house or farm through the trees...

She followed Steve along the ridge. He paused a few times, putting his hands on his hips and scanning around with narrowed eyes, obviously trying to remember the way he took before.

"I don't hear the sheep," Alex said, looking up at the sun. Thankfully, they still had plenty of time.

"They're not this close," Steve said. "We've got to keep going for a while. Ah! *This way*, I think..."

Alex followed Steve along the ridge, taking careful steps to avoid falling the long way down, cautiously navigating around the tall trees that reached into the sky. By the time Steve had led her down into the woods and they walked in shadow, Alex felt totally lost.

No longer able to look back and see *home*, she felt a cold dread growing inside her.

"Are you still going the right way?" Alex asked, trying to keep her voice from wavering.

"You lost already?" Steve replied with a laugh. He smiled broadly back at her. "Home is over there," he said, pointing at what felt to Alex like a random place in the forest, "the village is over *there*, and the cave is up there ... mostly."

Alex scoffed, trying her best to smile and hide her fear. "*Of course* I know that! I know where we are! I'm not lost!"

She was totally lost. It was a bald-faced lie.

Steve chuckled, smiling back at her. "Yeah, *okay*, Alex..."

The woman felt her cheeks turn hot with embarrassment, but she only shook her head—orange-red hair whipping back and forth against her face—and continued on.

Eventually Steve stopped again, deep in the shadowy woods. He scanned around, scratching his stubbly chin with his free hand. He twirled his wooden sword idly as he thought, looking around...

"Maybe we passed it," Alex offered. "It feels like we've been out here a while. Your stuff is probably gone by now..."

"I don't think so," Steve said, then smiled and pointed at a clearing full of sunshine. "There! There's the place where I stopped to eat an apple before I found the sheep. Come on!"

She followed Steve deeper into the forest, through the sunny clearing, then up the ridge again. Eventually, after another break to look around and think, Steve grinned back at her and pointed at a very dark place up ahead that made Alex very nervous.

"What?" Alex said.

"There's the cave," Steve said. "See, I *told* you I'd find it."

"We're not looking for the *cave*, Steve," she said. "Not really. We need to find our sheep before they totally disappear!"

"I need to get my *stuff* before *it* totally disappears!" he replied. "Besides—the sheep was on the other side. It's a tunnel that passes through out into the open again. I'll show you..."

Steve led Alex to the mouth of the cave and she looked into the darkness, gasping when she saw the bright spot of daylight on the other end of the tunnel.

"This is where you died?"

"Inside," he said. "There's a hole somewhere in there where I fell through. Gimme some torches..."

She did.

Steve smiled when he took them and led the way into the tight, dark tunnel. After a few steps, he put a torch on the stony wall, illuminating several feet ahead of them with a yellow glow.

"Be careful!" Alex said, cautiously following him into the tunnel.

"No hole yet," Steve replied, pushing through the narrow stone corridor and taking several more steps ahead until reaching the end of the light. Right when Alex saw the blue of her friend's shirt start disappearing into the darkness, she was about to call out for him to stop when he put another torch on the wall. "Here it is!" Steve exclaimed. "Watch out—it's a small hole."

Alex crept forward, holding a torch in her own hand until she caught up to her companion. Steve was standing over the edge of a hole in the rocky floor, looking down into what appeared to be an *infinite abyss*...

"That goes into a super-deep ravine?" she asked. "I can't see..."

"Hang on," Steve said, then suddenly leapt over the hole to the other side, making Alex's heart almost jump out of her chest! "Take a look..."

"OMG—be careful!" she exclaimed.

Alex crept up to the edge of the hole and looked down. It was indeed an *abyss*. Below the edges of the gap in the tunnel floor, she saw the blackest black. Shielding the torchlight from her eyes, Alex could eventually make out an orange glow coming from somewhere deep down there, as well as the faint glittering of firelight on water. The squeaks of bats echoed endlessly below them...

She looked up at Steve and saw him peering into the hole with a grin that almost split his head in two. The Minecraftian practically had stars in his eyes...

"I think my stuff's still down there," Steve said, marveling at the sight inside the hole. That was *adventure* down there...

"No way," Alex said.

"Yeah—I think I can see it! Let me have some of your dirt. I wanna make some stairs down into there so that I can recover my sword and armor."

"Steve," Alex said with a sigh. "We need to get the *sheep*."

"This'll just take a second," he said. "You have a pick axe? Of course—you're always prepared. Can you cut a path around the edge so we don't have to jump over this hole? And gimme some dirt. I'll go down there, get my stuff, and come right back up— honest!"

That bit about cutting a path around the hole was the first thing Steve said in a long time that made good sense.

Alex sighed, then plunked her torch onto the wall above the hole.

She pulled out her iron pick axe then gave Steve a lot of dirt. He'd need a lot.

As Alex started cutting into the stone around the hole, Steve balanced over the seemingly-bottomless pit, aimed carefully, then placed a block of dirt somewhere down in the darkness. He placed two more then lowered himself into the pit...

"Careful!" Alex said.

"You're like a broken record, Alex," he said. "It's fine. I'm making stairs."

She watched him—her heart suddenly pounding—then finished making a bypass around the deadly hole. When Alex was

76

done with the pick axe, she walked over to the abyss, examined Steve's dirt landing, and lowered herself down.

Now she could see a long ways in the darkness, even though it was mostly pitch-black. Far below, she could make out two brilliant reddish-orange lines of glowing light that shimmered and oozed. Those must be the lava falls that Steve was so excited about...

Steve was already fifteen feet or so below her, constructing a narrow, ramshackle staircase of dirt along the massive cavern's ceiling and one sheer, terrifying wall, lowering himself down one block at a time.

"Can you keep going like that all the way to the bottom?" Alex asked. Her voice echoed endlessly. A bat squeaked nearby, giving her a start.

Looking back up at her, Steve put a torch in the stone wall and smiled as its yellow light played across his face. "Looks like there's a cave mouth a little ways down. I can probably find a way down through there..."

"This is silly, Steve," she said. "There's *no way* you're gonna get down to your stuff before it disappears..."

"I can do it."

"We need to get the sheep back home before nightfall!" Alex's voice echoed loudly, and she realized that she sounded more than a little angry.

"We will!" he said. "Don't worry so much, Alex! I'll just go down and get my gear and come right back. How about ... why don't you just wait here?"

He turned and continued away, block by block, slowly heading down the sheer stone wall into the darkness...

"Okay, fine!" Alex said, listening to her voice's echo. "Just hurry, okay?"

"Alright!"

"And Steve, don't get *sidetracked!*"

"Okay, okay ... sheesh!"

Standing on the dirt platform under the hole for a while, Alex watched Steve work his way down the ridiculously tall stone wall of the ravine, delving deeper and deeper into the empty, black depths. It scared her to see him out on the wall so vulnerable, but what was the worst that could happen? If Steve fell, he'd drop a lot of her dirt, a cruddy wooden sword, and a handful of torches, then regenerate back home again.

Yeah, and leave me lost in the woods far from home, she thought.

Alex shuddered, looking out over the edge of the rickety dirt landing into the pitch black void...

"Well, I'm not waiting *here*..." she muttered to herself, then climbed up out of the hole and back into the dark tunnel.

The top of the ravine was barren and empty. There wouldn't be any hostile mobs there, but it was still possible that a giant spider might climb up to get them from the depths below...

At least the tunnel was closer to the sunlit world, though still dark.

Alex sat on the stone floor where she'd just cleared out part of the tunnel's wall. She was tempted to let her feet hang down in the hole, but decided against it.

She waited.

Alex waited for quite a while, eventually pulling out a loaf of bread and eating it when she became hungry.

Where the heck was Steve?!

Sidetracked, she thought. Either sidetracked or dead again.

After what seemed like hours—or several really bored, impatient minutes—waiting in the dark tunnel, Alex gasped when she heard the bleat of a sheep nearby...

"Ba-ah-ah-ah..."

She stood. It sounded like it came from the other side of the tunnel!

Alex looked down the deep, dark hole. She listened. For a few minutes, she didn't hear any sounds coming from down there other than bats.

"Steve!" she called into the hole. Her voice echoed down in the depths. "Steve! Come on!"

Nothing.

Alex sighed.

She heard the sheep *ba-ah-ah-ah* again from the other side of the tunnel.

"Fine," she said, kicking the ground. "I'll just do it *myself.*"

Taking out more torches, Alex skirted around the hole and continued through the tunnel toward the daylight showing from the other side. Whenever it became too dark to see, she put another torch on the tunnel wall, lighting her way. She had to make sure that she didn't fall through another hole like Steve had!

After several tense minutes creeping through the dark, torch after torch, Alex smiled and sighed when she emerged into sunlight again.

Looking down a rocky slope through spruce and oak trees, Alex saw a single white sheep tromping around eating grass. She had no idea where she was, but what used to be the ridge now looked like just a big mountain slope that rose up far on her right, and a large, grassy clearing led down from where the sheep was standing, extending into a wide, green field full of tall grasses and sparse trees.

"There you are!" Alex said with a smile, stashing the torch in her hand and pulling out some wheat.

Taking a few steps down toward the wandering sheep, Alex stopped when she heard a sudden cry of alarm and movement caught her eye.

She saw something strange down in the grass. There was a creature—something she had never seen before—running across the clearing *fast*; as fast as she and Steve could run! Alex had no idea what the sprinting, screaming creature was, but it didn't look like any mob she'd ever seen before. It looked mostly like a Minecraftian, but its *shape* was all wrong! Instead of her and Steve's blocky frames and bright, simple colors, the creature was soft and smooth, and so complex-looking in color and detail that it dazzled her eyes! The unknown mob held a small block of oak in one hand and it ran—screaming in unrestrained terror—babbling loudly in a high voice as it went!

"Help!" the creature cried, looking around with wide eyes covered with gleaming pieces of glass. "Oh Gosh—somebody help me! Help me *please!!* It's after me! It's *after me!!*" It had a black shirt and black pants and multicolored shoes, all rounded and smooth in a way that almost hurt Alex's head to look at. Long, dark brown hair flowed behind it like nothing Alex had ever seen! Its skin was colored like hers—not green or sandy or blue like the various zombies of the world. And it was a strange height; not as tall as Alex herself, but taller than the baby zombies that she saw sometimes...

Just then, Alex saw a creeper burst from the trees a distance behind the weird entity, following it as fast as the explosive, green mob could. The soft, Minecraftian-like creature was faster—easily outpacing the creeper—but the silent, frowning mob pursued it steadily across the glade...

Alex pulled her bow and nocked an arrow. She sidestepped toward a tree to help conceal her from the creeper.

Should she help the bizarre creature?

Did this strange, terrified thing have something to do with the words of the Divining Pool?

Alex made a decision and took action.

"Hey!" she called, drawing a quick, terrified look from the creature's amazingly complicated face. "Hey, *you!* Run up the hill! Get as high as you can!"

The creature seemed to understand her and crossed the field, pumping his smooth arms and running as fast as he could. When he reached the blocky slope, he paused to climb, looking back over his soft, rounded shoulder in terror.

Alex took aim at the creeper and fired at its frowning face. Her arrow whistled through the air across the clearing and struck it in one deep, dark eye. It reacted with a surprised *hiss*, lost its balance for a moment, then adjusted course and headed straight toward *her*...

"Oh dang," she muttered, nocking another arrow and drawing again...

Alex fired a second time, pegging the creeper square in the body. It fell back, quickly recovered on its four, stable little legs, and kept coming, frowning and glaring at her with an arrow stuck in its face and another where its stomach might have been if it was a man.

Feeling a thrill as the creeper closed the distance and began climbing up the slope, Alex focused, took a deep breath as she aimed, and fired a third time, striking it again in the head.

This time the creeper fell, let out a long, rattling breath, and crashed to the grass in a puff of smoke! It left behind nothing but a handful of gunpowder and a few glowing experience orbs.

Alex realized that her heart was hammering. She hardly ever fought mobs without Steve.

She did it. She'd killed creepers before, of course, but Alex hardly ever had to kill any hostile mobs without Steve's help.

Nocking another arrow, Alex peered around the clearing, scanning for any more threats...

The forest seemed quiet again.

She emerged from hiding, rushing quickly down the slope to collect the gunpowder. The pulsating, glowing experience orbs drifted toward her silently, alternating from green to yellow, and she absorbed them with the faint sound of tinkling bells. Alex searched for the strange creature and saw him half-hiding behind a tree near her. There was nothing about the creature that made her afraid. He wasn't scary at all—not like creepers or zombies or skeletons or other hostile mobs. He just looked ... afraid and confused...

When Alex turned toward him, lowering her bow, she smiled, feeling like she was approaching a scared animal.

"Hello?" she said. "Are you okay?"

The strange creature stepped out into the sunshine. She could now see that his pale skin was glistening as if he was wet. He was frowning, and his blue eyes—hard to see behind those pieces of glass on his face—darted around. He must have been frightened out of his wits!

82

His, yes, she thought. Even though he had long hair, the creature looked like a male. She could easily tell even though he was strange and curvy and soft. The creature's voice was deeper than hers at any rate...

"Alex...?" the creature said.

The woman felt a flush of fear. *How does he know her name?!* she wondered frantically.

"You know me?" Alex asked, then realized that he was still tense and ready to bolt away. She released the arrow that was ready on her bowstring and lowered her bow to her hip. With her free hand, Alex gently beckoned the creature toward her. "It's okay. You can come here. I won't hurt you..."

The creature took several unsure steps toward Alex. She closed the distance and approached him. Yes—he was definitely shorter than her. His head came up to her shoulders.

The bizarre creature looked Alex over, top to bottom, then he stared at the air around her as if looking at things that weren't there...

"Thanks for saving me," he said. "I don't have any weapons." The creature visibly relaxed a little, sighed, and reached up with his highly-defined fingers to pull the intricate dark hair out of his face.

Alex couldn't *believe* how complex this creature looked! She'd never seen anything even a fraction as visually amazing or beautiful. There were so many designs! His black shirt had letters and pictures on it. It read: *GAMER*. He had four little fingers and a thumb on each hand, and his arms flowed more smoothly than Alex could understand, thinning into wrists, then elbows. Gosh— his hair was made of countless fine threads, far thinner and finer than even cobwebs! She couldn't comprehend the level of detail in this creature's appearance!

"What *are* you?" Alex asked, staring at the little creature in awe.

"I'm a boy," the creature said. "I'm a *real* boy. Um—a human boy. My name is Jack Walker."

"Walker..." Alex repeated.

The Weird Walker...

Alex gasped.

"Jack," the boy replied. "Call me Jack."

So this was it. This 'boy' creature was the Weird Walker from the Divining Pool and Alex had found him! What did it mean? What was she supposed to do? Was this 'Jack Walker' supposed to go and live in the village like Steve's friend KittyPaws30 who'd appeared just as mysteriously?

Alex looked around. She glanced back up the hill where she'd run down from. From down in the clearing, she couldn't tell where the cave was anymore. Come to think of it, now she couldn't even remember which tree she had been standing behind when she'd attacked the creeper...

"How do you *know me*, Jack? I don't know you..."

Jack smiled. His face moved a lot like hers, but it was amazingly more elaborate and softer than anything she'd ever seen on this world.

"*Everyone* knows you, Alex," he said, which sent a chill up her spine. "Hey, um ... do you have a *sword* I can borrow? At least until we go ... um ... I don't really know where to go, really, but I have to find somewhere to hide before the sun goes down."

"Just craft a sword," Alex said, looking up at the sun. It was afternoon. She needed to get back.

"I ... um ... I don't know *how* yet," Jack replied, wrapping his arms around his curved, soft body.

"I guess, Jack, you can head back home with me—at least for tonight. There's something—" Alex stopped. She wanted to launch into a dozen questions about the boy's connection to the Divining Pool, but it'd be better to talk about that back home in safety. "We need to figure out why you're here..."

"I agree!" Jack said. "I don't know how I *got* here! I mean—I have some ideas, but ... yeah. Probably better that we should get to ... did you say *home?* You have a house near here?"

"I do," she replied. "With Steve—"

"As in *Minecraft Steve?!*" Jack exclaimed, his round eyes wide and his strange face cracking into a broad smile.

"Yes," Alex said, narrowing her eyes. This creature knew Steve too? "Steve the Minecraftian. Let's head home before the sun goes down."

"Okay!" Jack replied with a smile. He seemed to be in a much better mood already. "Lead the way!"

Alex sighed and looked around.

All around her were trees and rising slopes that Steve had said would lead to more mountains. She listened in silence, hoping to hear the sound of the stream, but there was nothing. Looking back up the slope, Alex realized that she had no idea where the cave was—she couldn't even tell where the big ridge was anymore!

"Sure thing," Alex said, eyeing the dark forest around them. "I'd be happy to but ... um ... well ... I don't know the way..."

S1E1 - Chapter 6 – Steve

The ravine seemed as deep as an ocean, delving into an abyss of utter darkness that Steve couldn't even see the bottom of...

"Oh gosh—this is so cool!" he exclaimed. His voice echoed endlessly. "I can't believe I fell all that way!"

There was definitely a bottom somewhere down in the pitch-black depths; a rocky ravine floor that had smashed Steve into oblivion when he plummeted down, down, down before!

Plopping another dirt block into the sheer ravine wall, Steve descended a little more, hopping down onto the next delicate platform that he hooked onto the stone. He peered down into the depths, trying to catch a glint of iron—anything that could tell him where in the underworld his armor was...

Checking the supply of dirt that Alex had given him, Steve figured that he had maybe a hundred more blocks. It probably wouldn't be enough. He'd have to find some tunnels or a cave network or something running through the side of the ravine that he could use to get to the bottom.

Maybe an abandoned mineshaft! he thought.

Even though most of the deep ravine was blacker than obsidian, there were some areas where Steve could see a little. There were the two lava falls far below him. Every once and a while, Steve paused to marvel at them. The burning magma was downright beautiful, constantly pouring out of the walls deep down in the world, oozing and glowing and glopping a long way down into darkness before finally colliding violently with a huge underground pool that Steve couldn't see from way up where he was.

Because of his deadly fall, Steve knew that the water was down there constantly hissing and spitting as the pool and the lava endlessly combined, cooled, and crumbled into cobblestone.

"There must be a fortune of stuff down here!" Steve said quietly to himself, his words echoing all over.

The ravine was pretty quiet. He heard a lot of bats squeaking. For a little while now, he'd been listening to the occasional echoing *clunk* of a skeleton's bones somewhere farther down as well as the infrequent *hiss* of a spider hunting on the walls. The farther he descended, Steve could make out more and more the constant spitting sounds of the lava meeting cold water far, far below him.

Steve paused to look back up.

His dirt staircase was perched dangerously along the sheer rock wall of the long ravine, going up and up all the way to the small, four-block landing he'd crafted under the tunnel's hole. He was surprised how far down he was from the surface already, and yet, he still couldn't see the bottom!

If he continued like this—constantly going down, block by block along the seemingly endless wall—he'd have to backtrack a long way along the ravine floor to find his gear...

"That's not gonna happen," Steve muttered in the darkness. He didn't have enough dirt to make it all the way down—he knew it.

Looking up at the landing again, Steve saw that Alex was gone.

"Huh..." he said, the word echoing on and on...

She must have gotten bored and left.

Steve really didn't understand Alex sometimes. Between the two of them, he was the one who couldn't keep still for long. Alex wouldn't have wandered off into the woods up there—she can't figure directions to save her life! She'd be totally lost, even as close to home as they were. Maybe she'd heard the sheep. *That* might draw her away...

The sheep, Steve thought. He needed to help her find the sheep!

He groaned. If they were as low on iron as Alex had claimed, then Steve really needed to find that lost armor. He needed his iron sword back. Even as beat up as it was, it was still loads better than the crummy wooden one he was carrying now.

Looking at the naked stone wall up ahead, Steve realized that he was standing in darkness.

He pulled out another torch and fixed it to the ravine wall, creating a big spot of yellow light in a huge, black space.

"I'll eventually run out of these, too..." he muttered.

He needed a pick axe. With a pick axe, Steve could make a stone sword and mine some coal whenever he found some. He could make more torches. Looking into his pack, Steve saw nothing but torches, dirt, a sheaf of wheat, his wooden sword, and a few blocks of oak.

Steve took a moment to build a larger platform of dirt where he was standing. He converted the raw oak into planks so that he could make a...

Didn't I just make a crafting table? He thought.

"Oh yeah," the Minecraftian said to himself. "Left it in the forest..."

With a shrug, Steve crafted another then plunked it down onto his precarious dirt platform. He pulled out the rest of his wood to make a wooden pick axe, then—

"Ah dang," he said. "Not enough..."

Steve put the scant oak planks remaining back into his pack, pulled out dirt and another torch, and continued down, leaving his hastily-crafted dirt ledge and crafting table behind.

For a while, Steve descended block by block, creating haphazard stairs along the ravine wall. Eventually, he could barely see the orange sparkling of the lava falls' light reflecting on the pool. He was ... maybe halfway down...?

How long had it been?

Looking back up to the hole leading to the surface, following his endless dirt staircase up along the stone wall and its random spots of torchlight, Steve found that he couldn't even see the top anymore. He'd moved along the wall in one direction down the ravine *too far*.

As he readied another block of dirt to continue, Steve suddenly noticed an opening in the wall ten feet or so below where he was about to place another step.

"Cave!" he exclaimed, his happy voice echoing all around him.

The ravine was longer than he could see, cutting through the world like a gigantic rift, but it was narrow enough that Steve could see the opposite wall in the darkness. Because of this, every time he talked to himself, his words bounced back at him then ping-ponged away up and down the ravine in both endless directions, echoing on for what seemed like forever...

Steve looked down at the tunnel extending into the wall.

It was too low. He'd pass over it if he continued his stairs gradually down as he was.

Putting his torch back into his pack, Steve grabbed a single block of dirt and crept to the edge of his perilous walkway. He hung down, trying to ignore the yawning, black abyss below him. Reaching for the tunnel's edge, stretching as far as he could, Steve strained to lengthen his bony arm, offering the dirt block further and further down until...

Plunk.

Steve barely managed to attach the block far below him in a way that it would act as a *ledge* leading into the tunnel.

"Phew," he said, grunting as he pulled himself back up.

Stepping over to the edge of his descending dirt steps, Steve looked down at the block he'd just placed far below him. He wondered whether or not he could jump down there without tripping and falling to his death, or maybe hurting his ankle if he managed to land on the small, dangerous space...

With a deep sigh, Steve stepped to the very edge, letting his toes hang off, then hoped for the best, aimed his body as best he could, and dropped down.

His feet hit the dirt block, making the treacherous ledge shake and tremble under his wait.

"Oh, yeah!" Steve exclaimed, his voice echoing on and on. He turned toward the tunnel and pulled his wooden sword from his belt, holding the weapon in one hand and a torch in the other...

The stone tunnel was dark. It was empty and turned down to the left.

"It goes down!" the Minecraftian said to himself dramatically. "The plan's working!"

Taking a few steps down into the tunnel, Steve smiled, letting his torchlight lead the way deeper into the world...

The plan, he thought suddenly, *was to get your stuff so that you could help get the sheep...*

Steve stopped, staring at the pitch-black tunnel leading to the unknown.

He'd been down in the ravine for what felt like a long time now. It took a lot of time to carefully make dirt steps down along a wall as far as he had.

Was his stuff still *down there* even? Or was Steve just wasting time exploring?!

"But exploring is never a waste of time!" he said out loud, grinning to make himself feel better.

But now, in the quiet tunnel, who-knows how deep underground, Steve was starting to feel bad. He needed to help Alex. They needed their sheep for meat and wool—for themselves and for trading with the village—and if they lost them, they'd have to travel who-knows how far to find more sheep again...

Alex needed him.

Steve sighed.

He *was* getting sidetracked, wasn't he? Alex had warned him not to get sidetracked. His stuff was gone now and he knew it. Steve had to get back up to the surface to help her find those sheep. The Minecraftian turned around, looking at the delicate dirt block he'd jumped down to. He could get back up by building a column of dirt under his—

A zombie suddenly gurgled nearby.

Steve gasped. He grinned. His sword suddenly felt *alive* in his hand...

That mob sounded like it was right down the tunnel!

Turning around again, Steve gripped the hilt of his wooden sword, put his torch before him, and continued deeper into the world. As he did, he heard the *thuds* of heavy feet wandering around below him. He heard a low moan from up ahead, then a gurgle right behind it.

"Two...?" he whispered, grinning from ear to ear.

Two zombies, Steve thought with an inner voice in his head like the dramatic announcer of a gladiatorial combat ring. *No armor. Nothing but a torch and a wooden sword...*

"Who will win...?" Steve said quietly to himself, hopping down a short drop.

He landed in a small cavern. Two zombies that had been wandering around in the darkness suddenly turned and looked at Steve with dead eyes and slack, rotten mouths...

"Yeah!!" Steve shouted, charging in at his first foe and slashing into it with his wooden blade. The Minecraftian struck the zombie hard, then clashed into the undead mob's body with his shoulder, knocking it to the ground!

The other zombie turned and raised its gross, green hands. It came after Steve, twisting its mangled face into a glare and a grimace, snarling as it approached! The warrior suddenly noticed that there were even *two more* zombies deeper in a part of the cavern that he didn't notice from where he'd landed.

"*Four* zombies!" Steve exclaimed, feeling a thrill fly through him.

When the second zombie came in at him, he parried a slow, swinging fist with his wooden sword, then punched the creature backwards with its crude, oak pommel. When the second zombie staggered backwards with a wet roar of surprise, Steve spun and quickly skewered the first one before it finished climbing up from the ground.

The first zombie collapsed, dead.

"Now *three* zombies!"

Steve rushed in with a deep lunge, thrusting his crummy wooden blade through the second zombie's chest while it recovered from the Minecraftian's knock backwards. When it reacted with a gurgling pain sound, Steve pulled his blade out of its body, rapidly spun it through the air, then took the creature's legs out from under it with a wide, low sweep of the blade. The moment the zombie fell to the stony cavern floor, Steve reversed his sword's grip and stabbed it through the chest, killing it.

He suddenly sensed movement coming in from behind and dodged like a cat, ducking out of the way as the third zombie—both of his remaining opponents were now in range—swung at his head.

Steve rolled to one side, giving himself distance from one and facing off with the other, then lashed out with two quick slashes, dicing up the undead mob and knocking it back.

"Take that!"

The wounded zombie's face was blank and it stared at Steve with dead eyes as it recovered its balance and pressed the attack, reaching for him with its green claws. The Minecraftian knew that he *had* to avoid letting those things get a good hold on him. The zombies were very strong—maybe stronger than Steve himself. If they grabbed him, they'd take him out easily...

Whipping up the blade of his wooden sword, Steve lopped off one of the zombie's hands. It punched Steve in the chest with its stump—knocking the Minecraftian backwards—then paused to stare at its *lack of hand* with a slow, confused face...

Steve laughed once then cleaved into the creature's head with a powerful, downward strike. It fell.

Facing off against the last zombie, Steve cast a quick look around him to make sure that there were no more mobs. He didn't want to be caught by surprise! When he was satisfied that the cavern was empty, he went to work on his last opponent, alternating between smacking it and stabbing it with his wooden sword and quickly dancing backwards out of the way whenever the slow, undead creature swung at him.

Eventually, the fourth one fell.

"Yes!" Steve exclaimed, grinning from ear to ear as a dozen or so brightly-glowing orbs of experience scattered around on the cavern floor casually drifted toward him, ringing like bells as he absorbed their power.

When Steve was left alone in the darkness once again, he pulled out another torch and collected several pieces of zombie flesh that hovered above the stone floor. Looking around the cavern, Steve saw two narrow tunnels leading away. One continued *down*, so he took it. He passed one offshoot tunnel, then another, but stayed on the same path—as long as it was continuing *down*.

After wandering through the winding, descending dark tunnel for a few minutes, Steve paused and held his breath when he suddenly heard several skeletons through the cave walls. Their bones *clunked* again and again.

"No shield," he said to himself.

The dramatic inner voice returned: *No armor. No shield. Armed with only a wooden sword...*

"Oh, shut up," Steve said to his overactive imagination.

Following the tunnel down several more steps, Steve paused when he heard a skeleton *clunk* right ahead of him. The instant he fixed a torch to the wall, he suddenly saw the gleam of bone in the darkness ahead and recognized a bow aimed right at him...

"Dang!" he cried, immediately ducking out of the way just as the undead archer let an arrow fly. The deadly missile whistled through the air and hit the stone wall where Steve was *just* standing, bouncing away into the tunnel behind him.

Looking out again, Steve saw the archer not very far in front of him, quickly reloading...

"Charge!!" he exclaimed with an explosive *burst* of speed, raising his sword high and desperately trying to close the distance to the skeleton before it shot at him again!

It worked. Just before the skeleton was able to nock its arrow, the mob looked up in surprise and alarm as Steve *crashed* into it, making its bones *clatter!* The Minecraftian laid into the archer, smashing at its bones again and again with his wooden sword. *Kill it before it shoots me!* Steve thought frantically. *Kill it before it shoots me!*

Under the third or fourth powerful blow of the blunt, oak blade, the undead mob broke apart and collapsed to the tunnel floor in a pile of bones and dust. Steve quickly picked up a stray arrow it left behind, as well as the biggest bone he could find, stashing both items in his pack.

Then he listened...

He still heard many bones *clunking* up ahead.

"There are a lot of skeletons up there..." he said quietly to himself.

Creeping ahead with a torch lit in front of him and his sword held ready, Steve took his time and listened as the sounds of moving bones grew closer and closer...

When he turned a corner of the tunnel and suddenly saw *cobblestone bricks*, Steve knew that he'd found a dungeon! He immediately saw a dim and small magical flame in the middle of a strange black cage with a tiny, dancing skeleton inside. He saw the brown color of a chest against a wall, then—

Several skeletons' bones *clunked* and Steve suddenly realized that many undead archers were standing in there ... looking at him. He saw several arrowheads aimed his way and backed up as fast as he could just as several bows twanged! As Steve scrambled backwards, he heard multiple arrows bouncing off of the stone walls.

"Dang!" he exclaimed, half-afraid, half-exhilarated. "A dungeon!" An instant later, several skeletons pursued him down the tunnel, their heels clanking on the stony floor and their bones scraping and *clunking* against the rocky walls. "Oh, double-dang!" he added.

Steve turned and ran. He scrambled up the tunnel, going up and up, hoping not to get shot in the back. There was no way he'd be able to conquer a skeleton dungeon with nothing but a half-busted wooden sword—it was getting pretty beat up by now—and no resources! He'd have to come back. He'd have to tell Alex about it and get her to—

"Oh, Alex!" he cried, stopping and whacking himself in the forehead. He heard the *clunking* of bones behind him so kept moving. Steve turned into the first offshoot tunnel he saw that he had passed before, then kept climbing. "The sheep! I *did* get sidetracked! Dang it!"

Steve felt bad. Alex needed his help, and he kept getting sidetracked. He was *always* getting distracted!

Rushing up the tunnel, climbing closer to the surface—Steve ignored the sound of a hissing spider he heard down another tunnel he passed—the Minecraftian wanted nothing more in that moment than to get *back up there* and help his best friend.

After a short while of climbing, Steve emerged into a fairly large cavern and stopped at a rushing river of cold, dark-blue water crossing his path. Looking upriver, Steve peered into the darkness...

He figured that if he followed the river it might lead him up to the surface again. Water rushed *down*, right?

Steve followed the shore of the river as far as he could before getting wet. He scrambled over boulders and leapt from rock to rock—sometimes having to ford water up to his waist that tried to push him over—and eventually followed the flow to a small waterfall leading to a pool farther above. Climbing the stone wall, Steve used Alex's dirt blocks to make his way up and when he crested the top of the cliff and the underground waterfall, the Minecraftian smiled when he looked up ahead...

"Daylight!"

On the other side of the small pool that siphoned into the waterfall, there was an underground stream winding up through a rising cavern, originating at the base of *another* waterfall that led up into sunshine!

Dang—these underground caves and caverns were *so cool!*

Steve ran along the stream—climbing and leaping from boulder to boulder—until finally reaching the small waterfall that would lead back to the surface world. Then—doing something amazingly athletic that he'd only done a couple of other times in his life—Steve plunged into the bright blue fall, held his breath, and swam *up*.

He swam, pulling and kicking—suddenly happy that he wasn't wearing heavy metal armor—and climbed the fall, holding his breath and focusing on one thing: getting to the top! After what seemed like a long time, Steve's muscles were burning and his breath was gone. If he held out any longer, he'd pass out!

Then Steve emerged into the daylight, his face breaking the surface of the water.

The Minecraftian took in a huge, triumphant breath and smiled.

"Yes!" he shouted, laughing as he treaded water and tried to avoid getting sucked back down into the hole again. All around Steve was a sunny mountain vale surrounded by tall spruce trees and the occasional oak. He'd emerged in a wide, slow-moving river—slow-moving at this part of it, anyway—that was snaking through the mountains.

It was amazing that a crevice under a river could lead to such an amazing underground place!

Steve swam for the shore, finally climbing up onto the grass when he felt like his body just couldn't go anymore. He turned and lay on his back, looking up at the bright, blue sky and the clouds drifting past. Craning his neck, Steve looked at the sun.

It was late afternoon.

He sighed.

Definitely time to get home.

But where's Alex? he wondered.

Eventually, Steve stood up and shook the water off of his skin, clothes, and out of his hair. He pulled out his wooden sword again and looked around for landmarks. Noting the sun heading toward the west, he quickly figured out directions. He had no idea whether he was north or south of home, but when he caught sight of the big ridge, he immediately hiked toward it. Steve knew that once he crested the big ridge, he'd be able to figure out where he was...

Soon, the warrior was standing at the highest point of the forest around him: on the top of the big ridge. The only way he could get higher would be to continue north into the taller mountains that led to snowcapped peaks and ice-spires that he hadn't bothered to explore yet.

The Minecraftian knew exactly where he was. Standing on the ridge, Steve looked out over the forest to the west and the vast desert to the east. He could see the village way out there—its glass windows sparkling in the low afternoon sun—and beyond it, from this vantage point, he saw *something else* out there in the sand dunes. There was a squarish structure far away in the desert; something he'd never seen before from his perspective near the homestead. It was colored just like the sand around it except for a few spots of orange-red that Steve could barely make out...

"A ... desert temple?" he said, feeling a grin spreading on his face.

He had to check it out!

Steve frowned and shook his head. "Don't get sidetracked," he said to himself. "Find Alex. Find the sheep..."

Now that he was oriented, Steve simply followed the ridge almost all the way home. Eventually, he saw the roof of their house and the wide, flat farm that Alex always worked so hard on. The entire time he was hiking along the ridge—occasionally needing to jump from rock to rock—Steve watched for Alex's bright green shirt and red-orange hair down in the woods. If she ended up not making it home before dark on account of getting lost, Steve would feel *terrible*...

He finally saw her near the house. Far below him, wandering through the trees, Steve saw Alex's bright shirt easily between the dark spruce trees and shadows of the woods. She was walking to the east through a clearing, holding her bow and looking around rather frantically.

Steve chuckled.

Alex apparently had *no idea* that she was right next to the house, just over a single hill! That girl was so clueless about direction—she had no sense of it at all! Steve laughed some more as he saw her talking, looking back behind her from time to time, then...

"What's that?!" Steve said, squinting his eyes and staring. He blocked the sunlight with one hand and peered down at the strange mob he saw following his good friend...

There was a short, slender creature a lot like a Minecraftian walking just behind Alex. It wasn't chasing her and she wasn't running from it. They were walking *together*. From up on the big ridge, all Steve could really see was that the creature was dressed in black, had pale skin and dark hair, and its body ... well, its body was *weird!* It was slimmer in every way than he and Alex and had bizarre, curving lines like nothing Steve had ever seen before!

"Huh..." Steve said to himself, lowering his hand.

He turned to intercept Alex and her new friend, then hopped and rushed down the slope into the forest. Before long, the ground leveled out and Steve was catching up behind them.

Alex suddenly cried out in surprise, spinning to face Steve with her bow held out, drawing an arrow with a trembling hand!

"Whoa!" Steve said with a laugh, holding his hands up. "Don't shoot!"

Recognizing him, Alex suddenly let out a huge breath in relief and lowered her bow. "Oh! *Steve!!*"

The creature with her also turned in alarm, then his weird, curvy eyes opened wide and his strange mouth stretched into a wide smile. "Steve! It's you! Steve!"

Steve walked up to Alex and the weird creature. His muscles were sore, but at least he wasn't wet anymore. He could tell that

Alex was positively terrified of the woods around them, but the nervousness pouring off of her seemed to relax as he approached.

"Where have you been?!" Alex asked crossly.

Looking over the strange mob next to his friend, Steve took in the bizarre sight completely. The creature was weird indeed— definitely some sort of Minecraftian—but so different and complicated-looking that merely looking upon it hurt Steve's eyes...

And it knew his name was *Steve*...

"Do I know you?" Steve asked, crossing his arms over his chest.

"Nope," the creature replied, grinning from ear to ear. "But I know *you*, Steve! I'm happy to meet you!"

"This is Jack Walker," Alex said, scowling as she looked at Steve. "He's the *Weird Walker* that the Divining Pool warned us about."

Huh? Steve thought.

"Weird ... walker ... what?!" he said, looking from Jack up to the lowering sun.

Alex scoffed. "Don't you remember? The Divining Pool? Earlier, after the *sun-shadow*, it said that *the time of the Weird Walker has begun!*"

Steve shrugged. Was that what she was talking about earlier? "Eh..." he said. "So, Jack Walker, where'd *you* come from...?"

The bizarre Jack-creature opened his soft, curvy mouth to reply, but Alex cut him off.

"We don't have *time* for that! We've been trying to find the way home from that stupid cave you brought me to for *hours!* The sun's going down soon. Let's talk when we get to safety..."

Steve laughed. He couldn't help it. He planted his hands on his hips and bellowed out loud and long, laughing into the hills.

"What's so funny?" Jack asked. Steve noticed that the creature had strange pieces of glass in front of his eyes. The Weird Walker's eyes were blue...

"Yes, please, Steve," Alex said, brimming with sarcasm and annoyance. "What's so freaking funny?! Today has been a *disaster!*"

Steve shrugged and smiled.

"The house is right over this hill," he said, turning toward home. He waved for them to follow. "Come on."

Alex scoffed, fuming in place for a while. When Steve looked back over his shoulder, he saw Jack trying to decide whether to follow him or to stay with Alex. Finally, the creature rushed to catch up then Alex did the same.

They crested the hill and Steve immediately saw the edges of the farm. To his left, the stream ran around the eastern side of the homestead.

"Oh my gosh!" Jack said with a laugh. "It really is right over the hill! This is your house??"

Alex followed, glaring at Steve. "Where have you *been?!*"

Steve turned to look at her and when he looked into her face, he felt a pang of regret when he saw pain and frustration in Alex's eyes. Her hard eyes immediately softened when Steve frowned.

"I'm sorry," Steve said. "I'm sorry we didn't get the sheep."

"We need to find them before they leave this forest," Alex said.

"We'll work on it tomorrow morning," Steve replied. "Together."

"No getting sidetracked?" Alex said.

"Right," Steve said. "No getting sidetracked. Oh—I've got to tell you about what I found down there! And farther away in the desert, I saw—"

Alex shook her head. "Let's get inside. We've got to figure out this stuff with Jack."

"I need a weapon," Jack said suddenly. "I don't seem to have an inventory or a crafting window."

Steve and Alex blinked.

"What's *that?*" Alex asked.

Steve smiled. "Well it's good to meet you, Jack. Welcome to our homestead."

"Yeah," Alex said, clapping the creature on its soft, curved shoulder. She seemed a little weirded out by what she felt there. "Welcome to our home."

With that, Steve led them through the farm, around the animal pens, and toward the side door. As he stepped inside, he looked up in the sky and saw the colors changing with the coming sunset.

The creature called 'Jack' followed them past their animals and newly-seeded wheat rows, staring around in awe. The *Weird Walker* smiled broadly as he considered stepping in through the door into the house.

This was going to be interesting...

Season 1, Episode 2:
One Block at a Time

One Block at a Time

Jack is stuck in a video game! And not just any video game. He's stuck in his own modded version of Minecraft in a new world he created called 'Vortexia' moments before a solar flare back in the real world somehow transported him into his school's new virtual reality system! Being inside this pixelated world is weird--Jack is a real boy with a real flesh and blood body surrounded by a digital world! It's a darned good thing that he ran into the famous Steve and Alex. Otherwise, he probably wouldn't survive the first night!

As Jack struggles to cope with being trapped in the game he loves without an inventory or crafting menu and missing critical controls that a player would normally have on a keyboard, how will the boy survive if he's reduced to working with one block at a time?? When a seemingly easy task of helping Alex and Steve gather some lost sheep becomes a lot more difficult than Jack anticipated, will the real boy--the Weird Walker--manage to cope with this bizarre, new world? And what wacky messages will the Divining Pool have in store for the trio today...?

S1E2 - Chapter 1 - Jack

Jack stepped into the digital house, following the pixelated and blocky form of Alex.

The wooden floor under his feet felt just as oddly-spongy as the outdoors had. Surrounded by bright colors and lots of light, the boy reached out and touched the doorframe—just a line of brown a few pixels wide—and walked into the hall.

Immediately on his right, Jack saw an opening into what might have been something like a kitchen. There were a few chests on the floor and hooked onto the walls next to a crafting table and a couple of furnaces. On top of the kitchen's crafting table was half of a big, white *cake*. Several slices were missing.

"Whoa..." he said, still amazed at the low resolution details unfolding before his eyes. He looked down at his hands again. Yep—they were still his normal human hands.

The kid suddenly felt a push from behind and gasped as Steve pushed past him, likely impatient and tired of waiting for the boy to *take it all in*.

Alex and Steve continued past the kitchen into the house.

"Close the door, will ya, Jack? It's *Jack*, right?" Steve called over his shoulder.

"Um ... yeah, okay."

"Night's coming!" Alex exclaimed from farther inside the house. "We need everything closed up to keep the mobs out!"

Jack turned, looked out over the farm and animal pens once more, then closed the door. It snapped shut quickly as if weightless with a loud *creak*. The boy looked at the hinges, down at the circular handle—this was a *spruce* door—and wondered how it all worked. Jack was inside a *video game*—and this was a game without physics! Blocks could hang in the air. He looked into the kitchen-type room and considered the chests hanging from the walls. How were they hanging there? Jack knew from experience that they'd simply been *placed* there, but he knew that if he walked over and cut the walls out from behind them that they'd still hang there in the air...

Looking down at the ring that served as a spruce door's latch, Jack reached out and touched it. The ring didn't really make sense. It wasn't something that he could wrap his real fingers around and *turn*. The latch barely stuck out from the door's surface, like it was just a decoration. How would he *open* this door? Was it even possible for—?

"Jack," Alex suddenly said from behind him.

The boy turned. Alex stood, her eyes green and her hair as bright orange as a carrot. The ponytail that hung down around her shoulder was literally *part* of her shoulder. Part of her Minecraft *skin*. Over her head was the Damage Indicator window, showing a little picture of her face, a bar that said 'Alex' and a green hit point meter that currently read 20/20.

"Hi, Alex," he said, looking up at the Minecraftian woman with an awkward grin. This was all so weird!

"Get lost, Weird Walker?" she asked with a smile. "Come on. I'll show you around. The sun will go down soon. We're gonna have some dinner before bed."

"Okay..."

Jack was still a little bothered by the fact that he was *short* in this world. Just like back in the real world, he was still a kid—though very close to being a teenager like his older brother—and only stood up to the chests of most adults. It was the same here.

In fact, he'd noticed that Alex and Steve themselves were the same height. *Of course*, he thought. All Minecraftians were the same height: 1.8 meters tall. Jack himself was probably somewhere around 1.5, which meant that the top of his head went up to these Minecraftians' chests as well. Which *also* meant that most hostile mobs would be taller than Jack too, and blocks wouldn't go up to his waist as if he was a player—they'd go up to his chest.

Ugh, he thought. *Everything's more difficult when you're a kid...*

If he was going to get stuck in this game, why did he have to be stuck as a human boy? He didn't have a keyboard with which to hit the 'E' key! How in the world would this work?!

Jack turned away from the spruce 'farm door' (as Alex and Steve called it), not knowing whether or not he'd ever be able to open it again.

"So, you already saw the kitchen," Alex said with a smile, pointing with a big, blocky hand at the small room off of the hall next to them.

"A kitchen in Minecraft?" Jack asked. "Why?"

"Uh ... Minecraft?" Alex replied, then smiled and shook her head. "Yeah, I know we don't need it. We do most of our crafting in the main room. But ... I like to cook, so I made a special room for keeping cooking ingredients and stuff. I also keep buckets in there. There's still some cake left on the crafting table if you want some...?"

"Uh, thanks," Jack said, looking at the digital half-cake again. What would happen if he tried to eat this food? Would it even be possible? If he could somehow get those pixels into his stomach, would they hurt him, or even be digestible at all?! "Maybe later..." he said with a forced smile.

"Okay," Alex said. "Come with me."

Jack followed Alex down the rest of the short hall and into the obvious 'main room'. The ceiling was high, the oak walls dotted with torches, and there was a big red rug in the middle of the room. Jack saw another door leading outside on one wall—facing the opposite direction from the farm—with a couple of large chests next to it on the floor. There were two more halls leading away on one wall—obviously going to the rest of the house—and the walls between the hallways and the other exterior door were lined with Minecraftian equipment. There was an array of nine furnaces along one area, a crafting table, some more chests, an anvil, and another crafting table, where Steve was standing now. The Minecraftian warrior was looking down at the device, moving his hand around. A stone sword suddenly *popped* into existence, held in one of Steve's hands. Along the wall near the other exterior door, there were two glass windows. Jack could see the sun low on the western horizon there, casting orange and pink colors and threatening to dip out of sight.

"Cool," Jack said, then spoke up to Steve across the room. "Making new gear?"

Steve looked back with a smirk. "Yep."

"This is the main room, Jack," Alex said. "Steve," she added, looking over at the warrior. "Take it easy on the iron, will you? We're low and can't afford to lose any more until we go mining."

Steve kept working on whatever he was crafting and waved a dismissive hand in the air.

"Yeah, yeah. I'm just makin *stone* stuff..."

Alex sighed and looked back at Jack. "Anyway," she said, "this is where most of our equipment is." She began pointing at all of the crafting gear that Jack already knew backwards and forwards as a player. "We have a bunch of furnaces for making ingots and glass and stuff, then there's a chest with materials for crafting tools and armor and other metal things right next to it. There's also a chest that we've been filling with coal but..." she crossed her arms over her chest and went on sarcastically, "*someone* tends to forget the furnaces running, so we're always trying to get more." Alex smiled and shook her head then went on. "There are also two crafting tables here, the anvil for fixing things and making magical items if we ever find any *books*, and through that hallway—" She pointed at the opening between the anvil and the crafting table where Steve stood, but Jack interrupted her.

"Do you have an enchanting table somewhere?" he asked.

"An enchanting table?" Alex repeated, cocking an orange eyebrow. "No, we haven't figured that one out yet." She spoke like she'd never heard of the concept before.

"You haven't enchanted anything before?" Jack asked, wrapping his arms around his body. He wanted to sit down, but looking around, he saw no chairs. The only place to sit was either on the floor or maybe on a chest or something...

"No," Alex replied, crossing her arms again and looking down at Jack suspiciously. "If you're familiar with such things, Jack Walker, perhaps you could help us with that."

"Gladly!" Jack said with a grin. "So ... what's in there?" he asked, pointing at the hallway where Alex had left off. With the intense torchlight illuminating this whole house—necessary to keep the mobs from spawning inside, Jack assumed—he could already see the brown shapes of many chests lining a wall. "Storage area, huh?"

"Yes," Alex said with a smile. "We have not been in this gulch for very long, but I figured that it would be a good idea to stay organized from the beginning, so I—"

"Oh, Alex *loves* being organized!" Steve exclaimed from the crafting table. Jack looked up and saw the Minecraftian swinging a stone sword and a stone pick axe around in tandem; dual-wielding. "And you'd better not put anything in the *wrong chest*, kid!" he said with a laugh and a smirk.

Alex scoffed.

"Well, at any rate," she said, "that's where we keep dirt and stone and mob drops, and we'll start filling that up with other things the more we gather as time goes on."

"What's through the other hall?" Jack asked, pointing at the other hallway leading away. He could see that it was a long wooden corridor.

If Alex and Steve hadn't been here very long, then how long had they really existed? They were in *Vortexia*—the new world that Jack had created *just before* putting the virtual reality headset on. Did they just suddenly *appear* here and start surviving and building while Jack was just getting into the game back before...

Back before you were sucked into a video game, body and all! he thought.

This was insane. Jack still wasn't sure whether or not it was real. Maybe he was lying unconscious on the floor, hooked up to the Vortex Wave system and dreaming this entire thing! He didn't want to think about it. It was too crazy—too bizarre. If he stopped to think about it, he would—

"Oh, that's where the bedrooms are," Alex said, snapping Jack out of his daydreaming. "If you're gonna stay with us, we'll have to build an addition, I suppose. Oh," she added, pointing at the oak door on the western side of the house near the windows. "That's the main entrance, by the way. We don't use it much, since we usually head out on the east side—what we call the farm door—but that's the way to my mine, which is across the field out front."

"Your access to the mine isn't in the house?" Jack asked.

That was odd, he thought.

Steve spoke up again. "She didn't want the tunnels coming up into where we sleep. Alex doesn't want any mobs wandering in..." He smiled as if teasing her.

Alex frowned and put her hands on her hips. "It's safer that way! Besides—we don't need to mine all that often." She lowered her hands and shook the anger off of her face. "Come on, Jack. I'll show you the rest."

"Okay."

Alex led Jack into the second hall toward the bedrooms. It was the longest hall in the house. There were two oak doors down the hall on the right and one on the left. All the way down the hall on the left side was another open doorway. Jack could see the shapes of chests just inside, so he figured that it must lead to the far side of the large storage room.

Leading the boy down the hall, Alex stopped at the first door on the right and opened it.

"My bedroom," she said. Jack craned his neck to look inside and saw a sparse room lit by torches that held a bed, a single large chest, an armor stand with a full set of iron armor, a green rug, and a frame on one wall holding an iron pick axe.

"Cool," Jack said.

Alex quickly closed the door with a *creak* and led Jack to the next door on the right. She opened it. Jack saw another bed, several chests, some randomly placed torches of varying heights on the walls, and three empty armor stands. There was also a single dirt block placed randomly on the floor, not quite in the middle of the room.

"Steve's room," she said.

"Okay," Jack said, looking across the hall into the storage room. It was indeed full of chests, and almost as big as the main room with another crafting table in the center. The storage room was also L-shaped, built around what must have been a small room—smaller than the bedrooms—on the same end of the hall. *That must be the other door on the opposite side of the hall from the bedrooms*, he thought. In real life, the small room would be a bathroom. "What's that?" he asked, pointing at the last door.

Alex shut Steve's door. "Something special," she said.

"Special?"

"Yeah. That's a special room built around the *Divining Pool*. Come on..."

Jack could recall Alex mentioning that term to Steve outside. Something about a prophecy involving a sun-shadow and the *Weird Walker?* So far, he'd figured out that *he*, Jack, was the Weird Walker that she was talking about. Heck—his *last name* was Walker. And it was pretty weird that he was here as a real boy. The sun-shadow that she was referring to must have been that strange solar eclipse that Jack had seen right before he was totally stuck in the game earlier that day. There are no solar eclipses in Minecraft. That must have been really weird for Steve and Alex...

Alex led Jack to the final door then opened it with a *creak*.

Jack first looked then stepped into a plain room with spruce plank walls (different than the rest of the house) with a torch up on each side. The room was empty save for a simple fountain in the middle: a basic ring of blocks with a single block in the middle full of clear, blue water. The odd thing about the fountain was that it was entirely composed of *bedrock*, including the blocks under it, which Jack could see glittering through the central pool. The indestructible stone was dark grey with black stripes and flecks of white that almost sparkled under the torchlight.

"Bedrock?!" Jack asked. This was strange. Normally, bedrock wasn't anywhere to be seen except at the bottom of the world. Well ... and on *The End* with the Ender Dragon. How was there bedrock up on the surface? "Where'd this come from?" he asked.

"You know bedrock?" Alex asked him, stepping into the small room and leaning up against a wall. "Have you seen it before?"

"Oh yeah," Jack replied. "I know all about this world."

"So it seems..."

"But I haven't seen bedrock on the surface before," Jack added.

"Neither have we," Alex said. "I call it the 'Divining Pool' because of the weird stuff it does sometimes, but it was here before I built this house. Some time back when Steve and I were passing through this gulch, we found it. I decided to build this house around it."

"What's it do?" Jack asked. He climbed up onto the bedrock, pausing the instant he touched it. "Holy chicken feathers!" Jack exclaimed when he touched the immovable stone. This was the first thing he'd touched in Vortexia that felt totally solid. It wasn't squishy at all. It was like solid stone back in the real world! He already knew that bedrock was indestructible but he figured that if he started punching it, he'd never break through it. Plus, he hated to think of how it would feel to the soft skin of his human hand. It would literally be like punching real stone!

"What's wrong?" Alex asked.

"It's ... um ... really solid!" Jack said, pulling himself up onto the fountain so that he could look into the water better. There were hazy white letters—a whole paragraph's worth of words—floating a few inches under the surface, gradually rising.

"Of course it's solid," Alex said. "It's bedrock."

"Hey, there are words in here!" Jack exclaimed, squinting to read it. He fixed his slipping glasses.

"Really?" Alex replied, stepping forward. When she saw them, she gasped. "Yeah—that's what it does! It makes words, and weird things happen." Alex turned over her shoulder. "Hey, Steve!! Words at the Divining Pool!"

Jack tried to focus on the words. They gradually became clearer and clearer as they approached the surface of the pool, but they shimmered and waved and were hard to read...

Steve suddenly appeared in the doorway, leaning against the frame while noisily eating an apple.

"What's goin on?" he asked.

"Shush!" Alex replied then leaned over the fountain to read the words with Jack.

Jack read the words aloud:

"*ok um let my character in here be poor. i am Braydon or KidOfCubes or Minecraft123. i use bows. my bow is modified and maybe it can shoot 2 arrows together. i don't have a house, i always move around in the forest. master in foraging in forests. - KidOfCubes*"

All three of them were silent for a moment.

What the heck?! Jack thought, scratching his head through his hair.

"Eh," Steve finally said, wandering away munching on his apple.

"KidOfCubes...?" Alex muttered. "Another new villager?"

"What's it mean?" Jack asked. Just as he did, the words— which had been drifting around on the surface of the pool— suddenly dissipated into the blue water and vanished. "Whoa! It's gone!"

"They do that," Alex said.

"Not very much time to read," Jack said.

"That's true. Really, I have no idea how often that happens while we're gone, but I see it almost every day."

"So weird!"

"I never really know what it means; *why* it's there," Alex said. "But usually it's kind of like a ... prediction. The Divining Pool says something strange, then something related to the words happens around us. Once, there was a similar bunch of words and another Minecraftian appeared one day and built a house in the village on the other side of the big ridge. This morning—just after the sun-shadow—it told me about ... well ... I guess it told me about *you*, the Weird Walker."

It was some sort of prediction device? A warning system?

"So does that mean," Jack said slowly, "that some Minecraftian will show up that can shoot two arrows at a time and lives in the forest?"

Alex shrugged, staring at the pool. By now, the words were totally gone and only bold, blue water remained. "Maybe," she said. "We'll see. Let's get something to eat. The sun's probably down by now and we need to get to bed. The longer we stay up, the more mobs will be around in the morning." She headed out of the room.

Jack followed, closing the door after one last glance at the Divining Pool. He'd never seen *anything* like that in Minecraft before; not even in a mod.

"Okay. Where should I sleep?" Jack asked. "I don't know what would happen to me if I die. I should probably make a bed." Something deep inside Jack told him to make a bed. Put down a bed and lie in it to set a spawn point, so that if anything bad happened, he'd respawn at the house; the *homestead*...

Assuming I can even respawn, he thought with a stab of dread.

Jack was here in his real body—not as an *avatar*. What would happen if a zombie killed him or a skeleton shot him or a creeper blew him up? What if he fell off of a cliff, or drowned, or slipped into some burning lava?!

Would he even come back to life again? Or would his real body be destroyed ... and he'd *die?!*

Fearful and brooding, Jack followed Alex back to the main room where Steve was rooting around in the various chests around the forges.

"Hey, Alex, where's the steak?" he asked, looking back at them.

"In the kitchen, doofus," she said. "Those chests are just for fuel and tool and armor crafting stuff. You're not putting random stuff in there again, are you??"

Steve smirked. "No. I know where stuff goes..."

Alex looked back to Jack. "Well, you *could* make a bed, Jack, but we're out of wool. We'll have to shear the sheep when we find them tomorrow."

String, Jack thought. Four string to each wool. "What about string? I can make three wool from twelve string."

"You really *do* know a lot about this world, don't you?" Alex asked. "Check the storage room. I don't know how much string we have, though. We haven't killed many spiders lately."

So he did.

Walking into the storage room, Jack saw rows of chests— some on the ground, some just higher than his head—and he immediately saw lots of wooden signs in between with pixelated words indicating the chests' contents. The room was highly organized. Looking over several signs, he stopped at 'mob drops' and opened the chest with a *creak*.

When he opened the huge, wooden container, Jack gasped as a large, glowing grid interface appeared in front of him. It was a lot like an inventory window, but it showed only the contents of the chest ... exactly as it would be in the game! He saw stacks of spider eyes, string (only two), rotten flesh, bones, gun powder...

"Wow!" Jack exclaimed, reaching out to the stack of string with the little number "2" next to it. He went to pick up both of them—snatching the stack out of thin air—but only managed to grab a single piece of string, leaving the other in the chest. Holding the string in his hand was like holding a large piece of plastic shaped like the blocky, white icon of string.

At any rate, two wasn't enough. He returned it to the grid, laying it on top of the other piece of string, and it disappeared from his hand, making the "1" change into a "2".

Weird!

Jack knew that his strange, 'real boy' condition would have some bearing on his ability to craft and manipulate the *stuff* in this world. He was suddenly certain that if he had an inventory, it would work the same way. Now, if he did, if only he could figure out how to *access* it...

The boy let the chest close again with a *creak* then went back out and across the main room to find Alex and Steve in the kitchen. On the way, he saw through the windows that the sky outside was black. When he went through the little hall toward the farm door and turned into the kitchen, he found Steve eating a steak. Alex was holding a loaf of bread.

"Hey," he said when they noticed him. "So, not enough string."

"It's okay," Alex said. "We'll make you a bed tomorrow. We just need to find the sheep first."

"Yeah..."

"So what do you want to eat?" Alex asked, opening one of the chests in the kitchen. "We have roasted chicken, steak, some apples, bread, and a few fish filets left..."

Jack stared at the food in their hands. It was the exact same as it was in the game: a thin, almost-two-dimensional pixelated picture of food. He didn't *smell* any bread or cooked steak; he only saw the icons that they were holding in their blocky hands.

The boy's stomach growled. When he'd snuck away into the computer lab and hooked into this game, it was right before lunch back in the real world. How long had he been here? He was already hungry when he arrived in Vortexia, and he was even hungrier now.

That said, staring at Alex and Steve's food—Steve was noisily munching on his steak while little pixels of what were meant to be *food crumbs* fell all over around him—Jack just couldn't imagine *eating* that stuff. He'd have to figure something out, of course. He couldn't simply *never eat*. Who knows how long he'd be stuck here?

Jack opened his mouth to ask for some chicken then he paused. He imagined biting and chewing the digital food and its pixelated pieces going down his very real throat and into his real stomach. Would those pixelated points hurt his insides? Would his body even recognize it as food? Or would it be like trying to eat cardboard or something?

"Uh," he said, trying to ignore his growling stomach, "I'm not all that hungry. I'll eat tomorrow."

Alex let the chest shut with a *creak* and shrugged, eating her bread just as noisily and messily as Steve ate his apple and steak.

"Whatever," she said, finishing her food. "Well, it's been a long *annoying* day, so, if you don't mind guys, I'm gonna hit the hay."

"Me too," Steve added between crunching bites. "Hey, you made a rhyme, Alex!" He smiled.

"Alright," Jack said, stepping out of the way as both Minecraftians left the kitchen and headed into the main room. The boy followed. "I guess I'll sleep in here ... if I have to."

Honestly, Jack wasn't all that tired. If the days were truly just ten minutes for him, then he could stay awake without getting tired for ... heck ... he couldn't even calculate how many days that was! If Jack's real body was still like back home where he was awake for fourteen or sixteen hours or whatever before sleeping, then here on Vortexia, Jack would be like a strange creature that seemingly *never* needed sleep! He chuckled to himself. Of course, if that was so, then when he finally *did* need sleep, it would be like he'd go into hibernation for many Minecraft days while he slept for eight hours or so...

Crazy!

The Minecraftians would think that he was *really* weird, hibernating like that...

"Jack, feel free to look around some more and make yourself at home," Alex said. "Don't let any zombies inside!"

"Yeah, good night, *Weird Walker*," Steve said with a laugh.

With that, the two of them ran down the hall to their bedrooms, each opened and closed their respective doors, and Jack was suddenly left in total silence.

He faintly heard a cow *moo* and stamp one foot outside.

Then he heard a plodding *thump* outside the front windows, followed by the distinct wet gurgle of a zombie somewhere out in the night...

"Oh gosh..." he said, creeping over to one window.

It was hard to see very well outside through the pixelated glass with all of the torchlight around him, but Jack could barely make out the dark blue and black forest. There was an area right in front of the door with light. There must have been a torch above the door on the outside of the house.

Jack heard a zombie walking around out there, its clumsy, heavy steps *thumping* around in the grass, but he didn't see the mob.

That would be his first zombie...

Imagining the hostile mob with green skin and rotten features and tattered, blue clothes was actually pretty scary, considering that the undead creature would be far taller and broader than Jack.

The boy walked away from the window. He didn't want to see the zombie.

How long would the night be? Less than another ten minutes, now...

He should make a *sword*.

Jack smiled.

He ran off into the storage room and started checking the chests. When Alex said that a lot of them were empty and just there for organization's sake, she wasn't kidding. Jack was able to find plenty of cobblestone and dirt, a good bit of gravel and sand, some glass, and a small collection of mob parts, flowers, dye materials, and other things that didn't have anything to do with swords, but he couldn't find any *wood*. He searched and searched but it looked like they were either totally out of raw wood and planks, or Alex and Steve had whatever was left in their inventories.

Jack suddenly remembered the two chests sitting around the front door.

"Dump chests, maybe?" he said to himself, running there and opening the first one with a *creak*.

There was a bunch of random stuff in there but no wood. The closest thing to wood was an extra oak door and some spruce saplings, but nothing that Jack could use.

He ran back to the kitchen and checked the chests in there. No wood.

Running back to the front windows, Jack looked outside. He waited for a while, watching and listening.

To make a sword, he'd need a stick. To make a stick, he'd need planks, and to make planks, he'd need raw wood from a tree. He'd found no sticks, planks, *or* tree logs in this entire house.

"Dare I...?" Jack said to himself, staring out of the window. He eyed the nearest tree: a small oak tree perhaps fifteen feet from the front door and the cobblestone porch outside. It would take sixteen punches from his fist to get an oak block, and he could make the rest of what he needed out of that. All he needed was a single oak block...

The last time Jack wondered '*Should I...?*' he ended up being transported into a video game.

Still, it was close. It was nighttime, and there were probably several hostile mobs around in the darkness, but Jack couldn't hear any *right here*, directly in front of the house...

He could do it.

In and out. Out and in. Just a few seconds...

Jack took a few deep breaths, jumped up and down on his toes to pump up his courage, then reached down to the oak door handle.

"The door problem," he said to himself, looking down at the shallow 'depiction' of a handle. How would he open the door? He reached for the handle to try and turn it, but it was very thin and didn't seem designed to actually *move*.

But how had he opened the chest? The chest was bigger and simpler. There was a top half and a bottom half, and he'd literally lifted the top half to open on hinges.

Jack reached for the handle again, imagining it turning in his hand.

Open, he thought.

And it did.

"What the...?!" Jack muttered as the door rapidly swung open toward him with a *pop*.

It was open. He was staring at the open night air. There were mobs around, so he decided to think about it later. Taking a quick glance left and right under the light of a single torch above the door outside, Jack ran toward the tree as fast as he could!

He immediately started punching it. *Punch, punch, punch, punch...*

Hitting the wooden tree trunk as hard as he could as fast as he could immediately started making his arm muscles start to burn. Jack couldn't see well enough in the dark to tell whether or not the block of tree was breaking, but he kept at it, hoping that he could harvest the block before some mob in the night noticed him!

Punch, punch, punch, punch...

Jack heard a zombie's groan from behind him on the right.

Dang!

Punch, punch, punch, punch...

He focused on the tree. Any second now, it would—

Pop!

A section of the tree trunk disappeared, shrinking down within a fraction of a second down to a block of oak log the size of a grapefruit, leaving the entire rest of the tree floating in thin air! Jack scrambled around on the dark ground, looking for the block as he heard heavy, plodding feet coming up behind him...

The approaching zombie let out a *growl* that turned the boy's knees to jelly!

"Dang it! Where—?!"

Then he found it, and immediately scooped up the block, turning to face the zombie. There it was—almost on him—tall and big and dressed in pixelated, dirty blue clothes that was ripped and untucked, approaching with a black, open mouth and dead, dark eyes, reaching for Jack with its long, blocky arms and claws. The mob was close enough that the Damage Indicator mod put up a window above its head with a picture of its green face, the word *Zombie*, and a green health bar that said 20/20.

"No! Oh no!" Jack exclaimed, feeling a burst of fright *flash* though his body from his head to his toes. He leapt backwards away from the mob! His knees felt wobbly and his body wasn't listening to his brain very well, but he focused on the block in his hands. He tried to ignore the approaching snarling zombie long enough to find the glowing, open front door of the house again, then Jack scrambled back home, trying not to trip on his own frightened, numb feet!

Jack stumbled on the way inside, dropped the tree trunk block onto the red carpet in the main room. Then he jumped back to his feet—heart pounding—and slammed the digital door just before the zombie stepped inside!

Crash!

The mob hit the door. The loud sound of crunching wood made Jack just about jump out of his skin!

"Dang!"

Crash!

Oh Jeez—did he make this game normal mode or hard mode? Would the zombie bash through the wooden door?! Oh, dang!

Jack ran into the storage room, threw open the chest of dirt, and grabbed a single block of dirt from the strange grid interface that appeared in front of him. He ran back with the miniature dirt block in his hand...

Crash!

Reaching the front door again, Jack threw the dirt block down onto the wooden floor in to block the door.

Plunk.

Then he took a deep breath.

Crash! Crunch! Crash!

The zombie outside continued bashing on the door. Every single strike scared the cornflakes out of Jack, but he knew—scary or not—that if the undead mob broke down the door, he'd be protected by the dirt block.

Hopefully.

That dang zombie stuck around all night.

After a few more seconds of trying to not have a heart attack, Jack turned back to the red carpet and picked up the oak block. He knew he'd also need stone, and didn't really have an inventory other than his little pants pockets, so he headed to the storage room to use the crafting table he'd seen there.

Taking two stone blocks out of the cobblestone chest, Jack balanced all three blocks in his arms and approached the crafting table. He tried to open the crafting table's interface.

"Open," he said, but nothing happened. He tried to touch it, imagine opening it, and thought *open* just like he did with the door, but nothing happened. Finally, Jack dropped the two cobblestone blocks and the log block, touched the crafting table with intent, thought to open it, then gasped and grinned when the familiar nine-block interface appeared in front of him!

"Yes!" Jack exclaimed with a smile.

Maybe he'd had too much in his hands...

All three blocks he'd dropped were just hovering gently up and down above the wooden floor at his feet. *If I had an inventory*, Jack thought, *that stuff would just automatically pop into it from being close to me*. Maybe he didn't have an inventory, after all.

Jack picked up the oak block and tried to open the crafting table again.

The interface pulled up.

"Awesome," Jack said with a smile. Then, he put the oak block into the first of the nine open spaces under the word 'Crafting'. The single empty space on the right of the arrow showed four wooden planks. Jack reached out, picked up the planks, and suddenly four miniature planks-blocks were tumbling from his arms!

"Dang!" he said, reaching down to grab them. The crafting table interface disappeared as soon as Jack let go of the device.

Picking up two wooden planks to make sticks, Jack tried to open the crafting table. He couldn't.

One at a time, maybe? he thought.

Jack dropped one plank next to him. Once he had just one plank in his hand, he was able to open the interface again. Jack put one plank-block into the nine-square, then carefully reached down to pick up another plank-block from the floor while keeping hold of the crafting table. When he picked up a second plank-block, he added it to the crafting table then smiled when *four sticks* showed up in the results box. Jack grabbed the sticks, which all promptly fell from his hands except for one.

One block at a time, he thought with a frown. *Lame.*

"Now, time for the sword," Jack said, putting the sticks down and reaching out for a cobblestone block that was hovering on the floor. He made sure that the second one was in reach then opened the crafting table again. Jack put one cobblestone block in, then carefully grabbed the other while still touching the crafting table.

When he had the blade crafted, Jack looked around for a stick on the floor, then released the crafting table to reach down and grab one.

The interface disappeared and both cobblestone blocks popped out and fell to the floor.

"Dang!"

Okay, Jack thought. *So I have to touch it the whole time...*

He started again, being careful to keep one hand on the crafting table the entire time. Reaching and placing one block at a time, Jack put in both cobblestone blocks to construct the blade, then added the stick for the hilt. He smiled when he saw the stone sword appear in the results box.

When Jack reached over and pulled the stone sword out of the box, the weapon appeared in his hand, light and apparently deadly to mobs...

Jack smiled.

"Finally!" he said.

Placing the sword on top of the crafting table, Jack put away the rest of the wood planks and sticks into Alex's designated 'wood' chest. Then he grabbed the sword, headed back into the main room, and stood in the middle of the rug.

Jack played with the sword. He swung it around, tried to parry with it, and alternated between fighting one-handed and two-handed. The handle was blocky and weird, so it was hard to hold, but he could make it work. Looking over and feeling the blade, Jack couldn't imagine this blocky, dull thing cutting through any enemies, but maybe things were different here. Maybe this blocky sword would go through mobs' blocky bodies just as easily as a sharp blade would back in the real world.

For the rest of the night, Jack stayed in the main room. Sometimes he stood, watching out the windows and trying to stay brave in the face of the zombie outside trying to bash in the door. Other times, he sat with his back leaned on a wall. He practiced some more with the stone sword—his first creation.

Jack smiled. He'd crafted everything there was to craft in this game as a player, and he knew Minecraft backwards and forwards, but somehow, he felt *very proud* of this simple stone sword...

Ten minutes wasn't very long, but when there was nothing to do—especially when a zombie was trying to bash in your door—it sure felt like a lot longer.

Jack spent some time trying to access his inventory and personal crafting window. He tried to imagine a ghostly keyboard in front of him; or at least just an 'E' key. He tried to summon-call the window into being just as he'd opened the door and crafting window, but he couldn't accomplish anything with his inventory.

Maybe he really didn't have one...

Eventually, Jack stood at one window—ignoring the loud and scary zombie close to him and seemingly splintering the front door—and watched the bright white (square) moon descend in the western sky.

The black sky eventually turned deep blue then began to lighten...

S1E2 - Chapter 2 – Alex

Alex opened her eyes with a sigh and a smile.

Sitting up in bed, she immediately looked at the window in her room to the outside and saw daylight streaming in. The shadow of a cow moved outside the glass.

She jumped out of bed then paused, remembering all of the crazy stuff from yesterday.

Jack! she thought. That's right! There was that weird creature living in their house with them now. She wondered if the *Weird Walker* had managed to sleep at all, or if he even needed sleep. What had he called himself? A boy. A kid...

They had to find those sheep today—it was super important! If the sheep wandered away too far and disappeared—forever lost in the vast surrounding woods and mountains full of hostile mobs in shadows—then she and Steve probably wouldn't see another sheep for a long time!

Alex frowned. She sure didn't want to have to make wool out of spider strings. *Gross...*

Checking her pack, Alex made sure that she had her trusty iron sword, a couple of pick axes, a wood-chopping axe, and all of the basic essentials that she'd need for a wilderness trip. Then she put on her iron armor, piece by piece. Alex hardly ever bothered wearing her armor when she was home working on the farm, but whenever she went down into the mines or knew that she'd be heading into the woods or on a trip, she made sure to always be prepared for battle.

Honestly, she hated fighting. But it was better to have her armor and not need it than to need her armor and not have it, right?

Alex felt well-rested and a little hungry.

Walking across the room to the door, she stepped out into the hall then turned to the main room.

Jack was there, standing by a window, looking out.

He was leaning up against the windowsill on his strange, soft and curvy arms with his chin on one forearm. Leaning up against the wall next to him was a stone sword.

"Good morning!" Alex called, stepping into the main room. Her armor clanked as she moved. She hated making extra noises.

Jack turned, adjusting the strange glass pieces that rested on his face and nose, then smiled when he saw her. He pushed the long, brown hair out of his face and tucked it behind his ears. *Gosh*—everything about this creature was so fine and intricate and complicated-looking! Just *looking at him* almost hurt Alex's eyes...

"Hey, Alex!" Jack exclaimed with a smile. "Look!" He reached down and hefted the stone sword by its handle, holding the blade in front of him. "I made a sword!"

She smiled. "That's great, Jack. Has Steve come out yet?"

"Here I come!" Steve suddenly shouted excitedly from behind her and down the hall. He closed his bedroom door with a *pop*.

Alex looked back as Steve rushed into the main room, dressed in his blue clothing with his shirt untucked in one spot. Her friend was grinning broadly and his blue eyes were bright and ready for action.

"Morning, Steve," she said.

"Morning!" he replied, stopping when he saw Jack standing by the front wall with a sword. "Hey—you have a sword, Jack!"

"Yeah," Jack said, seemingly happy that Steve had noticed. "I made it last night while you guys were sleeping." He looked at Alex. "It was actually really hard to do. For some reason, crafting isn't working like normal for me—I don't know why."

That's a strange thing to say, Alex thought.

"What do you mean?" she asked.

"Oh, well," the boy replied, "Usually I can just open up a crafting menu with 'E'—even without a crafting table—and make basic stuff, and I usually have an inventory too, but for some reason, I can't access those two things..."

Steve laughed. "What are you *talking* about?!" he asked with a smile. "You're weird, kid. Ha!" He looked at Alex with a chuckle. "The *weird* walker, huh? He's weird, alright..."

"You guys don't know what I mean by that?" Jack asked. "Inventory? Crafting menu? Tool belt?"

Steve smirked. "You don't *have* a belt, dude," he said.

Alex tried to comprehend whatever Jack was talking about, but couldn't make sense of it. "I don't know what you mean by that stuff, no," she said.

"How do you guys craft things?" Jack asked.

"We just ... *do it*," Alex said. "I can make a crafting table from four planks then make more stuff with it. Can't you?"

"No," Jack said. "I was able to figure out how to open the grid on the crafting table last night, but I have to like ... keep holding onto it ... and put in one item at a time, or it all comes flying off. And I can't seem to use it holding more than one block at a time..."

More weird words.

Alex had no idea what the kid was talking about.

"Sorry, Jack," she said. "I don't understand what you're saying."

"Are you a Minecraftian?" Steve asked him. "I figured that you were like us, but—I dunno—*shaped* different or something..."

Jack looked down at his hands, then down at the floor. He pushed up his strange face-item up his nose again and shrugged.

"I ... um ... I'm not sure," Jack said. "I guess I'm not. I'm a real boy; a real boy without a keyboard."

"Keyboard?" Steve asked with another laugh. "You sure say some weird stuff. So," he said, looking at Alex, clapping his hands together. *New subject.* "I was gonna head into the village today to help KittyPaws30 build a swimming pool. You wanna help?"

Alex felt her face turn hot.

Did he really forget already?! What about all of that talk of not getting side-tracked anymore and them working together to get the sheep first thing in the morning?!

"Really?!" Alex replied, putting her hands on her hips. Her armor *clanked*. "*That's* what you're doing today? Do you remember anything *else* that we were going to do first? Anything *super* important?"

Steve scratched his head and glanced back to the storage room. He finally muttered something about needing his own sword...

"Hey, uh," Jack said, "Weren't we gonna get those sheep?"

Alex suppressed the urge to glare at the newcomer. She was really curious as to whether or not Steve would figure this out without help.

"Oh yeah!" Steve said with a grin. "Yeah, let's do that little sheep thing. *Then* we can go to the village if there's still time."

134

"There's a village nearby?" Jack asked.

"On the other side of the big ridge!" Steve replied, pointing haphazardly toward the east. "So are you gonna be staying with us for a while?" he asked, his eyes immediately darting over to Alex with a look like a question mark.

Jack looked at her too. "Well," the boy said, lowering his stone sword. "Um ... I guess ... if that's *okay* with you guys. I don't really have anywhere else to be, and it'll probably take me a while to build my own house while I figure out this weird crafting stuff..."

Alex felt her irritation with Steve melt away when she saw the boy standing unsure.

"Sure, Jack," she said. "You can stay here. We can always build an addition. What can you do?"

"*Do?*" Jack asked. "Well, unless I have some other problems here I don't know about, I can do just about *anything* in Minecraft. I know this game backwards and forwards. I can—"

"Game...?" Alex asked. "What do you mean?"

The kid stopped, deep in thought. That look of uncertainty appeared again. He seemed about to speak then stopped himself. After a few more seconds, he smiled, pulled the hair out of his face, then spoke up again.

"Um, never mind that. I'm still figuring this out. I don't know how I got here, or even how long I'll be here. But yeah—*stuff!* I know *a lot* about this world. I know how to make a lot of things. I know a lot about villages and temples and dungeons and strongholds; I know about the nether and *the End* ... I even know how to enchant stuff!"

Alex felt one of her eyebrows rise.

"You can enchant?" she asked. "We've been wanting to try that, but we haven't devoted any diamonds to an enchanting table and we haven't collected any obsidian yet."

In all honesty, Alex hadn't yet figured out *how* to make an enchanting table. Steve was really big on reading every book he could find in libraries and anywhere else, and he was always talking about things like the nether or ... did Jack say *the End?* What was that?! She had no idea!

Maybe this kid would be a real help around here. Heck—at least she could rely on him to not instantly forget everything like Steve did.

"Oh sure!" Jack said. "I've made *tons* of magical items, enchanted weapons, armor, tools—even fishing poles! I can make magical books. You don't have an enchanting table in another house or anything?"

"No," Alex said. "This is our only house for many miles around."

"And our last place is nothing but an old, empty shack!" Steve added, giving Alex a playful nudge on one shoulder. Her armor *clanked*.

Alex glared at Steve. Their old house was a nice place. She could have happily lived there for a long time. Then she calmed down. Their *homestead* here was actually pretty nice too, and a lot bigger...

"Do you have any diamonds?" Jack asked.

"One," Alex said. It was in the chest in her bedroom.

"Well, you need two," Jack said. "And four blocks of obsidian, and a book. In fact, to make a good enchanting table, we need *lots* of books. It increases its power."

Okay, so maybe the kid wasn't kidding. He did seem to know a lot...

"Yeah," Steve said with a nod and a smile. "That's true." He turned to Alex. "The *Weird Walker* knows his stuff."

"That's good," Alex said, then, she looked at the daylight through the front windows. "Well, we need to get going and find those sheep. Let's eat, grab some wheat, then get searching."

"I need a sword and stuff!" Steve exclaimed. "Alex, can I have some wood and stone?"

"Storage room," she said. "Except there might not be any wood." She paused to open her pack.

"I had two sticks left," Jack said suddenly to Steve. "I put them in the 'wood' chest."

"Oh, good!" he replied then ran off into the large room full of containers.

Alex stopped reaching for her own wood supply and smiled at the kid.

"Hungry yet?" she asked him. "I was going to get some breakfast. Want a steak? Or some bread, maybe?"

"Yeah! Steak! I'm starving!!" Steve called back from the storage room.

Alex glared at the open doorway, then she sighed and relaxed.

Jack touched his soft belly under his strange, flowing shirt and grimaced. He looked up at Alex again and smiled.

"Nah," the kid said. "Not hungry."

"Okay."

With that, Alex crossed the main room toward the hall leading to the kitchen and farm door, then helped herself to a piece of bread and some roasted chicken. She added another piece of chicken and two apples to her pack for later.

Several seconds behind her, Steve burst into the room, ravenous and intent on eating the first thing he could get his hands on! He grabbed two pieces of steak and munched noisily on them until they were gone.

Steve burped. "Alright!" he exclaimed. "Let's rock!" He rushed out of the spruce door to the farm. Alex looked after him and saw that the warrior was dashing back and forth outside collecting bits of rotten flesh and other things left behind from the night's undead.

Alex left the kitchen and found Jack. "Ready, Jack?"

"Sure."

"Let's go, then. This way, through the farm door. We need some wheat for the sheep."

They stepped outside into the sunshine. Alex smiled and savored the warmth on her face. Steve—apparently finished collecting mob drops—was already sprinting across the wheat fields toward the stream. Jack closed the door behind him very carefully—as if he didn't fully know how—then stared around at the sky and their animal pens in wonder. The kid was carrying his new sword in one hand.

"Steve, wait up!" Alex called. The warrior stopped and ran back.

Walking over to the gardening chest, Alex removed several sheaves of wheat that she'd harvested yesterday during repairs to the farm and its *creeper crater*.

"Don't forget this," she said to Steve, handing him two sheaves of wheat. "Don't drop it. We'll need it, okay, Steve?"

"Sure thing!" Steve took the wheat and immediately threw the two items into his pack.

"Here ya go, Jack," she said, handing the kid two bundles.

He reached for them, paused, then replied, "I can only hold one." The kid took a single sheaf of wheat, holding it in his left hand as he still held his sword in his right. The boy then sighed, licked his lips, and peered around the farm. His eyes landed on the trenches between the crop rows. He stared at the water.

"What is it? What's wrong?" Alex asked.

"I'm so *thirsty!*" Jack replied. He looked across the farm again. "Did one of you say that there's a *stream* over that way?"

"Yes," Alex said, watching the strange creature.

"I really need a drink!" he exclaimed, setting off through the fields.

Alex and Steve shared confused glances. *What* was he doing exactly? Steve shrugged.

They followed Jack.

The boy found the stream at the edge of the homestead property. He carefully placed his sword and sheaf of wheat onto the green grass—they both began hovering up and down—then crouched down at the rushing water's edge.

"What are you doing?" Alex asked him.

"So weird..." Steve muttered.

Jack put one soft, intricate hand into the flowing blue water. He gasped then pulled it out again. Then he *cupped* his hands together—something that Alex had never seen before—and drew up a small amount of water in his palms.

"I need to drink!" Jack said, frowning at his small collection of blue water before finally bringing it up to his curved, complex mouth.

Drink? Water? Alex thought.

"What do you mean, *drink?*" she asked. "You mean like ... drinking milk?"

The kid slurped up the water noisily, thought about it for a moment, then reached down and brought handful after handful of water to his mouth. Eventually, he wiped his face, adjusted the glass-things on perched on his nose and ears, and stood.

"Yeah," he said with a smile. "Humans like me need to drink water to live."

Steve scratched his head. "Drink ... water?! You mean like drinking milk??"

Jack laughed, picking up his sword and wheat again. "Yeah, I guess," he said.

Alex looked up at the sun. It was still low in the air. They hadn't wasted too much time...

"Okay, Steve," Alex said. "Lead the way, please."

"Sure thing!" the warrior replied. He looked into the woods but before he did, he jumped down into the creek with a *splash* up to his waist, then played with the water experimentally for a moment. Jack and Alex watched him. Steve tried to bring water up to his mouth, couldn't, then shrugged and leapt back onto the shore again. "This way!"

Alex followed her friend into the woods. Jack struggled to keep up, running smoothly on his shorter legs, soon making heavy breathing noises. It wasn't long before the kid was really lagging behind.

After a little while, she stopped to let Jack catch up.

"Holy ducks, you guys are fast!" he exclaimed, gasping and breathing loudly. He leaned over his knees then stood, pulling the hair out of his face. Alex was surprised to see that the big mass of long, extremely-thin strands of brown hair were wet in some areas. That was odd. She didn't remember the boy putting his *head* into the stream...

"What's a duck?" Steve called back from up ahead. He pulled out his sword and swung at oak leaves trying to cut down apples.

"Let's take it a little slower, Steve," Alex said. "Jack doesn't move like us."

"Alright, whatever."

Alex looked around as Jack stumbled up to them, breathing loudly. She felt really nervous and uncomfortable in the forest. There were shadows everywhere. The stream continued deeper and deeper into the woods. At some point, she knew that Steve would lead them up to higher ground, then probably to that cave leading to the ravine where they separated yesterday. Alex had *no idea* where any of that stuff was from where she was standing. In fact, looking back, there was no sign of the *homestead* at all...

"Minecraftians are *so fast!*" Jack was saying, leaning against a tree. "And I'm really fast! At least—really fast compared to other human boys!"

"There are *more* of you?" Steve replied.

"Not here," Jack said, then, "Okay, I'm ready."

The three of them continued up a slope and through dense trees and shadows that gave Alex a chill. She pulled out her bow as they walked and felt a lot more secure than yesterday, wearing her iron armor. By now, she was completely turned around. From down in the forest, she couldn't even see the sun to know which direction was which. Jack tried his best to keep up, his skin glistening strangely with moisture. The kid was having a very hard time climbing the blocky inclines—each new level was as high as his chest, and it didn't look like he could jump like she and Steve could.

They climbed and traveled, leaving the stream behind. Alex was surprised when Steve suddenly led them into bright sunshine on top of a ridge. The trees opened up and they walked along the top of the sunny ridge for a while. Alex tried to make sense of the world around her and searched for anything she could recognize. On one side of the ridge was endless, sun-scorched desert. Alex saw a village down there. Was that *their* village? Or another? They'd already walked so far...

"Hey," Jack said, making loud breathing noises again. "Is that ... the village where ... *phew* ... you want to build the swimming pool?"

"Yeah!" Steve replied, pausing and standing on a boulder.

Jack climbed up onto a boulder next to him and stopped to breathe loudly and look around.

"So that's ... to the east, looks like?"

"Yeah," Steve said. "The village is on the other side of the big ridge to the east of the house," Steve replied.

Jack nodded. "So does that mean that *this* is the big ridge?"

"Yep."

"Cool."

This is the big ridge? Alex thought with a grimace. She could see the village clearly, but had no freaking *clue* where they were! How did Steve and Jack understand what they were looking at? The world around her was really confusing and mostly looked the same...

"Let's move on," she said finally.

They did.

The instant they dipped back down from the ridge into the shadowy woods, Steve paused when there was a loud, quick *hiss* from up ahead. The Minecraftian warrior crouched and put his stone sword up in front of him.

"What's that?!" Jack asked with a touch of fear in his voice.

"Spider!" Steve exclaimed then suddenly sprinted down the hill!

"Dang it, Steve!" Alex shouted after him, peering down into the murk. She could see the big black shape and the glowing red eyes, but it was obvious that the spider couldn't care less about their presence. It was daytime, after all...

Steve charged into battle anyway. The spider spun on its eight, long legs with another *hiss* just as Steve swung his stone sword and chopped into the mob!

The spider suddenly wasn't unconcerned anymore...

Alex saw the creature's red eyes narrow. It flexed its fangs, crouched, and leapt at Steve. An instant before the arachnid collided with her friend to tackle him to the ground, Steve dodged out of the way, slicing it with his sword again. The spider crashed down then immediately jumped back to its many claws and spun to face him. Steve rapidly *thrust* forward with his stone blade in response, skewering the mob through the middle. The monster fell, curling up its legs, then dropped dead.

A moment later, the spider evaporated into smoke and there was a *ding* as Steve absorbed an experience orb. The Minecraftian reached down and grabbed a piece of spider string.

"That was totally unnecessary, Steve," Alex said, crossing her arms.

Steve scoffed and walked up to both of them, grinning from ear to ear. He shrugged. "Hey—experience and a little bit of string. Not bad, huh?" He handed the string to Jack. "You need more string if we don't get the sheep back, right?"

Jack looked at Alex. "Can you carry it?" he asked. "I can't."

Alex sighed, reached out, and took the string, adding it to her pack.

"Can we *please* stay focused now?" she asked. "We've got to find those sheep!"

Steve groaned. "Alright..."

After the spider, Steve continued leading them through the forest, up and down hills that Alex didn't recognize. They finally stopped.

"What?" Alex asked, looking around and fingering her bow nervously.

She had *no idea* where they were...

"There's the cave," Steve said, pointing.

She looked ahead and saw a small black hole leading into the hillside. There was a softly glowing yellow light inside. Dang—she hadn't recognized it at all!

"A cave?" Jack asked, sitting on a boulder behind them. "The sheep are in a cave?"

"No," Steve said. "Well—probably not. But they're maybe around here *somewhere*..."

"It's a good start," Alex said.

"Let's split up," Steve said. "We can head in different directions past the cave and—"

"No way," Alex said. "We stick together. I don't know how to get home from here."

"I agree, actually," Jack added. "I lost track of where we are."

Steve rolled his eyes then pointed in different directions around them. "North, East, South, West," he said to Alex. "You don't remember?"

Alex glared at him then headed toward the cave. "Come on," she said. "Stick together."

Steve looked longingly at the cave. Alex could tell that he really wanted inside there again, but Alex insisted that they stay out in the forest this time. He led them over ground around the entrance. The plan was to follow the tunnel while up on the surface until they found the other opening where Alex had emerged and found Jack running away from the creeper. There was a sheep there yesterday...

That was the plan, anyway, but after passing the cave opening, Alex soon had no idea where they were heading, and just followed Steve.

"There!" Steve announced suddenly, pointing with his stone sword.

All three of them peered through the woods. Alex finally saw movement: a fuzzy, white shape in the shadows between some trees. She felt herself smile.

Finally!

A few seconds later, they were all running up to the single sheep. There were no other animals around at all.

"I hope we can find more than this *one*," Alex said, pulling out a sheaf of wheat and immediately drawing the sheep's attention.

"Ba-ah-ah-ah..." it said, tromping over to them through the trees.

She recognized the sheep. This was one of theirs.

"Five more to go, right?" Jack asked, walking up to pet the sheep's thick white wool coat. He smiled when he did, tucking his sheaf of wheat under one arm in a way that Alex had never seen before.

Alex peered around them and listened.

"This is *so* boring!" Steve exclaimed suddenly.

"Be quiet!" Alex snapped. "Let's listen..."

They did.

There was no sign of any more sheep around them.

Dang.

"Can we move on, please?" Steve asked finally. "Dang—this is gonna take all day!"

"Hey, we need to do it!" Alex replied, then, "Come on, girl..."

They needed to get this sheep home. One was better than none. Even if they didn't manage to find any more, they really needed to get *this* one back in the pen ... even if it meant going home for just a single sheep and coming back again. It would take time, but ... what was that saying? *A bird in the hand is better than three in the bush?*

She started leading the sheep back the way they'd come then realized that she had no idea where she were going and stopped. The sheep clomped after her, extremely interested in the wheat that Alex had in her hand.

"Where are you going?" Steve asked. "Let's find some more!"

"Let's get this one home first," Alex replied.

"What?! Just one?!"

"Yeah. That way, if we can't find anymore, we at least have *her*. We can't risk losing her while we keep searching for the others."

For a quick second, Alex had contemplated sending just Steve back with the sheep while she and Jack kept searching. Steve would be able to navigate straight home then back much faster than any of them. But it was doomed idea. Alex couldn't take the risk of him getting sidetracked on the way home and losing the sheep. Plus, she didn't like the idea of her and the *Weird Walker* roaming the woods, lost so far from home, waiting for Steve to just come back and find them again.

Steve scoffed. "This is a waste of time..."

"Don't worry," Alex said. "You can build that swimming pool tomorrow, right?"

Steve grumbled acknowledgement.

"It doesn't make much sense to go back for one sheep when there are still five out here..." Jack said carefully.

"Sure it does," Alex replied. "Steve, could you please lead the way??" She looked back down at Jack. "There are *no* sheep around here that we've seen. Steve and I *brought them here* from several biomes over. We can't risk losing even this one now that we have her. We can come back again after bringing her home."

Jack shrugged and walked along with them, swinging his stone sword idly.

Sometime later, they arrived home. Seeing the homestead miraculously emerge through the trees surprised Alex. She'd been just leading the sheep along—drawn to her fistful of wheat— through endless oak and spruce trees that all looked the same. Once they stepped out into the sunshine of the gulch, she tilted her face up at the sun and smiled.

Leading the animal across the fields and into the livestock area, Alex finally brought the sheep back into the repaired pen and closed it with a sigh.

"There's *one*," she said, smiling at the Steve and Jack.

Steve frowned. Jack touched his stomach, grimaced, and smiled.

"Well, let's go back," Steve announced dramatically, turning away, "...again! Walking around the forest *all day* when we could be chilling out in a nice, clear swimming pool before sunset!" He started leading them back to the woods.

Alex felt her skin grow hot.

Jack ran over to the stream, presumably to drink again.

"Hey!" Alex said, walking along after Steve angrily. "We never would have had to do this if you didn't go get the farm and sheep pen *blown up*, Steve!"

Steve scoffed and paused to look up at the sun, putting his hands on his hips.

"It's about noon," he said. "Maybe if we can find all five right away..."

Alex laughed and scoffed. "Yeah right..."

"I'm ready to go back," Jack said excitedly, catching up to them and wiping his mouth with the back side of his hand holding the wheat. "Let's get those sheep!"

The kid's positive attitude helped Alex's irritation melt away. She sighed.

"We'll try to hurry," she said.

They went back into the woods.

A long time and one dead skeleton archer later, the three appeared in the distant area where they'd found the last sheep.

They searched around, staying together.

They searched and searched.

Eventually, Alex found that the trees were changing, and the mountains were becoming steeper. The oak and spruce forest they'd been in all day was changing into a different forested biome: a taiga mountain forest. She recognized the massive, tall pine trees and the boulders strewn all around covered in moss.

Alex knew the biomes of the world—as much as she'd experienced, anyway—and she'd seen taiga forests before. However, taiga woods were terrible for being confusing and convoluted and turning her around, so she tried to avoid them. There were twisting gulches and rifts and ridges everywhere, and the trees were so tall that she couldn't make sense out of a bit of it. She wouldn't be surprised if even Steve became lost if they ventured too far into—

"A taiga forest?!" Jack exclaimed. So the kid knew what it was, too. "Holy snakes and beetles! Look at the size of these *trees!* I mean—I knew that they were big, but now? Next to the *real* me?! These things are freaking huge! They're like real trees!"

Steve smirked. "They *are* real trees, Jack..."

The kid said such strange words sometimes.

Snakes? Alex thought, then shook her head. She opened her mouth to speak then paused when she heard a faint but familiar sound from over a ridge:

Ba-ah-ah-ah-ah...

All three of them exchanged excited glances.

"A sheep!" Alex exclaimed. *This is great!* she thought. If they could get at least one more home, then they could at least breed more—even with only two!

"Come on!" Steve said with a grin, then ran up the steep hill around boulders and trees wider than the two Minecraftians put together. Alex and Jack followed. The kid instantly started breathing loudly as he struggled up the blocky incline, pulling himself up one level at a time.

"Don't lose your way back!" Alex called up at Steve as she pursued.

"This might ... be..." Jack stammered in between heavy breaths, "... a *mega*-taiga..."

She crested the ridge and gasped at what she saw on the other side. The taiga mountains went on forever, leading up and up toward an far-away area of huge, snow-capped mountains on the horizon. On the other side of *this* ridge, however, through the towering pine trees, she could see a sunny green valley full of mossy boulders.

In the middle of the valley were *five* sheep, all together in a herd and feeding on the mountain grass. Alex saw four white ones and one grey one. She smiled and let out a little *squee* of excitement. Those were *their* sheep!

"What?" Jack exclaimed, gasping for breath and pulling himself up block after block trying to catch up.

Alex smiled at Steve—who stood next to her with his arms folded on his chest, looking victorious—then she looked down at Jack.

"It's our sheep!" she exclaimed. "*All five* of them!"

As soon as Jack caught up, the three of them ran down the rocky slope to the valley where their animals were calmly feeding in the sunshine.

The five sheep all stood around without a care as she, Steve, and Jack ran up with wheat in hand. Well—she and Jack were holding the wheat. Steve was holding his sword, then paused—*oh yeah!*—and pulled out his own.

One by one, the five sheep looked up from the thick, green grass and stared at the wheat bundles in their hands with dumb eyes. They bleated and called out to their masters.

"Ba-ah-ah-ah-ah!"

"Come on!" Alex exclaimed with a broad grin. She felt a lot better. The thought of losing their sheep really scared her. They'd been with them for a long time. "This way, you knuckleheads! Let's go home, you guys!"

"Come on, sheep!" Jack added, smiling widely. He held the wheat up in his little soft hand and grinned up at Alex. He looked as happy as ... well ... a kid trying to feed a sheep. "Let's go *this* way! Up the hill!"

They started leading the sheep away from the taiga mountains. Between the three of them, it wasn't too hard to encourage the animals up the ridge and back into the spruce and oak forest.

As soon as they started their descent down into the woods that Alex was a little more comfortable in, a sudden sound filled her with fear and shot a chill up her spine...

Ah-rooooooooo!

All three of them stopped and looked around. The sheep stamped and *ba-ah-ah-ah'd* obliviously as Alex scanned the shadowy forest...

Then she saw a wolf ... then another.

There were grey shapes rushing around them in the distance like fleeting grey ghosts...

"Wolves..." Alex muttered with another shot of fright.

Steve immediately thrust his wheat back into his pack and held up his stone sword.

There was another howl from behind them, then a howl answered from a different direction in the woods...

"Oh, dang..." Jack said, holding up his sword like Steve did. "We're surrounded!"

"Keep moving!" Alex exclaimed. "Stay close to the sheep! Steve, which way?!"

"This ... uh ... *this* way!" he replied, pointing with his sword but watching an approaching beast that slunk through the shadows with gleaming fangs...

Then the wolves attacked, fast.

With another howl, Alex was shocked when three big grey and shaggy wolves burst forth from the forest to attack the group of sheep from a direction where she, Steve, and Jack weren't standing.

"No!!" Alex shouted, feeling fear choke up her heart as three fanged beasts all fell upon one white sheep at the edge of the group. They immediately tore it down to the ground and killed it. "No!" she screamed. "They're *killing them!!*"

S1E2 - Chapter 3 – Steve

Steve looked back and forth between the sheep, the attacking wolves, and his friends.

His sword arm flexed and he was suddenly full of energy!

With a wordless shout, the Minecraftian charged into battle, stone sword held high over his head! He flew into the three wolves like a wind blasting through dry grass. His sword was a bolt of lightning cutting through the air!

As soon as his carved-stone blade bit into the grey and brown hide of one of the wolves attacking the poor, lone sheep, all three beasts pulling the animal to the ground glared up and growled. Their eyes shone *red* like fire and their hackles rose, their teeth bared behind canine sneers. Growls and snarls rose like a volcano of wild predator sounds ready to burst!

Steve dodged to one side as soon as all three wolves forgot about the sheep and lashed out at him. He felt the slobber of one wolf's fanged mouth splatter his arm as it barely missed with its raging mouth. The Minecraftian was suddenly very aware that his arm was *bare*—protected by nothing more than his shirt sleeve. In fact, his entire body was exposed!

Dang! Steve thought, but only glared and focused harder. His meager stone sword felt like an old friend in his calloused hand...

As soon as Steve pulled his blade out of the body of one of the three wolves, he pivoted the tip around again with practiced ease and *thrust* into the same beast once more!

It yelped in pain, biting at the sword with long teeth...

Another wolf suddenly grabbed Steve around one leg with its jaws. The Minecraftian cried out in pain as the fangs pierced his pants and skin without effort.

"Aaaaugh!" Steve bellowed, kicking at the wolf. It held his leg firmly, digging in with more pain. The beast felt almost as heavy as Steve himself. The Minecraftian was *stuck*.

He pulled his blade up, changed his grip, then slashed down at the wounded wolf as hard as he could, cutting into its back just as the other wolf leapt up at him. Its jaws *snapped* in Steve's face—he barely dodged in time! The injured wolf under Steve's blade let out a short, painful howl and dropped to the ground.

"Steve!" Alex cried from behind him. Her voice was full of alarm and fear. "Look out!"

"One down!" Steve shouted back, trying to pull his leg free from the wolf that held him. "Two to—*ACK!!*" The second wolf bit his left arm. He was surrounded by a whirlwind of snarling sounds. The wolves yelped and barked, one of them muffled with its mouth around his leg.

There were two more wolves running in to join in, both of their eyes red as well. They growled as they ran up, and Steve saw their fangs bared and gleaming as they dashed through the shadows of the trees...

"Steve, get outta there!" It was the voice of Jack, the *Weird Walker*. The kid's voice shook with fright.

Steve was not afraid. He was wounded, but he was not afraid.

One of the new wolves leapt through the air at him, its paws spread out and its slavering mouth wide open, fangs reaching...

Steve ducked, pulling his leg against the wolf that trapped him, and the jumping wolf flew over him, landing somewhere out of sight with a snarl. As the Minecraftian looked to the wolf that bit him on the arm, he saw white fangs flying in at his face again and brought up his stone sword to parry just in time, sliding the blade along the incoming wolf's face. It *yelped* loudly and fell back.

"Steve, *come on!!*" Alex cried.

Looking down at the wolf holding his leg, Steve narrowed his eyes, let out a growl of his own, then stabbed it in the body.

The wolf finally let go.

Dodging out of the way of another beast suddenly leaping in at him from one side—it flew past him as a mass of grey fur and white teeth—Steve turned and ran back to the others.

Alex and Jack were trying to lead the four remaining sheep away. They each beckoned with bundles of wheat—Alex also held her bow and Jack held a stone sword—leading the dumb animals away from the fight. Both Alex and Jack had wide eyes brimming with fear.

"Go *that* way!" Steve bellowed, pointing to the south with his sword. Alex looked frightfully over her shoulder, nodded, and changed course.

Another wolf ran it at Steve. He blocked in time with his sword, whacking the beast's skull with the flat of his blade. It *yelped* and scrambled backwards.

There were many wolves around them. Steve could see them whirling around their position like grey ghosts in the shadows of the trees. Several hovered close to him and his friends, darting in and out, toying with the idea of attacking but only getting close enough when they had others rushing in with them.

Steve backed up to the tight group of stamping, half-brained sheep. He didn't care for the sheep. Steve felt like they didn't really *need* them, but Alex loved the dumb things. He was more than happy to make wool from spider silk. Steve loved hunting spiders. It was one of his favorite things to do in the woods in the morning, after the spiders became less aggressive. He was happy to hunt them at night, too—they were *really* aggressive then—but Alex didn't like him to go out at—

"Steve!" Alex screamed. She was pointing at the group of sheep.

Steve looked away from the circling wolves to where she was pointing just in time to see two wolves seizing one of the four sheep and pulling it away from the group, dragging it by its legs with their fanged jaws. The sheep bleated and cried out, terrified...

Rushing over, Steve raised his sword and narrowed his eyes, targeting one of the two wolves, but he knew that it was too late. By the time he closed the distance, the sheep was dead.

He stabbed one of the two wolves anyway. It *yelped* and snarled in response, then immediately lashed back out at him. Steve cried out in pain as its fangs nicked his sword arm. The Minecraftian felt red anger sweep over him, gripped his sword tightly in his fist, then swung down on the offending wolf *hard*. The chipped stone blade sunk into one shoulder and the beast whined and shrank away as the other one lunged in, seizing Steve's *other* leg.

"Oh no, you don't!" he shouted, immediately stabbing it in the neck. The wolf *yelped*, turned tail, and ran back into the circling pack.

"Here they come again!" the kid shouted.

"*Oh Gosh*—Steve!!" Alex cried. "Stop them!!"

Steve turned around with his sword ready to see that Alex and Jack had kept moving south with the three remaining sheep as he fought the two that had just killed the fourth. Now, the circling pack was moving in on the entire group; a half-dozen or more wolves rushing in at the three sheep from the trees!

"Get out of here!" Steve bellowed, waving his sword and other arm, sprinting in to save his friends and the animals.

He was too late.

The moment before the many wolves dashed in at the trio of sheep, the dumb animals must have seen *fanged death* running in at them, so all *bolted* and split up!

"Ba-ah-ah-ah-ah!" All three sheep bleated as they ran in different directions.

"Nooooo!" Alex cried, running after the grey sheep—the only one that was still close to them—waving her sheaf of wheat in front of her. Jack ran after Alex.

The other two sheep ran in different directions for a moment then converged again, surrounded by wolves on all sides.

For an instant, Steve didn't know what to do. Then, he saw that the wolves had all run together after the two white sheep and were leaving Alex, Jack, and the grey one alone—at least for the moment. He ran after the two white sheep, immediately crashing into the back of a wolf, swinging his sword down at it. It *yelped* and spun around to face him, red eyes fierce and enraged.

All heck broke loose.

There were chaotic sounds all around Steve: mostly a constant, vicious *snarling* from the many wolves, the bleating of the sheep, and Alex shouting at Jack to *keep going*.

One of the white sheep let out a bone-chilling scream of pain as the wolves around it attacked.

"Leave our sheep *alone!*" Steve bellowed, slashing into the same wolf again.

"Come on, Steve!" Alex shouted. "Stay together!!"

But he didn't. He wanted to save that last white sheep. He's screwed up yesterday, messing around in the ravine and stuff while Alex wanted to find the sheep. He'd let her down, and now they were losing their sheep because of it! He had to *save* these sheep—at least the ones that were left—and make it up to Alex!

The Minecraftian fought the wolves. It was madness. He let his finely-trained skills and strong, quick body do the work: dodging, slicing, thrusting, parrying—he even punched a wolf in the snout at one point when his sword was busy—and danced his dance of death with the six or seven beasts pushing and struggling and lunging at him. Steve felt light and as quick as lightning without his armor on, but his body paid the price. Every bite, graze, scrape of a beast's claws, and tug of hooked fangs caused pain and stung and made Steve cry out. It was a difficult fight— one that he would surely lose soon if he didn't—

An arrow suddenly appeared in the shoulder of a wolf fighting at his side. Steve stole a quick glance amidst the loud snarling and lashing of teeth over at Alex and Jack. He saw Alex in the distance with the kid and the grey sheep next to her, firing her bow.

They were safe. Steve would take the hits. That's what he was for.

It was okay, as long as Alex was safe...

The Minecraftian's sword flew this way and that; a dark grey blade of destruction. He saw that two of the wolves—at least— were dead. Many were wounded. *He* was wounded and ... starting to feel woozy...

Another arrow sank into a wolf with a *yelp*, and the beast immediately turned and ran off after Alex.

"No you don't!" Steve shouted, bounding after it. As he did, two wolves bit him smartly on the hip and on his left leg, but Steve caught the wolf going after his friends and skewered it mid-run...

"Steve, come on!!" Alex shouted.

Steve could barely hear her over the roar of his warrior heart and the snarling of the wolves trying to pull him to the ground.

Looking back, he saw six wolves bounding after him.

Wait, he thought, *weren't several dead?!*

The two white sheep were dead.

The only sheep left was the grey one. Steve knew that Alex really wanted to save the grey one. With that last sheep, they could at least breed some more...

But if he kept fighting like he was, the wolves would kill him for sure...

"Go!" Steve shouted. "Go south!" *Wait*, he thought. *They'd moved a little to the East*. "Go south and west!"

"What?!" Alex shouted back, fear wild in her eyes. "Come on!"

A wolf ahead of the pack reached him. Steve dodged to one side and thrust his blade into the creature's side as it sprinted past him with its mouth open. He skewered its heart and it collapsed without a sound.

Lucky hit.

Steve withdrew his blade and saw that his stone sword was in pretty rough shape.

The others would be on him in a second...

"I have an idea!" Steve exclaimed, pulling out his pack. He plunged into his disorganized mess of random stuff and started pulling out the rotten flesh that he'd gathered from the dead zombies that morning...

As the pack rushed in at him, Steve immediately threw a piece of zombie flesh at the face and open jaws of the nearest wolf. The rotten meat smacked it in the nose and fell to the forest floor. The beast immediately paused, sniffed it, then began wolfing it down.

Steve looked back and saw Alex, Jack, and the grey sheep getting farther away. They were heading in the right direction.

"Good!" Steve shouted, throwing another piece of meat at another wolf rushing in to devour him. "That's the way!" The wolf stopped to eat the meat. "Yes!!" Steve exclaimed, feeling his face stretch into a huge smile.

"Come *on*, Steve!" Jack shouted from far away. "That's not gonna work!"

"Steve!!" Alex cried. "Stay with us!!"

Six wolves came in at him. Steve tossed pieces of zombie flesh at them, one after another, smiling as they all paused to eat the rotten meat. When he ran out of the meat in his hands, Steve dove into his pack again and pulled out more. The wolves stayed with him. When the first two had finished eating, they came at him again with fangs bared and he gave them more. They stopped to eat more zombie meat...

This is working! Steve thought with a smile.

He threw the last piece of rotten flesh in his hands at another wolf approaching him for more, then reached into his pack. Steve pulled out a bone and threw it at a wolf, who happily took it, crunching through it with its fierce teeth as if the bone was only as hard as a carrot. Steve struggled to find more meat. He came up with a piece of string and tossed it to the ground...

There was no more zombie flesh.

The wolves all finished eating whatever they had, then all of them—one by one—put their eyes on Steve again, glaring and snarling and sneering, revealing their gleaming white fangs. They advanced on him, growling with fierce, red eyes...

Empty handed, Steve looked at his sword again. It would break soon. He looked back at Alex and Jack and the grey sheep, then felt satisfied with how far away they were. His friends watched him with fearful eyes...

Steve turned to the wolves.

"For the sheeeeeep!" he bellowed, and charged into battle!

Swinging his stone sword again and again, trying to ignore his many wounds, Steve waded into a mess of muscles and fur and fangs, snarling and cries of pain and growls, and he *fought on*. He sliced across one wolf coming at him, thrust at another, then was knocked to the ground with a *huff*.

Steve brought the sword up to protect his face, felt two wolves biting him on his legs, then stabbed another from the ground. Then, a fury shadow appeared above him, blotting out the sun, and all Steve could hear was a sea of snarls...

S1E2 - Chapter 4 – Jack

Jack watched as the wolves killed Steve farther up the hill.

The Minecraftian was an amazing warrior, but he was unarmored and trying to fight off a pack of wolves with nothing more than a stone sword.

Jack's stomach felt cold and he felt a heavy weight around his heart. He'd never felt this way before. Was that it?! Was Steve ... dead?

No, he thought. This is Minecraft. *He'll regenerate at home.*

Still, Jack felt cold fear swelling over him like a blanket of snow thrown over his body. He watched the wolves with red eyes all dodge in and out around Steve, eventually knocking the warrior down. He saw the Minecraftian disappear in a *puff* of pixelated, grey smoke. Jack felt a smothering terror.

What if Steve doesn't come back? he thought. It all seemed so real. Maybe it *was* real for him!

"Come on!" Alex commanded, her voice grim and dark. A shaft of sunlight piercing the trees made her iron helmet shine. "Dang it! Now we can't get back home!"

Jack suddenly realized that he'd been standing there, clutching onto a digital tree and staring at the battle with his mouth open.

He was so afraid.

Then, with Steve gone, the several Minecraft wolves were jerkily running and jumping around the area again, their eyes still red. It looked like a game again, and it wasn't as scary.

Still, what would those things *do* to him if they caught him??

"Is he...?!" Jack stammered. "Is he still alive? Will he regenerate on his bed?!"

"Yes," Alex replied, lowering her bow and holding her bundle of wheat in front of the grey sheep's face again. "He'll appear at home. Hopefully he'll come and find us before the sun goes down—*dang it!*"

Jack felt like his mind was stuck in a fog. He watched the wolves start wandering around together. It was as if they didn't notice the three of them forty feet or so away, hiding in the trees.

Their wolves' eyes were red. Jack understood what that meant. His skin broke out into goosebumps and he shivered even though the air was as mild and unmoving as if he was standing in a calm room. The boy finally snapped to.

"Let's go!" Jack whispered. "They're still hostile!"

Alex scoffed.

"Without Steve, I have no idea how to get home!" she said, throwing her hands up into the air for a moment. The grey sheep's head followed the up-and-down movement of the sheaf of wheat.

Jack looked around. He couldn't see the sun from inside the woods.

"He said south and east, right?" Jack said. "Let's find some high ground. If I can see the sky, I can figure out which way to go."

This was a video game. Jack knew how to find the way. Back in the real world, there was a mountain range running along the west side of town and open plains out east. Long ago, Jack's dad had taught him that if he ever wanted to figure out which direction he was looking at, to find the mountains. The mountains were always West back in Jack's town. Here in Vortexia, directions were even easier. The sun and moon would both rise and fall *exactly* in the east and west in Minecraft. The sky was a perfect compass ... if he could assess the sun when it was higher in the sky, harder to tell its direction.

Alex considered Jack, thinking for a moment.

"Okay, Jack," she said. "Let's go ... um..." She looked around and her green eyes landed on a hill rising through the forest away from the wolves. "Let's go *that* way."

It wasn't the way that Steve had pointed them to, but Jack knew he'd get them back on course soon enough.

"Alright."

Jack held up the bundle of wheat in his left hand. The grey sheep—its eyes stared dumbly in two different directions—started looking back and forth between Alex's and Jack's wheat. He looked up at the Damage Indicator window above the animal, noting that the sheep was still at full health. It hadn't taken any damage from the wolf attack.

Not *yet*...

They led the grey sheep, who *ba-ah-ah-ah'd* and stamped along slowly after them. It wasn't long before Jack was rolling his eyes. This was taking forever! How annoying!

"Don't you have any *leads?*" Jack asked as they started encouraging the sheep up the hill. Every time they reached a new vertical level, Jack had to stop showing the sheep his wheat so that he could climb up to the next layer of blocks. It was pretty difficult with Jack's *sub-adult size*; kind of like continuously climbing up onto a freaking *table* over and over again. Before long, his shoulders and legs were sore and tired.

"What's a *lead?*" Alex asked, nervously watching the wolves as the beasts explored the area a little too close for comfort.

"You make it with string and slime," Jack said.

"Slime?!" Alex replied, encouraging the grey sheep up the hill. "I didn't know you could do *anything* with slime."

"Have you killed slimes before?" Jack asked.

"Sure," Alex replied. "Sometimes they appear down in the mine, and there was one time when Steve and I traveled through a swamp. There were a bunch there, too."

"So you didn't try to craft anything out of the slime balls that they left behind?"

"No," Alex said. "That's gross."

Jack laughed, casting a wary eye at the nearby pack of wolves when he heard one of them howl. "Well if you had some slime, we could make a lead, and could just *pull* this sheep back to your homestead."

Alex paused and thought for a moment, nodded, then continued up the hill. Her armor *clanked*.

"You sure seem to know a lot about this place," she said.

That made Jack feel good. He was small and knew that he'd really have to keep away from hostile mobs or he'd get into *serious, deadly trouble*, but Jack knew everything there was to know about Minecraft, so would be very valuable to Steve and Alex because of it.

He saw a clearing up ahead with open sky.

"That'll do it!" Jack exclaimed, running up, pulling himself up block after block. Gosh—he was getting so tired! Walking around in Minecraft was like constant exercise!

Jack emerged into the sunshine under a blue sky with semi-transparent, huge clouds drifting by far overhead. He looked down at Alex. She was standing in the shadows waiting, watching the wolves.

Looking up again, Jack squinted against the brightness as he found the brilliant, square sun. It was pretty high in the sky—the time was somewhere around noon—and he watched it move, almost hurting his eyes. It wasn't the *real* sun, of course.

For several seconds, Alex watched the sun inch across the bright, blue sky, then figured out which way was south. Keeping *south* in sight, he looked down at Alex again and hopped down a few levels of grass blocks to join her.

"Okay," he said. "Let's go *this* way..."

So they did. Jack led them south, veering a little to the left—to the east.

Moving that dumb, grey sheep was hard work. Jack wasn't patient enough for this kind of thing. As the sheep watched the wheat, it sometimes followed and sometimes became distracted and wandered off until Alex hollered at it, waving the wheat, and got its attention again.

Jack felt like this whole thing was rather silly, but it was the only way to get the sheep home.

"What's this guy's name?" Jack asked at one point.

"He doesn't have a name," Alex said.

"Why not?"

"Eh," Alex said with a shrug, pausing to look nervously at the wolves running around nearby. The pack was drifting around, staying close to them for some reason. "Our animals come and go, and we use 'em for milk and wool and meat. There's no point in naming them."

"If you have just two sheep left, then you'll have 'em for a while now, right?" Jack asked.

"Yeah, I guess that's true," Alex said.

They both stopped and held their breaths when a wolf suddenly howled loudly from a little too close-by. Jack looked at the roaming pack—eyes still red and tails pointing straight in the air—and saw them wandering through the spruce and oak forest a little closer to them.

"Are they following us?!" he whispered, pushing his glasses back up his nose. He was sweating again after climbing up that hill, so had to pull the hair out of his face.

Alex peered at the wolves with her green eyes narrowed.

"I ... don't think so," she said. "I think they're just wandering randomly in our direction."

"Coincidence," Jack said.

"Yeah."

They continued trying to draw the sheep to the south, step by plodding, bleating step. Jack felt a constant, growing fear as the wolves stayed just behind them.

Jack never bothered moving animals this way. It was maddening and took too much danged time. In a Minecraft game, he never even bothered with farm animals until he'd killed some slimes and crafted lead-lines. Alex, on the other hand, didn't look distressed by the frustrations of leading the grey sheep with wheat at all, other than her nervousness about the approaching wolf pack. It looked like Alex dealt with animals this way all the time.

Eventually, Jack stopped when he saw a huge, taiga forest pine tree sticking out of the ground before them.

"What...?" he muttered, looking up the double-wide, super-tall tree to its boughs high above them. "What's *this* tree doing here?!"

Jack looked around the tree and saw the grass gradually change its color and consistency to a pixelated mix of dirt and what might have been meant to look like pine needles and gravel.

Where they heading into a taiga forest again? Or was this a *mega-taiga*, since the trees were so thick?

But they were supposed to be headed south and east...

Were they going north instead? Did he have it wrong??

Alex's face blanched. "Are we *lost?!*" she asked. "I thought you were leading us south!"

"I am!" Jack replied, looking up at the sky. He couldn't see the sun. "Maybe it's just a little piece of taiga coming in from the side or—"

"Oh, dang!" Alex cried, grabbing Jack's shoulder with an armored hand.

He looked up at her and saw the woman staring behind them.

The wolves were closer. They were frolicking and dashing around; pixelated blocky beasts practically bouncing to and fro on the choppy terrain

Two wolves were staring at them...

"Uh oh..." Jack whispered. He quickly scanned the area. If this was a mega-taiga with extra-thick and towering spruce trees, mossy boulders, and all the rest, then there had to be *caves* here and there, right?

There!

His eyes fell on a black crevice in the side of a steep, blocky slope.

"We can't lose this sheep..." Alex muttered, her eyes holding the gaze of now three wolves. Jack noticed an arrow sticking out of one wolf's side.

These wolves were all mostly wounded except for the fact that Steve feeding them would have healed them some—*dang!* Jack looked down at the sword in his grip. His small, kid hands seemed so very *small*...

"There's a cave!" he said. He pointed at it. "Let's get in there. Can you block us up?"

"*Block us up?*" Alex asked, not looking away from the wolves.

"Yeah, let's get the sheep in the cave and cover up the entrance with cobblestone or something!"

"Okay..." Alex said, backing away from the wolf pack. There were four of them watching them now, all slowly advancing. "Just back away slowly..."

Two wolves suddenly broke into a run. Another howled from somewhere unseen.

"Dang!!" Jack exclaimed, turning and pushing the grey sheep toward the cave. It moved a little, stamping its feet. "*Move it*, stupid!"

"Ba-ah-ah-ah-ah!" it complained.

"Come on!" Alex shouted, raising her bow and nocking an arrow. Her wheat was gone. "Lead him with your wheat! I'll cover us!" Her iron armor gleamed in the sunshine between shadows.

Jack raised his pixelated sheaf of wheat right in front of the sheep's silly face. It focused on it immediately and started walking. He heard Alex's bow *twang*, and heard one of the wolves *yelp*.

"Alright, sheep!" Jack exclaimed, wanting very much to yell and scream at the sheep to get its butt moving, but trying to stay calm. Alex's bow *twanged* again. There was another cry of a wolf in pain. "Let's go, sheep! Let's mooooove!"

"Ba-ah-ah-ah-ah..."

The sheep stamped along steadily as Jack led it toward the black rift in the mountainside. Alex's bow *twanged* a third time.

"Hurry!" she shouted. One wolf *yelped* and whined then fell to the forest floor, dead. The entire pack was after them now, rushing around and moving in closer. One darted in and backed out again. Soon those wolves would build up the courage to attack Jack and Alex directly, and they'd be finished...

"I'm trying!" Jack called back. He waved the wheat around in the sheep's face. His heart pounded in his chest. The boy felt cold fear flying around inside him again just like when they were attacked the first time. The air was filling up with the sounds of snarling and loud growling as the beasts circled around them— surrounding them everywhere except for the slope where the cave was waiting just a few more steps away...

Jack suddenly stepped backwards into darkness. He stopped.

"Keep moving!" Alex exclaimed, shooting again and again.

One wolf suddenly rushed in, jaws wide and fangs gleaming! Alex gasped in fright as she shot it in the face, stopping it dead in its tracks.

"It's dark!" Jack replied, suddenly worried about running into a zombie or falling down a hole.

"We're gonna be *dead* if you don't get in more!" Alex shouted back. She shoved the sheep into the hole behind the boy. Her armor *clanked*.

"Ba-ah-ah-ah-ah!"

Jack took a few fearful steps into the pitch-black space, making room. The sheep followed, still obsessed with the wheat in his hand, and Alex darted in to bring up the rear, dropping her bow and pulling out cobblestone. Two wolves snarled and rushed in, coming in fast with glowing red eyes and snarling loudly...

Plunk, plunk, plunk.

Alex threw down some blocks to barricade them in as fast as only a Minecraftian could.

The wolves stopped at the barrier, glaring and growling. One wolf a little farther way howled outside.

Relief washed over Jack. He let out a deep breath that he didn't realize he'd been holding. The boy suddenly felt terrified of the darkness behind them, turning to face the black space with his sword up...

Plunk.

The small cave was suddenly lit up with a yellow glow. Jack looked up and saw that Alex had thrown a torch onto the earthen wall.

It was a very small space—just a pocket in the mountainside, really. There wasn't any more to the cave deeper inside the hill. There wasn't enough room for a bed. There was hardly enough room for the two of them and the grey sheep!

"Ba-ah-ah-ah-ah..."

Jack and Alex both looked at the sheep and laughed. The tension poured off of the boy, and he dropped down to sit on the spongy, stone floor with a long, shuddering sigh.

There was still a small opening in the area where Alex had blocked them in; a one-block window to the forest outside. Jack assumed that she'd left it on purpose to serve as an opening too small for the wolves get in. He and Alex would be able to see when or *if* the beasts decided to leave. Outside in the sun, the two wolves that had almost reached them lingered for just a moment then wandered off to rejoin the rest of the pack. In that instant, the beasts were still close enough that Jack could see their

Damage Indicator windows. One of them had four hit points, and the other had seven. They had a maximum health of only eight.

Jeez, Jack thought. Steve had whittled most of them pretty far down, but was only using a stone sword. Peering out into the forest through their small, square window, Jack also saw several bright yellow and green experience orbs scattered on the ground here and there. Those glowing orbs must have been from the wolves that Alex had killed with her bow on the way into the cave.

"What are we gonna do?" Jack asked.

Alex sighed, looking down at her bow. "We'll wait for a little while for them to leave, then go outside again and try to get home."

"Steve won't be able to find us in a cave," Jack said.

"I know. That's why we need to get back out there as soon as we can ... unless you want to spend the night in this tiny place..."

"I'd rather not," Jack said. They'd have to block up that hole so they weren't killed by *baby zombies* in the night. Gosh—that would be terrifying. They were so fast—Jack felt that there'd be no way that he could fend one of them off...

So, they waited.

They waited for a while: Alex and the sheep standing around in the dark as Jack tried to get comfortable in all sorts of ways. He tried sitting on a stone block, but his feet dangled below his knees. With sore legs from climbing around all day, he couldn't keep it up for long. Jack tried to just sit on the stone floor, and that worked for a while, but then his tired muscles started getting stiff.

"Okay," Alex said finally.

Jack stood and looked out of the stone window. How long had it been? It couldn't have been long—the day was only ten minutes, right? *Weird*, Jack thought. They'd done a lot of stuff today—surely more than ten minutes worth, right? It wasn't evening yet! Time was passing by strangely in his head...

There were no wolves in sight from the view of the square block opening.

It was still daytime.

They heard no howls outside...

Alex put her wheat away and pulled out an iron pick axe. She rapidly cut through the cobblestone block below the window. The block she broke immediately transformed into a miniature, floating cube, flew toward her, and disappeared. Alex only made enough space for them to get out.

"Go take a look," Alex said.

Him?!

Jack felt a jolt of fear.

"Why me?" he asked. "I think ... um ... you can fight better than me. And you have armor!"

"Are you able to 'block up' the hole again if they're still out there?" she asked. When Jack couldn't reply, she went on. "Just creep out there a little and see if they're still out there or not. If they are, just run back, I'll block us up again, and we'll have to ... spend the night I guess."

Jack's knees suddenly felt like jelly. Those hostile wolves were scary, and he had no armor on. He hadn't even been in a fight with his stone sword yet!

"Okay..." Jack said.

Moving as carefully as he could on the slightly-spongy taiga forest ground, Jack slipped through the two-block opening in the cave with his sword gripped tightly in one hand. The blocky corners of the weapon's hilt felt weird and uncomfortable against his palm and fingers. He didn't know if he'd be able to fight well or not. Heck—the sword was dull. It was a lot like one of those foam Minecraft swords at Wal-Mart, but a lot bigger. How could this blade even *hurt* a mob, much less kill it?

Jack stepped out into the forest, immediately checking the slope above and behind him.

The coast was clear.

He took several steps away from the cave toward where Alex's experience orbs were sitting, glowing on the ground.

Jack looked back to call out to Alex, but paused when he heard a small growling sound.

Turning, he saw a single wolf approach him. Its eyes were red, and two arrows stuck out of its side...

The boy froze in his tracks, suddenly paralyzed with cold fear.

The wolf glared at Jack, sneering and showing its white fangs, slowly approaching with its tail held high in the air. It was still hostile.

"Oh..." Jack breathed, fear flushing through his body. He wondered what those digital teeth would feel like ripping through his human skin...

When the wolf came closer, its Damage Indicator window appeared over it:

Wolf. Two out of eight hit points.

Only two hit points, Jack thought, raising his stone sword before him...

The fear swallowing his heart fell back just a little. Jack could suddenly move again. He bounced the weird stone blade up and down in his hand...

If he could time it just right ... and hit the wolf before—

The wolf suddenly snarled, glared, and rushed at Jack with its jaws open wide!

"Aaugh!" Jack shouted, thrusting the big stone sword to catch the incoming beast with its blocky tip. He stabbed the wolf. Jack felt the weight of the beast fall onto his blade, almost knocking him down! It *yelped* loudly as a bold, red number "2" appeared over its head, floating up until disappearing as the beast fell to the side off of Jack's sword.

It disappeared in a puff of pixelated smoke...

He'd done it.

After the smoke cleared, two little glowing balls of light appeared on the ground. They slowly rolled toward Jack then *shot up* suddenly at his chest, disappearing without him feeling a thing! He heard the sound of tinkling bells...

He'd just taken in some experience points!

Jack laughed once. He stood in shock.

"Yes!!" he exclaimed, turning back to Alex with a huge smile!

He'd killed the wolf! He could defend himself! *Yes!* It might seem hard right now, but Jack could *learn!* He could learn to fight, and make armor maybe, and better weapons! And if he could gain experience, then he could probably enchant things!

He would survive!

"Alex!" Jack exclaimed, ready to call her out and tell her all about it...

Then he stopped.

The pack was there. While Jack was dealing with the two-hit-point wolf, five more wolves had circled around toward the cave and were now all standing there, wounded and angry with red eyes, showing their fangs, standing between Jack and the cave...

He couldn't see Alex or the cave, which means that she couldn't see *him*...

The wolves started growling.

Then, they started advancing on the boy slowly...

Five wolves. There was no way that Jack would be able to fight them off, and he sure couldn't run away. Even if Alex attacked with her bow right now from inside the cave, she wouldn't be able to save him...

The wolves snarled and growled.

Jack's stomach suddenly felt like it had a huge, cold rock stuck inside. His arms and legs buzzed with fear and he became so afraid that he wanted to just close his eyes and hope that it didn't hurt too much...

The boy cried out when two wolves suddenly leapt into action, charging him with their jaws open wide, their fangs gleaming in the sunlight! Even though Jack's whole body was almost numb, he raised his stone sword. He knew that it wouldn't help, but he couldn't just stand there and—

There was a sudden *twang* from a bow somewhere other than the cave. Both charging wolves were suddenly *stopped*, knocked backwards, each by an arrow to the chest! One of them instantly fell, dead, and the other *yelped* and spun around, confused and snarling, biting at the arrow sticking out of its body.

The other wolves rushed Jack.

The bow *twanged* again and two arrows whistled through the air, each hitting a wolf. One was killed, and the other wounded, falling and whining with an arrow sticking out of one shoulder.

The hidden bow *twanged* once more, and the remaining two charging wolves each took an arrow. All three surviving beasts—

each wounded by arrows from Jack's mysterious savior—turned tail and sprinted away into the woods, whining as they ran.

Jack watched them hightail it deeper into the taiga forest, dodging around the huge trees and mossy boulders, up and down two small hills, then they disappeared over a ridge.

Alex ran out of the cave, bow drawn, turning around a tree looking for Jack. She looked around in awe, scanning the woods...

"What's happening?!" she shouted. She eyed the dead wolves.

"Someone!" Jack called back. "Shooting the wolves from the trees!"

Jack turned and searched the woods. He saw nothing but trees and underbrush, and—

Something the shape of a Minecraftian suddenly moved, giving Jack a jolt of fear in his chest.

The boy gasped.

The unseen archer walked toward them from a hilltop, no longer hiding himself. He was decked out from head to toe in green camouflage, carrying a simple wooden bow in blocky hands protected by fingerless leather gloves.

Jack heard Alex's armor *clank*, and she was suddenly standing right next to him with one hand on his shoulder.

"Are you okay, Jack?" she asked. "I couldn't react in time, I'm sorry!"

Jack looked up at Alex for a moment then back at the quickly-approaching Minecraftian. He was like some kind of ... *ranger* ... dashing down toward them from where he'd sniped the wolves. Jack couldn't see more than just a little bit of skin—solely on his arms—and the man's face was just as camouflaged as the rest of his body. The ranger approached with long, quick strides, holding his bow down at his side. He held two arrows in his other hand. His full-camo clothing was stained with dirt and smoke. With that facemask, only his dark eyes were revealed.

"I'm okay," Jack said to Alex, then spoke up when the archer came close. "*Thanks* ... uh ... who are you??"

Cocking his head as he stopped before them, the ranger considered Jack for a moment without a word. Jack was so astounded that he didn't bother reading the Minecraftian's Damage Indicator window, which suddenly appeared above his camouflaged head.

"You ... are *strange*-looking," he said. "What are you?" His voice was quick with a touch of impatience.

Jack lowered his sword. He still couldn't believe that he'd just killed a wolf with it.

"I'm Jack," he said. "I'm a kid; a human boy."

"Jack the kid," the ranger replied, looking over Alex and her armor. "What are you two doing in that cave? Building a home?"

"No," Alex said. "We were just trying to get away from the wolves; trying to get my sheep home. *Who are you?*"

The ranger regarded them both for a moment then replied:

"I am Braydon. This forest is my home..."

S1E2 - Chapter 5 – Alex

The kid was shocked.

Alex was a little surprised, herself. She'd just seen that name in the Divining Pool ... how long ago?

"*Braydon?!*" Jack asked loudly, his voice high and full of surprise. He looked up above the ranger's head, then stared down at his face again. "Holy beetles! You mean ... um ... Braydon or KidOfCubes or ... Minecraft something-something-something?"

"One two three," Alex said. "It was Minecraft123."

The green-camouflaged archer watched both of them. Alex saw his dark eyes constantly flitting around, scanning the surrounding woods. He shook his head.

"I do not know of those other things," he said. "My name is Braydon."

"How long have you been here?" Jack asked, staring at the air above the Minecraftian's head as if something was there that Alex couldn't see.

Alex was wondering the same thing.

"I've always been here," Braydon replied. "Now, *you*..." he said, looking right at Alex. "You're the one that built a house with another Minecraftian to the southwest, right?"

"Twenty out of twenty..." Jack muttered to himself. Then, "South*west?!*"

Alex lowered her bow and let out a sigh. She was still so wound up from the wolf battle and from Steve dying! Up until just a moment ago, she and Jack were struggling to survive and save their last sheep from becoming wolf-food, and the kid was just nearly killed, himself. She'd sent him out to scope the scene. Was that wrong? It had made sense for her to hang back—only *she* could fill up the wall of the cave again if they needed to retreat. It didn't *feel* wrong—she felt like she'd made the right decision—but why did she suddenly feel so *guilty?*

"Yeah, that's me," she replied. "I'm Alex. The other guy you saw is Steve."

"Uh-huh," Braydon replied in a low voice. "Steve tried to fight a pack of angry wolves with no armor and using only a stone sword."

"Yeah," Alex said. "I know. His heart was in the right place..."

"But we've been going southeast," Jack said to himself, looking up at the sky. He tapped Alex on her armored arm. "I wasn't wrong about following directions with the sun, Alex! I was wrong about what direction Steve told us to go! We were going south*east* instead of south*west!*"

The ranger looked up at the surrounding trees. The pines towered over them, far taller than the spruce and oak trees of the forest surrounding the homestead.

"Still," Braydon said, scanning the woods. He bounced twice on his feet, seemingly antsy to get moving again. "This *Steve* was very skilled with a sword. I don't believe I've ever seen a swordsman take on a pack of wolves like that before. "

"He *is* skilled with a sword," Alex corrected. "He's still alive. He just regenerated back home. Hopefully..." She paused and looked around. The sun was a lot lower. They still had a few hours before dark, but it was late afternoon and they really needed to get home. She had *no idea* where to go. "Hopefully he comes to find us and lead us home."

"Wait a sec," Jack said, pushing up the strange item covering his eyes. The kid pulled his long hair out of his face. "You say you've *always* been here, but ... what were you doing last night?"

Braydon crossed his arms over his camouflaged chest. "None of your business, *human boy*." Then he looked at Alex again. "I take it you intend to bring that grey sheep with you?"

Alex felt a flush of anger for just a second. She suddenly felt paranoid that this forest man wanted to take her sheep. Then she sighed and shook her head. She was wound up tighter than a creeper...

"Yes," she replied. "He's *our* sheep. We lost six of them yesterday after a creeper accident damaging their pen. We've brought one home already, and this grey one is the only one left after the wolf pack attack..."

"I saw that," Braydon said. "Well—I saw the end of it. This taiga forest is full of wolves—not a very safe place for sheep, I'm afraid."

"Hold on another sec," Jack said, putting a little, soft hand of curves and lines in the air. "You saw the battle when the sheep died? You watched Steve get killed, and then you waited around and only came out when I was in trouble?!"

Alex could hear anger in the kid's voice. She reached down and grasped his soft, curved shoulder, feeling his strange muscles tense up at her touch. Jack looked up then softened.

"Would you prefer that I *didn't* help you?" Braydon replied with his dark eyes narrowed. "This is my home. I see almost everything that happens here. Yes, I saw the wolves attack the sheep, and I saw your friend fall in battle, but I was too far at the time to intervene. When I followed you two and your sheep, I was trying to help. When you took shelter in the cave, I was trying to determine whether or not you were *building* on this land..."

"But why didn't you—?!" Jack started, but Alex interrupted.

"We thank you, Braydon, for helping us. Little *Jack* here," she said, looking down at the boy with 'shut the heck up' eyes, "would have surely been killed if you weren't watching over us."

The ranger bowed slightly. "No problem," he said, bouncing lightly on his feet again. "Now, let's move on. I don't like to stay in one place for long."

"Why not?" Jack asked.

"When one lingers near the shadows, hostile mobs appear."

Alex and Jack exchanged glances.

"Can you tell us how to get home?" Alex asked. She wanted to ask Braydon more. She wanted to figure out the Minecraftian's connection to the Divining Pool and how he got here. Jack was probably wondering the same thing. If they could somehow figure out the ways that the Divining Pool pulled people into Vortexia, then maybe the kid could find a way back to ... wherever he came from. Jack certainly wasn't from here. He knew a lot about the world and the ways of things, but he was a *completely different creature* than the rest of them.

"You said the homestead's to the southwest?" Jack said. "We've been going the wrong way, to the southeast..."

"I'll do better than tell you how to get home," Braydon replied. With his heavy camo facemask, Alex couldn't tell whether the strange Minecraftian was smiling or not. "I'll escort you two and your sheep back before dark."

Alex and Jack both smiled.

"Thank you, Braydon," Alex said. "I'll go and get the sheep."

As she ran back to the cave, Jack ran after her, huffing and puffing as he slowed to a stop, putting his hands on his knees.

"Alex," Jack said quickly and quietly as she pulled out her bundle of wheat. "Do you think we can trust him? He helped me, yeah, but he knew that we ... were in trouble ... all of that time and..." The kid trailed off, trying to catch his breath.

"I don't think we have much of a choice, Jack," she said. "If anything goes wrong, we can always try to get away and spend the night in a dirt hut or dig into a hillside. Steve'll probably find us too, eventually."

"Really? We're pretty far away."

"He always finds me."

It was true. He did. Steve always saved her.

"Do you remember all of that stuff from the Divining Pool?" Jack said. "This is the guy from the message!"

"Yes, I remember."

"And the message said something about living off of the forest, right? And using a bow that can shoot two arrows at the same time. This guy doesn't have a house!"

"Yeah," Alex replied, drawing the grey sheep out of the cave. "So what?" The animal stamped and bleated dumbly. "I remember all of that. It's like the Divining Pool gave him life out of nothing, or pulled him here from somewhere else and tricked him into thinking—"

"—That he's always been here!" Jack finished. "But ... I wasn't created out of nothing. I was pulled into this world from the real world!"

"*Real* world?" Alex asked. This world of Vortexia was plenty real for her.

"I mean—my home world, I guess," Jack said, looking up at the sky. "I was definitely pulled here from somewhere else. So, was *he?*"

Alex shrugged. This wasn't the first time that the Divining Pool had done something weird, and she was sure that it wouldn't be the last. It was strange that Braydon thought he'd always been here, sure. At least KittyPaws30 had expressed a definite arrival point. She'd come from somewhere else and she knew it. Then she moved into the village and has been Steve's friend ever since.

"I don't know," Alex said. "Your guess is as good as mine, *Weird Walker.*"

Jack grimaced at that. As they approached Braydon again with the sheep in tow, Jack opened his mouth to say something more, but stopped.

"Are you ready?" Braydon asked with a clip tone, peering up at the sun.

"Yeah, let's go," Alex said. "Thanks for leading us home."

"No problem," the archer said.

They walked for a while, pausing here and there to earn back the attention of the sheep whenever it became sidetracked and tried to wander off.

"Braydon," Jack said. "Are you a *player?*"

"A player of what?" the ranger replied.

"I mean—are you a person playing this game, and Braydon is your avatar? Or are you more like a mob, living here and thinking that this is real?"

Alex stared at Jack for a moment, surprised by the utter weirdness of his question. Then, she shook her head and focused on the sheep again. Braydon also stared at the kid for a while, seemingly trying to understand what he'd been asked.

"I do not understand your question," the camouflaged Minecraftian eventually said. He reached up and scratched his hooded head with a gloved hand. "You are an *odd creature*, Jack the kid."

Jack frowned, shook his head, then hustled to catch up. Braydon walked very fast.

"No, I mean ... are you really there, in that body? Or are you playing and controlling that body from somewhere else? From a computer or a console?"

Braydon shook his head and moved on. "I do not know what you mean. Now, follow me this way..."

Soon after starting their journey home, the forest started to change little by little until they were eventually walking through the same familiar and uncomfortable shadowy woods that surrounded the homestead. The massive taiga trees eventually disappeared and gave way to spruce and oak, the boulders became more sparse, and the ground shifted from crunchy dirt and pine needles to soft, green grass again.

"How did we get turned around?" Alex asked at one point. "We ended up in the taiga again, but Jack thought we were headed southeast."

"We *were* headed southeast!" Jack said. "I know how to tell directions!"

"You were indeed going southeast," Braydon said, leading the way like someone who spends all day running through dense, difficult terrain. "You should have been going south*west*. You also passed through a pocket of taiga woods that extended into the normal forest."

"So we were headed the right way!" Jack exclaimed, smiling. "Um ... kind of..."

"If you were intending to go southeast, then you were, yes," Braydon replied. He paused, assessed the woods ahead of them, then he continued. "This way..."

"Hey, uh," Jack said, running to catch up. "How do you know these woods so well if you just showed up this morning?"

Alex felt a cold lump in her throat. The kid was going to annoy this ranger, and he'd leave them alone and lost in the woods.

"I already *told* you," Braydon replied. "I've *always* been here. I know these forests like the back of my hand."

"But how is that *possible?!*" Jack said. "If you just appeared here today, could the magic that brought you here somehow wire your brain to already have the knowledge—?"

Alex interrupted. "I'm sorry, Braydon," she said, rushing up and putting a hand on Jack's shoulder again. Her armor *clanked*. "Jack is *extremely* curious about this world."

Braydon looked down at Jack with his camouflaged head cocked. "I've lived here all my life, Jack the kid," he said, definitely sounding impatient. "I have *no idea* what you're talking about with all of these strange words and questions."

Jack sighed, furrowed his brow, and pushed up the thing on his face. Then, he looked away as they walked on.

"Don't worry," Alex said to Jack as they walked together. The boy looked up at her; his bizarre, intricate eyes covered with tiny pieces of glass contorted in uncertainty and frustration. "We'll figure this out, kid. I take it you'd like to find a way back to your ... real world?"

Jack stared at her for a moment then looked away into the surrounding woods. He didn't reply. After that, the kid didn't ask another question or say another thing until the forest finally broke open. The four of them—Alex, Jack, Braydon, and the sheep—all stepped out into the golden sunshine of the late afternoon, looking out over a huge vista of the land ahead descending all the way down to a massive, infinite desert of fiery sand...

"Wow..." Alex said. "I did not expect *this*."

"We've been heading south from where I found you," Braydon said. "Now, we'll head west to the—"

"Hey, is that the village?" Jack asked suddenly, pointing ahead with a slender, soft finger.

Alex squinted against the desert's glare and saw the glittering of the low sun reflecting off of the glass windows of a sandstone village far ahead and down amidst the dunes.

"Yeah," Braydon said. "That's *one* of the villages here—the one closest to your house." He looked annoyed at being interrupted, then pointed to the right of the village at where the land rose out of the sand, becoming a forest again and going up and up until creating a steep ridge running a long way in two directions. "We will head west now toward that ridge, then south until we can see your home."

"So that's the village Steve wanted to go to?" Jack asked, then pointed at the ridge, "And *that* must be the big ridge, huh?"

Alex couldn't quite tell. A lot of villages looked the same and the ridge didn't look familiar at all from their vantage point. Then again, just about *anything* outside of the homestead didn't look familiar to her.

"Maybe," she said.

"That is *a* big ridge," Braydon said. "It runs to the north and south, separating the forest where your house and farm are from the desert and village on the other side."

"Then I guess that *is* the big ridge," Alex said with a sigh. *Man*—Steve was right. She really *was* hopeless with directions!

"Cool!" Jack exclaimed. "We'll make it back before dark!"

"Yeah," Alex said.

They went on, heading west and following the quick, long strides of Braydon into the golden light of the lowering sun.

"How do you shoot two arrows at once?" Jack asked. "That's not something I've ever been able to do, and I haven't seen any mods that let you do that. In fact, how in the world do you do that at all without a mod on Vortexia to do it? I certainly didn't install anything like that..."

Braydon looked over his shoulder back at the kid as they walked. "I don't know what half of what you just said means, Jack," he replied. "My skill with a bow is a result of years of training and experimentation. I also modified this bow—it's of my own design."

They crossed the northern-most edge of the big ridge and headed down into the gloom of the trees once again. Starting down a slope, the three of them wound their way through the trees, down and down, all as Alex struggled to keep the grey sheep following. It stamped and bleated and sometimes turned around, at times losing interest in Alex's wheat. Each time that happened, they all waited as Alex waved the wheat in front of the animal's face again until it noticed, smelled it, then started following again.

Man, she thought. *I'll have to look into that slime-lead thing...*

As Alex encouraged the sheep down a steep spot of hill and rock, she saw Jack and Braydon suddenly freeze ahead of her.

"Did you hear that?" Jack asked.

Alex looked down the hill and pulled out her bow.

"What?" she said. "What is it??"

190

Then, there was a low growl from the shadows ahead—
something gurgling and wet.

"Get behind me, human boy," Braydon said, loading two
arrows into his bow and peering into the gloom with eyes like
daggers.

Alex felt a chill go up her spine. Jack moved as directed.

A few seconds later, there was a loud groan and a bubbling
gurgle from up ahead and two zombies emerged into the dying
light from under the shadows of spruce trees. Their dead eyes,
green skin, and tattered, soiled blue clothing suddenly made Alex
extremely nervous. They were just typical zombies, but ... where
was Steve?

As the undead mobs plodded toward them, groaning and
moaning with their green claws stretched out ahead of them, Jack
gasped and hid behind the camouflaged Minecraftian ranger.

Without hesitation, Braydon raised his bow and fired off a
single shot that launched *two* arrows at the same time! Each
arrow found one of the two zombies' skulls, sinking in right
between their dead eyes. Both mobs collapsed instantly, each
gurgling for a moment before vanishing into puffs of grey smoke.

Alex stared with her mouth hanging open.

That was *amazing*...

Jack gasped.

Braydon rapidly reloaded his bow with another two arrows as
if he'd done the action thousands of times before, then he
stepped forward to collect the rotten meat left behind. A handful
of glowing experience orbs drifted along the ground and merged
into the camouflaged Minecraftian with the tinkling sound of
bells.

"Holy beetles!" Jack exclaimed. "You just one-shotted *two* of them!"

"Stay sharp," Braydon replied, unconcerned. "There may be more shortly. It's getting dark. Those zombies were able to move freely in the shadows. Come on..."

They followed.

Pretty soon, Alex had stashed her bow and pulled out a torch, holding the flickering flame in one hand and the bundle of wheat in the other. The shadows of the forest deepened, and it was getting hard to see—especially hard to see a *grey* sheep in a darkening wood. Jack drifted to her side.

"Can I have a torch, too?"

"Sure," Alex said. "You don't have any?"

"I don't have an inventory," Jack said.

Inventory? she thought. Alex shrugged, pulled out another torch, and gave it to Jack.

"Here ya go..."

Instead of taking it, Jack handed her the sheaf of wheat he'd been using to help with the sheep. "Can you take this first?" he asked. "It looks like I can only carry what I can hold in my hands, and I've got two things already. I don't want to give up my sword..."

"Okay."

Alex traded the kid a torch for his wheat, stashing the extra bundle into her pack. When Jack held the torch before him—his soft face bathed in a flickering, yellow glow that made his glass-things sparkle—he smiled and moved on.

"Jack," Alex said. "What are those things on your face? It looks like two tiny pieces of glass...?"

Jack reached up to push the things up tighter onto his face with a finger of the hand that held his sword. "These?" he said. "These are my *glasses*."

"What do they do?" Alex asked. She imagined that they were some sort of enchanted item that allowed him to see strange things, like where dungeons were, or maybe something that would let him better find ore underground?

"They help me *see*," the kid replied. "I need them. Without them, my vision gets all blurry."

Alex nodded, slightly disappointed that they weren't something cooler. The kid was so knowledgeable, and from another world, so Alex was hoping that he had some fancy technology of some kind that could help them.

"Your eyes ... are broken?" Alex asked.

"Kinda."

"Here we are," Braydon said suddenly, stopping ahead of them.

Alex felt a jolt of joy leap in her chest. She smiled. Ignoring the sheep for a moment, she ran up ahead, armor *clanking*, until she could see through the trees where Braydon stood. There, in the beautiful light of the blooming sunset ... was *the homestead*. The young wheat sprouts of her recently-planted crop stretched up into the air, and the water of the trenches in between the rows sparkled. Their animals stood around in the cool air and the farm door to the house was closed. The torches illuminating the property glowed.

Where the heck was Steve?! Was he off looking for them? He'd died and regenerated *hours* ago!

Smiling, Alex ran back down to the grey sheep and caught its attention again with her wheat. She felt great to be home—and just in time, too! She grinned down at Jack.

"Hey, I think we should be able to make you a bed for tonight," she said.

The kid smiled up at her. "Cool!"

"Let's go," she said, smiling at Braydon as she led the sheep past. They stepped out into the open at the edge of the farm then she turned back to the ranger.

He was still there at the tree line, just inside the shadows.

Braydon raised one hand to wave. "Take care, Alex and Jack," he said. "Good to meet you."

Alex and Jack exchanged confused glances, then she looked at the camouflaged archer again.

"Come with us, Braydon!" she exclaimed with a smile. "We have plenty of food, and you can stay with us for the night. Head home in the morning!"

Braydon's face was covered, so she couldn't tell if he was smiling or what.

"Thank you for the offer, Alex, but I *am* home, and the forest provides me with all of the food I require."

"Hey, we walked a long way!" Jack replied. "That's a long way home in the dark with mobs out, dude. Come stay here for the night so you can go home in the morning when it's safe!"

"As I said," Braydon replied, slipping further back into the shadows of the darkening woods. "I *am* home. Goodbye for now..."

Then, he was gone.

Alex stared at the trees and scanned the shadows. She searched for movement or any shapes that might reveal the ranger, like the long line of his bow, or the lighter-colored exposed skin of his arms, but ... she saw nothing.

The two of them exchanged glances again.

"Weird guy," Jack offered with a shrug.

"Indeed," Alex said. "But it was a good thing that he found us, right?"

"Yeah."

Then, they smiled again and led the grey sheep toward its pen. Alex opened the gate and drew the sheep inside, shutting it behind her and leaving the kid out by the crops. She petted the face of the grey sheep, then patted the white one that had been in there for most of the day. They were her only two sheep left.

Reaching into her pack, Alex pulled out more wheat and fed both of them. As Jack watched, she gestured to the gardening chest.

"Hey, Jack, get me the shears out of that chest, will ya? Do you know what *shears* are?"

"Sure I do," he said, dropping his torch on the ground. The kid opened the chest with a *creak* and pulled the shears out, handing them to Alex, then he picked up the torch again. Man, he wasn't kidding about having a hard time carrying things.

Alex approached the sheep with the shears and quickly cut off enough wool to let Jack make a bed. Then she left the pen, closing the gate behind her, and placed the shears back into the chest. Looking into her pack, she pulled out three blocks of spruce planks that she'd made from the trees she'd chopped down yesterday.

"Here, Jack," Alex said, holding out three wool blocks and three blocks of planks. "Use these to make a bed. There's a crafting table there next to the door. Do you know how?"

195

"Yeah, I do," Jack replied. He put his sword and torch down onto the grass and collected the six blocks from Alex, shuffling awkwardly to the crafting table while balancing all of them in his arms. This 'human boy' sure was strange...

Alex watched as Jack struggled to use the crafting table. He uncomfortably juggled the six blocks, trying to use the device but failing, then he took to placing all but one block on the ground next to him. He worked at the table, picking up block by block while keeping one of his soft hands resting on its surface. At one point, he scoffed when he released the table by accident, and all of his wood and wool fell back to the ground.

"What do you think about giving the grey sheep a name?" Jack said suddenly while struggling to craft his bed. "You know— after all we've been through together with him?"

"Like what?" Alex asked.

"Something involving wolves."

"But he's a sheep," Alex replied, smiling and shaking her head.

"How about ... *Wolfie?*" Jack asked, pausing to look away from his crafting table to gauge her response.

Wolfie? Alex thought. That was just ... terrible...

She smiled and shook her head again. It didn't matter.

"What's the point in naming them?" she asked.

"Um..." the boy replied, fiddling with the blocks on the crafting table. "Ah! There we go!" Jack grinned as he pulled a miniaturized bed from the table, complete with a bold, red blanket. "Well, my people like to name things. We name *everything*. At least—everything alive. Although some people name cars and guitars and stuff, I guess..."

"What's a car?"

196

"Never mind," Jack said. "You're right. It's stupid."

Alex smiled down at him. "No, that's fine, Jack. Let's call him *Wolfie*."

"Yeah?" Jack asked, looking up at her with a smile. He pushed his glasses up on his face and picked up the sword again. The kid looked down at the torch and frowned. "I need to figure out a way to carry stuff."

"Maybe we can figure something out," Alex said, looking up at the darkening sky. The mobs would be out any second. "Come on. Let's go in. Hopefully Steve's already inside..."

Alex picked up the kid's torch, smiled again at her two sheep, then led the way into the house...

S1E2 - Chapter 6 – Steve

"Get off of me!!" Steve shouted, his voice much louder than he expected as he leapt up from his bed. Breathing and coursing with adrenaline, his eyes flashed wildly around the room.

His room.

You died.

With a gasp, Steve looked down at his empty hands. He was standing on his bed, its red blanket messy like always.

"Dang it!" he exclaimed, instantly looking into his pack and not surprised that it was empty.

He was back home. It was quiet, save for the noise that he was making.

Steve growled in frustration and jumped down to the floor. They were—Jeez, how far away were they?! Steve had to get back. He had to save Alex from the wolves. Oh—and Jack too...

He needed a sword.

Rushing around his room, Steve threw open all of his chests, searching for a weapon. They all had a random mishmash of stuff inside that he couldn't really use. There was a little bit of cobblestone in one, so he took that at least. All of his armor stands were empty. Some were getting dusty, even. Usually when Steve lost his armor by dying or whatever, he tried to replace it right away if he and Alex had the stuff. Some rare times, he put extra armor on the stands, but those stand had been standing naked for quite a while now.

"Isn't there any *iron* in here?!" Steve said to himself, searching through his chests again. There was none.

He did find a few bones in one and threw them into his pack. Maybe he'd need them to distract the wolves while he was saving Alex and Jack. Dang—she would be *so mad* if that last grey sheep of theirs got killed! What in the heck happened?! Steve knew that he was an awesome swordsman! He'd never met his equal! Surely he shouldn't have a problem with a few ... um ... six ... or maybe *eight* ... wolves...?

Okay, he thought. Eight-ish wolves were a lot for anyone, and he hadn't been wearing any armor. Defeat was understandable. And judging by the fact that he didn't hear Alex screaming and complaining right then in the next room over ... meant that she was still alive.

"At least I bought them some time to get away..." Steve said to himself, closing all of his chests and opening the door to the hall. "Hmm," he added, looking across the hallway into the storage room. "I wonder if there's any iron in there..."

It would be *way* better to go and kill the rest of those wolves with an iron sword than with a stone one.

Steve reached down and touched his stomach. He'd been really hungry before those darned wolves had killed him. Now he didn't feel hungry at all.

"Oh yeah," he said, running across the hall. "Because I died..."

Throwing open chest after chest, Steve searched for iron. Sure, the chests were all labeled, but he'd learned some time back not to trust the labels since sometimes he put the wrong stuff in the wrong chests, himself.

Steve grabbed a stick when he found it so that he could at least make a stone sword. For some reason, it was the only piece of wood in the whole danged room! Stopping his chest-searching for a moment, Steve ran to the crafting table next to him and made a stone sword. He looked at his handiwork and smiled, stashing the new weapon into his pack.

Putting his hands on his hips, Steve took a deep breath and sighed.

"Now, what was I doing again...?"

Sword. Wolves. Iron.

"Oh yeah!"

He resumed searching the chests and paused when he found thirteen pieces of leather, staring at the items for a moment before closing the chest again. He should ... *make something* out of those...

Remembering the search for iron, Steve ran out into the main room and checked the other chests out there too. He checked the container with stuff for the anvil and crafting metal and tools, then scoffed and smacked his forehead. He should have checked that one first! At any rate, there was no iron inside. Then he checked the dump chests by the front door—no success—then ran back into the storage room.

"There's no iron *anywhere!*" he exclaimed, putting his hands on his hips and shaking his head.

Steve thought about those pieces of leather again then realized that he should make some *armor* for going and fighting the wolves. Even having a little bit of armor would have helped tremendously in the last battle that killed him! If he'd been wearing armor, he'd probably still be out there with Alex and Jack now, helping them get that grey sheep back home...

Steve ran to the chest with the leather and pulled out all thirteen pieces.

He looked at the crafting table right there in the storage room and did some quick calculations in his head...

"Thirteen," Steve said, looking down at the pieces of leather. "I can *almost* make a tunic *and* leggings. Too bad there isn't any more!"

He stared at the leather in his hands.

Should he make the tunic? Or the leggings?

The tunic would provide better protection overall, but the wolves were attacking his *legs* a lot more...

Steve stood contemplating what to make for a minute, wandering out into the main room and toward the crafting table near the anvil. Then a sound from outside suddenly grabbed his attention. It was a little squishing *puff* sound.

Walking to the window, Steve looked and saw a single rabbit hopping around just outside in the grass. He noticed two more rabbits in the distance, further into the trees.

"Rabbits..." he said to himself, walking back to the crafting table.

He looked at the leather in his hands, then stopped.

If there wasn't enough leather for a full tunic and leggings, couldn't he *make* more by stitching together rabbit hides? He needed fifteen pieces of leather to make a tunic and leggings. That would be ... eight rabbit hides. Could he hurry up and kill eight rabbits...?

"You *bet* I can!" he said aloud with a grin.

Stuffing the leather into his pack, Steve pulled out his brand-new stone sword and opened the front door, immediately scanning for all of the rabbits he could see. He had to hurry, but killing rabbits was *easy*, right? Heck—he was fast enough, and these rabbits were next to a forest, so it would be easier for him to corner them against the trees!

With a broad smile, Steve charged out with his sword ready at the first rabbit—the one he'd seen out front from the window. As he sprinted up ready to swing, the little animal startled and looked at him with terror, then it *bolted* away! *Hop, hop, hop!*

Steve pursued, zig-zagging after the little guy until they both went running wildly through the trees. When he closed in on the little guy, Steve swung and *almost* hit it, but the rabbit had jumped in a different direction just as he attacked, and Steve chopped into the tree instead.

"Get over here!" he cried after it.

Chasing the rabbit through the woods, Steve eventually cornered it, found the second he needed to strike, then killed it.

"Ha!"

Picking up the meat and hide, Steve immediately started searching for another. It took a few minutes, but he eventually found one near the closed entrance to Alex's mine. The rabbit squeaked when it was discovered and frantically tried to get away!

Steve chased it down for a while around the mine then killed that one too.

Pursuing the rabbits in the woods was proving to be a little more difficult than he'd anticipated. Steve eventually took a break, sitting under a tree for a minute. He looked up at the sun. *Eh*, he thought with a shrug. There was still plenty of time before dark.

How many hides do I need? he wondered.

"Oh yeah—eight," he said, standing again and continuing his hunt.

Steve ran back and forth through the woods in the front of the house, hunting down one rabbit after another. The fourth one took a *really* long time to track down. Steve started thinking of a way he could corral them somehow—or make a trap—instead of wasting so much energy sprinting around swinging his sword!

When the third and fourth rabbits were dead, Steve looked over the four small hides in his pack and smiled. He also had three good pieces of rabbit meat that he could cook up and eat!

Steve's stomach suddenly growled at the thought, so he went back inside. Heading into the kitchen, Steve put the three pieces of rabbit meat into the furnace that Alex used as an oven, then added the two pieces of wood he had in his pack, igniting the fire.

As the rabbit meat cooked, Steve's stomach growled even more, and he watched the fire burning with hungry eyes. He stood, then leaned, then leaned against the corner, then stood on the food chest, waiting for the meat to be done.

When the fire went out and he knew that the meat was ready, Steve took out the cooked rabbit with a broad grin, licking his lips.

"Awesome!" he exclaimed, smelling the amazing scent of the cooked meat and carrying the three steaming chunks of goodness out into the front room. Steve stood and ate all three. He knew that he only needed two, and should save the third for later, but they were so danged good! Besides—he was still killing rabbits! He'd get more...

Stepping outside with a full belly, Steve smiled and looked up into the sun. He rubbed his hands on his stomach and took a deep breath of mountain air.

"Nice..."

Then he heard the soft *pat* of another rabbit hopping nearby, so pulled out his sword and got back to work.

"Four more!" he exclaimed, dashing after rabbit #5.

He had to chase it around the mine two times then into the trees for quite a while before the rabbit got itself stuck up against a steep ledge, giving Steve the split second he needed to kill it. After collecting its hide, Steve looked up at the sun through the trees and headed east again back toward the house. Partway home, he saw another rabbit and chased that one down too over several minutes.

Eventually—taking much longer than Steve had anticipated— he *finally* had eight rabbit hides!

"Yeah!" he exclaimed, looking at the hides in his pack.

He had thirteen leather and eight rabbit hides.

Why was he trying to gather eight rabbit hides? What was the significance of ... *eight?*

What were the rabbit hides for again...?

"More leather," he said with a nod, running back home.

As soon as he was inside, Steve closed the door and ran back to the kitchen, adding two more pieces of raw rabbit meat to the furnace. Man—after killing four more rabbits, he was practically starving!

Smelling the cooking meat, Steve smiled, holding his rumbling stomach.

"Now, what was I gonna make?" he said to himself, looking in his pack again at the leather and rabbit hides. The rabbits hides were going to be made into leather, and... "Oh yeah. Armor."

When the rabbit meat was done cooking, Steve pulled the two pieces out and ate them heartily while heading back into the main room. He looked outside. It was early evening. The sun would be setting soon.

Stepping over to the crafting table after a satisfying *burp*, Steve pulled out the rabbit hides and made them into more pieces of leather. Then he considered the fifteen pieces of leather and started creating a tunic. After a while at the crafting table, Steve finished and slipped on his new tunic. It fit well and creaked slightly as he moved.

"Nice..."

Then he crafted some leather leggings and put those on too.

Steve felt pretty good wearing armor again. He hadn't worn armor since ... well ... yesterday when he'd fallen into the ravine and died, right? Okay, so it hadn't been long. *But still*, he thought, reaching up and scratching his head. It would be better if he could make a leather cap and leather boots to go with the tunic and leggings...

He'd need ... nine pieces of leather for that.

That's...

"Thirty-six rabbits," he said to himself then let out a low whistle. "That's a *lot* of rabbits."

Why'd he *make* this new armor, anyway?

He'd been looking for leather ... and then had to hunt down some rabbits to complete this partial suit ... so that he could...

"Oh dang!" Steve exclaimed. "Alex and Jack!"

The wolves!

"Double-dang!!"

He had to get out there and help Alex and Jack get home with the grey sheep! Dang it—he got *sidetracked* again somehow! He needed to get up there and help them find their way home! If they were still trying to bring home that sheep, then they might still need help with the wolves unless—

Steve suddenly burst into a run toward the bedrooms and threw open Alex's bedroom door. Her bedroom was quiet. She wasn't inside. Her bed was made nice and neat.

"Still alive," he muttered. They were doing okay for now, but would likely be lost and need help getting back before sunset.

Looking down at his left arm, Steve admired the new leather armor, but felt like he needed a *little more* to deal with wolves...

"A shield," he said, running into the storage room.

Steve started searching for iron, but stopped after looking inside three chests.

"Oh yeah—no iron."

He wondered if Alex had stashed some iron in a weird place somewhere. Sometimes she hid things like iron and diamonds so that Steve wouldn't waste them by dying.

Well, those were *her* words, not his. Steve scoffed. He *never* wasted stuff!

For a brief moment, he thought about checking the chests in Alex's room, but thought twice about that. Those chests were *definitely* off-limits. They'd never broken each other's rules of not going through their private chests and he wasn't about to start now, even though he *really, really* needed a shield.

Stopping in the hall, Steve scratched his chin.

"Where could some iron be hidden...?"

He thought of the kitchen, then the gardening chest outside. He'd have to check there. Maybe down at the bottom of the mine's stairs, deep down in the ground. Alex had a place there for smelting ore deep underground. There was probably iron down there...

His eyes landed on the door of the Divining Pool room.

Maybe she had a chest in there...?

Steve smiled. It was decided. He'd check in *there*, then the gardening chest, then the mine. That would take a while.

Opening the door into Alex's weird, little room with that creepy bedrock pool, Steve immediately scanned the floor and all corners.

"No chest."

Then his eyes caught something white and shimmering in the blue water of the Divining Pool...

There were words deep in the water, floating slowly up to the surface. Steve drew in closer and leaned against the strange and dense bedrock thing, peering into the water and trying to read...

"*Can you add a ender Dragon fight later on and or or also can you add wither and last but not least can you add a fenix stone a fenix stone can bring a non immortal back to life? – Amy*"

Steve squinted and read the words aloud.

Fenix stone? he thought. What in the heck was a 'fenix stone'?!

He stood. The words 'dragon' and 'wither' bounced around very uncomfortably in his head. Just before Steve turned to run out to the gardening chest outside, he heard the farm door *pop* open then close loudly. He heard Alex's voice, then Jack's.

Steve gasped. He looked down at the pool and saw the words almost at the surface. He didn't really care about this weird thing, but he knew by now that when the words reached the top, they gradually faded away...

"Alex!" he shouted. "Jack!"

There was a moment of quiet where his friends were by the kitchen.

He heard Jack's voice going on and on: "Yeah, so, I don't know if you've done this before, but if we go fishing, you sometimes pull up a nametag, and we can use that to give Wolfie an actual name."

"But he already *has* a name now," Alex said from the main room.

"Alex! Jack! Come here!" Steve shouted, looking back at the rising words again.

"Steve...?!" Alex called. "You're *here?*"

"Come on!" Steve shouted back. "Hurry!"

"Where have you been?!" Alex snapped, storming across the main room. Steve heard her stomping move into the hall. "Where *are* you?!"

He stuck his head out of the room and saw Alex there, eyes angry and orange hair bright and fiery sticking out from under her iron helmet. She immediately and furiously put her hands onto her hips with a *clank*. She was still dressed in her full suit of iron armor and looked really funny with her armored hands on her armored hips like that. Jack was following behind her, looking at a miniature bed held in one of his strange, soft hands.

"Come in here!" Steve said.

"What are you doing in *leather armor?!*" Alex said. "Where the heck have you been?! You didn't try to come and *get* us?!"

"Hurry!" Steve said, waving his hands at Alex as if they could blow away her attitude. "There are words! Come see before they're gone!"

It took a second to process that, then Alex's eyes instantly transformed from angry to surprised and curious. She rushed into the room and the kid came in after her. All three of them bent around the pool again and Alex read the words.

An instant later, the waving, white letters all dissolved at the top of the pool and disappeared.

Jack the kid gasped, staring at where the words were, his bizarre, complicated eyes fluttering in thought, then in fear.

"An Ender dragon?!" he exclaimed. "And a Wither? As in ... a Wither boss?!"

"Does that mean something to you?" Alex asked him.

Steve had read about the dragon and he knew that it lived in some other weird world called *The End*, but he'd never been there. Apparently, the only way to The End was through a magical gateway deep underground ... or something...

What was a *Wither?*

"You don't know what those are?" Jack asked her, pushing his strange glass-eye things up closer to his curved and soft face. Steve still couldn't even comprehend all of those fine, dark hairs flowing around his head. The kid was really something else...

"I've heard of the dragon, but I've never seen it," Steve said.

Alex shook her head and smiled at him. "From those library books?" she asked sarcastically. "Those are just stories. They're not real. There are no *dragons*." She looked down at Jack. "I don't know what either of those things are."

"No!" Jack exclaimed. "Both of those things are *real things!* But neither of them ever come here, to the Overworld. Gosh— that pool said I was coming, and I did. And it said that Braydon would come, and he was there ... and he thought he'd always been here!"

Braydon?

"Who's Braydon?" Steve asked.

"Oh duck feathers...!" Jack said, running one hand through his hair. "Do you think...?"

"Who's Braydon?" Steve repeated.

"And what's a 'fenix' stone?" Alex muttered, staring at the pool.

Just then, there was a huge *boom* outside! Steve and the rest of them all crouched in surprise, raising their hands over their heads. Steve heard little bits of dirt, rock, and other stuff clattering down all around them on the roof and outside. It was like a creeper had blown up on top of the house, but the roof was still intact...

There was another huge *boom* then a loud low *roar*.

Then there were three airy *swish* sounds above them and another *boom!*

"*No way!*" Jack shouted then ran from the room.

"Wait!" Alex cried in alarm. Then she ran after him, her armor *clanking* with her frantic steps.

Steve pulled his sword and followed just in time to see the kid throwing his new bed down in the middle of the main room. Jack frantically lay down on top of it, stared at the ceiling for an instant, then jumped to his feet again.

Weird kid, Steve thought.

They all ran to the farm door. When Jack paused, Alex opened the door herself, and all three of them burst outside into the darkening evening. When Steve caught up behind his friends, he tilted his head back and looked up...

There was another *boom*.

In the dying light of the setting sun—the eastern horizon over the big ridge already dark—Steve saw two monstrous *beasts* battling in the sky! They were huge! In the last rays of the light and the silvery beams of the rising moon, Steve saw an actual *dragon*—huge and black with great wings and a horned face— circling around up there, dodging balls of gleaming grey fire being shot at it from another slightly-smaller monster with a big body of twisted bones and *three skeletal heads*. The *swishing* sound was coming from the three-headed thing spitting fireballs at the dragon, and whenever one of those missiles hit the huge serpent's body, it exploded with a loud *boom*, showering who-knows-what down all around them!

"Oh Gosh!" Alex exclaimed, covering her mouth with her hands.

"I can't believe it!!" Jack shouted, holding the hair out of his face.

"Where did they come from?!" Steve asked, crouching when another tremendous *boom* was followed by debris showering down around the farm. He had to assume that since one of the monsters was obviously a freaking *dragon*, the other terrible thing had to be that 'Wither' that Jack had mentioned.

"Look out!" Alex exclaimed, pulling Jack back as a chunk of rock plunged into the wheat near them.

The dragon suddenly lined up a straight pass at the Wither, gliding in on huge, black wings. It opened its mouth and *roared* as it passed, breathing out a sparkling cone of glowing purple fire all over the three-headed monster! The Wither howled in pain— covered with the stuff—and returned fire, hitting the black dragon with two fireballs as a third sailed off into the night. *Boom! Boom!*

"The dragon comes from the End!" Jack exclaimed. "And the Wither came from the nether!"

"They *both* came from the Divining Pool!" Alex said.

Just then, both monsters seemed to break apart. Steve watched them separate and head in different directions. The dragon propelled itself away from the battle with powerful wing strokes and the Wither floated—as if lifted by magic—toward the big ridge. Steve caught a glimpse of the dark, bony creature's eyes—all three sets of them glowed bright white in the dimming sky.

The air suddenly sparkled with purple light and Steve realized that what remained of the dragon's strange *breath weapon* was slowly floating down round them. He looked straight up and saw no motes of purple light over their heads, but some of the weird dragon-fire drifted down nearby.

"Look out!" Steve said, pushing both Alex and Jack backwards toward the farm door as the glowing stuff settled down into the farm, crops, and grass and trees outside of their property. He saw some land on sprigs of young wheat near them and as it settled, it hissed and bubbled and burned the growing wheat down to the ground.

"Whoa!" Jack exclaimed.

"The animals!" Alex shouted, pushing against Steve's arm, but he held her back. He saw more wheat burning down, and saw several areas of grass and the tops of trees sizzling just outside the farm. Looking over to their animal pens, Steve was relieved to see no dragon-fire settling down over their cows, chickens, pigs, or sheep.

Huh, he thought. There were *two* sheep.

"Hey, you got the grey sheep back!" he exclaimed, looking back up into the sky again.

"We had help," Alex said, relaxing when she saw that the animals were out of danger.

The dragon was still flying away, huge and black and menacing as heck. The Wither was heading off in a different direction. It seemed that the dragon was heading straight north, and the Wither was going east. The nightmare-creature with three skull-heads drifted over the big ridge...

To the village, Steve thought with a fright.

"Stay here!" Steve said. Then he dashed across the farm away from the others, heading toward the village. He had to make sure they'd be okay...

"Steve, *wait!*" Alex called after him. "It's nighttime!"

He leaped over the stream then began sprinting and jumping up the steepening side of the big ridge toward the village.

"I've got to make sure that—" he shouted back, but stopped.

Steve suddenly heard that *whishing* sound—three times—and his heart dropped. He heard three *booms* on the other side of the ridge, then the clattering of debris and rubble showering down all over.

No!

He climbed the ridge quicker than he ever had before, leaping from ledge to ledge expertly. He'd gone up this way many times by now, but never in such a hurry. When Steve reached the top and looked out over the desert to the east—silver in the light of the rising moon—he gasped...

The Wither was drifting steadily east—still just as high up in the air as it was before when it had been fighting the dragon—but it had slowed down over the village. Steve saw two sandstone houses destroyed. Villagers were running for their lives.

Launching another volley of fireballs, Steve watched in horror as the three burning projectiles streaked down through the air at the village. *Boom, boom, boom!* One of the larger houses was blown to smithereens—sandstone blocks and chunks flying everywhere—and another smaller home had its roof and one wall blown apart. Steve saw a villager thrown through the air and land in the sand.

He opened his mouth to shout out in alarm, but no words came...

Then, instead of finishing the village off, the Wither simply continued east, floating high in the air, and leaving the destruction and devastation behind.

Steve scanned the village. Several villagers were displaced and he saw a handful of zombies wandering up from the surrounding desert...

The village and its people were *exposed*...

"Dang!"

As fast as he could, Steve ran back home down the big ridge—dropping down and leaping where he could—then crossed the stream and farm back to Alex and Jack.

"What happened?!" Alex cried, distressed and clearly afraid.

"The Wither!" Steve replied. "It blew up a lot of the village! Come on—we've got to help them!"

"We can't fight that thing!" Alex replied.

"It's gone now!" Steve said. "But the village is really damaged and the villagers need our help! The mobs will be on them soon!"

"But it's nighttime!" Alex said. "Let's rebuild in the morning."

"They'll all be *dead* by then!" Steve replied. "Now, let's go!"

"I'll get my sword!" Jack exclaimed, running back inside.

With that, they all ran across the farm. Jack stopped to take a quick drink from the creek as he plunged through it. It looked like the boy couldn't just leap across it like Steve and Alex could. Then they climbed the ridge. Far away on the ridge to the south, Steve caught sight of a creeper heading toward them.

"Hurry!" he shouted—mainly down at Jack, who was having a very hard time scaling the slope.

Steve stood by with his stone sword in hand, ready to fend of the creeper if necessary.

He hoped that they could get to the villagers before the mobs killed them in the night.

He would sure try...

Season 1, Episode 3:
Save the Village!

Save the Village!

After a completely unexpected midair battle between an Ender Dragon and a freaking Wither, the village to the east of Jack, Alex, and Steve has suffered a lot of damage. The two Minecraftians and Jack the 'Weird Walker' head straight there to help repair the blown-up houses before sundown. If they don't, many villagers will likely be killed over the night!

Can they survive the night and save the villagers? And if they survive until dawn, what interesting things will Jack find in a Minecraft sandstone village as a real human boy? And will Steve finally get to help KittyPaws30 build a swimming pool?!

S1E3 - Chapter 1 – Jack

"I'll get my sword!" Jack exclaimed.

He still couldn't believe it. A freaking *ender dragon* and a *wither* both appearing out of thin air over this Minecraft house of Steve and Alex's, duking it out for no reason!

No reason other than that weird Divining Pool thing, the boy thought.

He ran back inside, passed the small pixelated kitchen, and grabbed his blocky stone sword from where he'd left it hovering on top of his brand new, red-blanketed oak bed. When the craziness outside had started, Jack threw that bed down—he'd just built it a moment before—right smack in the middle of the house's main room. Heck—he'd even tried to lie down in it! If Jack died somehow, would he even respawn on that bed?!

"Oh, beetles," he muttered, gripping the blocky weapon in his fleshly, human boy hand.

They were about to run out into the night to save the villagers.

The night would be full of mobs.

Jack was just a kid, and short for a twelve-year-old. The zombies would be taller and wider than him. The skeletons would tower over him. Even the creepers—imposing enough of a threat to someone unarmored like Jack—would be even more menacing. The boy thought back to first creeper he saw, quietly chasing him across the mountain glade like a cartoony, pixelated cactus-creature, intent on blowing him to *Kingdom Come*.

What would happen if I blow up? Jack wondered, his mind spinning. His head reeled as he gripped the sword.

"Oh, Gosh," he muttered, staring at the bed.

"Come on, already!" Alex exclaimed. "Steve's way up ahead!" The female Minecraftian stood in the hallway to the kitchen and farm-side door where Steve was no doubt waiting and jumping up and down for them to hurry outside. Alex's Damage Indicator window hovered over her head, showing her at full hit points of twenty and a profile of her face without her helmet on the left side of her name and hit point meter. "You okay there, Jack?"

Jack stared at the sword, tightened his grip, then turned back to her. Alex was wearing a full suit of iron armor and held her bow and arrow ready. Her hair was bright orange in the torchlight of the well-lit house, mostly contained inside her metal helmet.

"Yeah. Let's go."

The boy ran after Alex when she turned and sprinted back out into the farm. Jack followed her through the digital rows of wheat and carrots, dodging around the areas were the falling purple dragon-fire had burned up the ground when if drifted down onto the crops and trees from the battle in the sky.

It was night now. Pure, dark night.

Dang.

Before long, Jack found himself wandering into the strange water of the creek that ran along the eastern side of the homestead property. He felt wet, but not cold. The water slowed him down like normal water did, but it didn't really stick to his real-life clothes or his hair. He felt his glasses slipping in the dark and reached up with his free hand, pushing them back up his nose as he sank to his chest into the fast-moving creek.

Alex simply leapt across the water.

Jack looked up. He saw the blackened sky and the digital stars. He saw faint blocky clouds passing overhead, mostly transparent. Up ahead, up the big ridge, the trees and cube-like ledges and boulders were all a bunch of black shapes. He could hardly see. The square moon was low in the eastern sky behind him, almost full, but it provided no light that Jack could use.

A shape moved up ahead against the stars and Jack felt a stab of icy fear. Then he realized that it was Steve watching them catch up to him from high on the ridge.

Suddenly thirsty again, Jack dipped his face into the weird water and took a long drink.

"Come on!" Alex hissed. "Let's catch up to Steve so he can defend us from the mobs!"

"Okay," Jack replied, pushing his way through the water. He held tightly onto the grip of his stone sword to avoid losing it to the swift current.

Finally out of the flowing water on the other side of the creek, Jack did his best to climb. Each level of blocks was as high as Jack's chest. Climbing up was like continuously climbing up onto a kitchen table—or maybe up onto a school desk; desk after desk—and they were doing it in the *dark!* It wasn't long before Jack's shoulders and legs were burning again.

Feeling the digital grass under his free hand and his fist that held the sword, Jack struggled to keep up with Alex, who moved like the wind and *clanked* when she jumped. Jack tried to avoid looking back. He knew that he was climbing the ridge and already knew what he'd see behind him, but the ridge itself was too dark to see well. All he'd see behind him if he looked back now was the house, animal pens, and the fields lit with torches that—

Jack suddenly slipped. He'd reached up for the next level of blocks—another grass block too dark to see—and his tired hand and burning shoulder didn't reach far enough. When he tried to pull himself up, he fell back instead, and cried out as he slipped down into black, open space...

Two levels down, Jack hit the spongy ground with an *oof*, slamming his back into what felt through his shirt like another grass block. Terror flew through him and he wheeled his hands around to catch himself in the dark night, deathly afraid of falling all the way down the ridge and breaking every bone in his body! But the ground was soft. He bounced lightly, then managed to stay on that level without falling any farther down.

"Goose feathers!" Jack exclaimed when the back of his head smacked dirt that felt like the rubbery floor of a playground.

He was looking up at the stars, on his back.

The boy reached up and made sure that his glasses were still there. Yeah—he could see. *Of course* they were there. Otherwise, the stars would have been a bazillion blurry spots! He still had his sword in his hand.

"Are you okay?" Alex cried down from a few levels above him.

"I fell," Jack replied, struggling back to his feet and looking up the steep, blocky slope.

"Hurry!" Steve suddenly shouted from the top of the ridge. He didn't sound as far away as Jack had imagined he was. Maybe they were higher up that he'd thought.

"Come on, Jack!" Alex replied, and the boy's eyes were dazzled when she pulled a glowing torch from her pack. "Can't you see? Take this!"

He could see now. They were standing on a completely boring Minecraft hill—the slope leading up to the big ridge—surrounded by grass blocks and occasional patches of stone. Trees stood here and there. The yellow glow of the torch made Alex's metal armor gleam. Her face was worried.

Jack rarely wandered around in the dark when he was *playing* Minecraft safe at home or with his game pendant in the computer lab. It was easy enough to see fine in the game when playing in a dark room. The game world at night—or even deep underground in caves—was always dark blue and not *that* hard to navigate carefully ... assuming you didn't have to fight any hostile mobs in the darkness. But here, with his human eyes, Jack was surprised at how inky-black the night was!

"I need to up my gamma," he replied with a laugh, grunting as he climbed another level to catch up to Alex.

"What...?" she asked. "What's *gamma?*"

Jack laughed to himself and took the torch in his free hand. He suddenly felt a *lot* better having light. He was surprised they hadn't been attacked yet. He also thanked his lucky stars that he'd installed a mod to let torches cast light without having to *plunk* them onto the ground or a wall like in the normal *vanilla* game.

"Never mind," he said.

There was a *hiss* and a *clunk* from above. Both the Weird Walker and the Minecraftian woman looked up to see Steve fighting a creeper, both silhouetted against the night sky. The Minecraftian warrior—dressed in a leather tunic and pants and fighting with a crude wooden sword—danced in, stabbed the mob with his basic weapon, then dodged backwards again as the green creature let out a vicious hiss and *glowed* slightly, pulsating and shaking as it tried to reach him.

"Oh, dang!" Alex exclaimed, raising her bow and drawing an arrow. "Let's catch up!"

Jack did his best to move quickly. Each new level hurrying to the top of the ridge was harder and harder to climb as his muscles started to burn and become numb. Alex paused once to take aim at the fight between Steve and the creeper, but Steve suddenly struck the creature down with one last mighty swing, and the battle was over.

She lowered her bow as they continued up.

Then, Steve disappeared over the other side.

Jack could feel Alex's fear like a wave of cold immediately shooting out from her body.

"Steve!" Alex screamed. "*Wait up!*"

The Minecraftian didn't reappear. He was gone over the edge, on the village-side of the ridge.

Jack jumped when he heard a zombie suddenly moan from the darkness on his left as he pulled himself up another level. He raised his torch to the darkness. He could hear the plodding steps, but saw nothing past the glow of his light.

"He must have gone on to the village!" Jack said, hustling to keep up to Alex. She was fast and vaulted over the blocks with ease, but she was obviously slowing herself down to avoid leaving him behind. "We're almost there, aren't we?"

"I *don't know!*" Alex replied, her eyes suddenly wide and afraid in the torchlight. She eyed the warm, safe glow of the homestead below them and to the west. "I don't really know how to get to the village!"

"Don't worry," Jack said, huffing and puffing. Gosh—he was so out of breath! Alex stood in place, looking up for Steve, then down at the homestead and around them with her bow raised to

224

the darkness. "I know how to get to the village," he said. "But I meant: are we almost to the top of the ridge?"

"Yes," Alex replied, her even voice sounding not nearly as afraid as she looked. "It's right up there!"

"Then let's keep going. The village is on the other side. They have torches. All villages do. We'll be able to see it." The zombie on Jack's left gurgled again. Its heavy footsteps were surprisingly loud competing against Jack's heartbeat and breathing in his ears. Then, on the wind, Jack heard the *clunk* of bones. "The mobs are coming out. Let's catch up!"

Jack couldn't tell very well where the top of the ridge was from within his island of torchlight, but Alex was right. After several more grueling body-pulls up the seemingly-endless levels of chest-high blocks (chest-high to *Jack*, anyway), they emerged at the highest point. On the other side, past the tops of the trees that grew along the eastern slope of the ridge, Jack could see the distant glow of torches in the desert village down below. He could also see more than a few sets of glowing red eyes down there in the black sand dunes. *Spiders*. There had to be scores of zombies, skeletons, and creepers down there, too.

There was a sudden loud *zip* sound, and Jack saw a streak of purple light cross the darkness, stopping down the ridge just a few blocks away from him in a burst of glowing, purple motes of light! The tall and lean black form of an Enderman appeared—its legs alone as tall as Jack at its squarish hips—blocking out the stars. Two high-up purple eyes flared. It was carrying a block of dirt.

"Dang!" Jack exclaimed, suddenly looking down. He'd seen its eyes—just a glimpse of its eyes! Would it beat him into the ground? Oh Gosh—an Enderman could beat Jack to death in seconds! "Don't look at it!" he hissed over to Alex.

For a few more seconds, Jack watched the scary creature's thin legs without any obvious feet twitch in the grass at the edge of his torchlight. He saw the purple motes of light drifting down slowly to the ground where they winked out like embers from a campfire...

Zip. The Enderman suddenly took off, teleporting away somewhere else into the night.

"It's gone!" Alex said. "How did you know not to look into its eyes? They get very angry, you know, if you—"

She was interrupted by a zombie's gurgle and wet snarl from just ahead of them down the ridge.

"Look out!" Jack cried just as the pale blue shirt appeared at the edge of his vision.

The zombie climbed the blocks with ease that were so difficult for Jack to traverse, charging slowly at them with both green hands raised high. Its Damage Indicator window appeared over its head when it was close enough, bright in the darkness, showing a full-green health bar with twenty hit points. Jack raised his sword, but all of his joints felt like they were made of jelly...

Alex responded immediately with the *twang* of her bow. She shot the zombie right between the eyes! Her arrow appeared in its green forehead and the creature cried out in gurgling pain, stumbling backwards down two levels of blocks, down the slope. A bright crimson number "7" appeared over its head and floated up into the sky briefly before disappearing. Its hit points were now fourteen.

Jack watched as Alex pulled another arrow, loaded it, aimed at the zombie as it approached again—climbing toward them with a snarl—then pulled back her bow string as far she could. She fired again just before it reached them, smacking it in the face! A

226

red number "8" appeared, and the zombie was down to five hit points. It staggered backwards again with two feathered arrow shafts sticking out of the front of its rotten, green pixelated head.

Before the zombie could react and get close to them again, Alex had already reloaded another shot and fired one last time—quicker than the first two—and killed the mob.

The zombie fell down two levels of blocks and out of Jack's torchlight. In the darkness beyond its glow, all the boy could see were two greenish-yellow orbs of light, which fell to the ground and crawled up toward Alex until she absorbed them though her boots with the tinkling sounds of bells.

"That was awesome!" Jack exclaimed. "Why are you so afraid of fighting mobs, Alex?" he asked. "I've seen you kick butt every time you've tried!"

Alex reloaded her bow and swallowed. She took a breath and tossed the hair out of her face.

"*Steve* does the fighting," she said. "I'm not good at it."

"That's bull!" Jack replied with a grin. She did great. Jack had killed hundreds of zombies; at least, as a player on his computer. But face to face like that? That monster was freaking scary! He'd been paralyzed! If he was just playing the game, he wouldn't have thought twice about jumping in with his stone sword and cutting it to pieces before Alex even had a chance to shoot it! But here? *Here*, he might die! He might die for real! Alex would just reappear in her bed just like Steve had if she was killed in action, but for some reason, she was still afraid of getting hurt. And even as afraid as she was, she'd just kicked that zombie's butt! "You were great!" Jack exclaimed. "Let's—"

An arrow suddenly whistled past them in the dark, cutting him off.

"Dang it!" Alex replied, ducking slightly and scanning around the darkness.

Jack heard a skeleton's bones *clunk* from somewhere on their right, to the south.

"Are ... are we being *shot at?*" he asked, ducking.

Another arrow whistled through the air past them again. This time, Jack saw it in the light of his torch. He followed the quick white shape through the darkness and saw it *thunk* into a tree near them.

"There's a skeleton somewhere!" Alex exclaimed. "Let's get outta here!"

"Okay!" Jack replied, looking down at the darkness of the desert before them. He hopped down the first level off of the top of the ridge. He felt fear again. Soft ground or no, if he just went barreling down the ridge in the darkness and slipped, he'd kill himself before he reached the bottom!

"Run!" Alex shouted. "Come on!"

They did.

Jack hopped down block after block in the dark, barely seeing by the light of his torch as he rushed after Alex's gleaming armored form. When another arrow hit the ground next to him, its white fletching bright and buzzing as the shaft stuck out of the dirt, Jack imagined being stuck with it in his back and made himself go faster.

They ran down the ridge in the dark, around black trees and sounds of skeletons and zombies stalking the woods. Jack didn't hear any creepers around them, but he knew that they were out there ... creeping.

Through a mix of fear and exhilaration—but mostly stark fear—Jack pushed himself to keep going, trying as hard as he could to keep his balance as he almost overran the light in his path, vaulting through tall grasses. He narrowly avoided face-planting into a tree trunk. There was a time when he jumped off of a ledge that was two blocks high instead of one, and he yelped as he fell, crashing to the soft ground below. Once again, Jack was amazed and thankful that this strange video game environment was so *spongy*. Another time, he ran right into Alex's back, colliding with her iron armor with a *clatter*.

"Watch out!" she hissed, hiding behind an oak tree trunk. "There's another—"

An arrow *thunked* into Alex's shoulder armor. She grimaced and grunted in pain. Jack felt a stab of fear when he saw her hit points reduced to eighteen. An arrow shaft was now stuck in Alex's metal pauldron above her upper arm.

"Look out!" Jack cried. "Let's keep going before it reloads!"

Another zombie was approaching from somewhere, its heavy steps thumping through the night. It moaned lowly.

"We're at the tree line!" Alex replied. "It'll shoot us in the back if we run! There's no cover!"

"Make a wall, then!" Jack exclaimed. "Make some cover!"

The boy saw a light go on in Alex's green eyes.

"Good idea!"

She immediately put her bow down, pulled out dirt, cast a quick glance toward the village—Jack could see it now ahead and across an expanse of sand by the light of its own torch poles—and she immediately set to building a wide wall as tall as their heads.

Plunk, plunk, plunk, plunk...

Within a few seconds, there was an eight-block-wide, two-block-high wall of dirt where there was only nature before. Alex put away the dirt and pulled out her bow again.

"Okay, let's go!" she exclaimed.

"Wait—how do you know which direction—?"

"I *know* where it is! Come on!"

Jack obeyed. The two of them burst out from hiding spot and ran with the wall somewhat at their backs through the last of the thinning oak trees. The boy felt the sand under his feet; spongy like the grass, but hissing with his steps and strange in a way that he couldn't describe. They made for the village...

Alex had been correct in her assessment. The wall was Jack's idea, but Alex put it in the right place to give them the cover they needed to turn their backs and run away from the hidden archer without being vulnerable. It didn't fire at them again.

Soon, heaving his breaths and almost seeing spots from running so hard after climbing and fighting over the ridge, Jack watched the sandstone village appear before them in the torchlight of their scant 'street lights' and his own illumination.

He was surprised to see villagers running around, shockingly taller and bigger than him, with their hands folded together in their robes and their green eyes crazy with fear. The two of them found Steve fighting off a pair of zombies in the street.

Steve was fighting hard, several sandstone homes were ruined and broken open, villagers were scattered and fleeing through the streets, and the mobs of the night were coming in from all sides...

S1E3 - Chapter 2 – Alex

There were mobs everywhere!

Alex saw Steve dancing through the streets of the sandstone village, cutting down zombies left and right. He parried. He dodged. He jumped backwards when they came in at him, then flew in to skewer one hostile mob after another through their undead bodies. Little glowing experience orbs were piling up in the streets and slowly followed Steve, floating and rolling along like little pets of yellow and green light.

Jack the kid was clearly afraid. She could see it on his wildly intricate face and his wide eyes behind those things that he called 'glasses'. The boy's eyes flew around frantically. He held his sword, but the weapon shook in his strange, soft hand. By the kid's torchlight, Alex could see two zombies and a spider coming in at them from the sand dunes surrounding the village.

Alex's arm hurt a little where the arrow had hit her. Her iron armor had stopped most of the blow, but the tip of the arrowhead had made it through enough to pain her.

Jack wouldn't fight; not like Steve could. She knew it. She'd have to protect the boy. He was unarmored and inexperienced, even despite all that he knew about their world.

What an odd creature, Alex thought, looking down at Jack. To know everything about everything, but to be afraid of even a single zombie and have such a hard time climbing up the ridge!

"Cover me!" she exclaimed, raising her bow to help Steve deal with the many mobs assaulting the village.

Jack balked for a moment, then tightened his grip on his sword. Alex could see the boy's bizarre, intricate and soft fingers growing tighter around its hilt; even becoming white against the weapon. He narrowed his eyes and threw his round head to toss the hair out of his face.

"Okay!" he said. "What do you want me to do?"

"Protect me while I help Steve with my bow!" she replied, taking aim at a zombie that was coming up behind her Minecraftian companion.

Alex aimed at the zombie's back between its two heavy shoulders and let loose her arrow, which struck the undead mob soundly. It staggered, gurgled, and turned around to head toward her. She felt a spot of cold fear in her gut, but knew that she could take it. Heck—Steve had already killed over a dozen mobs by the look of it, and he wasn't slowing down.

The Minecraftian woman suddenly feared for Steve. She was afraid of what would happen whenever he became *hungry* and ran out of energy. She had some various pieces of food in her pack—she always did; Alex was always prepared—but Steve probably had nothing on him but whatever pieces of mobs he'd already picked up in the battle.

Steve never carried many items for long.

The zombie turned and stalked toward her. Its heavy, plodding steps made hissing sounds in the sand. With the mob facing her now, Alex couldn't see the arrow sticking out of the zombie's back.

She reloaded, drew, and aimed her arrow carefully at the monster's green forehead. When Alex fired, she hit her mark and the mob fell, dead, disappearing in a puff of smoke.

"Here comes another from the desert!" Jack exclaimed suddenly. Alex looked down at him and saw the boy hovering near her, clutching both his stone sword and torch while bouncing up and down in some sort of crouch. The kid could move in all sorts of weird ways that she and Steve couldn't.

Alex turned just in time to see another zombie coming in at them from the sand closest to the ridge—at least she *thought* that the ridge was there; she couldn't tell—and she took aim at its chest. Steve suddenly *whooped* loudly and she turned back to see him smashing a skeleton into bits. The mob archer fell loudly to the sandstone street into a pile of bones and smoke.

The incoming zombie snarled, almost making Alex jump out of her skin!

She turned and fired, smashing it in the chest with her arrow.

"Back away now!" she commanded to Jack, and the kid stayed with her as she reloaded and fell back from the still-advancing mob. When she could, Alex shot it again, making the creature stagger, but it didn't stop.

The zombie let out a low moan, struggled back to its feet, and continued on after them, both arms raised and two arrows sticking out of its heavy body.

"One more shot!" Jack shouted. "It's got three hit points left!"

Alex had no idea what the boy meant by 'hit points', but she reloaded and fired at the zombie's chest one last time. When her arrow hit home, the monster fell with a gurgling sigh, then disappeared into a puff of smoke.

Looking around for Steve, Alex found him with his back up against a broken sandstone house, fighting off two zombies and a vicious, nimble spider bigger than either of them. Its many red eyes glowed in the darkness of the night.

"Come on!" Alex said to Jack, leading him closer to Steve's battle.

Steve was struggling. He cut down one of the zombies, narrowly dodged the spider's fangs, and Alex could see that he was wounded. His leather armor—*was that rabbit-hide?*—only protected his body and legs, but seemed to be holding up okay. The Minecraftian warrior spared a glance in their direction, then he frowned and shook his head.

"The villagers!" Steve shouted, pointing into the night with his wooden sword. "Save the villagers! I'll stop the mobs!"

Alex raised her bow, shot the spider once in its fat, furry abdomen, then followed Steve's pointing weapon to see the pale form of a villager in a white robes running down the street, pursued by zombies.

"Watch out!" Jack cried. "The cartographer!"

Reloading, Alex changed her aim, swinging her bow toward the fleeing villager, but it was too late. The zombies caught the helpless villager, who made no attempt to fight back. As they tore into him and bashed him with their green fists, the villager squawked in pain again and again, but kept his hands tucked into his robes and only tried to flee. Within seconds, the zombies had pulled him to the ground, and the villager was dead.

"Dang it!" Alex cried, shooting one of the zombies in the face. It fell backwards from the body—which disappeared in a puff of smoke—then turned to face them, snarling with an arrow sticking out from under one black, lifeless eye.

"Save the villagers!" Steve was shouting. "Save the villagers or they'll be killed!"

Alex looked around. There were two zombies coming at them from where they'd killed the cartographer. Another was approaching them from the sands outside of town. She saw the menacing green of *another* appear from the shadows between two homes deeper in town. She saw one of the small houses with a huge, gaping hole blown in one wall. There was also one of the really big houses nearby with a full corner of its exterior walls blown to smithereens.

"Here comes more!" Jack exclaimed, hovering and bouncing around near her. His voice showed his fear.

Steve had killed the two zombies and the spider that had forced him against a wall and was now running around in the streets again, charging, slaying, dodging, falling back...

Alex thought of her cobblestone. She had plenty. Maybe they could fix the holes in the houses and somehow get the displaced villagers back inside before they were all killed...

"Stay with me, Jack!" she exclaimed, running toward the small house with the huge hole in its side.

Jack obeyed.

When they reached the small house, Alex checked around them to make sure that they weren't in immediate danger, then stashed her bow and arrow and pulled out her cobblestone. Looking inside the house through the gap in the wall, she saw two villagers scrambling around inside to get away from a single zombie that had invaded through the hole.

"There's a zombie!" Jack said.

"I see it," Alex replied, quickly plunking one cobblestone block onto the edge of the hole in the wall to start sealing it up. "Go kill it while I plug up this hole."

Jack balked again. He moved to follow the zombie through the hole, but paused. His sword shook in his soft hand and his eyes were wide. His intricate mouth was open and his face was fearful.

"I..." he stammered. "I ... um ... wouldn't it be faster if...?"

He was scared. Of course he was. He could hardly climb the ridge.

Alex frowned and put away her cobblestone after repairing only two blocks. She pulled her bow. "I'll shoot it once or twice, then you finish it," she said. "Hurry before we're overwhelmed!"

Aiming, Alex fired into the house, careful not to hit the panicking villagers, and struck the zombie in one shoulder. She reloaded and looked down at Jack, who stared back and forth between her and the zombie with wide eyes.

"Sixteen hit points," he said. "Another shot, maybe?"

Aiming again, Alex shot the zombie in the head as it climbed toward them through the hole. The zombie didn't fall, but Jack slowly approached, sword bouncing up and down in his grip, clearly afraid but somehow finding the courage to advance.

The boy shook like a leaf, but he drew himself up close to the hole, and when the zombie was in a vulnerable position climbing back out into the street, Jack suddenly *roared* with his little voice and swung the stone sword, landing the blade in the mob's chest!

Falling back into the house, the zombie let out a low moan, collapsed, and died.

There were more coming. Alex heard the steps in the street on either side of them, and the hissing of a spider was close up overhead.

Probably on the roof, she thought, squashing down the growing fear in her belly and pulling out her cobblestone again.

Jack was beaming. His eyes were big and his grin was bigger.

"I did it!" he shouted. "I killed it!"

"Watch our backs," Alex said, plunking block after block into the blown-apart gap in the wall.

"Okay," Jack said, suddenly wiping the smile off of his face and spinning around to face the street with his sword and torch held in front of him. He had a serious expression for a few seconds, but a smile crept back to his lips soon enough.

"Was the door closed inside?" Alex asked, putting away her cobblestone and pulling her bow out again. She did a quick ammo check in her pack. "I don't remember, myself."

"I think so," Jack said.

They both turned to see another villager running down the street, pursued by three zombies. The villager wore green robes and had an arrow sticking out of one arm.

"Let's try to get them into the big house," Alex said.

"Okay!"

But where the heck was the big house?

"Now, where *is* that place?" Alex asked, looking up and down the street.

"This way!" Jack said, leading the way.

Running down the street after him, Alex shot another zombie in the head as it came at them, killing it in one spectacular shot! She and Jack dodged through the crowd of slow-moving zombies and occasional skeletons that scanned4 for victims.

The big house was empty. No villagers; no mobs. The interior of the place was clearly visible through the collapsed walls and easier to see because of the torch inside high in the rafters.

A single zombie was near the huge hole in the walls. Alex shot it twice as they approached and Jack finished it off with his stone sword, clearly feeling a lot better about dealing final blows. The kid smiled broadly, though his hands still shook.

"Cover me while I block up the walls," Alex said, stashing her bow and pulling out her cobblestone.

Alex heard Steve suddenly grunt in pain from nearby, then there was the hiss of a creeper or spider unseen in the night. A moment later, a clattering *explosion* nearby shocked them both.

"Creeper!" Jack said with wide eyes.

Alex called out as loudly as she could. "Steve!! Steve, are you okay?!" She started sealing up the wall, trying to ignore the cold dread crawling across her body. This was *crazy!* She'd never been involved in a wild night-time battle like this before! There were mobs *everywhere!* She could understand Steve wanting to save the village, but this was downright reckless! If a handful of villagers were killed, would it—?

"I'm okay!" Steve called back from out of sight. "Save the villagers!"

Turning back to the wall, Alex repaired the damage as quickly as she could. She heard another villager squawk out in pain from somewhere deeper in the village, and the green-robed villager running past them again caught her eye.

"We've got to get them inside!" Jack exclaimed, hovering nervously around her as she worked. "They might not run back inside. Villagers don't really ... they don't defend themselves very well!"

Plunk, plunk, plunk, plunk.

"There we go!" Alex exclaimed, putting away her cobblestone and pulling her bow again. "Last one!"

"There are three villagers running around that I can see!" Jack said, pointing around the night wildly with his stone sword. "*At least* three."

"Let's try to help them into this house," Alex said. "Come on."

She led Jack running down the dark street after where she'd last seen the green-robed villager. The kid ran after her, his strange shoes flapping loudly as he did, heaving big, gulping breaths. The *Weird Walker* sure was weird.

They found the green-robe quickly enough. He was fleeing from a single zombie that had kept on his heels. Somehow, he'd lost the other two. Alex shot the pursuing zombie, plugging it in the chest and turning its attention onto *them*.

"Hey, you!" Jack called out to the villager. "Come on! This way!"

The zombie heading toward Alex let out a wet snarl. She reloaded and fired again, striking it in the skull and dropping it to the ground. Experience orbs littered the streets, crawling after her, Steve, and Jack whenever any of them ran past.

The villager stared at Jack for a moment, ran several more steps, then stopped dead in his tracks, looking around dumbly.

"Hurr," he said. "Hmph. Hurr..."

"Let's go, villager!" Alex shouted. "This way! Come on!" She waved her bow and pointed at the big house with the freshly-repaired corner of cobblestone.

"Come on!" Jack repeated.

The villager frowned, furrowed his brow, then turned away to walk down the street as if it was daytime and there weren't a billion zombies and other hostile mobs around.

"What the heck?!" Alex exclaimed. She felt her face scrunch up in anger. "Come on! Safety this way!"

Jack scoffed. "It's not gonna work!" the boy said. "They're villagers. They can't communicate with us. We've gotta *push* them."

"*Push* them?!"

"Like with Wolfie the grey sheep, remember? When we pushed him into that little cave?"

Now it was Alex's turn to scoff. Well, the kid hadn't led her wrong so far. It felt crazy, but this whole night was crazy, and they had to get the job done. If they could get the villagers all tucked away to safety, they could help Steve. His luck wouldn't last forever...

"Okay."

They both ran up to the green villager, who was trying to leave the scene, wandering down the dark street that was still teeming with hostile mobs.

"Look out!" Jack cried.

Alex felt a jolt of fear as a skeleton suddenly materialized from the shadows near them next to a sandstone wall. It was already aiming at her...

"Dang!" Alex cried as the mob loosed it arrow, which whistled through the night a hit her in the breastplate with a loud *clang.*

"Alex!!" Jack shouted in alarm.

The woman was knocked backwards a little, but the arrow had been stopped by her armor. She felt okay. Blazing with fear and anger, Alex aimed back and returned fire, smashing the skeleton somewhere in the ribs. It leapt in response.

Both she and the skeleton struggled to reload before the other.

"Take it out, Jack!" Alex exclaimed, taking aim again.

The boy was clearly terrified, but he ran up as fast as he could on his strange, soft legs and flapping feet holding, his torch before his frightened face and winding his stone sword back for a mighty swing...

The skeleton shot. Alex barely dodged to the side. She shot back, striking it in the ribs again. A second later, Jack crashed into the mob with his sword—almost with his body, too—and the skeletal archer collapsed into a pile of bones.

"Yeah!!" Jack shouted. Then, "The villager!"

They ran after the oblivious green-robe. When they caught him, Jack ran in front to cut him off, and Alex began pushing the villager back toward the big house. She felt awkward and uncomfortable doing it.

"Hmph!" the villager announced, frowning down at them and furrowing his thick brow. He seemed to not approve. "Hmph, hurr!"

"Sorry," Alex said, "but you've got to come with us! It's for your own good!"

They pushed him. He resisted. But eventually, they managed to get the green-robe around through the darkness, led by Jack's torch, to the front of the big house. Alex reached down and opened the door, then they pushed the villager inside.

"Hmph!!"

"Don't forget to close the door, or he'll come out again!" Jack said.

She did.

"There's *one* of them," Alex said, looking around, making sure that her next arrow was nocked on her bowstring.

This was crazy! She was normally so afraid of being out at night. They'd killed so many mobs, and there was no telling how many mobs Steve himself had killed by now! Even though Alex had been boiling with cold fear this entire time, ever since they'd left the homestead, she was somehow feeling a little more powerful; a little more confident. Maybe it was because she knew Steve was out there taking on most of their enemies. Maybe it was because Jack was with her, even though he wasn't much of a fighter.

Alex didn't feel alone.

"There's another villager!" Jack exclaimed suddenly, pointing at a fleeting, brown and black shape in the distant shadows near the middle of the village.

"Okay, let's get that one too," Alex said. "Stay close to me."

Then, as they started away from the big house, Alex paused when she heard Steve cry out from somewhere.

"Help!" he shouted. "Need some help now!"

Alex felt that cold fear bloom up in her belly again.

If Steve got himself killed, they'd be stuck here by themselves, surrounded by monsters with the dawn a long way away...

"Over there!" Jack announced, pointing his stone sword into the night. "Let's go!"

They ran.

"Where are you?!" she cried out into the dark village. "Steve!"

"Over here!" he shouted back. "By the library!"

The library?! Alex thought. Where the heck was the library? She'd been into this village several times, but now—in the dark, surrounded by the constant moans and clunking bones and hisses and sounds of battle—she had no idea what was where.

"This way!" Jack said. "I remember seeing the library when we got here!"

Really?! Alex thought. How could he remember that?

"Okay," she said. "Lead on!"

The boy led her through the dark streets. They had to pause to kill a zombie, but it only needed one shot from her bow. It was already really wounded; presumably from an encounter with Steve. Several seconds later, they emerged into a wide street next to the large library building. Alex saw another small house with a gaping hole in one wall. *How many houses are damaged?* she thought.

There was Steve, surrounded by several zombies and in the process of skewering a spider through its thorax. Mob parts were scattered all over the ground and a dozen or more experience orbs slowly rolled toward him; bright yellow lights drifting through the sand. The balls of light disappeared into his body whenever his fancy footwork put him into their path.

Steve was wounded but he was as deadly as ever, finishing off the spider that was collapsing before him. He directed his attention back on the horde. Every stab and swing of his wooden sword was precise; there was no wasted energy. Whenever the slow zombies counterattacked, Steve dodged with ease, light in his leather armor. He kept them moving and circling, and whenever they were all bunched together, Steve swung his blunt blade in a wide arc and hit several at once.

Gosh, he was good with a sword!

Then Alex noticed that the wooden guard of his sword was splintered and almost hanging off, and the wooden blade itself was breaking apart.

"Your sword!" Alex cried.

Steve shot a glance their way. "Almost broken!" he exclaimed. "Need another weapon, *pronto!*"

"Take mine!" Jack exclaimed, running up to the melee.

"No, take my iron sword!" Alex shouted, stopping Jack with one armored hand and drawing her weapon. Its metal blade rang out into the night.

Just as she did, Steve swung his sword at the head of a zombie and *shattered* what was left of it against the monster's green, rotten skull. It snarled in response and reached for him.

"Throw it!" Steve shouted, punching the zombie in the face.

She did.

Steve caught it from the air then was back in action, empowered by the superior weapon. Now, instead of a blunt and carved wooden sword, he had a sharped blade of iron, and the Minecraftian warrior began cutting down his attackers with ease!

Then, just as Alex was amazed by Steve's renewed fighting, she suddenly felt a cold stone in her stomach and terror washed over her.

Now, she had no sword...

If the zombies came in close to her and got past her bow, she'd be defenseless...

She needed to make another sword ... *right now*. And for that, she would need a crafting table. She could make a crafting table, of course. She had plenty enough wood, sticks, and cobblestone to create both things, but—

"Watch out behind you!" Jack exclaimed suddenly.

Alex whirled around and pulled her bow again. There was a creeper approaching from the shadows of an alley in between two sandstone buildings. Fear flashed through the woman's body. She aimed and fired, striking the green mob in its strange, tubular body. It hissed and fell back, then continued after her silently on four small, clawed feet with its deep frown and black eyes glaring...

"I need to make another sword!" Alex shouted. "Stay away! It's a creeper!"

Jack shot her a look in between expressions of fear. *I know what a creeper is*, it seemed to say.

"This way!" the boy exclaimed, leading the creeper in another direction down the street away from Steve's hot battle. "There's a crafting table in the library!"

Alex followed his lead, reloading and struggling to stay ahead of the creeper. For how quiet it was, it sure could move fast.

"How do you know that?" she asked.

"*All* libraries have crafting tables!"

She shot at the creeper once again, sinking an arrow into its strange form just below that deep frown. Alex expected the dangerous mob to keep coming after that, but that second shot did it. The creeper fell backwards with a hiss and a strange clunking sound, dissolving into smoke when it hit the sandy street.

Alex ran with Jack to the library. The kid hesitated for a moment at the door, then opened it with a strange expression on his face.

Inside, two librarians stared at her and the boy with wide, green eyes. Then, they frowned and began yelling at them with their strange language.

"Hurr! Hunh! Hurr!!"

"Excuse us for a moment," Jack said, pushing past them to the crafting table in a far corner.

Alex closed the door behind her, joined Jack, then made a stone sword from the components in her pack as quickly as she could. Several seconds later, she sheathed the new blade and looked down at the boy.

"Okay, let's get back to those other villagers in danger," she said, pushing past the angry librarians again. The villagers glared and stared with their hands clamped together under their robes.

"Good plan," Jack said. He turned to the librarians. "Thanks! Sorry to intrude!"

Then, they were out in the street again.

Steve and his many mobs were gone. Alex could still hear the sounds of battle. It appeared that Steve had killed all of his aggressors outside of the library and had moved on to another hot spot.

"Which way?" Alex asked.

She didn't want to bother pretending that she didn't know where the big house or the center of town was. She frankly had no idea. It was obvious that they were currently at the edge of town, but it would be a waste of time to figure it out the directions herself. Jack would know the way.

"Follow me!" he exclaimed.

They ran through the dark streets back to town. Alex recognized the town's water well when they passed it.

"Which way to the big house?" she asked, pausing to shoot a random zombie in the head. She reloaded as it turned its dull attention to them, then she took the mob out with two more shots as Jack looked around.

"This way, I think," he said. "And hey—there's another villager! A farmer, looks like!"

As they ran, Alex could suddenly make out the brown robes of a lost villager running through the night. The last one they'd seen was brown and black. This was a different one.

Then, a huge spider jumped onto the sandy ground in front of them both from a rooftop with a loud *hiss!* It was wide and low with a body bigger than Alex's and long legs. Its eyes were bright red, glowing maliciously, and by the light of the kid's torch, Alex saw the monster's fangs sliding back and forth in front of its weird and horrifying mouth...

"Duck feathers!!" Jack exclaimed with a jump.

He broke into a wild run away from the spider suddenly in his face.

The arachnid leapt to follow.

"Dang it!" Alex shouted, aiming at the fleeing boy and the monster that pursued him. The spider's legs drummed loudly against the sandstone street. "Stay with me! *Jack!!*"

In only a moment, the boy was running around the back of a small house as fast as Alex had ever seen him run, his torch and sword swinging madly, and the spider kept on right behind him. Alex tried to follow—tried to aim and shoot the mob in its fat, shaggy abdomen as it pursued—but when she rushed around a corner after them, the mob and the kid were already gone around the next corner.

Jack was screaming.

Alex changed direction, hoping that Jack was only running around the house and would be back around in a second with the spider in hot pursuit, then she bumped into the brown-robed villager who had also apparently been running her way.

"Watch it!" she shouted. "Jack!" She aimed around the other corner of the building, waiting.

"Hmph!" the farmer replied, putting his back to the wall. Alex suddenly saw that his green eyes were wide in fear. A moment later, she heard plodding footsteps and gurgling snarls...

Jack came running around the corner like she expected he would, his intricate hair flying around his terrified face, his glasses almost falling from his nose, his strange mouth pulled into a fearful grimace and eyes wide.

"Spider!" he screamed, huffing and puffing. "Spider chasing me!"

Alex aimed, waiting for Jack to pass, waiting for the spider to come running after him, but the sounds of the approaching zombies were loud and close, and she turned to see...

They were surrounded.

S1E3 - Chapter 3 – Steve

"Steeeeve!"

It was Alex's voice. She and the Weird Walker were somewhere near the center of town.

Steve parried the fangs of a spider leaping in at him, then skewered the mob right between its many red, glowing eyes. The creature let out a hissing sigh and fell away from his sword— Alex's iron blade, which was *far* superior to his now-broken wooden sword—and Steve was left holding the gleaming weapon as two zombies lumbered at him.

"You'll have to wait," Steve said to the incoming undead, then with a wide swing of his sword that knocked both of his attackers backwards, he turned and ran toward Alex's cry for help.

Sprinting past two more zombies wandering in the sandstone street and dodging through them and around small houses with villagers locked inside—Steve narrowly avoided being struck by a skeletal archer's arrow that whistled past him—he found Alex and Jack the kid in trouble.

He'd arrived just in the nick of time.

His best friend and their new companion were both cornered against the side of a small home. Alex had lowered her bow and had pulled out a stone sword—*where'd she get that?* Steve wondered—and both of them were fending off several zombies and a single spider that pressed in on them from multiple sides...

The spider, its red eyes narrowed and fixed on the strange, soft-lined boy, flexed its mighty legs to leap...

"Raaaawr!" Steve shouted, waving his arms. "Stop! Look here!!"

Two zombies turned and the spider was distracted from its impending pounce, fixing its glowing eyes on Steve.

The Minecraftian warrior charged in, Alex's iron blade light and nimble in his right fist. He was wounded, but he knew that he could take them on. He *had* to. The village was still in danger. There were still villagers out in the streets running for their lives; Steve could see two of them fleeing in the distance now. His friends were in danger, too. His skill and leather armor would protect him.

As soon as Steve reached the nearest zombie, he went in high, causing the mob to reach up for him, then ducked low at the last second to slice through the undead creature's legs. When Alex's fantastic sword cut cleanly through them, the zombie fell back against the nearest house wall and Steve pivoted the point of the blade to plunge into its chest, killing it with amazing speed.

"Help him, Jack!" Alex shouted from their position against the wall. "Steve's hurt!"

Steve was vaguely aware of Jack and Alex joining in the fight, both attacking a zombie that had been threatening them a moment before; a zombie now advancing on *him*. Both of his friends chopped at the mob's back, and when it turned to face them, Steve took off its head.

Now, the spider was advancing on him. Since Steve was wearing only leather armor, the arachnid must have through that he'd be a better snack than Alex, who was decked out in iron armor, or Jack, strange to this world.

The spider thought wrong.

It leapt at Steve, but Steve had killed *many* spiders and knew exactly how it would fight. As soon as the mob was close enough, he slashed at it with a powerful horizontal strike, cutting deeply into the mob and knocking it backwards with a loud *hiss* of pain. When it shook its furry head and glared at him with its glowing, red eyes, Steve was ready when it came at him again. As the spider pounced once more, Steve stabbed it right between its venomous fangs, knocking it back again, stunned. With that, he pressed the attack and finished the monster off. It fell away from him and crumpled up with a long, rattling hiss, soon disappearing in a puff of smoke and leaving some of its webbing string behind along with a glowing experience orb.

With that, Steve faced off against the two remaining zombies that had been attacking Alex and Jack.

He took a moment to catch his breath.

They came at him from different sides. When the first was in reach of Steve's sword, he ducked low and swung upwards, knocking the mob backwards after a vicious strike to its outstretched, green arms. Steve immediately spun and thrust his blade through the opposite zombie's chest, then threw his body weight into it behind the sword, knocking the mob backwards. As soon as the first zombie had recovered, Steve spun again and sliced it twice across the chest with two quick swings before collapsing the mob with a powerful vertical strike to its snarling face and head. The zombie fell, dead, and Steve turned and easily finished off the other.

"Holy beetles!" the kid exclaimed from where he and Alex were watching huddled close together against the wall where they'd been cornered.

"Thanks," Alex said to Steve, smirking under her helmet.

Steve looked at the two arrows sticking out of her armor. "Are you okay, Alex?"

"It's not bad," Alex replied as Jack looked up into the night sky. "Are *you* okay, Steve? You look like you've taken some hits. You hungry?"

Steve's stomach grumbled. *Of course* he was hungry.

There was a sudden *squawk* in the distance. One of the villagers was under attack! The thought of it turned Steve's stomach cold.

"It's the middle of the night," Jack said. "The moon's at its apex."

"Yeah, I'm okay for now," Steve said. "Much better now that I have a *real* sword. Now come on; let's save the villagers!"

He led the way, aware of Alex and Jack following. The kid had a torch in one hand, which helped, though Steve was accustomed to fighting in darkness and he wasn't bothered by it. Alex's armor *clanged* as she ran—now armed with her bow and arrow again— and the Weird Walker huffed and puffed out air from his small, curved mouth in a way that reminded Steve a little of zombies sighing in dark caves. He was a strange one, that Jack.

They ran to where a farmer was under attack. The poor guy was running down the main road with two zombies in pursuit and a skeleton firing at him from one side. The villager had two arrows stuck in his back as he squawked and cried out in the villager language for help, eyes wide and hands together under his robe.

Steve found the skeleton archer in the shadows and smashed its bones to pieces. His borrowed sword cut through the mob as if he was chopping through dry sticks. When the archer fell into a pile of bones and dust, dropping its last arrow onto the sandstone, Steve heard the *ding-a-ling* of its experience orb merging with his foot.

"Let's push the farmer just like the last villager!" Jack shouted, running up ahead with Alex.

As Steve ran after them, cutting into the two zombies pursuing the villager and catching the mobs' dead-eyed attention, he watched with interest as Jack and Alex proceeded to corral the poor farmer—pushing him from two sides—toward the big house that they'd had repaired.

"Hmph!" the farmer cried. "Hurr!!"

Steve fought the zombies and killed them with ease. Three more zombies suddenly plodded into their midst from outside of town, wandering in through the sands from the dark desert with their green claws stretched out toward him. Steve fought the three newcomers, killing all of them but taking one hit to his left shoulder that made him dizzy. Those zombies sure were strong!

Jack's voice rang out over the sounds of the night and the wandering mobs from nearby.

"No, you dummy! Get in! Don't come out!"

"Jack!" Alex added. "Don't let the green-robe out of the house! Watch out! He's—"

"Hurr!"

"I got him!" Jack shouted.

Steve ran toward the big house and paused to fight two more zombies in his path.

Nitwit, Steve thought. The green-robes were dummies, indeed.

"Okay, two more!" Alex shouted. "Close the door!"

"I'm trying!" the kid replied.

Time passed as the three of them struggled to save the remaining displaced villagers. As Jack and Alex tried to push along the remaining villagers that were still alive in the streets toward the big house where they were keeping the refugees, Steve hovered around them, killing any hostile mobs that he came across.

At one point, they were attacked by a creeper that Steve couldn't kill in time. The little green jerk blew up the side of another house, and the three of them were left staring through the smoke and the hole in the sandstone at a pair of villagers peering back out in horror from inside. No harm done, though. Alex promptly pulled out some cobblestone and repaired the wall and street that the creeper had damaged.

When Alex and Jack were chasing down the last vulnerable villager—the blacksmith of all people—Steve noticed when he was fighting a group of zombies that he was just outside KittyPaws30's house. His Minecraftian friend's home was different than all of the others: built from cobblestone and decorated with fancy blocks of wool and spruce wood.

As Steve finished the last of several attackers by stabbing it through the skull with Alex's iron sword, he looked up and noticed KittyPaws30 watching the fight from her second-story balcony. The balcony was protected from spider-invasion by an overhanging roof and rails around the outer edge to keep mobs from climbing up. She'd still have to deal with skeletons maybe taking potshots at her from outside if she stood out there during the night, but there were no skeletons around them at the moment.

Steve pulled the sword blade out of the dead zombie's skull just as the mob's body disappeared in a puff of smoke.

"Great job, Steve!" KittyPaws30 exclaimed with a sweet, high voice from up on the balcony. "You're such an *amazing* swordsman!" In the bright light of her balcony torches and the glow shining from inside her house, Steve could clearly see KittyPaws30's bright, blue eyes and bold, pink hair. She was wearing her typical white hoodie and three cats surrounded her, padding around on the balcony rail, swishing their white and black tails.

Steve almost felt himself blush. He grinned from ear to ear and flipped around the sword in his hand.

As several more zombies slowly plodded in at him from all around, Steve forgot all about Alex and Jack's work nearby and smiled up at his Minecraftian friend.

"Oh, you like that?" he said. "Then watch *this!*" Steve spun around and beckoned all of the zombies toward him. "Come on, you filthy mobs! Come at me!"

Four or five zombies closed in, moaning and snarling.

Steve took aim and *threw* Alex's sword at the nearest mob as they all closed in and surrounded him. The sword flew through the air, tumbling end over end, and its blade sunk into the zombie's face.

KittyPaws30 clapped her hands and laughed. "Delightful!" she exclaimed from above.

A second later, all of the zombies closed in.

Steve suddenly felt a rush of panic and launched himself at the mob with his sword stuck in its head. When he grabbed the hilt of his impaled weapon, he grunted as two heavy fists immediately bashed him in the back and shoulders. Then he lost his grip and fell.

Dang, Steve thought. *This isn't going like it should!*

All five zombies bashed on him from above. The leather armor he'd made from rabbit hide helped some, but Steve still felt the pain of every blow. He grunted and grimaced and tried to stand. He was suddenly dizzy again.

"Oh, be *careful*, Steve!!" He heard KittyPaws30's high voice drifting into his woozy head.

Somehow, Steve made it to his feet and broke away from the mob of mobs. The instant he was out from under the zombies, they turned to follow. He eyed the zombie with his sword stuck in its face and growled at it in anger.

"Okay, then!" Steve groaned. "One at a time! Fists to fists, huh?"

They came at him a little too quickly. Steve backed away down the street, trying to get them to approach him one at time in single file, but the zombies spread out. By the time Steve was no longer in view of KittyPaws30's balcony—*was she still watching?* He wondered—Steve rushed in at the first one and punched it heartily in its green, rotting jaw.

It retaliated with a heavy blow that knocked Steve down to his knees.

"Dang!" he grunted, but his voice sounded weird and slow to him.

Then, they were on him again. There were too many...

Stupid! Steve thought. *Had to show off!*

Then, under the fists of the small pack of zombies, watching Alex's sword gleaming in the light of the nearest torch pole as it bobbed around stuck in the face of one of his attackers, Steve died.

You died.

Steve opened his eyes and quickly sat up.

"That was *stupid!*" he exclaimed, clenching his fists and shaking his head.

He was back in his room, in his bed surrounded his messy red blanket and his empty armor stands and chests of stuff. The window showed him that it was still nighttime. He heard one of the cows stamp around outside his window. It let out a low *moo*.

"I've gotta get back there and help them!" he said to himself, shaking off the disorientation of regenerating. Steve stood and looked into his pack even though he knew that it would be empty. Without his leather armor, his body felt lighter and free, but he also felt more vulnerable. "Need a sword!"

Opening up chest after chest full of random junk that he'd piled up over time in his room, Steve looked for a weapon but found none. Amazingly, he found a single *stick*, then found two blocks of cobblestone from two different containers amidst lots of granite and diorite and gravel and spider eyes and leather saddles and other stuff he didn't need right now.

Steve threw open his bedroom door and ran down the hall to the main room where he did a double-take when he saw Jack's new bed sitting in the middle of the common crafting area.

"Oh yeah..." Steve said, smiling and shaking his head as he hurried to his preferred crafting table.

Standing before the crafting table, Steve wondered for an instant: *what was I doing?* Then, he pulled out the stick and cobblestone and made himself a new stone sword. Looking out through the front windows, he could see the sky lightening outside, and he hoped that Alex and Jack had survived the rest of the night.

Of course they're fine, he thought. If they'd been killed, they'd be here too. Well—probably. Alex would, for sure, but Jack? Who knows. The kid had made a bed, but he clearly wasn't of this world. What would happen if the Weird Walker got himself killed?

Steve took a few quick test swings with his sword in the big, open room. It was fine.

He turned to run back toward the farm door, intent on hustling past the crops and up and over the big ridge to reach the village again, but stopped.

Turning back to the hall leading to the bedrooms, he was suddenly curious about the Divining Pool.

Part of Steve wanted to ignore the draw of curiosity and head out, rushing to catch up to his friends and to help rebuild the village.

Another part told him to look at the mysterious waters inside that spooky little room...

Sheathing his new sword, Steve ran to the Divining Pool. In the hall, he quickly opened the door with a *pop*, then rushed up to the edges of the weird bedrock formation.

He was there just in time to see many hazy words floating in its blue waters, *seconds* before when the rising message would totally disappear...

Steve read the message aloud before it did:

"*I love Jack The Kid series. If my character gets picked, then please add me as Alice The Evil Ninja. She has black hair, is as sneaky as a fox, is intelligent as Albert Einstein, has black clothes, very secretive, secretly likes Steve, envies Alex, curious about Jack, has her favorite weapon on her back; her DevilScythe.*"

Steve stared at the words as they dissolved at the top of the pool and vanished.

"*Likes* me?" he said to himself. "What the heck is this?"

Turning away from the Divining Pool, Steve stared at the open door back into the hall, contemplating the words. This whole 'Divining Pool' thing was Alex's gig. Steve didn't like it one bit. Heck—the last time they'd read words from that thing, those huge monsters appeared in the sky outside, and that *wither* blew up the town!

Why did this message have to involve *him?*

And who the heck was Albert Einstein?!

Steve pulled his sword, shaking his head. There was no time for this. He had to get back to Alex and Jack and help them make the village safe again. Back when Steve had gotten himself killed like an *idiot* by showing off to KittyPaws30—he frowned down at the sword in his hand—Alex and Jack had been trying to corral the last loose villager.

I hope they made it, he thought. *I hope we didn't lose any more people.*

Alex was afraid of being out in the night, and now Steve was here, away from her.

"Well, at least it's morning now," he said, running back out into the main room then rushing through the 'farm door' toward the big ridge. "She's probably okay!"

I sure hope so, he thought.

Taking a quick look at the lightening sky and their animals stamping around in their pens, Steve took off again toward the village. He dashed through the farm rows, leapt over the creek, and started climbing the ridge as fast as he could.

Just before cresting the top, something in the shadows of the early-morning forest caught his eye.

Steve paused and looked north toward a copse of trees, expecting to see a zombie or something still protected from the morning's light. He saw something else instead. A *Minecraftian* stood there—a female—barely hidden inside the darkness of the woods still emerging from the night. She was dressed all in black with slick, dark hair and a face so pale that it was almost white. Blue eyes as cold as frozen oceans stared at him from the shadows. In her black-gloved hands, she held a strange, black *pick axe* or something that glowed faintly as if enchanted.

Was that—?!

"Are you ... *Alice?*" Steve exclaimed, shielding his eyes from the sun.

Those ice blue eyes stared at him for a moment longer, then, the mysterious female turned and vanished into the trees.

"Wait!" Steve shouted, changing course and running north to catch her. "Hold on! Where'd you come from?! Wait a sec!"

Steve caught up to where the dark woman had been standing, but there was no sign of her in the trees where she'd been.

Then, Steve caught a flash of shadow up on the ridge to his right. Looking up, he saw the barest glimpse of the Minecraftian female fleeing over the crest to the eastern side.

He followed, sprinting up the last bit of ridge.

From up on top, Steve could see the desert stretching out before him as far as he could see toward the east. The sun was in the eastern sky, blazing on the horizon and baking away the mist of morning. Many zombies and skeletons that had been caught by the dawn down in the sands ahead were wandering around on fire. They'd do that for a few seconds then all die, Steve knew. The village stood in the east and a bit to the south of Steve's position, its remaining windows glittering in the sunrise and several mobs around its edges and plots of crops walking around in flames.

Then, Steve spotted *her* again.

Alice the Evil Ninja who supposedly *likes* Steve—it *had* to be Alice, right?—was a black blip in the sand down and ahead, running to the east just to the north of the village's edge. She was passing the village and running away deep into the desert...

Why is she going there? Steve wondered.

Steve looked back at the village and searched for Alex and Jack. He didn't see them, but knew that the villagers would be emerging from their homes at any moment.

They had to be fine by now ... *right?*

Looking back down at the fleeting black form of Alice, Steve made up his mind. He was just too danged curious.

The Minecraftian warrior ran down the ridge's east side, leaping down and around the trees and boulders until he was briskly sprinting through the sand down below, holding his stone sword loosely in his right hand.

Then, toward the rising sun, Steve followed Alice into the desert...

Pssssst!!
Liking the story? Don't forget
to join my Mailing List!
I'll send you *free books* and stuff!
(www.SkeletonSteve.com)

S1E3 - Chapter 4 – Jack

"Don't let him get away!" Jack shouted.

The boy ran on with his torch leading the way, hoping that he wouldn't get shot by an arrow from the darkness. It was almost morning, but there would still be a good while of danger for him, Alex, and Steve.

They chased the blacksmith, who seemed to be fleeing from Jack and Alex as much as he was from the various mobs wandering the village trying to eat him!

"Hurr!" the blacksmith bellowed, running away with his hands together in his robes in front of his black leather apron. "Hurrrr!"

The villager didn't even seem to be injured. This was ridiculous!

"Wait!" Alex cried after the villager. "Wait up, you dumb villager! We're trying to help!"

"They won't understand you!" Jack replied, pausing to look around. The last thing he'd want was for a zombie or creeper to sneak up to melee range while they were chasing a dumb NPC.

Jack searched for Steve. This whole night had been scary as heck! He'd lost track of how many times he had to hit one zombie or another with his sword, but he'd only killed—or *finished*, at least—the two from before. There were several times where Jack had to use his stone sword to knock a mob back that had come in too close for comfort, and there was a constant sense of *danger* all night long!

He could hear the sound of Steve fighting somewhere—the grunts, zombie pain sounds, and clangs of Alex's donated sword—but the Minecraftian warrior was now out of sight again.

That made Jack's stomach turn cold.

Alex was a great fighter herself; a lot better than she cared to admit. But this night of terror and running around trying not to get killed was only made okay by Steve being nearby. Jack found that when the warrior was with him, the many hostile mobs advancing on them weren't as scary. Now, without Steve out of sight, Jack was starkly reminded that he was just a twelve-year-old boy from the real world with no fighting skills, and Alex was mainly an archer who was afraid to face mobs head-on.

"We lost Steve again!" Jack cried.

"He's gotta be right behind us," Alex replied, pausing to shoot a zombie that was getting too close to their path toward the blacksmith. "Dang it—that stupid villager keeps running away! We've gotta catch him!"

"Let's focus!" Jack said, drawing a firm nod from Alex. Her armor *clanked*.

They did catch the blacksmith. It was a harrowing chase, avoiding hostile mobs as they went, but when Alex was finally able to cut the villager off—gosh, Minecraftians were fast!—the two of them were able to keep the blacksmith under control as they pushed and bumped him toward the big house where the other survivors of this terrible night were waiting.

"Hmph!" the scowling villager complained as he tried to get away, furrowing his brow.

"Oh, shut it!" Alex replied. "We're saving your life!"

Jack looked all around them for Steve, but they'd totally lost track of the Minecraftian.

"Where *is* he?" Jack asked as the big house came within sight.

"Hurr!" the blacksmith bellowed as they pushed him. "Hungh!"

"Don't worry about Steve for now. We've almost got this guy to the house. Just a little further..."

When they reached the larger home, Jack opened the door. He'd done it a few times now and it was getting a little easier. Even though the door didn't have an actual working doorknob—what was there was just pixelated decoration, basically—he was getting the hang of ... *interfacing* with it ... and opening it with a touch and his intention. It was hard for the boy to understand, but he could open and close the doors easily enough if he didn't think about it too hard.

The green-robe immediately tried to push his way out. The villager was bigger than Jack and actually made the boy stagger backwards. For just a second, Jack was flush with anger as if a bully had pushed him on the playground.

"Get back, you dummy!" Jack cried, whacking the green-robe in the chest with his torch.

The villager squawked when struck and glared down at Jack, but backed away into the building.

For one panicked instant, the boy was afraid that he'd set the villager on fire! He didn't even think about it. In that moment, Jack wanted to *hit him* to make him back off, and he had to choose between his torch and his sword. Fortunately, the torch didn't ignite the villager's clothing. Torches didn't set fires in Minecraft, so why would anything be different here? It was a good thing, too. It would have been a ridiculous thing to spend all night trying to rescue these guys, then kill one of them with fire in the end!

As the green-robe backed away, glaring and furrowing his brow, Jack looked up at the villager's Damage Indicator window hovering above his bald head and saw that he was down one hit point.

"Sorry about that," Jack said.

Alex chuckled.

They pushed the blacksmith through the door and closed it with a *pop*.

Turning, Jack and Alex looked around the village. It was still dark. The sky was lightning in the east, but it would be a while yet before the daylight would protect them from the undead. Two zombies were in the street nearby, plodding toward them with outstretched green claws.

"I think that's all of the villagers," Alex said.

"I think you're right," Jack said. "At least—that's all of the ones that I saw, and I think Steve said that there weren't anymore, too."

"Now, where *is* Steve?" Alex asked. She shouted for him. "*Steve!*"

"Two zombies coming in," Jack said, pointing with his sword. He saw that one of them was a zombified *villager*, malicious and green but with the facial features of the village people. Something metal on the other one's face glinted in his torchlight. "Hey, what's that?" he asked.

Alex raised her bow and fired, plugging the zombie villager in the chest. It stumbled. She reloaded and fired again, hitting it in the shoulder. It didn't seem to care.

They were getting a little too close. Jack felt cold fear rising up in him again. What would happen if those monster hit him? How would his real body interact with a digital enemy? He'd been lucky so far—well, he got in serious trouble with that one spider—but Jack's luck wouldn't last forever. Would it be like getting punched really hard? Would the zombies try to eat him somehow? There were so many video games where your character could get hurt by merely *touching* bad guys. How were they damaged? Would the zombies' fists *burn him* or something? Would it be like being splashed with acid?

Jack's imagination went wild with horror as Alex fired upon the zombie villager a third time, killing it.

"It's a sword!" Alex exclaimed, reloading. "Get moving, Jack. It'll get you..."

The boy realized that he'd been standing still in terror while Alex was continuously moving away from the incoming zombies. He sprang into action, catching up to her, and when he did, he saw the second zombie from a different angle than before and realized that the hilt and part of the blade of an *iron sword* was sticking straight out from the mob's face! The pointy end of the blade was sticking out of the back of the zombie's skull.

"Holy duck feathers!" Jack exclaimed. "It's an iron sword impaled through its face! I've never seen *that* before!"

"Me either," Alex replied, firing at the zombie. Her arrow sank into its chest.

The zombie was suddenly close enough for its Damage Indicator window to pop up hovering over its head. Its health bar read *3/20*.

"It's almost dead," Jack said, cold fear racing through him and turning his joints to jelly.

"Finish him off, *Weird Walker*," Alex said with a smirk. "Just be careful."

Jack felt his heart hammering. His breathing was quick and deep. His head felt like he was floating.

As the zombie plodded toward them, a sword in its face and arrow stuck in its chest—three out of twenty hit points—Jack forced himself to take a deep breath to calm down. He gripped the strange, blocky hilt of his weapon and flexed the muscles of his right arm. His body was pretty sore.

When the mob was close enough, Jack cried out like a warrior—if only to make himself feel braver—and swung his sword in a vertical arc at the monster's wide chest as hard as he could! His stone blade struck true, and a bright crimson number "3" appeared over its head, floating upwards. The hit points reduced to zero and the zombie let out a gurgling sigh as it fell backwards under the blow. When it hit the ground, it disappeared in a puff of smoke, leaving behind a floating piece of zombie meat, a glowing yellow orb of experience, and the iron sword that had been impaled through its head.

Jack grinned.

The glowing orb slowly rolled along the sandstone street toward Jack's feet. The boy winced when it touched him, but it didn't hurt. It didn't feel like anything, really. Maybe ... maybe Jack felt a touch *stronger*, or perhaps that was just his imagination. The experience orb disappeared, absorbed into his foot; into his worn, dirty sneaker with loosely-tied laces.

"I've got XP!" Jack exclaimed happily.

Experience! He could level up! Couldn't he? Gosh—how could he tell what *level* he was??

"Come on," Alex said, gesturing at the dark streets with her bow. "Let's keep moving. We've got to find that last broken-up house." She approached warily and quickly picked up the iron sword, putting it into her pack.

"Okay," Jack said. He looked at where she was pointing and saw two more zombies approaching, followed by some glowing red eyes bobbing around in the darkness beyond. The fear returned. He suddenly remembered seeing the final blow-open house near the blacksmith's forge. Heck—that was probably the blacksmith's house, which was why he'd been running around out in the open. "This way," Jack said.

Alex followed.

Jack led them to the blacksmith's. When they turned a corner, the actual forge building was easy to see because of the reddish-orange glow of the lava in its smelter.

After avoiding more mobs, the two of them approached the small, empty house with the huge hole. Two of the walls had been blown apart.

"Let's stay inside here until morning," Jack said.

"Good idea," Alex replied.

Climbing through the gap in the walls, Jack stood by with his torch and sword as Alex sealed up the damage with cobblestone from inside. Seconds after she had the bottom two blocks of the exterior walls complete, Jack was startled by a zombie suddenly showing up just outside and snarling at them loudly.

As Alex continued her work, Jack looked around the inside of the small home. There was a torch in the rafters, so there was more light to see by, but there was nothing remarkable about the place. It was just a typical small village house. The boy tried to ignore the zombie outside then was startled again when it suddenly *bashed* the house's front door so loudly that it sounded like the wood was splintering.

"Duck feathers!" Jack shouted in alarm, then he faced the door, his heart hammering.

Alex looked to the door for a moment then went back to blocking up the wall.

"I think we're safe now," she said.

The zombie bashed on the door again with such a loud and terrible racket that it made Jack just about jump out of his skin.

"It's just a *sound effect*," he said to himself. "Just a scary sound effect..."

Several seconds later, the two damaged walls were completely blocked up and the inside of the house looked totally normal other than the fact that most of the walls were sandstone and a portion was now cobblestone.

"Now, we wait," Alex said.

So they did.

"You did *great* out there, Alex," Jack said, watching the sky brighten through the window. "I don't know why you're so scared of fighting mobs. You fight good."

Jack heard the voice of his mother in his head.

You fight well.

"Eh," Alex replied, looking around the scant interior of the tiny house. She pulled the arrows out of her armor. "I'm not that great of a fighter. I'm more of a miner ... and a builder."

"You fought well, too," Jack said. "Good bow and arrow work."

"Thanks," Alex said with a smile. "You got in some good hits of your own, too, didn't you?"

That warmed Jack's heart. Every time the zombie bashed on the door, they tried to ignore the scathing sound. It made Jack jump, but he was starting to feel a little better; a little less afraid.

"I don't know what's gonna happen to me if I die, Alex," Jack said. Saying the words filled him with cold dread.

They were quiet for a moment.

"Well," Alex said. "Let's hope that it doesn't come to that, okay? Just be smart and stay out of trouble."

"Like you?"

"Yeah, like me." Alex sighed and scoffed. "Where the heck is Steve? Probably got himself killed again."

"How about that sword in the zombie's head?" Jack asked. "I've never seen that happen before in this game. It's weird. Do you think it's *yours?*" He didn't know why he suddenly thought that; it was definitely a strange thought. But it had crept into his head just the same.

"Game?" Alex replied then shook her head. She pulled out the sword and held it in her hand. "I don't know. Why do you think it's *mine?*"

"I don't know," Jack said. "Can you tell? Can you see if it's yours?"

Alex looked at the blade, turning it over. "I can't," she replied. "It's just like any other iron sword."

Jack felt strange watching her. Alex was a Minecraft character; blocky and pixelated and full of straight lines, moving with a jerky quickness. But somehow, she was starting to feel more *real* to him.

They waited in the little house until the sun was fully up in the sky and the desert was bright again. At one point, Jack heard all of the zombies and skeletons scattered through the town and out of sight catch fire, and he listened to them gurgle and clunk and make pain sounds until they all expired.

271

Jack never felt tired. He just sat on the bed near the window and watched the sky lighten.

It was good to sit down. His thighs felt weak from all of the climbing.

He thought for a moment about back home.

What was happening there? Had time stopped for him somehow when he went into the game? Or did Jack just mysteriously *disappear* during the solar eclipse, and everyone was looking for him right now? Was he currently living in the circuits and electricity running through his game pendant, plugged into a USB port on the Vortex Wave Virtual Reality System 1.0? What would happen if Mr. Hayes suddenly *unplugged* his game pendant? Would Jack be ripped out of this world and reappear in the computer lab at school? Or would *he* wink out of existence as well when there was no more power to the drive??

Jack swallowed down the dread when Alex stirred with a *clank* of her iron armor.

They went outside when they heard the villagers all emerge from their homes.

When the first villager passed them by, Alex stood in front of the guy. He was dressed in the brown robes of a farmer.

"Hey you!" she said. "Have you seen Steve?"

"Hurr," the villager replied, seemingly annoyed at being stopped. He glared at Alex.

"Hang on," Jack said, approaching the farmer. "I gotta know if—" He stopped talking. How in the world would he interface with this guy? Jack was able to open chests ... because they were *chests* to be opened. They had lids. He'd figured out how to interface with a crafting table. But how would he *trade* with villagers? "Um ... what have you got?" he asked.

272

The villager frowned down at him.

"Hmph!"

Jack smirked. "Um ... *trade!*" he ordered.

The villager only looked down at him, his black furrowed brow heavy over his intense green eyes, hands together under the brown robes.

Forcing himself to overcome a wave of awkwardness, Jack dropped his torch to free his left hand and reached out to *touch* the villager. He touched the farmer's chest with the intent to trade, imagining the interface window that would normally appear if he was just playing; just like what would happen when he used the crafting table.

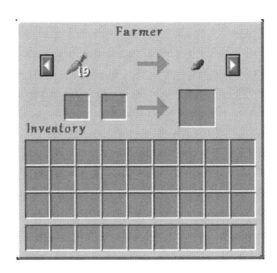

A familiar window suddenly appeared in front of Jack's eyes. It was huge, bright-grey, and imposed itself on almost his entire field of view. Jack had seen that screen several times over his years playing Minecraft—whenever he tried to trade with a villager as a player—but now, it seemed *huge* and really weird! It was completely flat, but also solid before him. It existed in his three-dimensional space, but seemed to be thinner than a single pixel!

"Haha ... *yes!*" Jack exclaimed. "Carrots!"

That was the first thing he'd noticed. The boy was ecstatic that he could even interface with the villager at all. He would figure this stuff out!

Then, when Jack noticed the big, empty 'Inventory' field below the trading area, he felt a thrill that made his heart buzz. He gasped loudly.

"What is it?" Alex asked. He could hardly see her with that villager's window blocking most of his vision. "What's wrong?!"

"My *inventory!!*" Jack exclaimed. "I can see my inventory! Holy beetles!"

Jack stared gaping for a moment before remembering the torch at his feet. He had to try this! Looking down, Jack saw the torch floating above the sandstone street where he'd left it and he almost just *grabbed for it*, but stopped himself. If interfacing with the villager was anything like using a crafting table, then he'd have to keep touching the farmer while he picked up the torch, and he'd have to keep only one thing in his hand at a time...

The boy dropped his stone sword to the ground. Then, carefully—trying to avoid releasing his hold on the villager—Jack bent down to pick up the torch. When he had it, he reached out with it to the huge, open and grey inventory area, and 'dropped it' into one waiting, empty square.

The torch appeared in his inventory!

Yes!!

Jack beamed from ear to ear. He now had an inventory!

"What's going on?!" Alex exclaimed.

Jack looked at her, unable to see her fully through the grey screen in front of him. "I'm ... uh ... I think I figured out a way to carry stuff, but ... I can only do it by interfacing ... um ... *trading* with the villagers."

He couldn't see Alex, but he felt her standing there silently.

"I don't really understand," she said. "But ... you're okay? You're just *staring* at that guy..."

Jack smiled. "Yeah, I'm great!"

He removed his finger from the villager and the screen suddenly vanished with shocking speed, leaving Jack standing in front of the farmer again.

"Hurr," the villager said, looking down at him with his chest puffed out and his hands clasped under his robes. Then, the farmer wandered away.

Jack stood, staring at nothing, and tried to feel in his head for anything *different*.

He now had a torch *somewhere* in his being. Where the heck was it?!

"This is *so weird*..." he muttered. Then, he looked up into the sky and said, "*E!*"

No inventory opened. It was just like before.

Maybe the only way to access his inventory would be through interfaces that let him see what he had? But ... why hadn't he seen his inventory when he'd opened the chests, or the crafting table? This didn't make any sense! Jack suddenly wondered if Alex and Steve would be okay with him pushing a villager *all the way* back to their house...

"Let's go," Alex said. "Let's find Steve."

"Okay."

They wandered through the village for most of the morning. Time and time again, Jack and Alex both tried to talk to the villagers, hoping to find their friend. Once, Jack interfaced with a butcher and confirmed that he still had the torch in his inventory. So he *did* have an inventory. He just didn't have an 'E' key. *Or any other keys for that matter*, he thought.

Eventually, they ran into KittyPaws30.

Jack looked over the strange Minecraftian. She was wearing a pixelated white hoodie, had pink hair, and blue eyes. In her blocky arms was a black cat with white markings and a red collar that regarded Jack with bright green eyes. Two more cats followed behind her, quick on their feet with long, skinny tails that bobbed up and down like levers.

"Why, hello there!" KittyPaws30 said in a sweet, sing-song voice down to Jack. "You are a very interesting creature, indeed!" She looked up. "Hello, Alex."

"Hi, KittyPaws30," Alex said. "Hey—we're looking for Steve. Have you seen him?"

"Oh, so *you're* KittyPaws30," Jack said, looking up to the taller Minecraftian woman. "Good to meet you. I'm Jack."

KittyPaws30 smiled down at him again. The cat in her arm *meowed*. "Indeed I am, Jack. Nice to meet you, too." Then she looked up at Alex. "I haven't seen Steve this morning, no," she said, then her toned excited. "But I *did* see him fighting zombies from my balcony, and what a sight it was! Steve is quite a warrior!"

"Yeah, he is," Alex said. "So you saw him before dawn? Haven't you seen him since?"

"I'm afraid not, Alex," KittyPaws30 replied. "But *please do* tell him, when you see him, that I enjoyed seeing him throw his sword

276

last night! That was quite a dashing move! He was happy to show me!" She laughed. "And I'm looking forward to him helping me build that swimming pool. Strange," she said, pausing and suddenly kissing the cat in her arms. They touched noses. "He was going to help me with that yesterday, or the day before, perhaps...? *When* will he come back?"

Alex rolled her eyes. "I don't know, KittyPaws30. We had some troubles with our sheep. Creeper troubles. I'm sure he'll come and help you when he can."

"KittyPaws30," Jack said, drawing her attention.

"Yes?"

"You're a Minecraftian, right?"

"Yes," she replied. "A Minecraftian *cat*."

"Uh ... *cat?*" Jack replied, sharing a concerned glance with Alex. "Um ... are you ... well ... are you playing yourself as a *character* ... you know ... from the real world? I mean—are you a player? Playing from your computer or *Xbox* or something?"

KittyPaws30's blue eyes narrowed in confusion for a moment. She considered Jack with a tilt of her head then laughed. It was a high sound.

"You *are* funny, Jack. I suppose we are *all* playing at something, right?"

"No—I mean," Jack said, "where did you come from? Where were you *before* you appeared in this village? Steve said that you just appeared here one day. Where'd you come from before?"

KittyPaws30 smiled down at Jack as if he was crazy. Her blue eyes and soft face became a look of patronizing patience. Jack had seen that look from adults all of his life.

"I'm afraid I don't understand what you mean, Jack." She smiled, then smiled up at Alex once more. "Now, if you'll excuse me, Alex and Jack, I must get my babies inside before they perish from this heat! I really do wish that Steve would come and help me with that swimming pool! Goodbye!"

With that, KittyPaws30 departed, quickly walking away, followed by two nimble, meowing cats.

Alex and Jack looked at each other.

Jack felt disappointed.

"Well, come on," Alex said. "Maybe that really *was* my sword in the zombie's head. Maybe Steve threw it like she said. He probably died, and is back at the house. Will you lead the way home?"

"Sure."

Jack did. They left the desert village, which was now bustling with villagers who acted like they *weren't* just attacked by a wither in the night. Village life as usual, except now, three of the sandstone structures were patched with dark-grey cobblestone and they were down at least one cartographer.

Up the foothills to the west and over the ridge, Jack led the way home, taking care on the steep parts and resting when he needed to. He was thirsty as heck, and when they went down the western side of the ridge toward the safe and comfortable-looking homestead, Jack eyed the blue, running creek with greedy eyes. He was actually getting pretty hungry, too. Sooner or later, he would have to try eating this weird Minecraft food. Hopefully, it wouldn't—

Something dark and fleeting suddenly caught Jack's eye. In the woods on the western side of the ridge, he thought for a moment that he saw the black form of a Minecraftian in the shadows; a Minecraftian holding a pick axe...

He stopped.

There was nothing there, now.

"Steve?" Jack called out.

No response.

"What is it?" Alex asked, peering into the shadows of the woods to the north where Jack had seen the figure. "A mob in the trees? They hide in the shadows of the trees sometimes..."

"No," Jack said, staring at the dark forest. He didn't see anything now. "I think it was a Minecraftian, but..." He searched around but saw no one. There was no Steve or anyone else. He called out again: "Braydon? Is that you?"

Who else was there? It had to be that odd, camouflaged survivor that lived in the woods north of here; the guy that had recently saved them from the wolves...

Alex raised her bow and stared at the spot where Jack's attention was fixed.

"It's probably Steve," she said. "Steve!" she shouted. "Steve! We're here!"

They waited. Cold, tingly fear began creeping up Jack's spine. The sun was bright and overhead now. The day was half-over.

"I guess maybe I was seeing things," Jack said. Really, he wasn't sure.

Alex shrugged. They moved on. Jack stopped to drink deeply from the creek. He drank the weird water-like not-water until he couldn't drink anymore.

When they reached the homestead and walked through the crop fields, Alex called out to Steve again. They went in through the farm door and searched the house, but he wasn't there. They did find the door to the Divining Pool room left open...

"He must have come into here," Alex said, going in.

Jack followed, looking around the brightly-lit spruce room. He walked to the pool and felt the bedrock structure, once again amazed at how solid and hard it felt compared to the relative sponginess of everything else in the world. He looked at the bold, blue water, and saw hazy, white shapes waving around deep inside.

"Hey, are these words?" he asked. "Another message?"

Alex immediately leaned over to see, super-interested, then said, "Yep. They're coming up from the bottom. We'll be able to read them in a moment..."

Great, Jack thought with a frown. *What now?!*

The many letters wavered and rose, eventually coming into focus. When the message was a few inches under the surface, Jack read the words aloud for both of them:

"*Can i be added in one of the jack the kid books as DarkestNight6441. I'm a good demon scavenger with a unique sword called a demon sword. it can shoot dark beams. (hence the name DarkestNight) can i also join jack and them on their adventure. i have black shirt and pants the shirt has short sleeves with a short cape that's jagged at the end. sorry this is very described well but i want you to know every detail.*"

Jack stared at the words as they wobbled and wriggled and rose to the surface.

He suddenly felt cold. His ears were filled with a *whooshing* sound that made him feel like he was in the vacuum of space or something. The boy realized that he wasn't breathing...

Jack the Kid ... books...?

He read the message again in his head, felt his eyes growing wider and wider, then finally managed to break his gaze away, looking up at Alex.

She was staring down at him with wide eyes and her mouth open as well.

"Books?" Jack muttered. His tongue felt paralyzed. "Jack the Kid *books?!*"

"What the heck is going on...?!" Alex whispered, staring down at the pool.

"I'm ... in a *book?!*" Jack said. His mind was a fog. He felt such a shock that he couldn't move. He didn't—it didn't make any sense! Where did this—? "Where'd this Divining Pool come from?!" he shouted up at Alex. "What am I *doing here?!*"

"I ... I don't know!" Alex replied, taking a step back. Her armor *clanged.* "What does this mean? We're in a book? That can't be..."

"We *can't* be in a book!" Jack exclaimed. "We can't be in a book, because we're in a game!"

"We're in a *game...?!*" Alex said, her eyes darting around the spruce walls. "What...?"

Jack couldn't stand anymore. He felt like he was floating above his body. He couldn't breathe. He sat, feeling his butt hit the soft floor as if he was landing on a firm mattress.

It didn't make any sense. What was the relation between a book and a game? Where'd the Divining Pool come from? What was *his* connection?!

"Oh, gosh..." he groaned, burying his face into his hands.

S1E3 - Chapter 5 – Alex

Alex watched as Jack the kid sat on the floor, falling into his personal despair.

The words in the Divining Pool dissolved and disappeared, leaving only the clear, blue water that was usually in there.

"Oh—what am I gonna do?" Jack muttered into his hands.

The message they'd just seen and all of the previous messages were starting to spell out some very strange things for Alex and her understanding about her place in this world. The kid seemed sure that Vortexia wasn't real. He called the place where he'd come from the 'real world', and a moment ago, when the boy had referred to Alex's world as a *game*...

Well, that wasn't the first time he'd said that.

It was strange indeed that the Divining Pool was continuously bringing new people and monsters into their world. The dragon and what Jack had called a 'wither' were terrifying! But stranger still was the way that that the messages seemed to be from *others*—other people somewhere, somehow—controlling her world with their words! Who was the intelligence behind the messages? Who were the requesters behind the requests?

Alex's mind boggled with it all. None of this made any sense, and it sure didn't make sense on this beautiful and bountiful (*and dangerous*) world that she'd lived in all of her life.

What she did see in that moment, despite all of the craziness, was a boy—a strange boy from another world, yes—upset and falling to pieces in pain and sorrow. Alex didn't know what Jack was or where he came from, but he was just a kid, and he was hurt ... and sad.

She didn't even understand *how* he was able to scrunch up his body on the floor like that, but Alex crouched and put a hand on Jack's shoulder.

"It's okay, Jack," she said. "We'll figure—"

"It's *not* okay!" he replied, shouting up at her and throwing her hand off of him. "I'm lost in this game that ... I thought I was making sense of it, but now I have *no idea* what's going on! None of these Minecraftians know anything, and I have no idea of how I'm going to get home! My mom and dad and my brothers might be looking for me, thinking that I'm lost or kidnapped! I'm hungry and I have no idea what will happen if I eat some of your weird food! I don't know what'll happen if I get hurt or if I die! Will I come back like you and Steve? In bed? Or will I just be *dead forever?!*"

Alex saw that the kid's eyes were now welling up with clear fluid that glittered in the torchlight. The fluid emerged from behind Jack's glasses—which were now steamed-up—and trickled down his soft, curved face.

Jack saw that Alex was looking down at his face closely, then he frowned and wiped away at the fluid roughly with his intricate fingers that were like nothing else on this world.

Alex was touched. Her heart swelled for the boy.

He was so afraid.

"I'll stick with you, Jack," Alex said, putting her armored hand back on his shoulder. "We'll figure this out. This is affecting my world too, you know. Don't be afraid. We'll get through this together."

Jack smeared the fluid away from his face again and pushed his glasses back up his nose.

"Can I...?" he asked with a small voice. "Can I *hug* you?"

Alex stared down at the boy. She had no idea what he meant by that, but she wanted to see him happy again.

"Sure."

The boy slowly climbed back to his feet as if his whole body hurt. Then, pausing to look up again at Alex, he approached with his arms wide. Alex gasped when Jack suddenly wrapped his arms around her waist and pressed his soft body up against her iron armor, turning his head to press one cheek against her metal chest plate. He was suddenly closer to her than any Minecraftian had ever been—aside from when she and Steve push each other around in mining tunnels, perhaps. Alex slowly followed suit, carefully wrapping her armored arms around Jack's soft and curved shoulders.

Jack sighed, long and deeply, then sniffed and shuddered. He made strange sounds that Alex hadn't heard before—like a sort of whining—and shuddered several more times before finally releasing her.

Afterwards, the boy stepped back and wiped his face again. He looked up at her, took his glasses off and cleaned them with his shirt—his eyes were *blue*—and sniffed.

"Thanks," Jack said.

"That's a hug?" she asked. "Do you feel better?"

"Yes," he replied, the let out another long sigh. "Now, let's go find Steve."

"Okay. Would you like some food?"

Jack frowned, thought about it, then shook his head. "Not yet," he said. "I'm not ready for that yet."

They left the house after Alex grabbed more arrows from her room and repaired her bow. Her armor was a little damaged, but they were mostly out of iron. Those repairs would have to wait

285

until later. She *did* have a secret stash of iron ingots, hidden away so that Steve wouldn't waste them, but she preferred to save them for an emergency; like if she needed a new sword.

With Jack helping with directions, they searched the immediate woods for Steve but couldn't find him. They eventually climbed the ridge again and followed it north and south for a while in each direction, calling for Steve and scanning the west and east from up high, but he was gone. In time, they headed back to the village—it was late afternoon by then—and couldn't find Steve anywhere. They tried questioning KittyPaws30 another time, but she hadn't seen him either.

Standing at the edge of the village in the golden light of the late day, Alex looked out into the distant desert to what Jack had told her was the east.

That *wither thing* was out there somewhere...

"Where *are* you, Steve?" she asked the distant dunes.

Jack stirred beside her. His shoes made a hissing noise in the sand.

"It's going to be night soon," he said. "You wanna spend the night here again?"

Alex shook her head. Her armor *clanked*.

"No, I don't," she said, looking back toward the setting sun. "But it's pretty late. We might be stuck here."

"I can get us home," Jack said.

"Yeah, but it'll be dark by the time we reach the ridge, won't it? We'll have to deal with more hostile mobs."

"I guess ... I guess we can handle it," Jack said.

They paused as the villagers started going inside, quickly opening and shutting their many doors with loud *creaks* and *pops*.

286

The night was coming. If they were going to stay in town, they'd have to find a safe place to spend the—

Something suddenly slammed into Alex with a ferocity that surprised her. Alex felt pain, and was knocked sideways as something stabbed through her armor and into her body. Then, she felt a wave of extreme *heat* and was blinded by orange light!

"Alex!!" Jack shouted.

She couldn't see where the kid was. She felt pain ... and burning! The orange light was crackling and writhing around her vision. She was *on fire!*

"Stay back!" Alex shouted, then realized that she was screaming.

"Get away from her!" Jack shouted. "Leave her alone!"

Alex couldn't see and it terrified her. Was she under attack?! Something had just smashed the heck out of her and set her ablaze, and the idea of Jack facing off against something so unknown and powerful filled her with fear. The fire raged around Alex and she felt herself *burning*. She realized that she was flailing around in a panic. Gritting her teeth against the pain, Alex dropped her bow to the ground and tried patting out the flames. Her armored hands clattered against her metal leggings and chest plate.

She was suddenly struck again. Something or someone smashed her again with a weapon—something hard and pointed—that *clanged* loudly against her helmet and renewed the flames! Alex spun, blindly trying get away, struggling to pat out the flames. She couldn't see her attacker. She was hit again in one leg! This time, the armor helped a little but the unseen weapon bit deeply into her, sending Alex's world exploding into pain! The fire around her flared brighter and she burned on, screaming and flailing...

A woman's voice screamed out into the evening over the crackling of the flames burning Alex's clothes and skin.

"You can't have him! He's mine!"

"Get off of her!" Jack screamed, his voice reaching new heights in pitch.

The boy grunted loudly and the woman shrieked in pain.

"*Back off*, weirdo!" the unseen woman screamed. "I have no fight with you! I must *finish her!*"

Then, as Alex backed further into the village trying to put out the flames, she ran into someone that was standing behind her; someone as solid as a cobblestone wall. She felt a strong hand easily push her out of the way.

"Stand aside, Minecraftian," a deep male voice said from behind Alex. She felt a new wave of stark fear. "I will handle this one!"

Then, there was a flurry of movement. Alex heard Jack's clumsy feet scrambling toward her. Were the flames dying down? That crackling wasn't as loud...

"Get out of my way, demon!" the woman shrieked. "You will not stop me! Steve will be mine! I must finish what I have started!"

"I will not let you harm them," the deep voice replied.

Then there were sounds of battle. Alex heard the clanging of metal. The woman screamed and hissed. Alex suddenly heard Jack next to her through the dwindling crackling of the flames. *Yes—* the fire *was* dying down!

"I don't know what to do, Alex!" Jack screamed, panicked. "Do you have a bucket of water? I can't put you out without catching fire myself!"

She hardly understood the words.

After what had seemed like a long time on fire, Alex began to hear the sound of her own screaming over the sound of the raging fire. The pain was remarkable. The flames were burning her up through her armor. She was done for. She could hardly hear the battle and the kid's voice. Her head was woozy and she was starting to feel like she was lying down...

Yet somehow, Alex eventually found herself standing in the twilight of the new night amidst the smoke rising from her body and clothes. There was a light-show going on in front of her, and two dark forms battled in the pale, sandy street: one of them lean and black, swinging what looked like a glowing pick axe that left trails of red fire behind it as it arced through the air; the other large and muscular, purple and black, with a long, ebony sword.

Just then, as the two fighting forms separated, the big purple guy pointed his strange blade at the dark woman and fired a brilliant dark-purple *bolt of energy* through the air! The dark beam streaked across the distance between the combatants and exploded against her. The dark woman—dressed all in black with a pale, white face and intense ice-blue eyes full of hatred—tried to block the attack by holding up her fiery weapon. The beam struck the weapon full-force, overpowered the woman, then knocked her backwards with a cry of pain.

When Alex expected the woman in black to leap back into the fight, she was surprised to see her completely vanish instead.

"Alex, you're alive!" Jack exclaimed. "The fire's out! Oh, gosh, you're at *two hit points!*"

She looked down to see the kid staring up at her, his face twisted into a complex expression of pain and concern, his eyes wide and white behind his glasses.

Alex tried to speak, but croaked instead.

She was alive, but only *barely*.

When she looked up at the battle again, the dark woman was gone, and the large figure with the black sword was confidently approaching her and the boy. He stopped before them, looking over Alex silently. The creature was shaped like a Minecraftian, but he looked very different. His skin was gnarled and purple, his form muscular, and his face frightening and covered in spikes. The 'demon' (as the dark woman had called him) was dressed in black leather and wore a black cape that was frayed and jagged at the edges, either from age or from the damage of many battles. The demon's eyes glowed bright red, just like a spider's. He held an elegant sword of pitch-black metal that shined like nothing Alex had ever seen before.

She tried to speak again.

"Thanks," she muttered. Her throat hurt.

"Who are you?" Jack asked. He gasped. "You must be that 'Darkest Night' character! Are you?"

Alex shifted in her armor, which hurt like heck to do. Her skin was burned all over. She was wounded in two places from that dark woman's pick-axe-thing, and she probably had a pretty big dent in her helmet.

"You live," the demon said to Alex in a dark, rumbling voice. "This is good. I feared that I was too late."

"Another hit and you probably would have been," Alex said, her voice hoarse from screaming and breathing in smoke.

The demon regarded Jack for a moment then sheathed his big sword.

"My name is DarkestNight6441," he said in his low voice. He was very intimidating. *Of course* he'd come from the Divining Pool. Alex wondered whether or not the demon knew that he did. "I have come to help you and protect you, Alex and Jack Walker. I am a demon; a scavenger that walks Vortexia to—"

"And you have a unique sword, right?" Jack said excitedly, interrupting him. "The Demon Sword?"

"Yes," DarkestNight6641 rumbled. "You know of me?"

"How do you shoot that dark beam?" Jack asked. "I didn't install a mod for that! How does it work?"

"My family sword has a unique ability to fire pure dark energy after it absorbs enough life to power it."

"Where'd you come from?" Jack asked. "Are you here to protect us forever?"

"I..." the demon paused, looking down at Jack, then up at Alex again. "I will help you how I can. However, I am a night demon." He pointed to the starry sky with a purple, clawed hand. "My ties to this world wax and wane with the strength of the moon. Jack, know that I will not remain with you always, but I will help you when I can, as I did tonight."

"But where'd you come from? Who sent you?"

DarknestNight6641 looked down at the boy for a moment, then looked up to Alex again.

"Alex, take this and heal yourself."

He offered her a glass flask full of pinkish-red liquid.

Alex had never imbibed a potion before. There was one time when she and Steve had fought a witch while traveling, and the witch had been throwing potions like this—though of a different color—but neither of them had ever tried to brew potions themselves, and they'd never found any as loot.

She thought about asking DarkestNight6641 about what exactly the potion would do, but she had a pretty good idea.

Alex uncorked the potion and swallowed the red liquid. It hurt her to do it. Immediately after, her entire core warmed up in a pleasant, cozy way. The crackling tightness of her cooked skin diminished, and she suddenly felt a lot better.

She sighed.

"Oh, gosh, thanks," she said. "That's *so* much better."

"Fourteen hit points now," Jack muttered. "*Healing II*, I think?"

"You are welcome," DarkestNight6641 replied. She could see him much more clearly now. Her wounds still stung but at least she wasn't dying anymore. "Now, I believe you two are wondering where Steve is...?"

That was a surprise. Then again, maybe this demon had been following them for a while. It was no secret that they'd been looking for Steve when they were asking everyone in town.

"Yeah, we are," Alex said. "Do you know where he is?"

"Hey," Jack said. "Can you at least tell me where you were *yesterday?* What were you doing before today around ... um ... lunchtime?"

DarkestNight6641 smiled down at the boy then turned his attention back to Alex once again.

"Steve followed Alice into the desert. She led him to the east before doubling back to attack you. From there, Steve went on to the desert temple in the sands toward the rising sun."

Alex scoffed. Why on Vortexia would he do that?! He probably got sidetracked...

"A desert temple?" Jack asked. "Who's Alice?"

"Alice is the woman who attacked you," DarkestNight6641 replied. "And she will likely attack you again." He said this to Alex, which made a ball of icy cold bloom in her stomach. "She will always attack you from the shadows. Alice is a *ninja*."

"Great," Alex muttered with a sigh. As if she wasn't afraid enough of the shadows already. "Will you come with us to the east and help us find our friend?"

"I cannot," DarkestNight6641 rumbled. "I have business to attend to here after tonight."

"What kind of business?" Jack asked.

"Demon business," he replied with a low voice. "I will be around. Be brave, Jack, and experiment with your uniqueness. It will serve you well in time."

"How do you know that?" Jack asked. "What do you know about me?"

DarkestNight6641 looked up at the mostly-full moon that was rising in the night sky. Alex suddenly noticed that mobs were in the village and wandering in from the desert, but they hadn't noticed them yet.

"I know what the moon tells me," the demon replied.

They all looked up at the moon. Jack suddenly gasped. When Alex looked down again, DarkestNight6641 was gone.

S1E3 - Chapter 6 – Steve

Steve pursued Alice across the desert.

The bright and sandy dunes stretched out in all directions, ending where the land rose hazily in the north and again to the west where Steve knew that the big ridge—and *home*—was fading into the distance.

At times, he turned back and looked at the far-off village. Alex and Jack were back there—probably—finishing the job that he had pulled them into in the first place after that wither had casually destroyed half of the town.

Dang—things were starting to get crazy! Maybe Alex was right about staying at that last place. They'd never run into crazy stuff like Jack the Weird Walker or a random ender dragon and wither showing up out of nowhere back in their boring, little hut in the middle of a flower-filled prairie.

Now, Steve was chasing 'Alice the Evil Ninja' into a deadly desert; a mysterious woman who had just appeared in their forest hours earlier!

But why was he chasing Alice?

"Now, that's the question, isn't it?" Steve asked himself. There was no one to talk back to him. The desert was barren of all but cacti and withered, brush plants full of thorns. He saw tan rabbits here and there hopping around in the sand, but otherwise, this land was hot, dry, and empty.

Was 'curiosity' enough of an answer?

This was the first time Steve had seen his own name in the Divining Pool. He hated being a part of that weird magic, but now that he was, he *needed to know*...

He was also intensely curious about this Alice that 'secretly likes Steve'. Even though his mind was normally a jumble of random thoughts and impulses to go this way and that, Steve remembered that message fairly accurately.

Steve wanted to know what a 'fox' was, and who 'Albert Einstein' was. And what the heck was her weapon, the *DevilScythe?* It looked like she had some sort of enchanted black pick axe.

He mostly wanted to understand what it meant that she 'liked' him. Those bold, blue eyes—as intense as fire but as blue as the ocean—stuck in his mind, staring at him from the shadows...

Steve smiled to himself, trudging on through the sand.

He was already getting hungry.

It was lunchtime. Looking up, Steve squinted against the blazing sun high in the sky. Of course he didn't think to bring any food with him. They had plenty of steaks and potatoes and bread and roasted chicken back home. Heck—there was even still some cake left over, sitting there in the kitchen waiting for Steve to pick up a slice ... or two ... or three...

Steve groaned against his growling stomach.

What the heck was he doing?! Alex was probably totally worried about him and wondering where in Vortexia he'd gone off to.

Just then, against the bleached, sandy world that was almost blinding him, Steve caught sight of a black shape.

"Alice!" he called. "Wait up!"

It was hot. He slowed down.

Steve looked around and saw a handful of sandy-colored rabbits hopping around the dunes that surrounded him. He could always kill some rabbits, he supposed, but he didn't have a way to cook the meat.

"Ha," he answered the thought. "I could barely catch rabbits back home! I can't catch them *out here*..."

Looking forward again, Steve searched for the black shape he'd seen and called out to, but there was nothing. He assumed that he'd just imagined it.

Turn back, he thought. *Go back to Alex.*

"Okay," he said to himself. "This is stupid. She's gone."

Steve wheeled slowly around, looking up at the blazing sun with a grimace. Then, he stopped when he heard a female voice call out his name.

"Steve!"

He spun back to face the east again.

There was nothing there. Just sand and cacti and rabbits.

"*Okay*, that's it," he said to himself. "I'm hearing things. Time to go home."

"Don't go, Steve," the voice said. Yes—it was definitely a woman's voice from nearby. "Let's talk, you and I..."

Steve opened his pack, looking for some food. He knew that there was nothing there, but he was hearing things. Maybe he'd hallucinate some food, too! Scanning the dunes and surrounding cacti, Steve searched for the woman in black, but saw nothing other than hot, shimmering desert all around.

"Why *not* go?" Steve said with a smirk. "I can go home where there's food and a nice cool creek ... and friends."

"Please stay and talk to me. I'll be your friend."

Steve looked around him, trying to pinpoint the voice's location. It seemed to be to the south, perhaps? The sun was straight up in the sky, so he was actually getting a little turned around and it was becoming difficult to tell directions. There were some cacti near him. Maybe Alice was hiding behind a cactus? She was a ninja, after all...

"Why are you hiding?" Steve asked. "Alice...?"

"Yes, it's me."

"Come out so I can see you. Are you behind a *cactus?*" Steve chuckled.

"Very well, Steve," she said, "but come no closer..."

Suddenly he saw her—or, part of her—leaning out from behind one of the cacti. It was the same woman from before: lean with black clothing from neck to toe. Her hair was black and slick, face pale, and eyes icy blue; very pretty. She was smiling slightly, but her pale eyes were wide with ... fear?

"Why are you hiding from me?" he exclaimed with a grin, heading her way. His feet were becoming heavy in the heat and the sand. Steve knew that he couldn't run anymore. "You should just come out so we can talk like *normal* people."

Alice's blue eyes widened then she disappeared behind the cactus again.

Steve reached her hiding place and smiled broadly as he leaned around the spiky plant...

The ninja woman was gone.

"What...?" he exclaimed. "Come on..."

"This way," Alice said suddenly from somewhere else. "Continue..."

Steve turned, shook his head with a laugh, and followed the sound of Alice's voice.

"Why are we going into the desert?" he asked. "Where are you leading me?"

"Somewhere *interesting*," Alice replied from her new hiding spot.

Steve followed the sound of her voice with his head and placed her hidden position behind another distant cactus. He was pretty certain she was there, but needed to be sure.

"Are we still going east?" he asked the general area of the cactus. "The sun's too high. I can't tell."

"Yes," Alice replied from out of sight. "East."

"So that means that the village and my friends are behind me. Why are you *hiding* from me, Alice? If you want to talk, let's talk!"

"I must talk ... I must..." she stammered slightly, and Steve pinpointed her voice's location again. "I must do this *my way*," she replied. "I wish to talk to you, but..."

Steve headed straight for the cactus where he was certain Alice was hiding. He smiled when she revealed herself for just an instant, her deep blue eyes peeking around the green desert plant. When he finally reached her and went around to find her, Alice was gone once again.

With a laugh, Steve stopped and put his hands on his hips. He looked up at the sun and squinted. Gosh—it was so dry and hot out here!

"Hey, uh, Alice," he said, continuing east. "If you want to be my friend, if you 'like' me, is this how we're gonna have our conversations? Kinda silly, don't you think?"

"I'm sorry, dear Steve," she replied from farther to the east. "A girl's got to be careful."

Steve scanned the area where the voice came from.

"But ... um ... what's a *fox*, Alice? I didn't understand that message fully. What's a fox? And who's Albert Einstein?"

She didn't answer immediately.

"I don't understand what you just asked, Steve," Alice said from up ahead. "What message? I don't understand either of those things you asked about. What's an *Albert?*"

He pinpointed another cactus where she *had* to be hiding. This time, he would be more subtle.

Steve grinned, slowly continuing, being careful not to alter his course. His eyes remained fixed on the spot where Alice was surely hiding.

"That's what *I wanna know!*" he replied. "That's what the words said."

"What words?"

"The Divining ... uh..." Steve trailed off. "You mean you don't know? Well, that's weird. And interesting."

"Steve, I'm very interested in *you*. I would like to know that I can trust you..."

That made Steve chuckle. "And I'd like to know that I can trust you too, Alice. I know you're curious about Jack and *envious* of Alex. I wouldn't want you trying to hurt my best friend, now would I?"

Just then, Steve was casually walking past the cactus where he was sure Alice was hiding. He suddenly changed direction with a burst of speed—as much as he could muster while he was hungry and tied, anyway—and turned around the cactus to catch her!

"Ha!" he exclaimed, then frowned.

Alice wasn't there.

The desert was quiet. A rabbit hopped around nearby, making hissing sounds in the sand.

Steve put his hands on his hips and looked around. The sun was a little lower now, so he could tell which was which once again. It was still hot and he felt like crud. If he didn't find food soon, he might die in the sand before reaching his friends again.

Was it stupid to follow Alice into the desert?

"Maybe," he said quietly to himself. "Probably," he amended.

But he *did* learn something interesting, if he understood correctly. He normally left the thinking and planning to Alex, but ... he felt like he was onto something here. The creatures coming from the Divining Pool *didn't know* about the Divining Pool. That meant that they also might not know that *they*—Steve, Alex, and Jack—knew what was in the message that brought them to Vortexia. The messages were more than just warnings. They were a kind of *intelligence*; secret information that might give them an advantage against whatever craziness came next...

That made Steve feel pretty smart.

Now, where was Alice?

"Alice!" Steve shouted.

There was no response.

"Alice, where are you now?"

Nothing.

"I thought you wanted to talk! Where are you?"

The desert answered with wind and blasting heat.

Steve peered to the east, searching for the woman's black shape. Maybe she ran up ahead again. As he scanned the shimmering distance, instead of seeing Alice, Steve saw bold red spots in a single location far to the east.

"What...?"

He continued on.

After a time, the red spots came more into focus and Steve realized what he was looking at. Up ahead, made of sandstone the same shade as the sand around it with a few colored clay blocks standing out against the desert ... was a *temple*. As Steve made out the distant shapes of the ancient structure emerging from the sand, he suddenly remembered that he'd already seen this temple from far to the west, back when he was on the big ridge searching for the sheep.

"Oh yeah!" he exclaimed.

Steve certainly didn't set out with the intention of finding and exploring that desert temple, but there it was, and here *he* was, plodding along through the sand dunes, dying under the midday sun. He could go back and maybe die, or he could go forward and see if that temple had anything that could help him and his friends...

He laughed. Who was he kidding?! Steve lived for this! He'd been yearning for more adventure, and there it was in front of him, beckoning at him with its promise of shade ... and maybe food inside!

Alex might be mad if he chose to explore the temple instead of returning to her and Jack, especially since they didn't know where he was. But, he'd already spent the majority of the day traveling the desert, and he'd probably die if he turned back now. Besides—he'd need a place to spend the night!

"That's that, then," he said. Maybe Alice was in there...

Steve looked back to the west. He could barely see the village. The big ridge was all but invisible in the haze of the horizon. How had he managed to see the desert temple from there before? It was so far away!

He hoped that his friends were okay.

Then, with ideas of adventure and riches and hopefully *food* in mind, Steve turned east.

He set off for the desert temple...

Season 1, Episode 4:
Shifting Sands

Shifting Sands

Our three heroes are separated. After a mysterious rescue following an even more mysterious attack on Alex in the desert village, Jack and Alex learn that Steve has traveled deeper into the wasteland toward a distant desert temple.

Will Alex and Jack be able to catch up to their friend, who's dying and trapped in the shifting sands? And what ancient horrors will Jack have to face in a desert temple as a vulnerable boy from the real world? Or is he really as vulnerable as he thinks he is? And what weird and probably terrible thing does the Divining Pool hold for Steve, Alex, and Jack the kid today?

S1E4 - Chapter 1 – Jack

The sun was going down. The demon had disappeared.

Jack and Alex were stuck outdoors and monsters would be invading at any moment...

The boy stood next to Alex in the dimming streets of the desert village.

They both stared at where the demon, DarkestNight6641, had been standing moments earlier before entirely vanishing into the coming night. Jack was still stunned from the crazy fight between the strange, purple-skinned Minecraftian in black and the evil ninja woman, Alice, that had tried to kill his new friend.

Alex looked up at the sky and gasped. Jack looked at her, close enough to see the Damage Indicator bar over her head. She wasn't completely back to full health. Alex had fourteen hit points out of twenty, and her armor was blackened and pretty beat up where that ninja had tried to break through Alex's iron defenses with her fiery weapon.

Jack didn't know *what* to make of any of this...

A Minecraftian ninja with a black, flaming pick axe? It looked like a pick axe, sure, but Jack had never seen a *black pick axe* before. Could pick axes even be enchanted with *Fire Aspect?* He could remember the ninja's intense, blue eyes, full of hatred. And that other guy—DarkestNight6641—looked like an outright demon! Jack could make sense of that to a degree. Minecraftians could look like just about *anything* within the limits of editing their 'game skin'—even appearing to be a purple demon like

DarkestNight6641—and his black leather armor could have been made with dye from squid ink sacs.

But that 'demon sword' of his, Jack thought...

DarkestNight6641 had shot some sort of purple beam of energy from his sword. How'd he do that?! *That* wasn't in vanilla Minecraft, and Jack hadn't installed any mods on his Game Pendant that would allow for such a thing!

He could imagine players creating those Minecraftians just fine on SkinDex.com or something, but that didn't explain those fancy weapons...

Could Jack craft something himself like that demon sword or the fiery scythe?

"Jack!" Alex exclaimed. "We need to *do* something! We need to get inside! It's nighttime!"

He looked around. She wasn't kidding. The villagers all around them were rushing into their homes and slamming their doors behind them. Jack looked out into the desert and saw their surroundings turn silvery-blue. The sun was down. The mobs would be out any second.

"We need to go after Steve!" Jack replied. "That demon guy said that he went into the desert."

Alex groaned, smacking her helmeted forehead with a *clang*. "What was Steve *thinking?!*" she exclaimed.

"He said that Steve was following Alice the ninja to a desert temple; toward where the sun rises. That's *east*." Jack knew exactly where east was. The moon was rising there now. He pointed at it.

"Well, we can't just run after him into a desert full of mobs!" Alex exclaimed, looking around nervously. "Dang it—where's the homestead? I'm totally turned around."

Jack pointed in the opposite direction through the village.

"That way," he said. "What are we gonna do?"

"We can't spend another night fighting all of the mobs invading the village again," Alex said, looking down and shaking her head. "I wish *Steve* was here!"

Jack knew that Alex was afraid. She didn't like fighting. Steve normally did all of the fighting for her. However, he'd witnessed Alex kicking some serious butt without Steve's help in the last day. She needed more faith in herself.

"Well," Jack said, looking out into the sand dunes to the east again. He saw the silhouettes of three mobs standing out there that weren't present a moment ago. They were just shadows against the rising moon. It looked like two zombies and a skeleton. Those mobs would start coming into town soon. "We can either hole up here in one of the houses, or we can hurry back home."

"But it's too late!" Alex exclaimed, sheathing her sword and pulling out her bow and an arrow. "We can't run home *in the dark!*"

"We did it before," Jack said. "If we stay here, the mobs'll keep spawning around us all night. They might cause more damage to the village. Besides—if Steve's in the desert, and we head home, then there'll be less spawns around us."

Alex looked at Jack like he was crazy. "What the heck are you talking about?! *Spawns?!*"

"Less mobs," Jack said. "Plus, if Steve dies tonight out in the desert, he'll regenerate back home, right? Wouldn't it be better if we're there, too?"

Alex looked back and forth between the sandstone homes around her and the two areas that Jack had pointed at. Her green eyes widened under her dented iron helmet as she looked into the desert and noticed the distant mobs.

It looked like she was torn; didn't know what to do.

"Come on, Alex. Let's go home," Jack said. "I know the way. Just follow me. Could you give me a torch again?"

He held his stone sword in his right hand then paused to push his glasses up tighter to his face. Jack pulled his long hair out of his sight. He extended his small, human hand to Alex.

She regarded him with uncertainty then seemed to steel herself. She nodded.

"Okay," Alex said. "Let's run home. You lead the way." She put her bow away again, drew her sword, then pulled out two torches. She gave one to Jack and kept the other one in her left hand.

"If we hurry," Jack said, "the only thing we'll have to worry about are skeletons, right? We can run away from everything else."

"Except spiders," Alex said. "Spiders will catch us."

"Then let's *hurry*," Jack said.

They did.

The sandstone village was simple and just like any other village Jack had ever seen in Minecraft—well, with the exception of KittyPaws30's house, which was custom-built. He knew where everything was already. The night before, they'd run all over, and he could easily recall where the library was, where the blacksmith was, where the big house was where they'd blocked up the huge hole in the wall, as well as most other small homes that they'd repaired with cobblestone.

Jack ran. Alex followed. Within a few moments, they crossed town and stood on its western border. Jack stepped up onto a wood stump that was part of a retaining wall around a farming plot full of wheat. He looked ahead. The ridge before them was already black with darkness. He heard the plodding *thumps* of a zombie wandering around nearby.

The monster gurgled from outside of Jack's torchlight, making him jump. It was a lot louder than he'd anticipated.

"Ready?" he asked Alex.

"Not really," she replied. "But let's rock."

They rushed into the dark sands west of the desert. The ground hissed under Jack's clumsy, frantic steps. Then, he was running on solid earth again. Well, it was more solid than *sand*, anyway. Nearly everything about this world felt a little bouncy and spongy to Jack's real body. By the light of the torch in his left hand, he saw their surroundings shift from desert to forest, then, they were running along grass. Oak trees started popping up around them.

Soon, Jack had to climb up to another level. If he remembered the layout of the land right, he'd have to head up a sloping hill, then climb over the ridge. Then, they'd be able to see the lights of the farm and the homestead on the other side.

Jack put his hands down on the next level—struggling not to lose his sword and torch in the process—and grunted, pulling himself up. Every time he had to climb a block, it was like pulling himself up onto a kitchen table, and he was short!

When Jack climbed to his feet again, he sighed, facing the black ridge ahead. He knew that he'd have to pull himself up like that a billion more times before crossing over to the other side.

He looked back to make sure that Alex was still there. When he did, he heard a zombie *snarl* from somewhere in the darkness on his right.

"Duck feathers!" he exclaimed in fright, holding his torch up. His heart was beating so fast already! He looked back at Alex again. She was just behind him, her iron armor gleaming orange in the torchlight. "You okay, Alex?"

"Don't worry about me, Weird Walker!" she replied with a half-smile, waving her torch to see their surroundings. "I'm a lot faster than you. I'll stay right behind you."

Jack turned and ran on. A few more blocks ahead, and he had to pull himself up again. Shortly after that, he pulled himself up to another level. He heard the plodding of zombie feet on both sides. There was the *clunk* of bones somewhere far on his left.

That sent a chill up Jack's spine.

Please don't shoot me, he thought as he ran forward and climbed to another level. *Please don't shoot me. Please don't shoot me...*

Then, there was a crack of thunder that made Jack just about jump out of his skin! He looked up and saw that the stars were *gone*. Above them was only blackness.

A moment later, the sky opened up and it began to rain.

"Dang!" Jack cried. "Why now?!"

"Oh, man! Oh, man!" Alex exclaimed behind him. He could hear the fear in her voice. "You can't tell direction anymore, right?! Oh goodness—we're gonna get *lost!* Are you lost?!"

"No, I'm not lost!" Jack called back. The rain obscured his vision, but he didn't feel wet. It was the strangest thing. "We just have to keep climbing! When we go over the ridge, we'll see the house!"

"Okay, lead on!" Alex said. "Please don't get us *lost*, Jack!"

He was already sore. His legs and back were burning. A cold, buzzing sensation was flying through Jack's arms and legs and his chest felt like it was freezing. Something made Jack not want to move at all. He wanted to find a tree in the darkness and curl up next to it, hiding until he didn't feel like that anymore...

"It's just fear!" Jack muttered to himself. "Gotta keep moving!"

He pulled himself up another level then another that came right after it. *Jeez*—it was turning steep! They must have reached the ridge itself. This seemed so pointless, *climbing it* like this! If this was his game, and he went back and forth between the house and the village a lot, he'd just cut a nice, well-lit tunnel through the ridge, and put a bridge over the creek.

"What'd you say?" Alex exclaimed from behind him. The rain was loud. She ran and jumped. Her armor *clanged* and shook as she moved.

There was another *clunk* of bones off to one side.

"Nothing!" Jack called back, pulling himself up another row of blocks. "It's just that ... have you ever...?" He struggled.

Suddenly there was a zombie on his right, appearing from the heavy rain. Its green face appeared in Jack's torchlight. The pale blue shirt and dark blue pants were a colorful contrast to the green grass and grey rocks of the ridge. It snarled and headed Jack's way with both green arms stretched out to catch him.

"Look out!" Alex shouted. "Run left!"

"Gah!" Jack cried, somehow obeying her even though his legs were buzzing. He was so tired! For a moment, he was worried about slipping on the wet ground, but the grass under his shoes didn't feel any different than usual. Jack had to rest, but they couldn't stop moving until they reached the safety of home on the other side of the ridge!

311

Jack ran from the zombie. He looked back for a moment and saw Alex running along with him, one row lower. Looking ahead of him again, he stopped just before running smack into a tree. The rain blocked his vision with blue streaks all over. He couldn't see more than a few blocks in any direction.

The zombie was slower than them. He and Alex had a bit of a head start to the left—*to the south*, Jack thought—then they turned and climbed up another row to get around the tree. Jack's heart was a jackhammer in his chest. He was breathing hard and suddenly thirsty as heck! The zombie's slow steps plodded along loudly behind them. It groaned.

"Keep going *up!*" Alex exclaimed.

Jack did, grunting as he pulled himself up another level. He looked up the ridge. It was black and completely obscured by rain. How much farther would he have to climb?!

Thunder crashed again.

Pulling himself up two more levels, making his arms and legs keep working when he desperately needed a break, Jack panted and hardly heard more than the pounding of his own heart in his ears. He almost dropped his sword, catching it when it fell out of his hand.

Then, he ran into a wall of stone that he couldn't climb. Looking up, the rain fell directly into his face and eyes. His glasses were fogging up, which didn't even make sense to him.

"Dang it!" Jack exclaimed then turned left again. This area was too steep. He'd have to continue south until he could turn west climb up again.

He hoped that Alex was still behind him. Jack heard the *clanking* of her armor as if she was, barely audible over the drone

312

of the rain. Looking back, he saw her looking at him, then up the ridge, then down. Jack looked ahead of him again and—

Suddenly a creeper was right in his face!

"*Beetles!*" he shouted. The thing was taller than Jack was, covered in pixelated green colors. It frowned with its big, black mouth and sad black eyes. The creeper immediately began shaking and pulsing with white light. Jack saw the Damage Indicator appear over its head, showing a small creeper's face next to some words and bars:

Creeper. 20/20.

"Look out!" Jack shouted. "Creeper!!"

Hissssssss....

Jack reflexively hit it with his sword as hard as he could. He was lucky. His strike only did three damage—a dark red "3" appear over its head, floating up into the rain—but he somehow managed to knock it down the slope. The creeper fell down the blocky slope, ending up at the edge of Jack's torchlight four levels down. It flashed for another second then stopped hissing. Turning, the green mob started climbing up after him.

"Run!" Alex cried. "Climb!"

Jack did. He ran and climbed like his life depended on it, because it probably did. What would happen if his soft, real-life body was blown up by a creeper? *Splat.* One of those things could kill an unarmored player at max health. It would be like a grenade or something going off in his face! Jack didn't want to think about it. He just climbed as hard as he could.

There was a bony *clunk* of another skeleton in the distance to Jack's left, to the south.

"Another skeleton!" Jack exclaimed. He was afraid. This wasn't fun. It didn't feel like a game. He didn't want to get hurt. He didn't want to die.

There was another crack of thunder then Jack heard another *hiss*. He thought that it was the creeper again, but then Alex shouted:

"Spider on the right!"

Jack turned to look, terrified at what he might see. Through the heavy rain, four glowing red eyes looked back at him from the darkness above and to the right of him.

Dang.

That was something that could catch them.

He looked up and saw the black sky. Rain fell down constantly. He had no idea how far they still had left to climb, but the top of the ridge *had* to be close! They might have only a few more levels to go!

"Hurry!" Jack shouted. "I think we're almost at the top!"

He heard Alex cry out in surprise, then the *whoosh* of her sword. Her armor *clanked*, and there was the sound of a zombie snarling in pain.

"Then keep going!" she cried. "I'm right behind you! Are you sure you know ... ugh!" She grunted. Jack heard the *clang* of her armor. "Are you sure you know where you're going?! I have no idea where we are!"

Jack knew. Even though it was dark as heck and the night was thick with rain, he knew that the ridge ran north and south. They were almost at the ridgeline. Hopefully, after just a few more levels, he'd see the light of the farm...

Looking to the right in fear, searching for the spider, Jack saw it scuttling their way. He heard its feet drumming on the ground.

Adrenaline shot through his system when he saw its pixelated, glowing red eyes standing out from the pitch black ridge and the dark blue streaks of rain.

It was so hard to see!

"Yes, I know!" Jack cried, pulling himself up another level with a grunt. "We're almost at the top!" He *hoped* that he wasn't lying.

This was crazy.

It was your idea! Jack thought.

It was, yeah, but Jack had no idea how freaking scary this would be!

He pulled himself up another level, grunting and moving slowly up the block of grass, certain that he couldn't do the action again until after a rest; after he had something to drink and relaxed for a little—

Jack suddenly saw the yellow glow of the homestead peering through the storm. The sky was still full of rain and dark as pitch before him, and he was looking *down* onto a landscape of black shadows, but in the middle, a good distance ahead ... was *home*. The farm was well-lit. The animal pens, with a torch on every post, were easy to see, even through the rain! Jack could see the shadows of every animal shuffling around in the distance. The house was like a beacon of safety. It was down the ridge and not far ahead...

"There it is!" Jack exclaimed. "Here's the top! It's down from here!"

"Be careful!" Alex called back, running up behind him. "Don't fall!"

Right, Jack thought, looking down. Falling could be a problem.

He looked to his right and saw the spider approaching. Its claws drummed against the ridge—still climbing up from the other side behind him—and its eyes glared red in the dark rain.

"Let's get outta here!" Jack shouted then jumped down to the next row of blocks.

When he landed on the spongy grass, he held his torch out before him to guide his way before jumping down to the next. Then the next. Then the next. Before long, Jack felt himself losing control and groaned as he struggled to keep from falling too far forward and tumbling the rest of the way down!

He caught himself, slowed down, then looked up and behind him. Alex was descending with ease and that spider was navigating the top of the ridge and heading their way!

"Home!" Alex exclaimed with a grin. Her green eyes were wide. Her armor *clanged* as she jumped down without any trouble. "We're almost there!" Her torchlight cut through the rain around her. Jack was surprised that their torches were still *lit* in such a storm, but he also couldn't remember rain ever snuffing torches out before.

"Spider chasing us!" Jack called.

Then, he turned and hurried down again, jumping, landing, jumping, landing, trying not to drop his sword or his torch; trying to see through the thick storm.

Several rows down, he heard the spider *hiss* at them again. Jack turned mid-jump to see it then landed wrong. He tumbled over the side of the block he was landing on and fell with an *omph* onto the block below that. With the rain in his face, Jack bounced, rolled down two more rows—out of his mind with fear and now completely disoriented—then found himself falling through space...

He cried out in a panic for just an instant, then *splash!* He fell into rushing water.

The digital water enveloped him, surrounding Jack's face and putting out his torchlight. Fear flashed through his mind. He was in the creek. He felt himself tumbling still, probably pulled along with the current. Jack held onto his sword and torch for dear life and struggled to get his feet under him, but he couldn't tell which way was up! He was going to drown!

Then, Jack hit something hard and metal that moved when he collided into it. He felt strange fingers grasp his shoulders and pull him up.

His face was suddenly out of the water. In the torchlight outside the creek, he could see again. It took Jack a second to realize where the heck he was, and he looked around frantically for landmarks. The glow of the homestead was strong on his left.

Behind him—the hard, metal thing—was Alex. She'd jumped ahead and stood in the water to stop him, and was now pulling him up, her sword sheathed and her torch in one hand. Her eyes were in a panic. She looked afraid, but focused on *him*. Her Damage Indicator hovering over her head said that Alex was at *twelve* hit points now. She'd been hit on the way home...

"Are you okay, Jack?" she shouted above the roar of the rain.

"Yeah," Jack said, trembling with fear. "The spider...?"

"Still behind us. Let's go!"

Alex helped Jack out of the small creek that ran between the farm and the big ridge. When he made it to dry ground again, he was glad that he was still holding his torch—lit again as soon as he was out of the water—and his stone sword.

It was easy to run across the rows of farmland. Jack had to jump over a few trenches of water, but that was easy after pulling himself up that stupid ridge. His heart was still pounding and his lungs and body hurt, but he ran anyway. That spider was out there somewhere behind them, but Jack didn't look back. He watched the little spruce door of the house's farm area grow closer and closer. Just on the other side of that door was *safety*. There'd be the kitchen, then the crafting room with his bed. There were no mobs inside. It was *bright*...

They ran through the young sprigs of wheat. Alex was suddenly in front of Jack, moving with great speed. She threw open the back door of the house and leapt inside, out of the rain.

Jack followed her in, immediately diving into the kitchen so that she could close the door again.

She did.

Jack was seeing spots. He felt his heartbeat pulsing in his skin all over, and his muscles and his lungs burned.

That was *crazy*.

He slid down along the pixelated wall to the wooden plank floor and sat.

"Oh my gosh!" he blurted, panting heavily. "Holy duck feathers, that was *hard!*"

Alex stood in the hall next to him, watching the door for a moment. She looked down at Jack—clearly not winded at all—and smiled wearily.

"Well, your plan worked, Jack," she said. "I'm gonna get some sleep before morning. You should do the same."

Alex pulled a piece of roasted chicken from her pack then turned and walked away toward the main room, munching heartily on the digital food.

She needs it, Jack thought. Alex needed to heal. Eating that food was a good way to do that. He wondered what would happen if he was ever hurt—hurt *for real*—in this world. Would the Minecraft food heal him, too? Jack really had no idea, and was honestly more than a little afraid to try. What if he the bits of fake food hurt his insides?

He sighed. His heartbeat was almost back to normal and he wasn't panting for breath anymore.

Jack was surprised that running around in Minecraft was so hard on his real-life body. After all, Jack was a runner. He loved to run fast. He did *Track and Field* at school. He could run faster than anyone else in his class even though he was shorter than most of them.

Still, he'd been doing a lot of climbing and jumping; much more than he'd ever done at home in a long time. He used to run around and explore outside with his little brother, Dex, a lot, but nowadays, he mostly just did homework and played on his computer and read books.

Well, at least he'd get in better shape while he was stuck on this game world, right?

Alex's voice shouted from across the house.

"Jack! Jack! Come here!"

With sore legs, Jack climbed to his feet and ran into the front room. Alex wasn't there. He threw his torch and sword onto his bed.

"Where are you?" he called out to her.

"Divining Pool! Hurry!"

Jack ran to the hallway leading to the bedrooms then took the open door on his left, rushing into the bright room with the spruce walls. He saw Alex bending over the Divining Pool, leaning up against the bedrock fountain and looking inside. She looked at him with her green eyes wide and waved him over with one armored hand.

Running up to the mysterious artifact's edge, Jack stood tall and looked over. The bedrock under his hands was hard with sharp edges. The water inside was deep blue. White words wavered in there, almost at the surface. He'd almost missed it! Without a sound, Jack read the message silently, intent to finish before the ghostly words vanished:

"I wonder if you can add me as Liamfrey and he has a sword named the Inferno Sword and it sets fire to the enemies it hits. It also has the ability to create a Fire Whirlwind. The sword's blade is hotter than the sun's surface. Also, can I have an iron and wooden airship that I live in? It is powered by redstone and fire and propellers and has a bombing hatch. However, the airship is completely optional, but it is what I really want to be added. As a character, Liam helps Steve, Alex, and Jack fight monsters in the temple and helps them cross the big desert. – Teslageek"

When he finished reading, he looked up again and read over the part about the airship again.

Airship? Jack thought. Was that even possible?!

Optional? Where did these messages come from?

The words hit the surface of the pool and dissolved. Only blue water remained.

"What the heck?" Jack said.

Alex looked across the fountain at him and shrugged. Her armor *clanked*. Jack could see the Damage Indicator above her again. She was back to full health. Good.

"I don't know," she replied. "I thought I'd check on it before bed and I almost missed it! What's an *airship?*"

320

Jack stared at the water. He knew what an airship was, but had never seen one in Minecraft; not a working one, anyway. He'd seen plenty of them on *Mario Brothers* and other games. Any airships in Minecraft would have to just be some kind of player *build* that looked cool, but didn't actually *move*, right? It couldn't be an actual *bomber*. It couldn't travel the skies, powered by redstone and fire from coal or wood or whatever, right?

This world of Vortexia was weird. Jack had already seen several things that didn't make sense existing on the lightly-modded world of his Game Pendant.

Then again, it sure didn't make sense that he was stuck here, himself, did it?

"It's a ship. Which is ... a ... uh ... big house on the water with weapons and stuff. An *airship* is ... you know ... the same, but in the air. It would travel through the sky. This 'Liamfrey' would live on it."

"That's interesting," Alex said. "I suppose we'll be finding out soon enough."

"Yeah..." Jack said, turning away from the Divining Pool.

It was a good thing that the pool was giving them another ally instead of another *Alice*. This Divining Pool stuff was getting a little out of hand. Dragons, Withers, and evil ninjas...

"Well," Alex said, stepping away from the Divining Pool as well. Her armor *clanked*. "I'm gonna get some sleep. You okay, Jack?"

Jack looked up at her and forced a smile. "Yeah, I'm alright. Good night."

"Good night."

Alex left, crossed the hall into her bedroom, then closed the door.

Jack stared at one of the spruce walls for a while, imagining an airship. He wondered who was writing these messages, and how *he* was involved. Jack was the *Weird Walker*. Why was he here?

Leaving the Divining Pool room, Jack closed the door by pushing on its fake, flat doorknob and 'willing' it to shut. Then, he walked back into the main room, to his bed, and sat down. His sword and torch were floating above the mattress and its red blanket. Jack figured that they'd time out and disappear eventually, so he brought them one at a time to the dump chest on the left of the front door. He put both items inside after accessing the chest's interface.

Then, he returned to his bed, lay down on his back with his hands behind his head, and stared at the ceiling.

The bed was spongy just like the ground. It wasn't like a real mattress. It felt *exactly* like the ground, actually.

Jack sighed and fidgeted. He crossed his ankles and stared at one torch on a wall. It was bright in the main room. He'd have a hard time falling asleep with all of that torchlight, but they would need the light to keep the mobs from spawning inside.

How long had Jack been here now? It had been days in the game, but game days weren't like real days. Technically, an entire daily cycle—sunup, daytime, sunset, and night—lasted twenty minutes in the real world. Still, the timing was weird. Sometimes, Jack felt like he was passing through time very quickly; like the sun really *was* up for only ten minutes. There'd been other times where a day or night felt like it had lasted for *hours*. He didn't understand it.

Jack *was* starting to feel a bit tired. It was probably all of the running around and fighting. He was also getting *really* hungry. He

322

didn't know how much longer he'd be able to put off trying to eat some Minecraft food.

He closed his eyes.

A few seconds later, Jack heard the heavy, plodding footsteps of a couple of zombies out front. One groaned just on the other side of one window. Jack tried to ignore the sounds.

Then, he heard light footsteps outside and opened his eyes again. A chill ran through him. Sitting up, Jack jumped out of bed and crept to the window. He put his hands against his face on the glass to block the light of the many torches inside...

The frowning, green face of a creeper stared back at him.

"Holy beetles!" Jack exclaimed, leaping away from the glass. He sighed. Looking outside again, he saw the moon high in the western sky. At least the rain had stopped, and morning wasn't too far away. "Well, so much for sleep," he said, going back to his bed.

He lay down again, laced his fingers behind his head, then stared up at the oak ceiling.

Jack thought about his family. His older brother, Joel, was going to have soccer practice after school. Mom had told Jack and Dex to *not be late* getting outside after school to be picked up.

Did they already have soccer practice? Did Dex go home with Mom, and his whole family was going on without him, wondering where the heck Jack had disappeared to? Were Mom and Dad freaking out, thinking that he'd been *stolen*, or hurt and lost somewhere?

"I *am* lost somewhere..." he muttered at the ceiling.

Or was time standing still back in the real world while Jack was stuck in Vortexia?

That *had* to be the answer. Otherwise, Mr. Hayes, the Computer Lab teacher, would have found his Game Pendant in the *Vortex Wave Virtual Reality System 1.0*. He would have yanked it out of the USB drive by now; shut down the program.

"But what if it's not the answer?" Jack asked himself.

What if everyone was wondering where he was? What if he was stuck here ... *forever?*

Jack stared at the ceiling and waited for the morning.

S1E4 - Chapter 2 – Alex

When Alex woke in her bed, she forgot for a moment that she and Jack the kid had both run for their lives the night before. The sun was shining through her windows and she heard her animals outside stamping around. A cow *mooed*.

A normal, beautiful morning.

She jumped out of bed and put on her battered iron armor, looking it over piece by piece as she did.

"Getting pretty damaged," she muttered to herself.

Alex's armor would need to be repaired soon, but she had almost no iron. She was down to two ingots, and she *always* saved two ingots in case something bad happened to her gear and she needed to make a new sword. After finding Steve at that desert temple—or wherever he was now—they'd really need to go mining.

Alex smiled. She loved mining.

But not today. Today, they needed to go on an expedition into the desert, and she wasn't excited about it at all.

With all of her armor on, Alex sheathed her iron sword, grabbed more arrows from her personal stash, and opened the door to her bedroom. She stepped out into the hall with a sigh and found the Weird Walker still lying in bed with his hands behind his head and kicking his feet up and down over the edge; a very strange way of moving that she could never do herself.

"Morning, Jack," she said.

The boy sat up, folding his legs together under him. Gosh—he could move in so many complicated ways! He pushed his glasses higher up his nose and smiled.

"Morning already?" Jack said. "I guess Steve didn't die?"

"I suppose not," she said. "I'll check his room."

Alex looked back at the hall leading to the bedrooms. Steve's door was closed, and she hadn't heard him at all through the night. If he *had* died and regenerated in his bed, he would have probably made a heck of a lot of noise, running around the house trying to tell them all about the temple.

Returning to the hall, Alex opened the other bedroom door and looked inside. There was a messy bed, three empty armor stands, a bunch of chests, and randomly-placed torches on the walls. What a mess. No Steve.

She stopped on the way back to the main room to check the Divining Pool. Opening the door and stepping into the brightly-lit room, she approached the bedrock fountain and looked inside. The cool, blue water was still and empty. Alex was still rather perplexed about the message they'd seen yesterday. She tried to imagine an airship, but couldn't. *Well*, she thought. *I guess we'll see it eventually*. They seemed to be coming across everything from the pool so far. What wacky magic. Maybe one of these days, she'd see a message about her making friends with an intelligent horse. That'd be pretty cool to have a horse that could talk...

" Steve's not here?" Jack asked from the main room.

"Nope," Alex called back, shaking her head with a smile and leaving the Divining Pool room. "Let's pack for a desert expedition, Jack. Gosh, I wish he'd just come back already. I'd rather not go out there at all, not with that ninja *Alice* on the loose." Alex realized that she was hungry and headed to the kitchen. "Are you hungry, Jack?"

As Alex passed Jack's bed—placed in the middle of the main room—then turned into the hall leading to the kitchen, the kid made a sound behind her like he was starting to say *yes*, then stopped himself. Jack paused. "No, I'm not hungry. Not yet."

"We need to get some gear together. We might be out in the desert for a few days if it takes a long time to find Steve." Alex opened a kitchen chest and pulled out some roasted chicken. She hated the idea of camping in the desert, but as long as they gave themselves plenty of preparation time, she could simply craft a small dirt hut for them to spend the night in, protected from the mobs. There weren't any dangerous things in the desert during the day, right? There were only rabbits out there. The biggest risk was running out of stuff to eat. "I'll take a lot of extra food," she added.

"You should take an extra crafting table," Jack said from the main room, "and lots of torches, extra tools, sticks, wood, and dirt and cobblestone. Maybe a furnace."

"Now, *that's* a good idea," Alex replied, munching on a piece of chicken in the kitchen. "I didn't think of an extra furnace. We'll be able to cook stuff." She pulled a lot of food out of the kitchen chests; more than she typically took with her outside. For a moment, Alex contemplated whether or not to take *even more* food for Jack. She hadn't seen the kid eat a bite since he arrived here. Did he even *eat?* Or did he get all of the energy he needed from 'eating' the water in the creek?

Alex took a little extra food. At the least, if Jack didn't need it, Steve might. He was never prepared.

Wood was a problem. They were very short on wood. They had been ever since before Jack had arrived. Alex could remember going out into the forest past the animal pens to get more wood the day that Steve was looking for the escaped sheep.

It would be good to have plenty of materials for making more tools. Who knows what they might run into out there? Heck—if they had to hole up somewhere, she might end up spending the night mining under a little, dirt hut.

Jack was pulling his sword and torch out of the left dump chest by the front door.

Why did he put them there?

Jack must have seen Alex giving him a questioning look, because he shrugged and spoke up.

"I don't have an inventory, Alex," he said. "I can only hold stuff in my hands."

That was so strange that he couldn't carry things like she could. Jack was weird. The *Weird Walker*.

"I need to get some wood out front," she said. "Wanna help?"

"Sure," he said, stretching his arms and legs in a way that looked very odd to Alex. He stretched his little, round mouth open for a moment, then closed it again. "I'm actually starting to get a little tired."

"You didn't sleep?"

"Nope. Not really," Jack said, looking at the front windows. "The mobs out front were distracting me."

Alex smiled then walked forward. She passed Jack and opened the door.

"Well," she said, "they should all be burned up by now. Let's go to the trees by the mine and chop down a few to—"

Alex stopped in her tracks when she turned to face the sunlit field out front. She'd taken only one step outside. A creeper was there, turning to head her way. It was just ten feet away, frowning and hurrying toward the house on its creepy four little legs...

With a gasp, Alex jumped back inside and slammed the door.

"Oh yeah," Jack said. "There was a creeper out there last night. Sorry. I forgot to say anthing."

Alex felt a flash of anger at the creeper for interfering with her plans. She frowned. For a moment, she was tempted to run out there and fight it, but the idea made her extremely uncomfortable. Steve always did the fighting. True, he was so unpredictable and scatter-brained that he was just as likely to make the creeper blow up the house than to kill it, but still, *he* was the warrior. Alex wished that he was here.

"I guess ... we'll get some wood from the other side of the house," she said.

Jack smiled. "Sounds good to me."

"You sure you don't want to eat before we go?" Alex asked. "We'll probably be walking out there for a long time. I always get hungry when I travel."

"No," Jack said with a shake of his head that was a little too eager. "I'm fine. Not hungry *at all*."

"Okaaaaay," Alex said. "You ready to go?"

"Um ... almost," Jack said. "I've got to ... um ... I'm gonna go around the southern side of the house real quick when we go outside."

That was weird thing to say.

"Okay...?" Alex said.

With that, they went to the farm door. Alex opened it and looked back and forth before stepping out. No creepers. The coast was clear. She walked out into the farm, being careful not to step on the young wheat, while Jack ran to the right around the edge

SKELETON STEVE

of the house. She made sure that the spruce farm door was *closed*. Sometimes Steve forgets to close their doors. That means that, every once and a while, they'd find a random zombie wandered around in the main room or storage room.

"I'll be back in a sec!" Jack called back. "Don't look, okay?"

What a strange creature, Alex thought. "I'll just wait here!" she replied.

While she waited, Alex went to the farm chest, pulled out dried wheat and seeds, and fed the animals. She grabbed two carrots; one for each of their two pigs. The cows, sheep, pigs, and chickens were all very happy to eat. She petted the grey sheep that she and Jack had rescued from the wolves.

"Hi, Wolfie," she quietly said to him.

A minute later, Jack came back.

"Okay, let's go!" he exclaimed.

"What was all *that* about?" Alex asked.

"Um ... real life *boy* stuff," Jack replied. "Let's go! Gosh—I sure am thirsty!"

Jack led the way across the farm to the creek. Alex followed. There, the Weird Walker dropped down to his curved knees, reached into the water, and scooped some out with both hands put together like a bowl. He brought his hands-bowl to his mouth and drank, repeating the process several times. Like usual, Alex was amazed at the bizarre ways that the kid could move his body.

"Why do you do that?" Alex asked. "Why the water?"

"I need to *drink*," Jack said.

"You mean ... like *milk?*" she replied. "Why?"

"Real people need to drink," Jack said. "Otherwise, we get dehydrated and die."

So strange.

330

Alex looked up at the sun. It was low in the sky over the ridge before them. The day was young.

"Are you sure you know the way to follow Steve?" she asked. She sure had no idea how to get there. Alex figured that the desert and the village might be on the other side of the ridge—if she was remembering correctly—but she wasn't totally sure. She had absolutely *zero idea* how to find the desert temple.

"Oh yeah, sure," Jack said, standing and wiping his hands on his shirt. He pushed up his glasses then pulled the hair out of his face. "The village and desert are to the east. DarkestNight6641 said that Alice led Steve to the *east*, then he went on to the temple, right? Toward the rising sun? That's east."

"Oh."

"You know," Jack said, looking down at the creek. "I have an idea, if you have a spot in your inventory to spare..."

Alex didn't really know what he meant by that. *Room in her pack*, maybe? "What idea?"

"Do you have a bucket?"

"Yes," Alex replied. "It's back in the farm chest, for the cows and fixing the crop trenches."

"Could you bring it with you? Fill it with water from the creek first?" Jack asked. "I have a feeling that if we bring a bucket of water, I can drink whenever I'm thirsty by pouring the water into a hole, then putting it back into the bucket again after."

Alex didn't really understand what he meant, but the concept seemed important to Jack. After all, he said that he'd die from dehy ... dehy-something if he didn't drink.

"Sure, okay," she said.

Alex ran back to the farm chest, grabbed an empty iron bucket, and returned to the creek. She filled the bucket and stashed it away.

They set off, back up the ridge again. Jack had a hard time getting up the blocky slope, but he kept moving. The strange creature was huffing and puffing, but he pulled himself up block after block. He couldn't just *jump* up like Alex could. They paused to rest at times. Soon, they were on the top of the ridge. Alex looked down at the homestead on one side and the desert and village down on the other. Looking out over the huge desert made her feel very uncomfortable.

Jack stood on the top, peering out into the endless wasteland. He put one hand over his eyes for some reason.

"I can't see a desert temple from here," he said.

Alex sure hoped that he'd be able to find their way. Jack had already proven himself very capable of navigating, but it would be terrible to get lost in the desert. She looked up and down the ridge in both directions at the nearest trees. There were some out in the open here and there, but most were within thicker woods with shadows. Shadows meant mobs. Alex felt a chill run up her spine and she thought about Alice the ninja. That friendly demon, DarkestNight6641, had mentioned that Alice would always be looking to attack Alex from the shadows.

Still, she couldn't see any hiding mobs, and no black-suited ninja with blue eyes either...

"Come on," Alex said to the boy. "Stay close, and watch out for ... you know ... mobs and ninjas while I make you an axe. Then, you can help me cut some wood."

Jack smiled. "Okay," he said.

332

Diary of Jack the Kid
FULL SEASON ONE

Alex led Jack in one direction along the ridge until they were close to a smattering of trees separated from the main forest. She plunked down her extra crafting table. Using some cobblestone and the low supply she had of sticks, she made the kid a stone axe.

"Here ya go," she said. "Let's chop wood fast together so we can get away from the woods and find Steve."

Jack looked at the axe she was offering, then looked at his sword and torch in each hand.

"Will you hold my things while I chop?"

"Sure."

He dropped his stuff and took the axe. She picked up his stone sword and torch.

Then, they went to work. Jack chopped a lot slower than Alex did, but in time, big blocks of dark oak started falling to the grass all around him.

"I can't pick up the blocks and still use the axe," Jack said, so Alex made sure to follow behind him every once and a while to collect their wood.

When they'd chopped down five trees, and the wood was all stashed into Alex's pack, they replanted the saplings and continued. Once Alex was standing solidly in the sunshine again, she felt a lot better. She looked down at homestead one last time, then back at Jack.

Jack seemed to be having fun. When she returned to him his sword and torch, the boy tried something very weird indeed. He attempted to slide the handle of his axe into the collar of his shirt behind his neck, as if using his strange, soft clothing as a sheath for the tool. It didn't work very well, so he gave the axe back to Alex. Jack took back his weapon and torch.

Then, they started down the village-side of the ridge.

Alex was tempted to ask Jack again whether or not he knew the way, but she didn't want to nag. As soon as the homestead was out of sight, she became completely turned around and had no idea which direction was which.

The boy moved like he definitely knew the way, so Alex hoped for the best and followed.

"Wanna stop in the village on the way?" Jack asked. He was leading her through the sand around the outside edge of town. Up ahead was a vast, empty waste of sand dunes, scraggly bushes, cacti, and occasional hopping bunnies.

"No need," Alex replied.

At one point, a big black shape in the bright sands came out from around a cactus, giving Alex quite a fright with it *hissed*. She aimed her bow the instant she recognized it to be a big, eight-legged *spider*. Even in the glare of the desert, Alex could make out the red glow of its eyes. The mob was very close and would be on them in a second if it charged their way!

"Don't shoot!" Jack said, putting a soft hand on her armored arm.

"It's a spider!" she replied.

"It's okay," Jack said. "Let's keep walking. Spiders get passive in the daytime. If we leave it alone, it'll leave *us* alone."

Alex lowered her bow and walked on, following Jack and keeping an eye on the spider. The kid was right. The scary mob was just wandering around in the sand. It looked at them from time to time but didn't pursue them.

Jack really knew his stuff. Alex was impressed.

They continued into the desert, leaving the ridge and the village far behind. Soon, all they could see were dunes and cacti. Rabbits made little *hissing* sounds as they leapt around

"Are we still going the right way?" Alex asked, peering ahead and seeing nothing. "I don't see a desert temple."

"I don't see it yet either," Jack said. "But yeah, we're going directly *east*."

"What if we get lost?" Alex asked.

"If we need to go home," Jack replied, "we'll turn around and go *west*."

Alex sighed and walked on through the sand next to the kid. She was a little embarrassed at her total lack of direction. She had no idea how Jack and Steve could be so good at finding their way around. She preferred to be home, tending her farm and animals, or down in the mine.

They walked on with the sun high overhead. As the day went on, Alex saw the shadows behind the cacti moving. She looked around, watching out for Alice the ninja, but saw nothing alive other than rabbits.

Steve was somewhere up ahead. Alex continued deeper into the desert with Jack, hoping that Alice wouldn't attack them again while they were alone and in the middle of nowhere...

S1E4 - Chapter 3 – Steve

Steve sat in the dark, exhausted, tapping his hand repeatedly on a block of sand until it almost broke, then allowing it to regenerate back to normal. He did this again and again, waiting for morning.

He was *so* hungry.

How in the world did he get here? He didn't understand what had happened. One moment, he was heading toward the desert temple, which he clearly saw in the distance, standing tall and decorated with bright, red blocks of terracota. He was searching for Alice. Then, all of a sudden, he'd totally lost track of the place!

What a crazy night.

Heading east over endless sand dunes, Steve had been heading *straight toward* the ancient structure. Just before he lost it, he'd been walking for a while since he last saw Alice, and was intent on reaching the place before the mobs came out. He needed food. He needed shelter from the night.

Then, at one point, he'd staggered down one sand dune, unsuccessfully chased a desert rabbit that came a little too close to him—so hungry!—then, by the time he went up the next dune, the desert temple was *gone!*

What was worse was that as soon as night settled in, the sky became full of clouds so thick that he couldn't see the moon all night! Steve couldn't tell one direction from another, so he *tried* to head east, but there was absolutely *no way* to tell which way he was going.

Now, Steve tapped against a block of sand with his weary fist. He really had to resist the urge to fidget with his sword—the only belonging he carried other than freaking *sand*—because he didn't want to break it. His weapon wouldn't last much longer.

When the sand block was about to break again, he stopped, letting it regenerate back to normal once more.

There was sand and sandstone all around Steve. The night had been desperate. He had to fight off and flee from many mobs and he could barely stand. He was *so hungry*. Now, he was starving, wounded, and totally, hopelessly *lost*. The only way he'd been able to survive at all was to dig a quick hole into the sand by hand then bury himself.

So there he was, under the desert and enclosed by tight darkness, waiting for morning in a cocoon of sand.

Looking up, Steve struggled to raise his hand high enough to beat on the block above his head. He whacked it until it broke...

The sky was orange and pink. The cloud cover was clearing, and he could see some empty areas still full of stars.

"Oh, goodness!" he exclaimed. His mouth was dry and he could hardly concentrate.

Morning was finally here!

Steve could still hear zombies and skeletons moving around up their—the plodding steps, occasional gurgles, and *clunking* of bones—so he knew that he had to wait a little while longer. He was in no shape to fight anything. Besides—he didn't have to. The sun would kill the undead mobs for him ... except for the *husk* zombies.

He's seen a couple of husks over the night and knew from experience that the special desert zombies were immune to the scorching, wasteland sun. Heck—it was a good thing that those clouds were clearing. Otherwise, Steve would have to spend all day in this stupid hole! In bad weather, if the sun couldn't get through, then the undead mobs would no doubt stick around.

Steve waited.

Maybe this was a stupid idea. He wondered what Alex and that kid were doing. By now, he couldn't even remember how they became separated.

"Oh yeah," he said to himself. "I died."

Still, maybe he should have tried to find them in the village instead of running after Alice the ninja. Why the heck did he *do* that?! That was stupid.

"Because she *likes* me," he answered. "The Divining Pool said so."

Well, now he was starving, almost dead, and hopelessly lost, far from home and away from Alex. Steve hoped that she was doing okay and not huddled up frightened somewhere.

Eventually, Steve heard the sounds of zombies and skeletons bursting into flames, burning to death in the morning sun. The undead above him in the dunes all rushed around, crying out in gurgling pain or clattering their bones. Several seconds later, the sounds of the sizzling mobs died down.

Okay, Steve thought. *Time to look around.*

Willing his exhausted body to move, Steve climbed out from the hole he'd dug above his head. He emerged into the desert surrounded by nothing but dry sand dunes and cacti. He looked up into the pale blue sky of morning. The sun was dazzling as it rose in the east. Steve also saw a few piles of mob drops here and there. Nearest him, a chunk of rotten flesh was all that remained of a burned-up zombie. Farther away, he saw bone dust and an arrow hovering above the sand. He also saw ... a *carrot!*

"Whoa!" Steve exclaimed. "Score!"

Leaping out of his hole, Steve's body couldn't keep up with his mind. He tried to run for the blessed food, but instead, slowly trudged through the sand, desperate to grab the carrot! He was so hungry. He *needed* it. He had to—

A rabbit suddenly leapt up from nowhere to the carrot, landing into the sand with a *hiss*. It grabbed the carrot and hopped away.

Steve felt despair *explode* inside him.

"No!" he cried, immediately trying to run after the little animal, but he was left in the dust. "You furry little jerk! Bring that back! I'm *starving!*"

After a few exhausted steps, Steve stopped. He turned around and eyed the hovering piece of rotten flesh.

Zombie meat, he thought with a frown.

Slowly approaching the disgusting remains of a dead zombie, Steve reached down, picked it up, and looked at it. He resisted the urge to smell it. He knew that he wouldn't want to smell it.

Steve ate the rotten flesh. It was very, very gross. Choking it down, trying not to throw up, he put his hands on his grumbling belly and ... was surprised to find that he felt a little better! He felt a little stronger! He might even be able to run again!

Then, he felt *green*. The rotten flesh turned in his belly and he felt terribly sick.

Steve groaned. "Food poisoning," he muttered to himself.

He held his belly, trying not to be sick for a while. In time, the 'green' feeling started to subside, then, Steve found himself able to focus again.

Looking up into the sky, Steve found the sun low on the horizon.

"Let's get this over with," he said, then set off toward the east.

Steve pulled out his sword. He watched out for creepers, which might look a lot like cacti in the desert. Any creepers from the night before would still be around. One might follow him. He thought back to last night; running through the desert all over, looking for the desert temple in the dark while trying to avoid the many mobs coming after him. Steve had killed five zombies, two skeletons, and a spider over the night, trying to survive. He still hurt because of those fights, and he knew that he might not survive another skirmish—especially with a creeper.

He slogged east through the sand.

Dune by dune, the little bit of energy that Steve had received from that nasty rotten flesh whittled away. He continued east, exhausted again.

"How freaking far east *is* this place?!" he eventually shouted up to the sky.

Over one dune, he came across three husk zombies standing together in the sand. They were dried out and brown, their clothes tattered, and they stood making dry, raspy moaning sounds. Steve quickly backed up and hid behind a cactus before they saw him. Then, he went down the dune, took a short detour to the south to skirt around the mobs, and continued on his way.

When the sun was a little higher—still not high noon, though—Steve had run out of energy entirely. He moved slowly, trudging east through the sand, step after slogging step.

Every time he passed over a dune, he hoped with all of his heart to see the desert temple and its red accents among the sand.

Each time, he was disappointed.

It was really starting to feel like maybe Steve had only *imagined* seeing it before; that there was no desert temple.

He wondered what Alex and Jack were doing. He wondered about Alice.

Then, not really believing his eyes, Steve came across the strangest thing...

Crossing over one dune, trying not to trip over a dry, thorny bush in his path, Steve looked down at the sand in front of him and saw ... a *hole* in the ground. There was a trap-door propped open at the top of the hole, and the top of a wooden ladder leading *down* into the darkness. Right next to the hole, a torch was stuck in the sand, still burning.

"What the heck?" Steve said.

He stared at the hole for a little while, not knowing whether or not it was real.

Weird.

After one look to the east again to make sure that the desert temple wasn't in front of him—it wasn't—Steve shook his head, smiled weakly, then headed down the ladder.

"Well, it's more interesting than anything up here," he said to himself.

Maybe he'd be able to find some *food*.

Steve climbed down. He descended a long ways. The ladder went down and down, and every time he looked up, Steve saw the bright square of blue sky getting smaller and smaller above him. As he climbed down the ladder, the surrounding walls shifted from sandstone to grey stone, then began alternating with gravel and other types of stone like granite and diorite. Sometimes, he passed patches of dirt. Once, he saw some iron ore in the shaft wall, but since he didn't have a pick axe, he passed it by.

Who built this? he wondered.

Then, finally, Steve's feet touched the ground. The shaft with the ladder had been dark all the way down, but now, the bottom of the shaft was lit up by more torches. There was a small, hollowed-out room with two tunnels leading away into the darkness in two different direction. Steve saw that the ground under his feet was *bedrock*.

"Whoa," he said quietly to himself. He was *deep*.

Then, he heard a voice. It was a male, singing to himself from far away:

"*Not afraid of the Herobrine, that's completely undead. Keep away from the voices, creeps under your bed...*"

At first, Steve couldn't tell which direction the voice was coming from. Then, he figured that it was the tunnel on his right. *Is it another Minecraftian?* he wondered. He set off to follow the singing voice, moving slowly because he was so exhausted and hungry.

"*We're trying to kill you, stop wishing us dead. We're going crazy. Yeah, we're going crazy...*"

"Hello?" Steve called. His voice echoed.

The singing stopped.

Steve continued through the low tunnel, hoping that he was right about it being a Minecraftian. He hoped that the guy would be friendly. Hopefully he wasn't that ghost, *Herobrine*. The walls around him alternated between natural grey rock and purposely-laid cobblestone. He passed a torch every several feet.

343

"Who's there?" the singing voice called out, not singing anymore.

Steve stopped.

"My name is Steve!" he shouted back. His voice echoed. "I'm a Minecraftian. I'm lost in the desert. I found your hole."

Further up the tunnel, a head poked out of a hole in the wall that Steve hadn't seen. It *was* a Minecraftian. Steve caught a quick glimpse of a weathered man with brown hair and blue eyes. He wore a leather helmet and some sort of *goggles* over his forehead. The Minecraftian smiled and stepped into the tunnel, quickly approaching.

Now, in front of him, Steve saw that the man was dressed in a white shirt, black pants and boots, and wore a brown leather jacket. A bright red scarf was wrapped around his neck. He held an iron pick axe in one hand and was holding some redstone powder in his other. He was covered in redstone and rock dust. An iron sword hung on one hip, its grip gleaming purple as if enchanted.

"Well, *howdy!*" the Minecraftian said. "Steve, huh?"

"Yes," Steve said. "I came across your *hole* up there, and—"

The man stashed the redstone into his pack and stuck out one weathered hand for a shake. "My name's Liamfrey, Steve. Nice to meet you. Quite *random* for you to find me here, I reckon. You're lost, you say?"

"Uh ... yeah," Steve said, taking the man's hand. Liamfrey shook his hand firmly, frowning when he felt Steve's exhausted grip.

"You a bit *tired* there, Steve? Been wandering the desert long? Care for some food?"

That caught Steve by surprise. He smiled and nodded. "Oh, yeah. That'd be real nice of you ... Liamfrey?"

"You can call me Liam if ya like. Or Liamfrey. Doesn't matter." He stowed his pick axe and reached into his pack. "Let's see. How about ... some steak? It's a little old. No cows in the desert, right?" He laughed, pulling two pieces of steak out of his pack and offering them eagerly.

Steve's mouth immediately watered at the sight of the meat. He didn't care *how old* those steaks were. They were better than freaking rotten flesh!

He took the steaks and ate them as fast as he could. "Thanks!" he exclaimed between bites. The meat was gone within seconds and Steve could feel the *life* flowing back into him. "Oh gosh—thanks, Liam! I've been wandering without food for a long time!"

"Where'd you come from?" Liamfrey asked. "Where ya headed?"

Steve leaned against the tunnel wall with a sigh, feeling his body heal. All of the woes of the previous night and day were slowly fading away.

"My friends and I live west of the desert, near a village. I was heading east to the desert temple, but last night ... I somehow got turned around. Where'd you *come from?*"

Liamfrey clapped the dust off of his hands and crossed his arms over his chest. He looked like some kind of old-fashioned *pilot* or something. Steve liked him immediately.

"Well, I'm down here just getting some *redstone*. My airship is a little to the east. I've been in this desert for ... well ... I don't know how long now, but I had to stop to refuel and resupply. Had an accident down that other tunnel and lost all of my gear, ya see." He sighed. "Turns out I might be stranded here for a little while, I reckon."

Airship...?

"Did you say *airship?*" Steve asked. "What's an airship?"

"Well," Liamfrey said, looking back at the tunnel behind him. "I suppose I may as well *show ya*. It's about time to take a break, anyway. You'd best come with me."

"Okay..."

Steve followed Liamfrey back up the ladder and back out into the bright desert. He felt amazingly better after those two steaks but was already getting hungry again. His body was mostly healed. Looking up in the sky, Steve saw that it was almost high noon. Maybe Liamfrey was thinking of having *lunch*.

The interesting Minecraftian led Steve farther east over several more dunes. As they hiked through the sand, Liamfrey's red scarf fluttered in the desert wind. After a pretty good walk, something truly bizarre and unlike anything he'd ever seen became visible in the sky before them. It *amazed* Steve. He had to stop just to take it all in:

Ahead, low in the sky but well above the reach of the tallest dark oak trees back by the homestead, was a massive, floating house. It was more than a house; it was some sort of ship, like a huge *pirate ship* made of iron and wood with four great propellers aimed down at the ground—one on each corner—whirling with a low *whup-whup-whup* sound that was completely new to Steve! A long rope-ladder hung down to the desert, stopping too high for Steve or Liamfrey (or any mobs) to reach.

"What on Vortexia is *that?!*" Steve asked, awestruck.

Liamfrey smiled and put his hands on his hips, standing tall on his dune.

"*That*, my friend Steve, is my airship. I call her the *Thunderbird*. She's a bomber, and she's my home."

"The Thunderbird?" Steve repeated. "And your ship's a *she?*"

"All ships are *she*," Liamfrey replied. "Now come on. The ladder's off the starboard side. I'll show you around up top."

Steve followed, smitten with wonder, as Liamfrey led him to the ladder hanging in the air. The ship was bigger than Steve and Alex's house, and the propellers were *huge*, sticking out of four different corners, constantly pushing air down with that *whup-whup-whup* sound. Steve could feel the air on his head from below. The Thunderbird *loomed* over them, blotting out the sun.

Liamfrey threw down some dirt blocks so that they could reach the ladder.

"Go on up, Steve," he said. "I'll follow, so as I can break the blocks again."

Steve climbed the ladder, unafraid as he ascended through the sky up to one side of the ship far above him. What had Liam called that side? Starboard? What the heck was that? Steve had done plenty of crazy stuff in his life, but he'd never seen an *airship* before; much less *boarded* one.

He climbed the ladder past the bottom of the ship—rounded like a giant boat made of wood and iron—then eventually pulled himself up over the side in an area surrounded by guard rails. He found himself standing on the wooden-plank floor—or roof, depending on how you look at it—of the ship, near the middle. There seemed to be a front and a back. Steve had seen pictures of pirate ships in library books, and he even saw something once about strange, purple ships in a far off realm called *The End* with the heads of dragons on their front ends. This airship was a lot like those, but there weren't any sails. There weren't any masts (poles) or nets. The top half of the ship was fairly flat and open, with many crates and chests stacked up near the back, a trap-door hatch leading into the ship's body in the middle covered in a small roof in the middle near him, and a raised area in the front with a strange metal and glass contraption that Steve wasn't familiar with near the forward-most tip. Near the very back of the ship, surrounded by the crates, was another raised platform with a huge wooden *steering wheel* standing in its center with a chair behind it. There were also some furnaces in one area near the middle on the other side of the roofed hatch, and more chests on the wooden plank floor near the ladder, where Steve was standing now. The propellers made their constant *whup-whup-whup* sound, but now, he also felt the wind in his face.

When Steve realized that Liamfrey was coming up under him, he moved out of the way.

The Minecraftian pilot stepped up onto the top of the ship as if he'd done it a thousand times, put his fists on his hips, sighed and smiled. The wind made his scarf flutter behind him.

"So, what do you think, Steve?" he asked.

"It's amazing!" Steve said. "What's under the floor?" He pointed at the hatch.

"This is called the 'deck', Steve; not the floor. And inside my ship, there's my living quarters and the big engine that runs the propellers. I mainly use redstone for fuel, but she can take coal and other combustibles, too. Redstone's the most efficient."

"That's amazing!" Steve repeated. "What's that metal and glass thing up near the front tip of the ship?" He pointed.

Liamfrey laughed. "The 'front tip' is called the *bow*. That's my telescope. You can use it to see far. Wanna take a look? You can see that *desert temple* with it from up here. I reckon that's the temple you were talking about."

The desert temple was within sight?!

"Yes!" Steve exclaimed. "Yes, please! Where the heck is the temple?"

Liamfrey smiled. "You say you were heading east looking for it?"

"Yes."

"Well, my friend," he replied. "Looks like you overshot it by a goodly margin. Let's aim the telescope portside and see what we can see..."

"I walked *past it?!*" Steve shouted over the wind, which was suddenly gusting through them. "How the heck did I miss it?!"

Liamfrey shrugged, smiled, and took a minute to dump a lot of redstone and other things into one of the chests near the ladder. Then, he led Steve toward the front of the ship. Steve walked along the wooden deck, marveling at all of the vessel's parts. He peered over the edge, past the guard rails, and watched the propellers. Then, he caught up to Liam near the telescope.

"Alright, now," Liamfrey said, "just put your eye up against that there *eyepiece* and take a look. Try not to jostle it, alright?"

Steve complied. When he looked into the little hole, he saw an area of desert inside, bright and full of dunes and cacti. It was as if he was looking from up high and up close; as if standing down on the ground and high up in the air both at the same time. *Wild!* But, there was no temple.

"Where's the desert temple?" Steve asked, stepping away from the contraption.

"Oh—just a second there, let's see..." Liamfrey stepped up, looked inside, and made the thing move with levers that turned golden wheels. He stopped and stepped back. "There ya go. Take a gander."

Steve did. Looking through again, he saw the same desert temple that he'd seen before sundown, clearly visible through the device. He was looking at it from another angle, but it was definitely that desert temple. He looked up from the eyepiece and peered at the distance, trying to see it with his natural eyes. He couldn't. Looking at the desert temple again through the telescope, Steve could barely make out some movement down there. When he concentrated on holding *perfectly still*, he saw that the movement was a dozen of more *husk zombies* wandering around the structure on the outside in the sun.

Lots of zombies, he thought.

"So, that's *west?*" he asked.

"Yep. Feel free to look around and see what you can see down there, Steve," Liam said. "Just move the controls *slow*, and take her easy. Don't break my telescope, please. I'm gonna set up some *lunch*."

That made Steve smile. "Thanks. I'll be careful."

Steve looked through the telescope some more as the *whup-whup-whup* sound of the propeller blades around him continued endlessly. He played with the telescope's controls and found that he could make it move from side to side. He watched the landscape move as he did.

He was just starting to really have some fun scanning the desert when he stopped the telescope on two figures hiking across the dunes in the far distance. They were so far, in fact, that Steve could barely see them through the device. He held perfectly still again and waited to see...

The sunlight glinted off of iron armor. It was either a Minecraftian or a rare husk zombie walking around wearing armor. Then, he saw a bit of a green shirt. The other figure was a very strange shape and moved very fluidly; soft and rounded on the edges with a sword in one hand...

Gosh! he thought. *It's gotta be...*

"Alex and Jack," Steve said quietly to himself.

He looked beyond the telescope with his eyes, but couldn't see them.

Of course, Steve thought. They were even farther away than the desert temple.

Then, the realization hit him like a ton of cobblestone.

"The desert temple!" Steve exclaimed. "They're headed to the desert temple!" Alex and Jack probably thought that Steve was in there, but he wasn't. Instead, the temple was crawling with husk zombies!

Panic flew into Steve's heart. His friends were walking into an ambush!

"Liam!" Steve shouted. "Liam!" He looked toward the back of the ship but didn't see the man. He must have gone below. Steve rushed toward the hatch, quickly slowing down when he almost stumbled and remembered that he was on a flying ship high in the air. "Hey, Liam!"

A moment later, as Steve reached the open hatch, Liamfrey stuck his head up out of the hole, his blue eyes perplexed.

"What is it?" he asked. "What in tarnation is the matter?"

"I just saw my friends, Alex and Jack, down there!" Steve replied. "They're heading to the temple—probably looking for me—and they're almost there!"

"So, what's the problem?" Liamfrey held up some food. "Would ya like some lunch? I have some pork chops that I was saving for a special occasion, but I reckon that meeting a new friend is—"

"The desert temple's crawling with husk zombies!" Steve exclaimed. "They're walking into a big fight! I need to get down and help them!"

Liamfrey stepped up out of the hole and closed the trapdoor. He looked west as if he could see the desert temple and Steve's friends, then smirked and turned back to Steve.

"Well, I reckon we'll make this lunch *to go*."

"Thanks!" Steve replied. "You'll come with me? Are we gonna *fly* there?"

"I'll help you out, Steve," Liam replied. "But we've gotta walk, I'm afraid. The Thunderbird is almost out of fuel. That's why I was down there mining for redstone. I won't be moving her for quite a while; takes too much fuel to get going again, and I want to make sure that she can stay in the air." Liamfrey handed Steve a pork chop. "Eat up, my friend. Let's go save your buddies."

Steve took the pork chop with a smile then followed Liamfrey back to the rope ladder. They urgently started down...

Pssssst!!
Liking the story? Don't forget to join my Mailing List! I'll send you *free books* and stuff! (www.SkeletonSteve.com)

S1E4 - Chapter 4 – Jack

Jack led the way across the desert.

It was so strange, walking through the Minecraft sand. His very real shoes were squishing into the strange, spongy surface, making a *hissing* sound with each step. If it was real sand, the stuff would have gone in through the tops of his shoes and gotten all over in his socks and between his toes. But here, in the digital world of Vortexia, there was no such problem. For that matter—thinking back to his dunk into the creek next to the Homestead—when Jack fell into the water, he didn't really stay wet after he'd climbed out of it.

So weird, he thought.

Walking along with his stone sword in his right hand and resting on his right shoulder, Jack began to whistle. He watched the sun and headed straight east, knowing that as the day went on, the sun would get higher and higher, and it would be harder to tell. Eventually, they'd have the sun on their backs. It wasn't hard to tell directions in Minecraft, as long as you could see the sun or the moon. They rose *exactly* in the east and set *exactly* in the west; not like back in the real world. There, back on Earth, last summer on a camping trip, Jack had played around with a compass that his dad had given him. He recalled that the sun rose in the *northeast*.

He looked back at Alex.

She still looked nervous. Alex walked with her bow and arrow drawn and ready. The bright sunshine glinted off of her beaten-up iron armor, and she glared at every cactus and every sand dune capable of hiding a Minecraftian behind it with her wary, green eyes.

She must be afraid of Alice, Jack thought.

Alex looked Jack's way and saw him watching at her.

"Are we still going east, Jack?" she asked, trudging through the sand. "Please make sure. I don't want us to get stuck here."

Jack looked ahead at the sun halfway between the horizon and high noon. They were headed straight for it.

"Yep," he replied. "Still east."

It was odd. Alex was acting like she was hot and a little fatigued by the desert, but Jack didn't feel a thing. The wasteland was like a huge, empty bouncy-world. He didn't feel hot at all.

They continued on.

After a while, Alex started taking potshots at desert rabbits with her bow. When she killed one with a *squeak*, Jack looked back, wondering what in the heck she was doing.

"So many rabbits," Alex said with a shrug that made her armor *clank*. "We may as well get some extra meat while it's available and save the cooked food. Whenever we camp for the night—*if* we camp for the night—I'll cook these guys up." She deviated from their path to collect the rabbit meat and its hide, floating above the sand. A single yellow experience orb rolled into her foot with a tinkling sound. "We can also use these rabbit hides to make leather."

"May as well, right?" Jack said.

They walked and walked. Jack passed everything that he would normally expect to see in a Minecraft desert. There were the cacti that grew taller than mobs and Minecraftians, those prickly bushes that would leave *sticks* if he tried to break them, and rabbits. Lots of rabbits, hopping around in the sand. Every once and a while, he saw a small hole in the ground—usually shored up with sandstone and extending into darkness—but he didn't bother with them. Mostly, it was just dry desert with dunes rippling endlessly into the distance. Eventually, he couldn't see anything around him *except* for desert. The village disappeared behind them. The rising mountains and forests to the north faded from sight.

All around the two of them was nothing but bright, sandy wasteland.

Jack and Alex moved ever-east, up and down the dunes, one at a time.

With nothing around them but sand, Jack started to feel thirsty again. He wasn't thirsty because he was hot or dry, but just because time was passing, and a lot of time had passed with them walking on and on.

Jack's stomach growled. It was an unpleasant feeling. Back home, he never really got hungry. He ate breakfast that his mom made, he ate lunch at school, usually had a snack in the afternoon there, then had an after school snack at home and dinner at night with his family.

How many hours had it been since he'd eaten back on the real world?

He'd have to take care of this soon...

Eat the weird food, he thought, *or starve*.

Jack was afraid.

So far, he'd managed to avoid hurting himself. There'd been plenty of times now where he could have fallen down too far, or been hurt by a mob, or even drowned, but he'd stayed safe for the most part. Jack was scared of what might happen to him if the Minecraft food was bad for him. What if eating a piece of Alex's roasted chicken was like eating fake food made of plastic or rubber? Or what if it broke down into lots of sharp, tiny cubes in his stomach and hurt his insides?

If Jack became sick or hurt here, well, there were no doctors or nurses to help. No Mom.

He was by himself. Well—he and *Alex*.

Jack held out as long as he could before suggesting that they take a break. He needed to drink some water, but he didn't want to deal with the 'food' thing.

Finally, continuing ever-eastward, Jack saw something familiar materialize in the hazy distance. It was a desert temple, standing blocky and tall with red terracota blocks for decoration built into the sandstone walls. It was just like the thousand other desert temples that Jack had seen in his time playing Minecraft on his computer or at school.

"Hey!" he shouted, looking back at Alex with a smile. He pushed his glasses up. They were slipping down his nose. "There's the temple up ahead! See it?"

Alex stopped and peered at the distant, sandy horizon. She squinted her green eyes then grinned.

"There it is! Great!" she exclaimed. "Good job, Jack! You got us here!"

That made Jack feel good. Even though he was just a twelve-year-old kid, and couldn't really fight or do amazing feats of strength and agility like his Minecraftian friends, he knew a *heck of a lot* about this game.

"Well, DarkestNight6441 *said* that it was east, didn't he?"

Alex lowered her bow. She seemed relieved and watched the distant temple as if looking for Steve. "Still, you got us here across the desert, Weird Walker." She smiled. "Let's take a break and have some lunch."

Jack groaned.

He was super-thirsty, and *nearly* super-hungry.

"Okay."

So they did.

When Jack saw Alex start pulling food out of her pack, he walked over and bent down to consider the sandy ground. Putting down his torch—it hovered several inches above the ground—he punched one block of sand with his hand. It was a strange sensation. He did it again, then again, then whacked it over and over until it *popped* out of place, leaving a block-shaped hole. He didn't bother to pick up the single block of sand that had shrunken to a fraction of its normal size, floating above the ground near his torch.

"Alex," he said. "Could you pour the water in here, please?"

Alex was munching on a piece of chicken. *Crunch, crunch, crunch, crunch.*

"Sure."

Reaching into her pack, Alex pulled out the bucket of water from the farm then carefully dumped it into the sandy hole. The recess that Jack had made was immediately filled with blue water.

Jack dropped his sword and dove at it, cupping his hands and drinking quickly. He took several long drinks then asked Alex to collect the water again. She did, and it stayed in the bucket just fine. His idea had worked. Jack made a mental note to always have Alex carry a bucket of water in her inventory whenever they went on long trips.

"Thanks," he said, sitting on the sand and putting his stone sword and torch in his lap.

Alex watched him from standing. She was a Minecraftian. She couldn't sit. "Would you like some food, Jack? I have chicken, steak, and bread. Oh—and a few apples."

A little spike of fear twisted around in Jack.

Then, his stomach growled in response.

"Uh," he said, very worried, "How about some ... bread?"

Alex smiled and handed him a loaf. It was flat, shaped like a crude, pixelated loaf of bread, and smelled like nothing. Jack carefully tried to break a piece off of one blocky corner, and it came off easily in his hand as if he was breaking Styrofoam.

Gosh—I hope it doesn't taste like Styrofoam, he thought.

Then, Jack took the small piece that he'd broken off and slowly put it in his mouth. Just before he bit down on it, the piece of bread dissolved onto his tongue. It tasted ... *like bread!* It tasted like one of those white bread rolls that he sometimes got from the lunch line at school!

Jack smiled up at Alex. She was watching him and smiled back.

"It's okay?" she asked.

Jack looked at the rest of the loaf in his hand. It was large but thin. It would be kind of like eating a big, thin *book*.

He raised the bread to his mouth and bit off a piece as if biting a chunk out of a huge cookie.

The same thing happened. The piece broke off easily then dissolved into his mouth quickly, tasting vividly of bread. Jack grinned, looking up at Alex again, then quickly *devoured* the rest.

When the loaf was gone, Jack thought about his hunger. It *felt* like he'd eaten something. He didn't feel sick. He didn't feel weird.

"Can I have a piece of chicken?" he asked.

"Sure," Alex said, fishing out a pixelated cooked chicken, roasted and tan, drumsticks and all. She gave it to him.

The chicken was the same size, thinness, and consistency as the bread. Jack took an experimental bite, savoring the amazing *chicken flavor*, then quickly ate the entire thing! It dissolved in his mouth just as easily as the bread did, and it tasted *amazing*; like a roasted chicken from the Wal-Mart deli! Dad brought those chickens home on his way back from work sometimes and Jack loved them. *Rotary chickens*, Jack called them. They weren't really called 'rotary', but he couldn't remember the actual 'R' word. He liked to help pick apart the entire chicken body until it was nothing but bones. They was so good, and this Minecraft chicken was like a digital version of that!

Jack didn't feel stuffed or ill or weird afterwards.

He stood.

He felt the huge worry about how he was going to eat here in Vortexia just *drop* off of his shoulders. It was great. He relaxed. He'd be able to eat this food just fine!

Grinning, Jack looked at the desert temple to the east. Then, he looked back at Alex.

"That was awesome!" he said. "Very tasty, thanks!"

"No problem," Alex said. "I make the bread from our wheat and the chicken comes from our coop. The chickens breed quickly, so we slaughter some sometimes and use them for meat and feathers for arrow fletching."

"Even better since you made it," Jack said.

Alex smiled. "Ready to go on?"

"Yeah," Jack said. "Let's go find Steve."

They set off to the east with the desert temple in sight.

As they grew closer, Jack watched the temple, mostly with disinterest, but Alex gasped and stared at it from behind him. Jack had seen a billion desert temples, it felt like. They were all the same. You go in through the middle, clear out the mobs, then dig out around the blue square to get down to the treasure, careful to avoid setting off the trap between the four chests at the bottom of the pit. Desert temples were an easy way to find things like iron, gold, horse armor, magical books, and even a diamond or two. Many chests held nothing but sand and bones. Still, it was no big deal. Desert temples were all alike.

Still, when they approached the structure, Jack found himself a little overwhelmed as the sandstone exterior with the red markings loomed over them.

Maybe it was different going in there as a real boy. The place felt a lot bigger than it ever had when playing Minecraft as *just a game*.

They walked together through the open sandy plain in front of the ancient building's entrance. The main archway looked like a mouth with two blocks of red terracota for eyes.

"Wow," Alex said as they stood before it.

Jack clenched his fist around the blocky handle of his sword. He bounced the blade in his hand a few times and swung his torch twice, warming up his arms.

"Be ready," Jack said. "There's a hole in the middle of the pyramid that lets in light, but there won't be any torches inside, so there might be mobs in the shadows."

"Unless Steve is in there and set up a bunch of torches," Alex said.

"Yeah," Jack said, but he didn't think that'd be the case. "You think he's in there?"

"Well, there's one way to find out," Alex said. She took a deep breath, and called out, "Steve!!" She waited for a few seconds. "Steve! Are you in there! Hey, *Steve!!*"

They waited.

Jack and Alex watched the yawning archway. It was dark inside.

Nothing happened.

"I don't think he's in there," Jack said.

"Well, there's *another* way to find out. Let's go in." She put away her bow and pulled her iron sword and a torch.

"Wait!" Jack said. "We need a plan. There are ... three exits from that place. There's the one *here*, and then there are those two towers..." He pointed at the two towers with red markings that each flanked the main entrance. "They have stairs going up, and you can get out from there onto the top-sides of the pyramid. There might be mobs in there. Well, I guess there's *four* entrances, actually. There's also the entrance to the upper level, but I never go in that way."

"You sure know a lot about desert temples," Alex said.

"They're all the same," Jack replied.

"Really?"

"*Anyway*," Jack said. "If we go in there, and mobs start coming after us, we should probably just run right back out the front again and fight them out here, outside, if we can."

Alex nodded. Her armor *clanked*. "Good plan, Jack. Ready?"

"I ... I guess so."

Together, they went into the temple. Alex led the way through the open archway. As soon as they were out of the sunshine, Jack felt extremely nervous. He couldn't think of a single time that he'd ever come into one of these and didn't have to deal with at least a mob or two in the main chamber. Was this place empty or were monsters waiting inside? Or ... had Steve already been here and killed them all?

When Jack stepped into the main room, he saw the shaft of light coming in from the hole in the peak of the pyramid. The beam of sunlight lit up the blue and red markings on the floor between of the four columns in the center of the structure. That's where the treasure was; down under there. He also saw that the many alcoves and spaces in between other columns around the outer walls of the temple were bathed in shadows. There were no torches.

Steve wasn't here.

Jack felt his heartbeat quicken. Fear buzzed in his arms and legs but he stayed by Alex's side, holding up his stone sword and illuminating the area to his left with the torch in his other hand.

"Steve?" Alex called. In the enclosed space, she said it a little too loud and her voice made Jack jump.

"We can check the stairwells, I guess," Jack said quietly. He could now hear his heartbeat in his ears. "I've camped out in them before."

"Okay," Alex replied quietly. Her green eyes were wide. Jack figured that she was afraid, too.

They backtracked from the main room and found the tunnels extending to each side from just inside the entrance. Each sandstone corridor led to a separate tower. Jack headed toward the left tunnel. Alex followed. They crept quietly, aside from the metallic shuffling of Alex's armor. The tunnel was very cramped and narrow, and when Jack saw the stairs emerging by his torchlight ahead, he stopped.

"Steve?" he called out more quietly than he meant to.

There was no sound. The light of day filtered down from above, up where the doorway to the outside of the pyramid would be.

"I don't think he's here," Alex said.

"Okay, let's go back," Jack replied. He raised his voice a little. His heartbeat was slowing. Maybe there were no mobs here, after all. They started back to the center. "We should loot this place while we're here, I guess," he said. "I know exactly how to do it without getting us blown up. We'll need torches, and to make totally sure that there are no shadows left where mobs can spawn. Then, you can use a pick axe to ... um..." Back near the main entrance, Jack looked outside into the bright desert, then, he looked down the other tunnel to the other tower. "Wanna check that one?"

"Nah," Alex said. "Let's step out for a sec. Steve's definitely not here."

"Okay," Jack said. They started out. He stopped. "Eh ... I'm just gonna check it real quick. Be right back."

Starting down the other tunnel, holding his torch before him against the darkness, Jack held his sword and moved quickly. Alex shrugged and followed. Within a few seconds, he reached the stairs, looked up, and saw the light shining in from outside.

No Steve.

"You were right," Jack said, looking back.

Alex was waiting halfway down the tunnel back to the entrance. She smiled to say something then both she and Jack gasped when there was a sudden, raspy *groan* from very close by...

Jack's heart leapt up into his throat, immediately pounding again.

Alex turned and screamed.

"Augh! Jack! Come on! Get out!"

The sound was loud in the cramped tunnel and shocked the boy. He jumped, and suddenly everything went *blurry*. The dark tunnel lit up by their torches became muddy and muddled.

Alex was suddenly fighting. Through her flailing, armored form, Jack saw a zombie or something fighting her between him and the main exit. She was close to getting out—it was only one zombie—but it snarled and gurgled with a drier-than-normal, crackly voice and bashed down at her armor. The Minecraftian woman grunted and struggled in Jack's blurry vision, stabbing the mob again and again with her sword. Finally, the zombie fell back into the main hallway and Alex pushed her way through its dissipating remains to the entrance.

"Come on, Jack!" she cried, appearing as a bright blur as she stood before the exit, bathed in the sunlight from outside.

Jack ran to catch up. *Was that a husk zombie?* he wondered. His brain was frantic with fright—almost in a total *panic*—and he—

"Wait!" Jack shouted, stopping in his tracks. He couldn't see! He reached for his face with the back of his torch hand, and realized that ... his glasses were gone. "My glasses!" he cried.

Jack turned back toward the stairwell, crouching low and waving his torch over the sandstone floor. Several feet away, back where he'd jumped in surprise, he saw the gleam of firelight on a lens. He scrambled toward his glasses, being careful not to stumble or step on them. *That* would be a disaster in a world like this...

"Jack!" Alex screamed. "Oh gosh—*Jack!* Come on! They're coming!"

Amazing himself, Jack managed to swoop down and pick up his glasses from the floor. He quickly put them back on and swept the hair out of his face.

He turned to run out...

Husk zombies were pouring through the tunnel toward him. He could already see their Damage Indicator windows above their heads:

Husk. 20/20.

Jack's heart and stomach went as cold as ice. Alex was screaming in alarm. The sound of it washed away in a drone around the edges of the boy's senses. For a second, all he heard was the moaning and raspy groaning of the husks coming in at him, their dark-brown arms stretched forth and their slack, withered faces dancing with shadows as his torchlight flickered. His suddenly couldn't feel his arms and legs. He couldn't move...

There were at least four of them—maybe more—pushing through the narrow sandstone tunnel toward him single-file. Their skin was brown instead of green and they were dressed in torn rags the color of sand instead of the normal *zombie blues*. Jack tried to scream. He tried to move, but all he could do was stare in cold terror as the husks' plodding feet filled his senses and the one at the head of the pack snarled loudly in his ears...

Jack finally found his feet again when the lead zombie almost caught him. He stumbled backwards then turned, fleeing toward the stairs that he knew would lead outside. He felt like he was running in slow-motion. He could feel the spongy floor moving under his sneakers. When he reached the stairs, he looked back—expecting to see the zombies far behind him again—but they were *right there*, flooding into the stairwell all around him. More were still filing in through the tunnel. He had no idea how many husk zombies were after him...

With a scream that he hardly heard—Jack could dimly hear Alex shouting his name in the background—Jack made for the stairs. He climbed one, then another, then *tripped*, falling over the edge down to the floor!

"No!" Jack shouted, landing on the floor on his side. He jumped back to his feet, holding his sword and torch in front of his face. The zombies were coming around at him from both sides, flowing over the lowest stairs. "No! Stay back!"

Jack felt more scared than he ever had in his entire life. Fear blazed through him and he felt like his heart was going to explode out of his chest! The edges of his vision were black. As he looked at the zombies looming over him in horror, he looked into their dull eyes and wide-open jaws and knew that he was *doomed*.

He was about to die...

He thought of Mom and Dad. He thought of Dex and Joel. Images of his friends from school and the girl he liked flashed through his head. He thought of Grandma and Grandpa who lived far away in Arizona. He thought of Mom and Dad again...

Finding some last, wild bit of strength inside him, Jack lashed out at the nearest zombie with his stone sword, striking it across the chest with a careless slash. The creature flashed red and Jack barely noticed the big, dark-red "4" drifting up over its head. *That* husk was down to sixteen hitpoints. There were too many of them. Jack was trapped. He knew that he wouldn't be able to fight them off. He was going to *die*.

When the first hit came, Jack was so scared that he almost passed out. One husk zombie that he hadn't hit swung its big, dark brown fist down at Jack as he was recovering from his sword swing.

The zombie's fist smacked him on the shoulder.

Jack didn't feel his skin burning. He didn't feel his bones breaking. Why, the hit wasn't even as hard as when his older brother, Joel, sometimes punched him on the shoulder! It was as if the zombie had whacked him with a square-shaped *soccer ball* or something.

Heck—it didn't even *hurt!*

Jack stood shocked for an instant, thinking about it, as another zombie swung in and conked him on top of the head.

Smack.

It was as if his little brother Dex had hit him on the top of his head with a pillow.

"What?!" Jack cried. "Duck feathers! *What the heck?!*"

He stood and faced the zombies, still blazing with fear; his heart still pounding like a jackhammer. The first one husk him again on the chest. It pushed him back a little, but didn't hurt him. It was nowhere *close* to hitting him hard enough to leave a bruise. The husk zombies snarled and sneered in Jack's face and bared their rotten teeth—they were scary as *all heck*—but they just *smacked* him again and again, not hurting him!

Alex was screaming his name from outside.

There were so many freaking zombies in here with him! They mobbed him from all over, but their hits weren't doing *squat!*

Jack felt himself being knocked around by the many zombies that could reach him, but he wasn't being hurt! He was *invincible!* A weird feeling rose up in him like a crazy mix of anger and excitement and the same insanity that made him feel really fast and full of energy after drinking a big *Slurpee*. He found himself screaming, too! Jack screamed, then took in a big breath, and shouted out his *mightiest battle roar!*

He was in *God Mode!!*

Setting his eyes on the zombie with 16/20 hit points, Jack raised his sword, ignoring the many soft fists battering him around, and *attacked!*

S1E4 - Chapter 5 – Alex

"Jack!!" Alex screamed. She felt helpless. Standing just outside the temple in the sun, Alex hurt from the two hits that she'd taken from that husk. She felt like she was poisoned or something, becoming more sore and weaker by the second.

Alex looked into the temple in horror as maybe a *dozen* husks rushed out of the main room—they must have been hiding behind the pillars near the outer walls—and flooded into the tunnel, all of them going after Jack!

She could hear the kid screaming.

It was terrible.

Alex had to do something, but ... what could *she* do against a dozen freaking zombies?!

She stood screaming his name, working up a fire in her blood, telling herself that she needed to charge into there; to run into battle and save the poor boy!

Wishing that she had a shield, Alex rushed the doorway screaming Jack's name. She heard the boy screaming and the raspy snarling and hissing and gurgling of the many zombies pushing through the tight, sandstone hall. Two husk zombies immediately turned to face her just inside. There were three still in the main chamber—seemingly waiting to get their turn to attack Jack the kid—and Alex couldn't even tell how many were crowded into the corridor heading to the rightmost tower, where the Weird Walker was under attack.

"Jack!" she screamed. Alex immediately thrust her iron sword into the nearest husk. "Jack!!"

She fought. A few seconds in, Alex felt the battering blows of the zombies in front of her as they bashed her with their withered, dark-brown fists and snarled, showing sharp, black teeth. Her armor took more and more damage.

With fear flying through her like a storm, Alex slashed at the first husk again and again, cutting into its tough, dried-out body and slicing through the ancient rags of cloth covering it. She bashed another zombie with the flaming torch in her other hand—splashing it with sparks but not setting it on fire—until her torch broke and disappeared into the chaos. She could hear Jack screaming and shouting. It was amazing that he was still alive!

Her torchlight was out. Alex quickly found herself fighting in darkness with the light of day behind her. She tried to dodge, but they zombies in front of her seemed to forget about Jack. They pressed in at *her* instead.

Clang!

One zombie's fist landed on her helmet. The blow made Alex's ears ring and her vision double.

"Jack!" she screamed. "Oh, Jack!"

She backed out into the sun. Alex hadn't fought these husk zombies before, but she knew what they were from Steve's stories. She hoped that they'd burst into flames when they followed her into the sunshine, but she also suspected that they wouldn't.

Two husk zombies immediately poured out of the temple's mouth after her. They did *not* burst into flames.

Fear flushed through Alex's body. She already hurt all over. Those monsters had mostly battered her armor, but she'd felt a little of each and every blow.

A third husk followed the first two, stepping through the smoke of the first zombie she'd killed as it disappeared on the sandstone floor of the temple with a *poof*.

She could still hear the kid screaming, but the sound had changed. Now, it was more like ... fierce *shouting*. It was shocking that poor, little Jack wasn't dead!

Alex watched the three zombies approaching her from the darkness of the desert temple. They didn't care about the sunlight; not one bit. They were dark and terrifying, plodding through the sand with their twisted arms and claws outstretched, opening their dry mouths and staring at her with dried-out eyes. They made raspy sounds as if their bodies were full of sand...

Looking back, Alex saw empty dunes behind her.

She could run.

She could run away...

Then, she heard Jack let out a mighty cry. His voice cracked. He was still alive. Jack wasn't screaming in terror; he wasn't crying in pain. He was shouting at the zombies.

Alex had to help him.

Eyeing the three zombies clustered together and approaching her through the hot sand, Alex adjusted the grip on her sword, took a deep breath to calm her nerves, then burst into a sprint, rushing around the right side of the trio. The mobs began changing course, watching her charge with their dull, lifeless eyes and turning to catch her, but Alex was far faster.

As soon as she was around their sides, she leapt in and slashed at the closest zombie's leg and body. One of her strikes knocked it backwards. The monster let out a scratchy sound of pain. Then, before it could catch her, she darted away out of reach.

The zombies snarled and gave pursuit.

Alex repeated the process again, focusing on the same zombie. This time, when she hit its leg, she cut through it. The monster stopped, immobile.

The other two zombies flowed around it, snarling and reaching for her.

Backing away again, Alex ran several steps out of reach and waited. She was getting tired. Jack was still shouting inside. Whatever he'd done, he was still alive. He had to be trapped up high or something. Maybe he'd climbed up to a ledge, and now had zombies all around him, clawing at the walls to pull him down...

Alex rushed in and attacked one of the two intact zombies. She stabbed it through its husky chest—it was tough on the outside and empty on the inside—then spun on her heel and surprised herself by lopping off its head!

"Yes!" she cried then immediately grimaced as the other zombie bashed her on one armored shoulder. "Dang it!"

Then, Alex heard the strangest thing. She couldn't believe it. Jack was *laughing*.

The boy was laughing as if he was having fun.

Alex shook the pain off of her and leapt backwards *barely* out of reach just as the zombie's other fist came sweeping down at her. It missed. She had no idea how much longer her armor would last, and she was pretty wounded herself, but she knew that it was getting pretty beat up. Alex had made that suit of iron armor a long time ago—back when she and Steve first settled in the valley that became their homestead—and she'd taken good care of it, repairing it when needed. But now, she'd been in more battles in the last few days than *ever* before, and they were just about out of iron.

She circled the remaining zombie that could still walk. It took plodding, uneven steps through the sand, constantly spinning and trying to reach her as Alex struggled to stay ahead of it. She was out of energy. She needed food. But she needed to kill this zombie and help Jack! Whatever was going on, there had to be ... maybe ten zombies or more in there!

A sudden snarl over Alex's left shoulder made her jump in fright. The zombie that she'd crippled was *slowly* making its way toward her, still trying to reach her...

"Looks like you could use my help now!" a voice suddenly called out from above the temple.

Alex looked up and saw Steve and an unknown Minecraftian standing above the entrance on the blocky slope of the pyramid. Steve looked fine—healthy and well-fed—and stood tall in the sun with a stone sword in one hand. The Minecraftian was a man, dressed in black pants, a white shirt, and a leather jacket. He had a weathered complexion as if he spends all of his time outdoors, brown hair and blue eyes, and was wearing a leather helmet with some sort of goggles pushed up over his forehead. A bright red scarf was wrapped around the guy's neck, fluttering and waving in the desert wind. He held a sword with a red-hot, glowing blade...

The zombie next to Alex snarled and she barely dodged its blow. She tried to raise her sword to parry, but she was too tired and missed her chance. She was lucky that *it* had missed as well.

"Steve!" Alex cried. Jack was still laughing and shouting inside the temple. "Thank goodness!"

She backed away from the zombie as Steve and the mysterious stranger jumped down into the sand. As soon as they were on ground, the unknown Minecraftian stabbed Alex's crippled zombie with his glowing blade and the mob *burst into flames!*

"Back off, Alex," Steve said, rushing up with his sword ready. "I'll take care of that husk for you."

"Help *Jack*, not me!" Alex exclaimed. "He's stuck inside the temple, surrounded by zombies! I don't know what's going on in there, but he's still alive!"

Both men ran up to the Alex's opponent, ignoring her words as they flanked it from either side, then cut it to flaming pieces with ease. Every time that strange Minecraftian stabbed or slashed at the husk with his red-hot sword, he set it on fire. A few seconds later, both flaming zombies dropped to the ground, burned up into cinders, then disappeared as bursts of grey smoke. Only rotten flesh and glowing experience orbs remained.

Jack was still laughing and making battle sounds inside.

"You look tired," Steve said with a smirk.

"Help Jack!" Alex repeated. "Come on!"

She set off to the temple entrance again, hurrying as fast as she could, but she was exhausted. Steve and the other Minecraftian easily outpaced her and rushed into the darkness. The red-glowing sword was bright in the dim temple interior, almost like a torch. Alex eyed the stranger again, looking over the way he was dressed. Something about him seemed familiar, like the way that his sword was hot and set enemies on fire, and the way that he was dressed, almost like—

Alex stopped. She gasped.

It was the guy from the Divining Pool! It was—what was his name?—*Liamfrey!*

374

Pausing, hating that she needed to stop, Alex pulled a piece of bread out of her pack and wolfed it down as fast as she could. She had to help Jack, but she couldn't do squat to save him if she couldn't even raise her sword or dodge her enemies.

Feeling an immediate boost of energy, Alex rushed in after Steve and the Minecraftian. Her armor *clanked* as she bumped against the sandstone arch leading inside. Steeling herself mentally for more battle, Alex turned to the right—toward the tunnel where Jack was being swarmed—and she waited for her eyes to adjust to the darkness...

"Holy smokes!" Steve called out from up ahead in the main chamber. "Check out Jack!"

"Well, I'll be!" the Minecraftian exclaimed. "What in tarnation is *that?!*"

Looking down the tunnel, Alex saw nothing. The corridor and the room with stairs beyond it was dark—too dark to see—but she could tell that no one was fighting down there.

Up ahead, in the central chamber, Steve and the Minecraftian were standing—waiting—with their backs turned to her. Ahead of them, in the shaft of sunlight piercing through the hole in the top of the pyramid, Jack was fighting off a half-dozen husk zombies *by himself*. They were all around him. The boy was hard to see, being shorter than them all. Alex saw zombie fists flying and arms bashing in at the boy again and again—they surrounded him—and the sight of it made her feel sick. But, she also saw zombies flying backwards, wounded, as Jack's sword danced and swung and slashed around from the middle of the crazy mobbing. The boy whooped and shouted and laughed as he fought them back, being pummeled from all around.

375

"What's going on?!" Alex cried, running up to Steve's side. "*Help him!* Come on!"

Jack was laughing as if he was playing a game.

Scowling at Steve and the Minecraftian stranger, Alex shoved her way through them to help Jack. She raised her sword, full of fear again.

Steve grabbed Alex's arm from behind, stopping her. Her armor *clanked*.

Alex looked back, furious.

"I think ... I think he's fine!" Steve replied with a quick smirk. "Liamfrey, do you have any idea what's going on there?"

Liamfrey. So it *was* Liamfrey.

"*You're* Liamfrey?!" Alex exclaimed.

The Minecraftian looked at her and gave a curt, dramatic bow. "Yes, ma'am. Pleased to meet you, little lady." Then he looked back at the battle. "I don't rightly *know*, Steve," he said. "I reckon that this strange creature killing all of those husks *cannot be killed!*"

"Jack, are you okay?" Steve shouted.

Another husk fell back away from the pile of flailing zombie limbs and the flashing sword blade. The monster collapsed to the sandstone floor and disappeared in a puff of grey smoke. Jack grunted and laughed.

"Oh, Steve!" Jack shouted from inside the fray. "I'm actually ... getting pretty tired! Can you guys help me out?"

Alex shared glances with Steve and Liamfrey, then they all ran into the lit-up area, surrounding the zombies that surrounded little Jack. Alex started hacking at the backs of the husks, being careful not to hit the boy by mistake. The others did the same.

After several carefully placed shots, she saw when a zombie near Liamfrey burst into flames.

Jack immediately cried out when the fire flared. Alex saw him push his way through the remaining husks to get away from the flames.

"Hot!" Jack exclaimed, panting and gasping for breath. "Duck feathers! Watch it with the fire!"

The kid looked fine, indeed. He wasn't wounded. His stone sword appeared to be in pretty bad shape, but Jack seemed *uninjured*. His skin glistened all over with some kind of fluid; something that Alex didn't understand at all.

When he was safely away from the flaming zombie, Jack turned and charged into the nearest husk, swiping at it with his sword again and again while shouting some kind of *battle cry*. Alex watched the zombie swing its mighty fists down at the kid— she flinched when it hit him—but Jack seemed unmoved. He didn't seem bothered by the blows at all!

What the heck?!

Working together, they all finished off the rest of the husks in the main chamber. At one point, Alex caught sight of Liamfrey doing his 'signature move' from the Divining Pool: spinning around in a circle with his red-hot sword out, cutting through three husks at the same time and setting them all ablaze.

Soon, all of the husk zombies were destroyed.

They all stood in the quiet desert temple. Jack was huffing and puffing for breath.

The kid smiled from ear to ear. He showed his little, curved white teeth. Bending over, he rested his hands on his knees as his entire body swelled and deflated over and over again with his huge, loud breaths.

"That was *awesome!!*" the boy exclaimed. "Did you guys see that?!"

"I saw *something*, kid," Steve said. "Those husks weren't hurting you one bit!"

"I know, right?!" Jack excitedly replied. "What's up with *that?!* I don't understand it! Oh, gosh! Have I been immune to zombies this whole time?? What else am I immune to? I'm *invincible!*"

"Not invincible, son," Liamfrey said, stepping forth. "Not *totally*, I reckon. What manner of creature *are* you? Why, I've been all over this world of Vortexia, and I—"

"In your *airship*, right?" Jack exclaimed, interrupting him with a wide smile. "You must be Liamfrey, is that right? Is that your *Inferno sword?*"

Liamfrey looked surprised at that. He sheathed his sword and crossed his arms over his chest, cocking an eyebrow at Jack.

"I'm afraid you have me at a *disadvantage*, little fellow," the Minecraftian said. "*Yes*, my name is Liamfrey. This is, indeed, my Inferno sword. But who the devil are *you*, and what manner of mob or Minecraftian are ya, and how on Vortexia do you know *me?*"

Alex rushed up to the kid. "Jack! Are you okay? What happened?"

The boy smiled up at her, still huffing and puffing.

"Well, I lost my torch, so ... I ran out here to fight the husks under the light." He pointed up at the sky, which was visible through a bright, single-block opening at the top of the dark temple.

"How are you still *alive?!*" Alex exclaimed.

378

Jack looked at all three of them, shrugged, and produced a shy smile. "I don't really know," he said. "I thought that I was dead meat for sure! But ... when those zombies hit me, they just sort of ... *shoved me*. I don't get it. Maybe it has something to do with the game programming. I mean—I didn't really know what to expect, right? In Minecraft, mobs hurt you just by touching you, but it's not like they actually have teeth and claws, right? What would happen when they touched *me* since I'm real? Would they burn me? *Melt me?* I had no idea! But I guess that since they're programmed to hurt *you*, and you're programmed to get hurt, then if I'm hit, since I'm not part of the program ... and I have a *real body*, then ... *nothing happens...?*"

Everyone stared at Jack for a moment.

Alex didn't have a *clue* about what any of that jibber-jabber meant.

Steve suddenly laughed and turned away.

"What?" Liamfrey exclaimed. "What are you *talkin about*, boy? Programming? *Melting?!* That all doesn't make a lick of sense."

"They just..." Alex said, "*shoved* you?"

Jack looked up and smiled. He took a deep breath, making his entire curved, smooth form swell for a moment in an odd way. "Didn't you see?" he asked. "They were just pushing me around! But, with my sword, I could still hurt *them*." He smiled. "This is great! I don't have to worry about mobs hurting me!"

"I reckon you still have to watch out for certain things," Liamfrey said, staring at Jack with intense curiosity. "You felt that *fire*, didn't you, kiddo?"

Jack stopped smiling.

"Yeah," he said. "I guess I did."

"But ... you're okay?" Alex asked. "I thought ... well, I thought I *lost you* for a moment there."

Jack smiled again. "Nope. I'm alright." He looked up at the leathery Minecraftian. "Thanks for the help, Liamfrey. So, do you have your airship? Is it around here somewhere?"

"No problem at all, little fella," Liamfrey replied with a smirk. "I *do*, yes. What do you know about it? How do you know me?"

Steve called out from near some columns close to one outer pyramid wall. He was looking behind all of them with his sword drawn. "Hey, Alex, is Liamfrey another *Divining Pool* thing?"

"Yes," Alex replied. She looked at Liam. "We knew you'd be coming, Liamfrey. We have an artifact that warns us about ... certain things."

For some reason, she didn't want to outright tell this stranger about everything involving the Divining Pool. What if Liamfrey and his airship didn't *exist* before she and Jack had seen that message? How would he take it? He'd already mentioned *being all over Vortexia*. Liamfrey clearly believed in his own mind that he'd been around for a while.

"An *artifact* you say?" Liam replied, both blue eyes widening. "Well, that's just downright *fascinating*."

"Hey," Steve said, drawing everyone's attention. "Did everyone forget that we're standing in the middle of an *ancient freaking desert temple??*" He grinned, standing in the shaft of light coming down in the middle of the chamber. The floor was decorated with red terracota. Steve was standing on a single blue block in the very center of the entire place. "How about we all talk about this stuff later and get to the treasure? It's *right below us!*"

380

Liamfrey rolled his eyes and turned back to Alex, putting his hands on his hips. "Now, Alex, I hear y'all have a village next to your house out west. Is that so?"

"Alex, can I borrow your pickaxe?" Steve asked, reaching for her.

"Sure," she said, handing it to him then turning back to Liam. "That's right. The desert starts near our house, and there's a desert village there. There's actually a Minecraftian living there, you know ... in the village, I mean."

"Really?" Liamfrey replied, cocking an eyebrow. "Well, I might just have to come with you three back to that village. I lost a lot of important equipment that I require in order to get the *Thunderbird* on her way again. I might have to do some *trading* there."

"Her?" Alex said. "Your ship is a *she?*"

"Now, the thing about desert temples," Jack said to Steve, "is that ... um ... have you been in one of these before, Steve?"

"Oh, I've read about them, kid," he said. "This is the first time I—"

Alex heard him start picking into the sandstone. She turned back to Liamfrey.

"Wait!" Jack shouted. "Don't!"

Alex jumped in surprise at the boy's alarm, looking around, expecting to be on the receiving end of some kind of *trap*. Instead, she saw Steve suddenly *drop through the floor* where he'd been standing on that block of blue terracota!

Steve let out a yelp as he fell through the hole.

Then, he was gone. Alex heard the *smack* of Steve landing somewhere far below. He didn't cry out.

"Steve!!" Alex screamed.

They all ran to the hole and looked inside.

Steve was deep down in a pit below the floor. In fact, the floor under their feet was suspended over a deep and wide shaft going down through the sand. At the bottom, Alex caught a glimpse of four chests. Steve was sprawled in the middle of the sandy floor down in the darkness.

"Steve!" Jack shouted, his eyes wide in fear. "Watch out for the—"

BOOM!!

There was a massive explosion. Alex protected her face as the force of it flew up through the hole, strong enough to make her eyes water. The floor under her feet shook, and the air was filled with dust and smoke.

Liamfrey started coughing. As the smoke cleared, Alex saw that Jack had fallen away from the hole and onto the floor. He was pushing up his glasses then scrambled to his feet and reclaimed his sword.

There was no way that Steve survived that, she thought.

They all stood around the smoking hole, staring in shock for a few moments.

Finally, Liam spoke.

"I reckon that's not good for the treasure," he said.

"Watch out for the *pressure plate*," Jack muttered.

Alex sighed.

Poor Steve...

"I guess we'd better head home to meet him," Alex said.

"You might want to hold off on that thought for just a tick," Liamfrey said, waving one hand at the smoke in their faces. "Take a gander down there in that *hole*."

Alex did. She peered through the dusty, smoky haze, looking for what remained of the trapped treasure room where she knew that Steve would be nothing more than some grey smoke, his stone sword, her iron pick axe, and whatever junk he'd picked up along the way...

Steve's stuff was gone. The treasure room ... was gone.

What *was* down there, past the bottom of the sandstone shaft, was a vast, yawning abyss with a distant reddish-orange glow and the glittering of water far below them. Alex heard the sound of bats squeaking. As she peered more intently into the depths of the world, Alex could just barely make out some sort of structure far down there. She saw what might have been mine cart tracks and ... wooden scaffolding...

"What's the structure down there?" Alex asked.

"I know what that is," Jack said, adjusting his glasses. "That's an *abandoned mine shaft*..."

They were looking into a ravine; a *deep* one. There was a huge ravine directly under the treasure chamber of the desert temple—likely including some easy-to-gather resources and who knows what else down in that mining structure—and Steve's blunder had opened it all *right up* to them...

S1E4 - Chapter 6 – Steve

You Died.

Steve woke in his bed. He had dreams of falling, then there was a *click*, and...

Wait. He *wasn't* dreaming. There was Alex ... and Jack! There was Liamfrey and the Thunderbird, and the desert temple!

"I died?!" he said, sitting up in bed. Steve threw his covers off and leapt to his feet. "Dang it! Nuts! The treasure! Was the treasure blown up?!" He groaned and punched his mattress. "Stupid! Stupid!"

After a minute of calling himself names, he settled down and took a deep breath.

Steve looked at his window. It was dark outside. At least it wasn't *raining* again.

How did he screw that up?! He'd read all about desert temples back in that one library. He knew that he had to dig where the floor was blue! That's what everybody said! Also, that was the only treasure in the whole place! Did he blow it up?! *Terrible*...

Steve sighed.

He looked around his room.

Several empty armor stands looked back at him. He approached one of his chests, opened it with a *creak*, and looked for something that would help him get back and find his friends again, but it was all just junk. The other chests were the same.

Eventually, Steve opened the door of his room and stepped out into the quiet hall. He looked across at the storage room. That'd be his next stop.

"So Liam came from the *Divining Pool?*" he said to himself. "Figures..."

Steve looked down the hall at the door to Alex's bedroom, then, he approached the Divining Pool room, reached down, and turned the handle.

That 'artifact' (as Alex called it) was really starting to creep him out. Jack came from it. That dragon and Wither came from it. That weird ninja-girl, Alice, came from it. Now, Liam had come from it, too? Oh—and there was some forest guy that Alex had mentioned. What was his name? *Braydon?*

Steve stepped into the spruce-walled room, staring at the bedrock fountain with disdain.

What weird thing would show up next?

"Well, that's also where *KittyPaws30* came from," Steve muttered, considering the blue water with a shrug. She was his friend. For good or for bad, one thing was for sure: that Divining Pool was definitely filling his and Alex's lives with *adventure*, and before Jack had arrived, Steve was *dying* for some adventure. He sure was tired of farming.

Steve approached the pool. He didn't know what to expect. It would probably just be blue water. The pool hardly ever spoke to *him*.

He looked deep into the water for a moment then sighed. He really needed to get some gear together and get back to the desert. He needed a *sword*.

Then, Steve saw something white glimmering deep down in the calm, blue pool...

"What...?"

A moment later, he saw words.

Smiling, feeling a surge of excitement inside, Steve stared at the pool, trying to read the words as they drifted slowly to the surface...

They came into view:

"*It would be amazing if you could add me! I am a Minecraftian called HelloDance4436 that just moved into the village and has some really cool stuff to trade.*"

Steve read the message, read it again, then repeated the words aloud.

HelloDance4436? he thought.

Disappointed that it couldn't be another mighty warrior to help Steve again, or another airship—what if there were *two??*—he turned away from the Divining Pool when the words dissolved on the surface.

"Well," Steve said to himself, "a cool trader *could* be useful."

Nice, new gear was always a good thing, but it seemed that Steve never held onto anything for long. Plus, he never really traded, because he never had enough resources that he could trade *with* most of the time. Still, he recalled Liamfrey saying something about needing to do some trading just before he—

Steve suddenly gasped. Something else came back to him.

Alex's *pick axe!*

"Dang it!" he exclaimed, thumping the wall with one fist. The wood broke slightly in the middle then rapidly regenerated itself. "I lost her *iron pick axe!*"

Steve was suddenly flushed with embarrassment and a little bit of shame. That was *her* iron pick axe. She'd told him that they were low on iron, and now he went and lost her pick axe.

"That's okay," he said. "I can make another one."

Rushing to the chests in the main room, Steve began searching for iron. He found tons of coal and a little charcoal, but no metal ingots; not even metal *ore*. They had no iron. They didn't even have any gold. What in the world had happened to all of their iron, anyway?! He searched the dump chests on either side of the front door—both empty—then ran through the archway into the storage room and went scouring *chest to chest*. He needed some iron ingots to make things right to Alex; to make her a new pick axe. There *had* to be iron around here, somewhere!

After searching each and every chest—man, they were really low on building and crafting supplies!—Steve leaned up against the crafting table there to think.

He'd checked everywhere except for the kitchen ... and Alex's room.

He wouldn't check Alex's room. *Nope*. He'd already decided to never invade her privacy there.

"Are we *really* out of iron?" he said to himself.

Come to think of it, Steve didn't find any *sticks*, either. He didn't even see any wood! The only thing close to wood was a chest full of saplings for planting.

Well, if he was going to head out into the desert, he'd at least have to make a sword. Alex and Jack were probably still back at the temple, and it was nighttime! They had to be dealing with invading mobs left and right! It was a good thing that Liamfrey was there with them, and could help protect them, but still...

He couldn't make a sword. There were no sticks.

Wandering back into the main room, Steve looked out of the front window.

He could probably run out into the night, collect some wood, then run back, right? He'd done it before. That wasn't too hard, was it?

"Piece of cake!" he exclaimed aloud, smiling and setting his sights on a particular tree. "I can do this, no problem!"

Steve watched outside for a few minutes to make sure that there were no zombies around at all. He listened for their heavy, plodding feet but heard nothing. At one point, he thought that he *might* have heard some quiet footsteps, but when they stopped, Steve figured that he was just hearing things.

With a shrug, Steve approached the front door, intending to quickly sprint out there, punch that tree until he had three blocks of wood, then run home again.

He opened the front door with a *pop*.

A creeper was standing there, right in front of him...

It looked at him.

He looked at it.

Steve gasped and felt his heart jump up into his throat! He immediately went to close the door again as the creeper began to sputter and *hiss*, pushing its way inside. Its weird, green body crackled and pulsed as if building up with gasses under its skin. It flashed white.

"Dang it! *Get out!!*"

He couldn't close the door. The creeper was in the way! Steve ran forward and pushed on the thing, immediately feeling the bubbling reaction under its crinkly skin with his hands. The mob frowned at him and hissed as Steve frantically tried to push it back outside again so that he could close the door...

Hisssssssssssssss ... *BOOM!!*

There was a tremendous explosion. Steve was thrown sideways, immediately losing track of which way was which. He heard pieces of the house, wall, chests, windows, roof, and floor clattering all over as his vision faded to black.

You died.

"Again?!" Steve shouted, sitting up in his bed. "Dang it!"

He looked outside.

It was still nighttime.

He needed to get to his friends!

"Stupid creeper!"

Jumping out of his bed, Steve checked the several chests in his room for anything that could help him get back to his friends through the desert. He *had* to have a sword or some iron ingots around here somewhere. Maybe he could at least find a *stick* so that he could make another stone sword...?

Oh yeah, he thought, then stopped. No iron. No wood.

Steve closed the chest with a *creak* and frowned.

Opening his bedroom door, he suddenly remembered the creeper blowing up the front of the house. *That* was unfortunate. But, it also meant that he'd have to be careful not to run into any zombies or anything *inside* the house. Gosh—Alex was going to be so mad at him!

The hallway was clear. Steve closed his bedroom door and crept toward the front room.

When he reached the end of the hall, he saw that the creeper's explosion had destroyed a good-sized piece of the front wall, both windows, both dump chests, and parts of the wooden floor and ceiling. There was nothing floating on the floor. The pieces were all gone.

"Dang," Steve muttered. "I could have used the wood..."

Scanning for mobs and seeing none for the moment, Steve quickly crossed the damaged room and turned into the kitchen and farm door area. Experiencing a quick moment of clarity, he stopped into the kitchen, opened a chest, and took three pieces of roasted chicken, stashing them into his pack. He'd need that for the desert.

"Look at you!" he said to himself. "Thinking ahead! Alex would be proud..."

Then, popping a torch off of the hallway's wall to take with him, Steve opened the spruce back door of the house and stepped out onto the farm.

The wheat was getting pretty tall. Soon, it would be time to harvest. The moon was high overhead and a cool breeze blew through the valley from north to south, making all of their crops wave and whisper. The animals stamped and stood around in their pens. One cow *mooed*.

Steve could hear the plodding of zombie feet nearby, but he didn't see any mobs. He was empty handed. The night was dark, but the moon was bright. He'd have to avoid fighting anything until he could find some sort of weapon. At that point, he needed to make it to the desert. Once he stepped into the open wasteland of endless dunes, he would be able to see enemies coming from far away. He'd have to constantly run away from them, sure, but he'd *see* them; not like standing like this in the farm or surrounded by the trees all over the big ridge.

As if answering his thoughts, a zombie suddenly appeared from behind a tree at the edge of the crop fields. It stared around dumbly, dressed in blue, with green skin and dull, dark eyes. Lit up by the many torches of the homestead, the undead creature started plodding his way...

"Great..." Steve said. "Time to start running."

Then, he saw that the zombie was holding a bright and shining *iron shovel* in one hand.

A weapon.

Steve took several steps away from the house. He limbered up his muscles and clenched his fists, preparing for a duel. He stashed the torch he'd been carrying from the house into his pack and raised both fists before him...

The zombie reached for him with its green claws and let out a long, low snarl. It walked forward slowly, grasping at the air and extending both arms, groaning as its heavy feet plodded through the wheat rows.

When the mob was close enough, Steve punched it once in the face then danced backwards, light on his feet.

The zombie moaned in either pain or annoyance—Steve wasn't sure which—then kept coming.

As the undead mob closed with him again, Steve was ready. He punched twice—*one, two*—hitting it in the face with a jab then again with a powerful right cross!

The zombie staggered then snarled and came after him as Steve darted out of the way again.

"Ha!" Steve shouted. "Take that!"

Then, he danced back into range and punched the thing *three* times. One, two, three to the face! When the zombie swung back at him, Steve barely dodged out of the way.

"Urrrgh!" the zombie exclaimed, carrying around its shovel as if it didn't know what to do with it. It tried to hit Steve with its available fist again but failed. Steve dodged with ease.

"I'm too fast for you!" Steve exclaimed with a grin, dancing on his feet. He darted in to hit the zombie *four* times. Jab with the left, *cross* with the right! Jab with the—

The zombie suddenly *smashed* Steve in the chest, knocking him to the ground. The Minecraftian warrior rolled through two plots of wheat then scrambled back to his feet.

With a low gurgle, the zombie continued toward him.

"Okay," Steve said, shaking his head. "Maybe not *too* fast."

More cautious now, Steve made sure to dart in and out of the zombie's range whenever he was ready to strike. Two punches at a time, he wore the zombie down and down, careful to get out of its reach before it could counterattack.

Finally, after one last powerful *one-two* combo, Steve punched the zombie so hard that it collapsed backwards into the wheat, dead. It disappeared in a puff of grey smoke, leaving behind rotten flesh, a brand new iron shovel, and an experience orb that quickly rolled toward Steve and absorbed into his foot with a *tinkling* sound.

Steve left the rotten flesh on the ground this time. He took the iron shovel.

Seeing motion on his left on the other side of the animals, Steve looked up and scanned the woods. He expected to see another zombie coming, but instead saw a shadowy black form blending into the darkness of the trees beyond the torchlight...

Could it be...?

"Alice?" Steve called.

He squinted against the glare of the torches, but whatever he was looking at was gone.

Steve shrugged. He must have been seeing things. There were definitely hostile mobs in those woods. He looked back at the house and saw that he'd left the back door open. For a moment, Steve thought about going back to close it, but then he remembered that there was a huge, gaping hole in the front wall. Closing that door wouldn't make any difference.

Armed with a shovel and pulling out his torch again, Steve ran across the farm, leapt over the creek, and started up the big ridge. He ran like the wind, staying away from the sounds of nearby mobs. He stayed extra far away whenever he heard the *clunk* of bones.

On the other side of the ridge—looking down at the torch-lit streets of the village up ahead to the east—Steve paused to gather some wood. He punched several pieces of oak out of a tree in the dark, collected them, then ran on.

For a moment, Steve was tempted to spend the night in the village. There was that new trader there, HelloDance4436, after all. Was he or she there *now*? Moved into town already? He really wanted to know.

Better not, Steve thought, shaking his head.

Jack and Alex were out there in the desert, probably trying to defend themselves all night long against husks and other mobs, holed up in the desert temple and waiting for him. He needed to hurry on.

There'd be time to find HelloDance4436 later. Maybe he'd introduce Liamfrey to the new trader. Steve hoped that Alex was doing okay. He thought back to that bizarre battle between Jack the kid and those husk zombies. The boy had fought like he was invincible. How on Vortexia was that possible?!

There were many questions, but the answers waited ahead in the endless dunes...

Steve ran to the desert. He ran east with a shovel in one hand, a torch in the other, and he hoped for the best.

He had to catch up to his friends...

Season 1, Episode 5:
The Quest for Iron

The Quest for Iron

Once again, Jack and Alex are separated from Steve, but they're not alone! A mysterious Minecraftian brought to life by the Divining Pool, Liamfrey the airship pilot, is with them in the desert temple. And as Steve struggles to catch up to his friends, Jack the kid, Alex, and Liamfrey all delve into the massive ravine under the temple's blown-up treasure chamber in search of iron, redstone, and maybe even some treasure!

But, as they explore deeper and deeper into the dangerous ravine, constantly striving to reach the precious resources at the bottom, will our heroes be able to survive the many mobs stalking the darkness? Can Jack's strange new-found immunity to zombie attacks save the group from skeletons, creepers, spiders, and other hostile mobs?

S1E5 - Chapter 1 – Jack

Steve was dead. He was dead *again*.

Jack stood at the edge of the hole that his warrior friend had cut through the floor of the desert temple. The Minecraftian had wanted to find the treasure, but he *didn't listen*.

He went down through the blue block.

Never go through the blue block, Jack thought.

Steve fell right smack into the middle of the treasure chamber down below, then *KABOOM!!*

Now, Jack stared through the dense, pixelated smoke. He couldn't see Steve's *Damage Indicator* bar. The guy *had* to be dead. He was unarmored. There was no way that he could have survived that explosion.

Jack was still on his hands and knees. The TNT had shaken the floor when it went off.

Pushing his glasses up his sweaty nose, the boy looked around the sandstone floor until he found his stone sword. He picked it up, sighed, and crawled back to the edge of the hole where Alex and Liamfrey were both peering down through the smoke.

The airship pilot cleared his throat. He looked like some kind of World War II pilot and talked like a cowboy.

"I reckon that's not good for the treasure," Liam said, obviously referring to the explosion.

Jack felt like laughing, but he was more annoyed than anything.

"Watch out for the *pressure plate*," he muttered to himself. That's what the boy was *going to say* before Steve went ahead and cut through the floor faster than Jack could react.

Jeez.

Dang.

Alex straightened up and put her hands on her armored hips. The iron armor all over her body was really starting to show a lot of wear and tear, but according to her Damage Indicator, she was at full health.

"I guess we'd better head home to meet him," she said with a sigh of her own.

Liamfrey smirked and waved his blocky, gloved hand through the thick, grey smoke rising up from the hole. "You might want to hold off on that thought for just a tick," he said. "Take a gander down there in that *hole*."

Alex drew in close to the hole and looked down. Jack scrambled to them and looked over the edge as well, holding his glasses to his face so that they didn't slip off of his nose and disappear into the smoky pit.

He immediately saw an orange glow pushing up through the smoke.

It didn't take long for Jack to realize that the treasure room was completely *gone*. Amazingly, it looked like this desert temple was built on top of a huge, underground ravine! The floor of the treasure room had been hanging out into the open space of the ravine's ceiling. Now, with the bottom blown out, Jack was looking down a smoky, sandstone shaft that opened up to a massive *void* in the world. He saw the glow of lava falls far below; the glittering of the fiery magma reflected on blue water and waterfalls, too. Ravines often had waterfalls and lava falls near the bottom. The boy didn't really see any bedrock. Heck—it would be really hard to identify bedrock anyway from this far up. Jack knew from experience that the bottom of naturally-spawned ravines were usually *above* the bedrock; at least by several layers. It was deep enough to *maybe* find a diamond or two in the chasm's floor, but likely not. They'd have to go even deeper for bedrock and diamonds...

That wasn't the only interesting thing that he could see, though. It was amazing enough that there was a huge ravine under the desert temple, but, deep down in the lower levels of the abyss was something even *more* unlikely.

Jack saw the shadows of wooden poles and rail tracks and cobwebs. He saw the outer edges—sticking out of the ravine's wall here and there into the open space—of a freaking *abandoned mine shaft!*

What were the odds?! A ravine directly under a temple's treasure room ... with an abandoned mine shaft in it??

Opening his mouth to express shock and delight, Jack was interrupted by Alex.

"What's that structure down there?" she asked.

Jack looked up at her, adjusted his glasses, then peered down into the gloom again.

"I know what that is," he said. "That's an abandoned mine shaft."

"What ... what in the heck is that?!" Alex replied, narrowing her green eyes and staring deep into the hole. "Holy cow—is that *lava?*"

"Lava that is, indeed," Liamfrey said with a smirk. "Now, this is just downright *fascinating*. I don't know how much you two know about mining, but where there's lava, there's—"

"Diamonds?" Alex offered, smiling at the two of them.

"Well, *yes*, little lady," Liam replied. "I reckon it's likely that we can find diamonds down in the deepest part of the ravine. Heck—we can probably find a tunnel or two going even deeper and find a few diamonds there. *However*," he said dramatically, "what I really need to keep my *Thunderbird* flyin up in the air instead of dilly-dallying down on the sand ... is *redstone*."

That caught Jack's attention. He remembered the message in the Divining Pool mentioning that Liamfrey's airship would be powered by redstone, fire, and propellers. *It has a bombing hatch*, the message had said.

Jack found himself *desperate* to see the ship.

He *had* to see this 'Thunderbird' for himself. He'd never seen an 'airship' mod before, and had no freaking idea how this was even happening. If he was, indeed, stuck in his own Vortexia—the world he'd spawned on his Game Pendant—then there was no way that this could be possible, unless these mods were (he scoffed) *installing themselves*...

Jack frowned.

What if they were??

Liam was still talking.

"...and when Steve found me before we came to rescue you two, I was in a mine of my own making, *gathering* redstone. But, you know, that's a slow going process. I reckon that if there's redstone in the walls of that ravine down there, then I can gather a good bit of fuel for my ship *real fast*."

"Okay," Alex replied with a sigh. "We should really try to meet up with Steve again. There's bound to be a lot of hostile mobs down there. He's a really great fighter..."

"Worry not, little lady," Liamfrey said with another smirk. "I'm a pretty darned good fighter myself. Plus, little Jack here can deal with the zombies, *can't ya, Jack?*"

Jack looked up at the two of them. He clenched his fist around the strange, blocky handle of his stone sword.

Oh yeah. The zombies.

He was invincible!!

That made Jack smile. He smiled bigger than he thought possible. Not only was he in this game in his real life body, but he was in some kind of *God Mode?* Jack didn't understand it, but he had an idea that maybe he wasn't part of the game's *code*. It's not like the zombies had any weapons that could break his bones or cut him, right? They just *touched* players to cause damage. And here, in the temple, Jack had been *touched* by all of those scary husks ... and that's all they did—*touched* him! The zombies might have pushed him around a little, sure, but they didn't hurt him. Jack could hurt *them* with his Minecraft stone sword, but they couldn't hurt him back! He wasn't a Minecraftian. He wasn't *programmed* to take damage when an enemy touched him. Jack smiled so wide that his cheeks hurt.

"I can!" he exclaimed. "I'll fight *all* of the zombies! They're no problem anymore!"

Alex made an uncertain face. She winced.

"I dunno, kid," she said. "Maybe you got *lucky*. How can you really know if—?"

"I know it!" Jack replied. "Those zombies were bashing me repeatedly and they didn't hurt me at all! I think it's with the programming of the ... um..." He wanted to tell them about game programming, but he didn't want to freak out either of them. Alex and Liam were part of the program, after all. "Just don't worry.

I'm sure I'll be fine. Now," he said, looking over the hole. "I know where we can cut down and follow along the walls down there." Jack scoffed, shaking his head. "You *never* just go down from the blue block. There's *always* a pressure plate trap down there."

"You've seen these before?" Liamfrey asked.

"Yep," Jack replied. "Dozens of 'em. I've also seen loads of ravines and plenty of abandoned mine shafts. I know *exactly* what's down there." *Unless there's some weird new mob or something strange spawned from the Divining Pool that we don't know about*, he thought. "Let's cut through the floor *here*," he said, pointing at the ideal spot on the temple floor, "and start making stairs going down out of cobblestone or whatever. Then, once we reach the top of the ravine, we need to carefully get to the wall across the ceiling until we find a ledge."

"Alright, partner," Liamfrey said, looking at the block he'd pointed out and drawing an iron pick axe. "You sound like you know what you're talkin about. Follow me."

"We should explore that mine shaft, too," Jack said. He wondered what cob webs would feel like. "We can get some good loot from chests in there."

"Not yet," Alex replied. Liam and Jack both looked at her. "We need to meet up with Steve again. This temple's not far from home, right? Let's get some redstone, and hopefully some iron, and head back up. We can explore the mine later."

That made sense. Jack didn't argue, even though he *really* wanted to see what the abandoned mine shaft was like in person. What would riding fast in a mine cart be like...?

They dug down exactly as Jack had suggested. With Liam in the lead, the trio made their way down along the shaft wall, plunking down block after block of cobblestone (Alex had plenty), until breaking out into the very top of the ravine.

Bats squeaked and fluttered around. Whenever they came close enough, Jack saw their Damage Indicator bars appear over their tiny heads:

Bat 6/6.

With the agility that only a Minecraftian could pull off, Liamfrey managed to hang out into the dark space so far that Jack was sure that he'd fall, but instead, the airship pilot somehow connected a handful of blocks to the nearest ravine wall and built a narrow walkway to where they had to drop down.

Liam went first. Jack followed. Once the boy touched down onto the one-block-wide cobblestone catwalk, he felt an immediate dizziness sweep over him. His legs suddenly felt like jelly. Looking down, Jack let out a long groan and lowered himself to his hands and knees.

He accidentally dropped his torch. It fell over the edge and disappeared into the darkness.

Jack let out a little yelp. He couldn't help it.

For a long time now, he'd been holding his stone sword in one hand and a torch in the other.

Now he had no light.

Duck feathers—he was high up! Jack realized that he was on a very small bridge over what seemed like hundreds of feet of empty darkness. At the bottom of the ravine was a solid stone floor broken up by pools of water and lava flowing from falls and mingling with a constant *hissing* sound.

"Are you okay, Jack?" Alex asked, stepping down onto the platform behind him. Her armor *clanked*. She seemed unafraid.

"Yes, I'm..." He paused. His voice was shaking. Jack was certain that if he slipped and fell, he'd go *splat* down at the bottom of the ravine in a very real way, even *if* the blocks were bouncy like everything but bedrock. He tried to sound brave, but his voice was so small. "I'm okay. We're just ... really, *really* high."

"Just follow me to the wall, little fella," Liamfrey said.

Jack looked up and obeyed, crawling along the bridge until he found himself behind the pilot again. Liam had stopped at the ravine wall and was carving out a space for them to step into.

Once there was a big enough ledge cut out of the raw stone, Jack crawled into it and took several deep breaths. He felt better already. He could *feel* the solid stone below him, above him, and to the one side. Back when he was on the one-block-wide bridge, he felt nothing but open air all around him. Alex followed.

When Liam had carved out enough space, Alex suddenly produced a crafting table from her inventory, plunking it down. She also put a single torch on the wall, which really lit up the darkness around them. Jack stared at the pixelated smoke constantly rising from the little fire. He listened to the bats.

Maybe this wouldn't be as easy as he thought...

"Jack," she said. "I'm going to make you a stone pick axe. I've got to make myself another one, too." She sighed. "Steve lost my iron pick axe in that explosion."

Jack looked at his stone sword. What would he do with it? He didn't have an inventory. He could hold his sword in one hand and a pick axe in the other, but then he wouldn't be able to carry a torch...

The boy suddenly recalled all of the times playing with toy guns and foam weapons with his little brother when he was younger. He used to stuff all sorts of weapons down the back of his shirt as if his collar was a great, big scabbard.

Jack tried to do the same thing now. He was wearing his black 'gamer' shirt. It was a little big, and the collar had some room in the back. Carefully slipping his stone sword in behind his neck, he lowered it against the skin of his back until its cross-guard became caught on the top of his shirt. He moved around to test it. It was a little uncomfortable and made it harder to turn his head, but it would work for now. Just like when he used to carry toy weapons in the back of his shirt, Jack stood, carrying his sword in his collar on his back. He reached up and found that he could grab the blocky handle to draw if from his shirt too, but it would take a little while to draw that blocky blade free of his collar.

"Okay," Jack said. "I'll try to help."

His voice echoed over the edge out into the darkness.

When Alex handed him a brand new stone pick axe, he took it. Jack wondered whether or not he'd be able to use it with one hand like *they* did. He needed to, if he was also going to hold a torch.

"Thanks," he said. "Can I also have another torch? I dropped mine."

"Sure," Alex replied with a smile. "Her damaged armor reflected the firelight of the one torch on their ledge.

Thunk, thunk, pop. Thunk, thunk, pop. Thunk, thunk, pop.

Jack looked at Liamfrey and watched as the Minecraftian quickly carved his way through the stone, making a stairwell out of the ravine wall, heading down. He was making their path two blocks wide, cut right into the rock.

They all followed the stairs down. Jack stayed as far away from the edge as he could.

When Liam suddenly stopped, Jack almost ran into him. He looked up.

"Found a ledge," Liamfrey said, looking back with a smile. "Y'all ready for some *exploring?*"

Jack tried to remember that he was immune to zombies. Heck—he was probably immune to every mob here. Still, he was pretty scared of falling.

"Let's do it," the boy said, trying to keep his voice from shaking.

It was no big deal, right? They'd follow the ledge until they found a tunnel or something to take them farther down. If there was no tunnel, they could keep digging into the wall, going farther and farther down, all the way to the bottom if necessary.

Jack realized that he was thirsty. He'd have to take a big drink from one of those waterfalls. He knew that he could stop and ask Alex to do the thing with the bucket of water, but he didn't want to slow everyone down.

They all stepped out onto the ledge. It was a natural rocky walkway, following around the ravine wall on just the one side. Jack could see across the ravine, and the other wall was blank and sheer. He'd seen a million ledges like these. If they kept—

There was a dark green face up ahead on the ledge that they were standing on. It was a broad, pixelated block of green with deep, sad black eyes and a wide, gaping frown.

The creeper started heading their way from the darkness. Jack could hear its light steps on the stone.

Liamfrey had his back turned. He hadn't noticed.

"Creeper!" Jack exclaimed, feeling a sudden *surge* of emotion to protect his friends. Holding his pick axe before him, he rushed past Liam, ignoring the cliff for the moment, and stood in between them and the incoming mob.

"Oh, Jack, watch out!" Alex cried. He could hear the fear in her voice.

The sudden yellowish-red glow coming from behind him told Jack that Liamfrey had pulled his burning sword. As the creeper approached, staring at Jack with empty, black eyes, Jack stood tall, expecting fully that the mob could do him *no harm*.

He waited, holding his pick axe like a baseball bat. When the thing came close, he'd try to bat it off of the edge. If it blew up ... oh well. They'd just have to repair the ledge and keep going.

"Get back, in case it blows up!" Jack exclaimed, winding up for a heavy strike...

The creeper approached with a steady quickness on its stubby, blocky legs. The instant its Damage Indicator bar appeared over its head—*Creeper 20/20*—it also started *hissing*. It sputtered like something wet on fire. The mob's body started glowing here and there as its crackly, green skin began to stretch and shake...

Jack felt something *wrong*.

He suddenly *knew* that he'd made a mistake. Maybe it was the way that the creeper created a charge in the air that made all of Jack's hairs stand straight up. He felt the tiny hairs on his arms moving. Jack's blood was suddenly full of *fear*, cold and wild and heavy, coursing through his body and making his elbows and knees buzz. He felt terror.

Something's wrong, he thought again.

But he was invincible!

The creeper continued. It would be in his face in the next moment.

But something's not right...

This was a terrible mistake. Jack's ideas of invincibility suddenly flew straight out of his head and he was *completely* overtaken with naked fear. He'd screwed up. The creeper was coming, bubbling and popping and hissing, and it was going to *kill him*. Jack thought of his mom and dad. He thought of his brother, Dexter. Images of his bedroom came to mind. He thought of his friends from school. He didn't have many friends, but *some* kids liked him. He would never see any of them again. He'd never see his *family* again...

This was the end.

Then, much to Jack's surprise, Liamfrey zipped past him with amazing speed. As the creeper's skin-prickling *hiss* reached its peak and the mob seemed ready to burst with unspeakable violence, Liam's fiery sword slashed through the air. The red-hot blade hit the creeper where its shoulder might have been if it had any arms, and the creature let out a surprised, hissing sound as it was knocked off of the ledge, out into the ravine! The instant the mob was over the edge, there was a tremendous *BOOM!!*

The force sent Jack flying toward the carved wall of the ledge. Liamfrey was thrown as well. There was a feeling in the wind that hit Jack in the face so hard that he didn't understand it: like someone smacking his entire body with a gigantic fly swatter and flicking him through the air.

When Jack landed—crashing against the stone wall—he dropped his pick axe and fell to the ground. Thankfully, the stone wall and floor were both slightly spongy to the touch, and he didn't break anything in the impact.

But that *force*—that concussive force—was nothing to sneeze at.

Jack sprawled out, his ears ringing, dizzy, and tried to figure out which way was up. A moment later, he felt Alex's blocky hands grabbing his shoulders and pulling him to his feet. Jack's head was spinning. His hearing was weird.

Then, the world came back to him as if he'd popped up from underwater in a swimming pool.

"—okay?!" Alex was screaming. "Jack! Jack! Are you okay?! Say something! *Jack!*"

He coughed.

"Oops," he spat.

Alex paused, staring at the boy with wide, green eyes. Then she laughed.

"*Oops?!*" she replied loudly. "You almost blew up! Are you alright?"

Finding his feet under him, Jack stood and steadied himself against the wall. He looked for Liam and saw the airship pilot climbing to his feet as well, still holding his flaming sword.

"I'm ... I'm okay, yeah," Jack muttered, wincing at a sudden pain in his head. It was like a terrible headache. "What the heck *was* that?!"

Liamfrey laughed. "Hey, I'm okay too, just in case y'all are wonderin." He sheathed his sword, straightened up, and pulled out his pick axe again. Jack saw that the ledge was, indeed, partly destroyed. They'd have to fix it before going on. "*That*, little boy, was a *creeper*. It nearly killed you."

Jack stared at the blown-up ledge.

But ... he was *invincible* ... wasn't he?

This didn't make since. How could zombies not be able to hurt him, but a *creeper* could?

411

Because, Jack thought. *Creepers don't hurt by touching you. They blow up, and it's the explosion that hurts you...*

"I know what creepers are," he said. "But ... *blown up*..." Jack trailed off into mumbling then looked back to Liam, who watched him with a cocked eyebrow. "Thanks, Liamfrey. Thanks for saving me. That was stupid of me."

"Indeed," the pilot replied then smiled broadly. "Don't tempt the fates, kid. Now," he patted a lot of rock dust off of him. "I reckon that we should head on."

Jack smiled up at Alex, who was still staring down at him with concern.

"Yep. Moving on," he said.

She cleared the worried look off of her face. "Moving on," she echoed.

Jack picked up his dropped pick axe. They repaired the big crater in the ledge then continued.

The ledge eventually hit a dead end. When it did, Liamfrey continued digging down, making a ledge of their own leading deeper. After a while, they found *another* ledge and continued along it, farther down into the black depths of Vortexia. They passed a blazing lava fall. Jack could definitely feel its heat on the skin of his face and arms. Twice, they saw zombies walking around on cliffs on the other side of the ravine, but with no way to cross, the undead mobs couldn't reach them. They only reached helplessly for them, groaning and growling and staying put.

After a while, Jack started to hear the repeated *hissing* of spiders; *lots* of spiders.

When they continued past the loudest spider sounds—once Jack could still hear the many angry hisses move to appear behind them—he stopped.

"Let's go back this way a little," Jack suggested. Liam and Alex shrugged and humored him.

Jack found a place on the ledge where he could hear many spiders somewhere in the ravine wall pretty close to them. If they were to keep going, the sounds moved away. If they went backwards, the sounds moved to be in front of them again.

There was a *spider spawner dungeon* through that wall. Jack was sure of it...

"Liam?" he said.

"Yeah?"

"Let's cut into this wall here. Just go block by block."

The Minecraftian cocked his eyebrow, considering it, then shrugged and began carving a tunnel toward the spider sounds.

"What? *Why?!*" Alex exclaimed. "Why are we going *toward* the spiders?!"

"Don't worry," Jack said, unable to keep from smiling. "Trust me. I know the ways of this world backwards and forwards, remember?"

They followed Liam's narrow tunnel deeper into the ravine wall, ever moving *toward* the frightening sounds of spiders. Before long, Alex looked openly terrified,--her green eyes wide— as she peered at the stone all around them. Eventually, it sounded like the spiders were *literally* all around them.

For just a moment, Jack felt a little uncertain. He wondered whether or not he was immune to spiders bites. The attack of a spider *had* to be just like the attack of a zombie, didn't it? They had fangs, but weren't those fangs harmless blocky things? They probably couldn't hurt Jack at all...

What about poison? he wondered with a chill. What if they were venomous?

"They can't bite me," he muttered to himself, pulling his sword out of the back collar of his shirt. He slid the handle of his pick axe into its place.

"What?" Alex exclaimed a little too loud. "*Why* are we going to fight spiders?! I thought we were going to find *redstone!*"

"Don't worry, Alex," Jack repeated. "I have a strong feeling about what we're about to find, and we'll be seeing it any second..."

As if on cue, Liam's careful picking stopped.

Thunk, thunk, pop. Thunk, thunk, pop. Thunk—

"Hey there, Jack," he said. "Take a gander at *this*."

Moving around Liam—it was a tight corridor—Jack looked at where the Minecraftian had stopped his work.

There, revealed through the hole That Liamfrey had just dug, Jack saw a block of cobblestone covered in *green moss*...

S1E5 - Chapter 2 – Alex

This is crazy, Alex thought.

This is crazy.

This is crazy!

Liamfrey and Jack the kid stood before her, examining a strange block of cobblestone covered in old, green moss. All Alex could think about were the bazillion *spiders* on the other side of that wall! It sounded like they were all around them!

Looking back, Alex peered through the darkness back into the ravine. Their ledge there was precarious at best. This was nuts. More mobs—another creeper maybe—could be coming around that corner from the ledge at any moment. They'd be stuck in this tiny tunnel trying to ... get to a bazillion spiders for some reason?!

Spiders weren't all that useful. Sure, they dropped silk, but it took a *lot* of silk to make rope, and their beds, bows, and fishing rods were all *fine*.

She wished that Steve was here.

Steve always protected her. He was a great fighter. And now, Alex was deep down in the world, exploring a hostile, dark ravine with Jack and another Minecraftian who she didn't even know.

Still ... Jack seemed pretty excited about that abandoned mine shaft down there, and they'd definitely be able to find some *iron*. He looked at the mine greedily, even though they'd agreed to stay out of it for now.

What they *really* needed was more iron...

Looking down at her armor, Alex groaned. She'd had that armor for a long time, and in just the last week, she'd been in so many fights that it was bashed up to heck. It wouldn't hold out much longer. If they could find a good bit more iron, she'd be able to repair it at the anvil when they returned home.

The hissing of the spiders was loud and frightening. One *hissed* violently right over Alex's head, which made her gasp and look up.

There was only a low, stone ceiling. The thing must be in the dang *walls*.

She heard the intense drumming of many legs on the rock. The spiders *had* to know that she, Jack, and Liam were down there. They were trying to get to them—through the natural stone—and it seemed that they were *all around*; even below her feet.

Jack and Liam were talking. Alex hadn't been paying attention. All she could focus on was the loud noise of the eight-legged mobs.

"Why, *yes*," Liamfrey said with his odd, drawling voice. "I *have* laid eyes on dungeons before, Jack, but I do not recognize your term ... *mob spawner*."

"Okay," Jack replied, pushing up his glasses and tapping on the mossy cobblestone block with his torch. "*This* is the outer wall of a dungeon. You both have seen dungeons before, right? Alex? Have you seen a dungeon before?"

She stared down at the otherworldly creature with the round, smooth features. The boy smiled up at her.

There was a time when she and Steve had gone deep into a cave next to their old house, back on the prairie. Steve was always crazy-interested in exploring dark places. Well, back then, after following tunnel after winding tunnel deeper and deeper into the dark, they found a place chock *full* of skeleton archers. It didn't make sense how they kept coming. Steve happened to have armor and a shield at the time—he would end up losing that armor later when he carelessly fell into lava—so was able to fight them off pretty well while Alex put up some torches so that they could *see*. Eventually, the skeletons stopped coming and they looted a couple of old, dusty wooden chests. She *did* remember the walls of that place being made of the same moss-covered cobblestone...

"Um ... yeah," she replied. "I think I have. I think it was a 'dungeon' as you put it, Jack."

"I reckon that I've come across a good *dozen* of em underground at times," Liamfrey added. "I agree with ya, boy. This looks and sounds like a dungeon. Now, what's this ya say about a *mob spawner?*"

"Well," Jack said, "Every dungeon—there are *tons* of em all over underground—is the same like this: they have walls like this, they're dark, they each have a mob spawner, and they each have one or two chests full of loot."

"What's a mob spawner?" Alex asked.

Jack laughed. "That's what I'm trying to tell you! In the middle of the dungeon, there's gonna be a black cage with a little flame inside. This one is obviously a *spider* spawner." The spiders all around them—their legs drumming on the stone—seemed to answer the point with several vicious *hisses*. "There's gonna be a tiny spider inside the cage. All of *these* spiders...?" the boy gestured to the terrifying sounds all around them. "They're coming from that cage; the spawner."

"So," Liamfrey said, cocking his eyebrow and leaning on the tunnel wall. "We should destroy the spawner cage doohickey, and the spiders will stop coming...?"

"No," Jack replied. That confused Alex. "Those things are valuable! We'll disable it and kill all of the spiders that are there now. Then, we can loot the chests, and if we ever need spider eyes or string in the future, we can come back here and farm 'em."

"*Farm* ... spiders?" Alex asked. She imagined her farm on the homestead and trying to grow spiders in the fields, or maybe keeping them in the cows' animal pen. That was ridiculous. They'd just climb out of the animal enclosures and wreak havoc.

"Uh ... kill em for string and stuff," Jack replied. A spider *hissed* very close to them, making Alex jump again. "You know— take advantage of the spawner being here so that we can kill as many spiders as we want...?"

She understood.

"I think Steve will like this a lot," Alex replied, wishing again that he was here. "He loves fighting spiders."

"Great," Jack replied with a smile. "Now, here's the plan." He turned back to the mossy cobblestone block. "Let's clear some more stone outta the way so we can get right up to the cobblestone. Then, we'll break a small hole into the dungeon, throw some torches in, and kill all of those spiders through the hole. Then, we go in, kill the rest, torch the place up, and loot it."

"That's a mighty fine plan," Liamfrey said, "but how are you so sure about what's on the other side there, Jack? How do you know *so danged much* about this world?"

Jack smirked. "Didn't you say that you've seen a dozen of these, Liam?"

"Yep."

"Think about it," Jack said. "Weren't they pretty much all the same?"

The airship pilot stood for a moment staring at the tunnel wall. Then he smiled down at Jack. The torchlight glittered in his blue eyes. "That's right," he said with a nod. "I reckon they all fit the pattern you described."

"Let's do it," the boy said. He stood back, motioning for Liam to continue with the pick axe.

He did.

As Liamfrey exposed more of the cobblestone wall covered in old, green moss, Alex looked around at the rock walls and ceiling, listening to the many spiders scuttling around, hissing at them. She felt scared—especially without Steve—but having Jack and Liam with her made her feel a little better.

"Okay, now the hole," Jack said.

As Liam nodded and cut one block out of the wall—one up from the floor, so they'd see through it without crouching down—Jack muttered something to himself that gave Alex a chill.

"Hopefully they're normal spiders," he said, "and not *cave* spiders. I'm pretty sure that cave spiders can fit through a one-block hole..."

She had a brief mental image of a swarm of small spiders *pouring* out of the hole and crawling all around them...

Alex frowned and shook her head.

Everyone switched to swords. When the block was destroyed, Alex found herself looking through the dark hole around Liam and over Jack's round, hair-covered head. She saw many sets of glowing red eyes inside that injected cold fear into her belly.

The *hissing* grew louder. Many hostile spiders were rushing around in the dark through that hole, in and out of sight, pausing to look at them with those glowing, red eyes...

"I hope you know what you're doing, Jack," she said quietly.

"Let's kill em through the hole!" he exclaimed with a grin. When it became obvious that he wouldn't be able to reach the hole with Liamfrey in front, he added, "Liam, please?"

The pilot sighed, smiled, and stepped forward with his red-hot, flaming sword. Alex watched as he stabbed several spiders through the hole. The mobs tried to get to him, but Liam had more reach, and he killed one after another from relative safety. Once, she saw a spider reach through the hole with its scraggly legs and tear at Liam's leather armor, but the Minecraftian shrugged off the attempt and stabbed the arachnid through its fierce, fanged face.

Eventually, it seemed like the tide of furry legs and glowing eyes and clicking fangs subsided. Alex could see the dim green and yellow glow of many experience orbs rolling around on the floor inside.

"Now some torches," Jack said.

Liam looked into his pack then looked back at Alex.

"I have some," he said, "but I reckon you've got plenty, don't ya, little lady? You seem like the *prepared type*, aren't ya?"

Alex smiled. "You reckon right, Liam."

They changed placed. Alex moved up to the front—up to the frightening hole to the spider dungeon—then dug into her pack.

Using her ability to place things far out of her own reach—something that surprised Jack but had always felt perfectly normal to her—Alex set up several torches around the inside of what appeared (through the hole) to be a relatively small cobblestone room. The floor was littered with spider eyes, hovering bits of string, and experience orbs. Through the hole, especially now that the place was a little better lit, Alex saw a strange, block-sized black cage in the center of the room exactly as Jack had described. It even had a tiny spider bouncing around within the dim fire that danced inside.

"Weird!" Alex exclaimed.

"That's better," Jack said, clenching his stone sword and standing just behind Alex. "Now, just break the lower block, and let's head inside and torch it up some more."

"It's safe now?" Alex asked.

The hissing had stopped.

"For the moment probably," Jack said. "Those spawners need a lot of torches around to not make any more mobs. More spiders will appear shortly."

"Then we'd best hurry," Liamfrey said from the back.

Alex grimaced. She was in front. She sheathed her sword and pulled out her stone pick axe. Looking down at Jack—he smiled up at her and pushed his glasses up his little, smooth nose—she stepped forward and broke the dungeon wall enough for them to climb inside.

As soon as she did, Jack grinned and darted through the opening, heading straight for the spawner. "Come on! More torches! Quick!"

"Be *careful*, Jack!" she exclaimed, switching to her sword again.

Then, Alex gasped when several bulbous, furry bodies descended from the ceiling above the hole. One of the spiders immediately turned toward her, reaching out with its long, bristly legs to attack her at their improvised entrance. Fear bubbled up inside Alex as she raised her sword.

They were on the ceiling.

Now, Jack was trapped in there. There were several spiders between her and Jack. The boy was on his own until she could kill this one...

"Jack!" she screamed. "Look out! Behind you!"

Battle broke out in a loud, chaotic blend of spiders' legs drumming on stone, the monsters *hissing* loudly, and the clanging of Alex's armor as she struggled to kill the mob in front of her as quickly as she could. The beast leapt at her. Alex tried to block it with her sword—which cut the spider across its furry belly—and there was a *thomp* and a *clank* as the arachnid clashed into her iron chest plate. The creature tried to bite her. She narrowly avoided its fangs.

"Duck feathers!" Jack screamed from inside, amidst many *hisses*. "Oh Gosh! Help!"

"Push inside, Alex!" Liamfrey bellowed from behind her. "I can't help from behind ya!"

"I'm trying!" she shouted back, wincing as she felt something sharp scratch her left leg.

She stabbed at the spider hissing in her face—if was big and angry and making lots of noise—and it shrieked in pain as she struck it, falling back enough for Alex to push forward a little more.

Alex fought. She struggled with the spider that was trying to eat her, hoping that her armor would hold up for a little longer and that she could get *in there*; get in there and save Jack.

"Ha!" the boy suddenly exclaimed. "Yes!! I'm *invincible!*" He let out several crazy laughs.

Oh Gosh, Alex thought. *Not again.*

But Jack wasn't kidding. As Alex pushed into the spider she was fighting and into the dungeon—as Liam pushed past her to rush in and save Jack with his flaming sword—she saw the boy surrounded by dark legs and glowing red eyes, and he was *laughing*. Jack—so small compared to the big arachnids—had dropped his torch and was swinging his stone sword back and forth with both hands wrapped around its hilt. He cut through the spiders like a warrior that didn't care about being hit back. He *was* being hit back. Alex watched in astonishment as several spiders fighting the boy threw themselves at him, seeking to pierce his soft, curved skin with their fangs, only to push up against him harmlessly instead.

Jack killed three of them by the time Alex had skewered her own spider through its multi-eyed head. When her spider opponent fell and stopped moving, Liam had rushed into the fray and killed the last spider attacking Jack with a spinning move that set the creature on fire before it perished an instant later.

They all stood in the room full of rolling experience orbs. The dead spiders disappeared in puffs of grey smoke. Alex instinctively picked up several bits of string and spider eyes without thinking about it.

"More torches now!" Jack exclaimed. He had a huge grin plastered over his face. His strange skin glistened with moisture in the firelight. He was breathing heavily.

Alex and Liam worked together, setting up several more torches in the room, including on and around the spawner thing as Jack indicated.

Finally, all of the excitement died down and the mossy cobblestone room was quiet.

It was quiet and *bright*.

Jack and Liam went straight to a single wooden chest that was sitting in cobwebs in a corner of the ancient room. Alex stared at the 'spawner', watching the tiny spider inside dance and flip among the small flame burning in there under their many torches.

Where'd this come from? she wondered.

It was a terrible thing. Alex wanted more than anything to break it. Looking down at the sword in her hand, then back at the evil spawner again, she almost did. Sure, Jack wanted to save it for later, but Alex couldn't possibly imagine *wanting* to bring more scary, hostile spiders into this world.

"Spider farming!" she muttered then scoffed.

Jack opened the chest with a loud, echoing *creak*.

Alex stayed her hand. She decided to listen to the boy's wisdom and preserve that terrible spider spawner. With the twenty or so torches they'd scattered throughout the room, it seemed to be under control. It was disabled.

Heck—back when she'd first met Jack, they had almost lost all of their sheep. What if something bad happened to their animals and they didn't have access to wool anymore? Spider silk could be made into wool in a pinch. As unnerving at it was, as much as the idea of it made Alex shudder, Jack might be right about saving the spawner for possible use in the future.

"Huh," Jack said suddenly. "Not bad."

He stepped away from the chest. Alex looked up. Liamfrey was leaning over the container, looking in.

"What's in it?" she asked.

"What we've got here," the airship pilot said, "is some old bread, three ingots of *gold*, lots of old bones, and ... *what in tarnation?!* This looks like a *golden apple* that glows..."

Liamfrey reached into the chest and pulled out an apple that gleamed in the torchlight with a surface of solid gold. It emanated a magical purple light...

"Whoa!" Alex exclaimed. She suddenly didn't feel as bad anymore. *That* was interesting. "What's *that?!*"

Jack moved over to the spawner cage and sat down on top of it. "It's a magic thing, yeah," he said. "It's like a normal golden apple, but better. Makes you regenerate, have extra hit points, immune to fire and resistant to attacks for a while."

Alex didn't know what he meant by 'hit points', but that sounded *amazing*.

"Gosh..." she said. "That sounds valuable!"

"It takes nine blocks of gold to make, so yeah," Jack said. "Kind of a rare find, actually."

"Well, you two know what I figure?" Liamfrey said, holding the glowing apple and looking back into the chest. "I reckon we should eat the bread, take the rest, and move on."

"Good plan," Jack said. "And look." He pointed at another break in the cobblestone wall that Alex hadn't noticed before. There was a tunnel leading down into darkness; the only way into this dungeon before they'd cut through the wall. "I bet that tunnel will take us deeper into the ravine. If I'm right, the direction of that way out follows the ravine, and it's going down!"

Alex approached the chest and looked inside. Liamfrey immediately handed her the enchanted golden apple.

"For me?" she asked.

"Well," Liam replied with a smirk. "Not *necessarily*. But since you're the one with the most armor and yer also the most *careful*, I reckon you should hold the loot."

Alex smiled and sighed. She looked down at her armor. It was in poor shape. That spider had yanked on her left shoulder pauldron, and it was hardly hanging on now.

"The most armor *for now*," she said. "We need to find some iron so that I can fix it back at home at our anvil."

"Alrighty," Liam said, grabbing the gold and handing it to Alex. "You want these bones, too?"

"Sure. They make good fertilizer for the farm."

"So," Liam said. "Let's head down to the bottom and see how much redstone and iron we can find, okay? And, so you know, we don't have to go all the way back across the desert to fix your armor, little lady. I have an anvil on my airship, too."

"Really?" Alex smiled. That made her feel better. She'd be able to fix her armor sooner, and they had a reason to take a look at Liam's *Thunderbird* now, too. "Okay. Let's go there after this."

Alex stashed the gold, the enchanted golden apple, and the bones.

They all gathered around the spawner block and ate the bread. There was a piece for each of them. It was old, but it was still edible. As soon as Alex had some of it in her belly, she started to feel a little better; had a little more energy again. She didn't realize that she was feeling so tired.

She watched Jack eat the bread. He appeared intensely curious but also repulsed. It was the second time she'd seen the boy eat food from this world. With his small, curved mouth full of tiny white teeth and a wet, soft tongue inside, he took little nibbles, breaking it into pieces. After a few bites, Jack sighed and smiled. When he caught Alex watching him, he grinned up at her.

"Tastes good," he said. "I'm still surprised."

"What'd you expect?" she asked.

"I ... I don't know," he replied, and finished his bread.

When they were done, they pulled their swords and torches, faced the tunnel leading down into darkness through the break in the wall, and continued down...

S1E5 - Chapter 3 – Steve

Steve ran through the desert.

He ran and ran. He had to reach his friends. It wasn't *his* fault that he'd blown himself up. How was he supposed to know that there'd be a freaking pressure plate trap in the middle of the treasure room?! How could he have known that the blue block was the wrong one to cut through? That book he'd read about desert temples told him that the treasure lay beneath the blue block; that's all. There was nothing about *traps* in there!

The sand hissed around his feet as he ran. The sky shifted from pink and orange to silvery as the moon rose in the east.

"Well, hey!" Steve said to himself between breaths. "I'm an adventurer, right? I try new stuff! Now, I know not to cut through the blue block!"

Every once and a while, Steve looked up at the rising moon. He tried to keep moving east. The iron shovel he'd taken from that zombie danced in his hand. It wasn't the best of weapons, but at least it wasn't made of wood or stone, right? In his other hand, he had a single torch.

That's *all* he had: a shovel and a torch.

Dang—he hadn't even taken any food! All he had to do was check Alex's kitchen chests on the way out. Man, he really needed to start slowing down and thinking things through a little more...

"It's *fine!*" Steve said to himself, jumping over a dip between sand dunes. "I can find ... food ... out here! There are plenty of rabbits, and probably other stuff!"

In fact, he heard the rabbits jumping around in the deepening night around him. As he ran farther and farther away from the homestead—passing wide around KittyPaws' sandstone village— he heard less and less rabbits moving around.

The desert animals were quickly being replaced by the mobs that come out at night. Instead of seeing a rabbit hopping around in the dying light, Steve saw the silhouettes of zombies appear in the distance. He heard the *clunk* of a skeleton's bones. As the desert turned black under the silvery night sky, Steve saw multiple sets of glowing red spider eyes searching the darkness.

"Oh dang," he muttered to himself, strengthening his grip on the shovel in one hand and his torch in the other.

It wasn't long before Steve ran down a dune and recognized the dark figures of three zombies coming straight at him from below.

"Whoa!" he cried, peeling away to the left and trying to avoid the undead mobs.

He heard a loud, croaky snarl and another growl. His warrior's senses narrowly saved him from being snatched by two strong, undead hands. The sounds were dry and raspy.

Husk zombies.

Steve swung his shovel as he dodged a desiccated zombie that came out of nowhere.

Clang!

He wonked it in the head and kept going.

Steve fled. He ran and ran, then dodged out of the way of a spider that came bouncing his way along the dunes from up ahead. Its glaring red eyes regarded him hungrily as it leapt along the sand to catch him.

"Dang!" Steve cried, turning and running the other way.

He had to get ahead of all of these mobs; had to continue east and reach the desert temple. He knew that he'd get tired eventually. He'd only be able to stay ahead of the mobs for so long...

"Nonsense!" Steve replied to his thoughts. "I'm a great warrior! I can handle anything!"

Looking up at the moon, Steve did his best to get his bearings—he was all turned around—and continued east.

Before long, running through the sand, he heard the *clunk* of a skeleton's bones in his path.

He dodged out of the way just as he heard the *twang* of a bow. An arrow whistled over his head in the darkness. Steve didn't even see it.

"Hey! No!" Steve shouted. "Leave me alone!"

He turned and ran at an angle that would make it harder for the skeleton to hit him on its follow-up shot, then was surprised when he heard the bow *twang* again and he felt the arrow strike his arm.

Steve bellowed in pain and kept running.

He sprinted in a zig-zag pattern away from the skeleton, then—

"*He he hee...*"

There was a high-pitched voice in the darkness ahead; a laugh that sounded female and scratchy. It sounded like...

"A witch!" Steve shouted, turning ninety degrees off of his path again and running toward whatever direction would take him away from the dangerous creature. He sure didn't want to be hit by a *weakness potion* or something and made to slow down! He didn't want to deal with zombies and spiders with his muscles weak, unable to fight...

Running as fast as he could, Steve tried to make tracks away from the witch and the skeleton, but was stopped several big sand dunes later when he ran into a group of zombies again.

They groaned and growled and reached for him, lit up only by his yellow torchlight.

If Steve wasn't such a warrior, he was sure that he'd be terrified.

That would have scared the pants off of Alex.

Instead, Steve screeched to a halt with a hiss of sand, started running another way, then grunted as one of the zombies bashed him on the side. He tripped and fell. They immediately fell upon him, bashing and trying to bite him, growling and rattling with their dry, raspy voices...

"Get off of me!" Steve shouted, feeling a fiery rage build up in hit guts. "Back ... *off!!*"

With that, he shoved three zombies off of him with his strength and the shovel. When the zombies let him up and immediately pressed in on him again, Steve jumped to his feet— his muscles were on fire!—and swung his shovel at the closest one.

Clang!!

The zombie groaned in pain and paused. Maybe it was dizzy. Steve didn't care. He beat it outta there, running away from the group as quickly as he could.

Several steps away, he heard the *twang* of a bow and felt an arrow pierce his left leg.

"Ow! Dang it!"

Maybe running through the desert at night wasn't such a good idea, he thought.

"Doesn't matter!" he said. "I'm here now! I can handle this!"

He ran on, ignoring the pain. Steve was already hurting all over from the arrows and the zombie hits, and each furious stride through the sand was sapping his strength. He was getting tired.

Steve paused for a moment to look up at the moon but couldn't find it.

"What...?!" he exclaimed, glaring at the sky, then he heard the *hiss* of a spider and many legs drumming along the ground. "Dang it!"

Stave ran on, hoping that he was heading east. He had to get to his friends. He had to help them, and heck—he needed to get out of the open or he was going to get killed again!

At one point, dodging from one group of mobs to another, Steve saw something weird on the shadowy horizon. Across the pale desert night he sighted the black shapes of buildings. There weren't any lights—no torches—but it looked a lot like ... a village!

"What the heck?!" he exclaimed, pausing to peer at the dark collection of structures.

Yep. *Definitely a village*. Where the heck *was* he?!

Steve looked up at the moon again and saw that it was high enough in the sky that he couldn't make heads or tails of directions.

"Freaking *great*..." he muttered then started running again when he heard a low, raspy groan and plodding steps heading his way in the sand from somewhere out of sight.

If it was a village, he'd be able to hole up for the night. That was *exactly* what he needed. If definitely wasn't *his* village; the village next to home with KittyPaws30 and his other friends and that new Minecraftian from the Divining Pool that he hadn't met yet. What was his name? *HelloDance* something or other...?

Steve set his sights on the dark village and ran. He ran like he was going to die if he didn't, because he very likely would. He could already imagine the many houses and shops with villagers locked up inside for the night, sleeping until the morning, when they would all emerge and go about their villager duties. Some of the houses would be small and cramped, but *anything* would be better than getting beaten to death in the desert. If he ran to the first house he found and it was one of those tiny shacks, if he had to share the floor with two other villagers, he would. It didn't matter. Steve wanted to live! He had to get to his friends!

There was a burst of pain when Steve was suddenly hit by another arrow. It struck him square in the front of one shoulder. He stopped, staggered. The shooter was somewhere in the darkness ahead of him...

Looking up and ahead, Steve gasped when a very tall mob made of bones and lots of legs rushed into his path. It was wielding a bow, already nocking another arrow, and—

Holy smokes, Steve thought. It wasn't some weird, unknown creature. Once it closed in on Steve and his torch, the mob was revealed to be a skeleton archer riding on the back of a big, black spider with glowing red eyes.

"A spider jockey!" Steve exclaimed, partly in great pain, partly intensely curious (he'd never seen one of *those* before), and a little afraid. The spider-rider was between him and the village.

Without a second thought, Steve charged. He didn't give the spider jockey a chance to fire at him again. If it did, he hoped that it would miss. There was nothing else to do.

When he drew in close to the spider—it hissed and widened its many red eyes as Steve rushed them—the Minecraftian warrior wound his shovel back for a mighty blow then swung it at the skeleton with all of his might!

Clang!!

Bones crunched. His shovel connected heavily and followed through. Then, Steve realized that he'd knocked the skeleton off of the spider's back.

Steve roared. There was a fire in his blood. He lifted his shovel and smashed it into the spider, who'd crouched, confused and surprised with its fangs spread wide.

Splat!!

The spider's eight legs flailed out in all directions then it collapsed to the sand, dead.

There was a *clunk* and *clatter* of bones, and Steve turned on the skeleton archer, who was standing nearby. Its skull was cracked. It loaded an arrow into its bow and aimed at him...

Steve tumbled to the right, dodging the shot, then swung his shovel again as he popped up again on the skeleton's left side.

Crunch!!

Bones flew everywhere and the rest of the skeleton dropped to the sand.

Steve took a quick breath. He looked down at the iron shovel, smiled, then back at the distant, dark village.

He ran on.

By the time he reached the edge of town, Steve was totally exhausted. He'd dodged three more groups of mobs and had tried as hard as he could to avoid getting into any more fights. He was so wounded. Somehow, he'd managed to pull the three arrows out of him along the way, casting them down into the sand as he hustled on, but he was pretty badly hurt and he knew it.

Leaping over the dry water trenches of a dead farm on the outside of the village, Steve immediately felt better when his boots hit the hard, gritty street. This village was made of sandstone, just like the one east of the homestead, but it was totally *dark*.

Steve ran through the narrow road, stopping at the first house he reached. He leapt up the two stairs and pounded on the wooden door.

"Hello?!" he called. "Please, let me in! I need help!"

There was no answer. No *humph* or *hurrr* of a villager replying grumpily through the door.

Steve pounded on the door some more.

"Please open up! I need shelter! I'm very wounded. Please!"

There was no answer.

"Okay, I'm coming in!" Steve shouted.

He opened the door.

As soon as he did, several husk zombies *poured* out at him from inside, all teeth and growls and dry, strangling hands.

"Aaaugh!"

Steve cried out in shock and fear as they came at him. He immediately backpedaled into the street and ran farther into the village. As he did, he looked back once and saw three zombies emerging from the dark shack, all turning to follow him.

He stopped at another door, went to pound on it, but just opened it instead.

A zombie just on the other side snarled so loudly in his face that Steve almost dropped his shovel. There were more zombies inside this one, too. They all pushed through the doorway, reaching for him.

"Dang it! Is this a *zombie village?!*"

What am I gonna do?! Steve thought frantically, immediately kicking the nearest zombie back into the house. He backed up. He was boned. He was gonna die again and start back at the homestead again. He'd *never* get to Alex and Jack!

Looking around through the streets, a chill ran up Steve's spine as several more zombies emerged from various other houses; the ones with open doorways that he hadn't noticed before. The streets were quickly filling up the walking dead.

He looked up. If he could get to a roof, he could get away from the zombies. There'd still be spiders to deal with, and some skeletons might be able to take shots at him, but—

A husk zombie suddenly bashed him on the back. It came out of nowhere.

Steve grunted, fell forward, then scrambled to get away.

He dropped his torch then, when he turned to go back for it, he saw that three zombies were already walking over it.

"Dang!" he cried. "Dang it, dang it, dang it!!"

Besides, Steve couldn't get to the roof. He had no blocks. He didn't even have any freaking *dirt*, and everything around him was just *sand*.

The blacksmith.

He didn't know why, but Steve figured that he might be able to find something to help him there. Blacksmiths always had gear inside their shops; maybe even a *sword*. If only he had a sword...

Steve ran through the streets until he saw the orange glow of the forge. When he reached the blacksmith's—running several steps ahead of the zombies—he immediately rushed up onto the upper deck and made for the little shop where a chest would be waiting inside for—

A green zombie villager wearing a blacksmith's apron emerged from the building ahead of Steve with dead eyes, growling fiercely and reaching for him. It had a big, green nose and a heavy brow over its black, sagging eyes...

Steve felt fear.

He recoiled, leaping backwards just before the ex-blacksmith grabbed him.

He raised his shovel, backing into the little nook next to the forge full of lava.

I'm screwed, Steve thought. *I'm gonna die...*

The many zombies gradually following him—plodding through the sandstone streets with growls and yowls and raspy snarls—were already just down the stairs. The ones closest to the blacksmith's were already climbing the porch.

Steve held his iron shovel in front of him. He'd have to take them on, one by one, but he was exhausted. He wouldn't last for long. If he was wearing armor and was fresh—not exhausted from fighting and running all night—he could *maybe* take on all of these zombies one at a time in a chokepoint like this ... *maybe* ... but not now. Not like this. Not wounded and exhausted, unarmored and wielding nothing but a *shovel*...

He raised the shovel anyway and waited for the first undead monster to rush him. The first time he made a mistake, he was done for, but he'd take some of them out with him...

There was a sudden, orange flash of fire. In the pitch darkness of the night, Steve saw an arc of a fiery blade slicing through the air and something landed lightly on the platform in front of him.

In the red glow of a flaming black blade, Steve saw the pale shrouded face and ice-blue eyes of ... *Alice the ninja!!*

What?!

438

The flashing blade that he'd seen was her *DevilScythe* swinging through the air as she dropped down from the roof. The exotic weapon cut straight through the first zombie, lopping the creature into two pieces and dropping it to the ground.

An instant after Alice's nimble arrival—touching down in front of Steve to protect him from the undead horde—she spun her black scythe again with a flare of red fire and sliced off another zombie's head!

Alice had dropped in to save him, but the many husk zombies emerging from the village and the desert night were still pressing in.

They were surrounded...

Psssst!!
Liking the story? Don't forget to join my Mailing List! I'll send you *free books* and stuff! (www.SkeletonSteve.com)

439

S1E5 - Chapter 4 – Jack

"Here comes another zombie!" Jack exclaimed, grinning from ear to ear.

It was dark. They were at the bottom of the ravine, following along its floor. Ahead of and behind them, the orange glow of lava falls gave the entire deep space an eerie atmosphere. The echoing of Jack's steps and voice was downright creepy to the boy, but this was *his* game. He'd been in a bazillion ravines like this one, and being in one for real was the same, only ... *bigger*.

The grey, stone walls stretched up and up endlessly on both sides, reaching into darkness. Bats squeaked frequently, flapping their little pixelated wings and wandering around the open, cool air. They'd long since left behind the abandoned mine shaft, whose dilapidated tunnels of rotten wood and cobwebs popped out of the ravine walls here and there.

Jack looked forward to exploring the mines at a later date...

An incoming zombie slowly plodded up to the group. Jack put his torch down onto the ground—it went into a slow hover above the ravine floor—and grabbed sword's hilt with both hands as the undead mob headed his way. The creature groaned lowly and reached out with its blocky green hands...

Jack drew the sword back like a baseball player waiting for the pitch...

"Batter up!" he exclaimed.

The zombie snarled. The Damage Indicator window over its head was bright in the darkness and read: *Zombie. 20/20.*

As it closed the distance, Jack swung with all of his might. When he connected with the mob's body, it grunted in pain and jumped back. A red number "4" appeared over the zombie's head and floated up until vanishing.

Dang, Jack thought. No matter *how hard* he tried to hit them, he only did the damage that a stone sword could do. He really needed to get himself an iron sword, or even a *diamond* one if possible. Since he was immune to the zombies' attacks, he figured that he'd probably be killing most of them from now on to keep his friends from risking any harm.

When the zombie mindlessly came at him once more, Jack struck it again and again, ignoring the little bumps the hostile mob gave him on the head and shoulders as he did.

Jack wasn't afraid; not one little bit.

He knew that he could now take on zombies and spiders without a problem. Creepers? Those were dangerous. Those could likely really hurt him, or even kill him. Skeletons and other mobs? Jack had no idea, but he figured that they wouldn't be able to hurt him either. Would blocky arrows hurt him? Or would they just bounce off of him like *Nerf* darts? And what about Endermen? They were big and strong. Would they hit him harder? Or would it be the same as with zombies?

As the one zombie fell into a puff of grey smoke and the resulting experience orbs rolled over and merged with Jack's foot, another approached from around a blocky rock. Jack fought it too while Alex and Liamfrey watched.

Jack ignored the first ineffective punch from the zombie and swung his sword twice, back and forth, cutting down its hit points with each swing.

What about ghasts? he wondered as he fought. Those shot fireballs. And blazes. Oh—and magma cubes. What would happen if a magma cube touched him? Were they hot like lava? Would they burn him? He could probably fight zombie pigmen without a problem, although their gold swords might hurt a little more than a zombie's fist.

Jack paused his fight to look at his stone sword's blade. The zombie in front of him whacked Jack again, but the boy ignored it. The sword was wider than a normal sword, and it had those bumpy points. *That might hurt a little*, he thought, but it wouldn't hurt him seriously.

"Uh, Jack?" Alex said from behind as the zombie shoved the boy again on his chest.

"Yeah?"

"Are you okay?" she asked, pointing at the zombie he was ignoring. "The zombie...?"

Jack turned back. He saw that the zombie had two hit points left. It whacked him gently on one shoulder.

"Oh," he said with a laugh. He killed it then turned back to his friends. The zombie fell to the ground with a low groan. "I was thinking about other mobs," Jack said. "If these guys can't hurt me, and spiders can't hurt me, do you think that skeletons can? Can their arrows?"

Both Minecraftians shared concerned glances then shrugged.

"If I were you," Liamfrey said, cocking an eyebrow, "I wouldn't put that to the test, boy. I reckon that you should just assume that *everything* can hurt you. You know—the mobs that you don't *know about* just yet. Then, if you're ever in *bad trouble*, and you take a hit, if you're immune, it'll be ... a pleasant surprise!"

"You thought that creeper wouldn't hurt you," Alex added. "If Liam didn't knock it off of the edge, well ... that could have been the end of the *Weird Walker*, you know?"

She looked uncomfortable saying it.

Jack swallowed. A chill ran up his spine. She was right, of course.

"Yeah, I guess that's a good way to approach it," Jack said. "I'll just try to avoid getting hit by everything but zombies and spiders."

They continued walking.

At one point, Jack had to swim against the current of a spreading pool of water at the bottom of a waterfall. The entire bottom of the ravine there was full of it. He took the opportunity to drink as much as he could, which made him feel a lot better.

When Jack pulled himself out of the water and onto solid ground again, he yawned. He realized that he was actually starting to get a little tired. At some point, he'd have to sleep for real. Jack had been unable to keep track of time *at all*, and had no idea how long he'd really been awake. If many days passed on Vortexia while he was still awake, then, when he finally went to bed like he would back on Earth, would *days and days* pass while he was sleeping?

Next time we go home, Jack thought, *I'll try to sleep then*. Maybe he'd make his own room attached to Alex and Steve's house where he could move his bed to and actually turn off the lights. He needed a dark room. He couldn't imagine sleeping surrounded by burning torches...

From time to time, they came across veins of iron ore, coal, and gold. The three of them always stopped to mine it out together. Jack helped, picking through it all with the stone pick axe that Alex had made for him, but he couldn't pick up the ore blocks or chunks of coal as he went. Instead, Jack ended up cutting through veins in the rock walls of the ravine and accumulating lots of ore around his feet. Alex would come and collect it all behind him.

"Hey, Liam, when do you want to go deeper to get redstone?" Jack asked at one point.

The airship pilot responded by putting his hands on his hips, taking a deep breath of the cool, underground air, and scanning the darkness.

"Eh ... I reckon we'll get to that eventually. We should finish exploring the bottom of this here ravine first. *Then*, we'll head lower."

Whenever they found iron, Alex's green eyes seemed to sparkle. Jack knew that she was excited about fixing up her armor. With Jack's normal eyes, he had no idea how damaged Alex's armor really was. He didn't see any sort of green health bat like when he was just *playing* the game. Maybe if he had the ability to access some sort of 'inventory', he'd be able to see an item's health. *Come to think of it*, he thought, looking down at his pick axe, he had no idea how damaged his own tools were, either. His stone sword could have been three swings away from breaking, and he had no way to know. He recalled that stone pick axes never lasted very long when mining, but *hey*—it was stone. They could make more.

Later, the three of them were following the ravine floor as it curved to the left, and two arrows suddenly whistled past them from the darkness up ahead.

"Incoming!" Alex said. "Look out!"

Before the next shots flew past, all three of them broke for cover. Jack ended up hiding behind a big, blocky boulder with Alex while Liam took shelter behind another rock formation on the other side of the ravine.

They all pulled their swords. The red glow of Liamfrey's sword looked mean in the darkness.

"How's my sword?" Jack asked, holding it up to Alex.

She took a moment, pulling away from peering over the boulder to look down at Jack. Her green eyes flitted to the sword, then back to him.

"What do you mean?" she asked.

"How's its *durability?* Is it going to break soon?"

She looked again. Sheathing her sword, she took Jack's, then handed it back to him again.

"It's a bit below half," she said. "Can't you tell?"

"No," Jack replied, taking his weapon back. He heard the faint *twang* of a bow up ahead. An arrow landed on the ground next to them, sticking in the rock with a *plunk*. "Hey, you have arrows, right?"

"Yeah," Alex said.

"Let me see one."

Alex stared at Jack in confusion for a moment, then reached into her pack and produced a single arrow. Jack took it.

The missile was straight and solid, but the big, blocky arrowhead was just as spongy as the ground, trees, and everything else. The fletching on the other end felt the same.

"What ... are you doing?" Alex said.

Jack looked up at her, then back at the arrow, then gave himself a few experimental *jabs* with it on the arm and chest. He stabbed himself in the belly. It wasn't sharp at all. It was like ... maybe like a tennis ball, but not as hard. *Would it hurt him to get shot with one of these...?*

"Just testing," Jack said. Two more arrows flew by them, whistling away into the darkness.

"*Oh* no..." Alex said with a frown. "You're not thinking of...?"

"Oh, yes I am," Jack replied with a smile.

He felt afraid, but also excited. They were pinned down and they had to try *something*. Jack already felt pretty certain that the skeletons wouldn't be able to hurt him. He *had* to be immune to them too, right? Their attacks were physical, just like with zombies; just like with spiders. He'd be okay...

Looking down at the arrow near him sticking out of the stone floor of the ravine, Jack felt a chill. What if he was wrong? The arrow was strong enough to stick through *solid rock*.

But is it, really? he wondered. Is the arrow strong enough to pierce the stone? Or is the stone just *programmed* to let arrows get stuck in it...?

Jack felt sure that he was immune. He'd be fine.

Well ... he felt *pretty* sure...

The boy stared at the open area in the middle of the ravine where he'd have to run through. He took some deep breaths, dimly aware that Alex was sheathing her sword and readying her bow. Jack raised his own sword, felt all of his muscles flex—it felt like a fire was flowing through his blood!—then he *charged!*

He was suddenly out in the open. By the light of the torch in his left hand, he saw the pale bones of two skeletons ahead of them in the shadows. One was aiming at him. Jack gritted his teeth as he ran as fast as he could to close the distance. As he drew closer, he saw their Damage Indicator windows appear over their heads, making it much easier to find them.

Skeleton. 20/20.

"Help him, Liam!" Alex shouted from behind.

There were bow *twangs*. Jack hardly noticed one arrow flying past his face. Then, he felt like he was hit with a hard-thrown beanbag on his right leg.

"Ow!" he cried, launching himself into the skeletons.

He swung his sword at the first mob, crashing into its bones with a *clatter*. A red number "5" appeared before it, and the archer's hit points dropped to fifteen. Jack swung again and again, making the skeleton fall back and let out a loud *clunk* every time he hit it. The numbers fell as the other skeleton calmly walked toward him, passing around to behind Jack's left side as if to flank him.

There was a *twang*, and Jack felt the arrow pelt him on his left shoulder blade. That one hurt more than the one on his leg, but it was like getting punched.

"Ouch!"

Well—like getting punched *not very hard*.

He could handle it. It wasn't too bad. It was like getting hit by a dense, soft ball. Not a *softball*, and not like a baseball. Jack had once seen a sports show on TV that his dad was watching, where a big, muscular dude was shooting some kind of tennis ball *cannon* at a normal looking dude that was trying to rush to the front of an obstacle course. It was like *that*. It felt a lot like how Jack imagined being hit by a tennis ball cannon would be ... if the tennis ball was also *soft*.

He killed the first skeleton. When its hit points dropped to zero, it fell sideways to the ground in a clatter of bones and grey smoke.

Jack faced off against the other.

When he ran to attack it, it turned its bony back to him and tried to walk away.

"No you don't!" Jack shouted, rushing up and slashing across its bones. The skeleton jerked away with a *clatter* then turned.

He battled the skeleton with ease. The mob shot him once while Jack was battering it with his stone sword—pelting him once in the chest with an arrow that immediately bounced away into the darkness—then in a flash of red fire, Liamfrey entered the fight from behind.

When the skeleton fell under both of their swords, Jack smiled and turned, about to thank Liam, when Alex shouted:

"Jack, *look out!!*"

He saw it at the same time as he heard it: a creeper emerging from the darkness up ahead, already almost close enough to hit with a sword. It was *hissing* and shuddering, shaking as it rushed up on its little, blocky legs.

Jack felt a jolt of fear and panic—it was like ice water suddenly in his stomach and his guts—and scrambled backwards, bumping into the stone ravine wall.

"Duck feathers!!" he shouted, turning and running like heck.

As he did, the moment he turned away from the creeper, he saw an arrow streaking past him from Alex. It whistled through the air and struck the explosive mob, which yelped and jumped back with an angry *hiss*. The shuddering stopped for a moment.

Liamfrey crouched, changed his hold on his sword, then he shouted, "*Fire whirlwind!!*" as he launched a violent spin attack that lit up the area with a blazing, red light! He cut through the creeper's crackling green body and set it *on fire!*

"Get out of the way!" Alex shouted. Jack ducked and kept running toward her. Liamfrey followed suit, changing his grip on his sword again and retreating from the burning creeper.

She fired her bow once more.

Jack heard a *thunk* and a dwindling *hiss*, and when he turned to look, he saw the flaming body of the creeper falling down to the ravine floor. It disappeared in a puff of grey smoke.

They all cheered.

Jack felt amazing.

He gasped, thinking of taking those three hits from the skeletons, and immediately reached up to touch his chest. The spot where the third arrow had hit him point blank felt a little tender, but yeah—it was like being punched by his little brother.

The three of them took a break after that. Alex gave Jack a piece of roasted chicken from home, and when he ate it—it tasted so good!—he oddly began to feel a lot better.

They moved on.

Continuing along the bottom of the ravine for a long ways, Jack, Alex, and Liamfrey collected ore and coal wherever they found it. Before long, they were really starting to get quite a collection of iron ore, which seemed to make Alex very happy.

The ravine became narrower and narrower, eventually stopping altogether.

They reached its end.

"What now?" Jack said as they turned around. "Go deeper?"

"Yep," Liam replied. "There was a tunnel a good ways yonder direction headin down. I reckon we should take a gander *there*."

"Okay," Jack said.

"Sounds good," Alex said.

They backtracked for a little while, killed a few more zombies and a spider, then found the tunnel that Liamfrey was referring to. It was wide but short, and Jack could see that it obviously went down.

There wouldn't be much more of this world under them. The bottom of the ravine had to be really deep already. They'd find lava soon. And redstone. Any maybe *diamonds*.

"How much redstone do you need, Liam?" Alex asked.

"Well, as much as we can get our hands on," he replied. "The *Thunderbird* always needs more. She's a hungry ship. Takes a lot of energy to *fly*, you know. But ... I reckon if we find as many veins of redstone as we did iron, that'll keep her in the air for several more days."

They followed the tunnel down. Like Minecraft tunnels tended to do, it wound left and right, dropping at times and sometimes revealing a hole here and there leading into other higher caverns. Jack could hear mobs all around them, sometimes more than others.

Eventually, going lower and lower, they found lava.

When Jack saw his first lava pool down there, he had to stop and stare at it for a while. It was hot. *Blazingly* hot. The constant, loud bubbling, spitting, and frothing made him more than a little afraid. He could feel the dry heat blasting his skin. It made his eyes water.

Back when Jack was a noob playing this game, he'd made a handful of mistakes at times—cutting through the wrong blocks under him or being too careless—that resulted in his character falling into lava and quickly burning to death.

Here, he could *feel it*, and it was freaking terrifying! If he made one bad move down here and fell into this lava, it wouldn't be an *oops*. It would be a kid burning to death. It would be Jack dying horribly. He knew it.

He wanted to go back. He wanted to stay away from the lava. The lava was *bad*.

Instead, Liamfrey led the three of them onto a ledge that went around the big, terrifying and intensely hot lava pool.

Jack hesitated, but when the others looked back at him to make sure that he was okay, he tried his best to hide his fear. He gritted his teeth and followed Liamfrey and Alex into the deep, deadly depths full of lava...

S1E5 - Chapter 5 – Alex

It was hot.

Alex had seen plenty of lava pools before. Heck—her own iron mine next to the homestead had an area deep underground where she'd carved nice, wide walkways around a huge underground lake of magma. After the second time Steve had run through the area too quickly and accidentally plunged to his fiery doom, she'd even built cobblestone guardrails.

Still, every time she passed by lava like this, she treated the glowing, hot stuff with intense respect. Alex hadn't died in a *long* time, and she planned to keep it that way. However, one careless step—one slip next to this magma—and she'd lose her entire inventory.

Jack appeared fascinated. He also looked scared. The strange, curvy creature was glistening with moisture that Alex didn't understand. He had to keep stopping to wipe 'fog' from his glasses.

As the three of them followed along the side of the blazing, twisting lava pool, they stopped from time to time when the rock wall drew in too close to the magma's edge. Liamfrey would then take the lead—he kept his iron pick axe ready—and eagerly cut through whatever was in their way to keep them walking along in relative safety.

Twice since finding the lava pool, the odd Minecraftian who had spawned from the Divining Pool let out an excited *hoot* that Alex could barely hear over the constant loud bubbling and spitting of the lava as he stopped to collect redstone dust from glowing, red veins of ore in the deep stone. At one point, they actually found two veins at once.

"Hey, Alex, help me out with this, won't ya?" Liam said.

"I can't," Alex replied, looking down at her stone pick axe. It wasn't strong enough to mine redstone. "Steve lost my iron pick axe when he ... well, *you know*."

"Dang it," the airship pilot replied with a smirk. "So I have the *only* iron pick axe? I reckon I'll be doing *a lot* of pickin..."

"Sorry. Wanna stop to smelt some iron ore?" she offered. "I can build a furnace and make another..."

Honestly, Alex didn't want to use *any* of the iron they'd collected if she could help it. She wasn't sure exactly how much they had now, but she really wanted to fix up her armor and didn't know how much iron it would take.

"Nah, that's okay," Liam replied. "It's infrequent enough. I'll just do it myself. You know? It's a pity that we couldn't *find* that pick axe of yours. That trap that blew Steve to *holy tarnation* opened up the floor, so I reckon it should've been down on the ravine bottom somewhere."

"It probably was," Jack said, staring at the fiery lava. The intense, orange light of it reflected in the strange pieces of glass in front of his eyes. "Objects de-spawn after about five minutes though," he added. "I'm pretty sure it took us longer than that to get down here."

De-spawn? Alex thought. The kid sure said weird things.

Strange thoughts wriggled through Alex's head. Jack had made multiple references to her world—her entire existence—being some kind of *game*. Heck—even the Divining Pool said stuff alluding to that sometimes. She recalled something about this being a 'book'.

Alex shook her head and looked at the lava.

She didn't want to think about it.

Once they finally left the lava pool behind and started exploring a deep, silent cave, they were back in the dark, so Alex scoured the black deep for hostile mobs sneaking around waiting to do them in.

It wasn't long before they had to start defending themselves.

Now that Jack knew that he was 'immune' (as he said) to zombies, skeletons, and spiders, *everything* changed. The kid was no longer afraid of mobs. He began charging into battle with a grin on his strange, smooth face, swinging his stone sword with abandon and going toe to toe with multiple opponents as if certain that he was invincible.

Perhaps he really *was*.

It was uncomfortable, watching Jack battle the many mobs that they found in the darkness. The zombies towered over the boy. The skeletons seemed to hurt him a little, but after killing a few more after those two in the ravine, he seemed to ignore their pelting arrows with an excited grimace as he launched himself into their bony forms. Jack didn't fight well. If he was a Minecraftian, he would have died several times over from counter-attacks or from being hit first. By all means, he should have been overwhelmed many times, but when the zombies mobbed him, the kid only laughed and cut through them with ease, shouting taunts and saying things like 'now *four* hit points' and other stuff that Alex didn't understand.

Every once and a while, a creeper slid out of the darkness on padded feet that crackled like dry leaves. When it did, Alex shouted for Jack to *look out*, and Liamfrey would step in to kill it.

It was crazy. Alex had never seen anything like this before.

Eventually, Jack's stone sword broke. He beat on his zombie opponent with his fists when it did, calling out for help as he was harmlessly battered back and forth. When the mob was dead, Alex pulled out her crafting table again and made Jack a new stone sword.

They made their way through the deep tunnels and caverns until eventually hitting bedrock, which appeared in patchy areas of the ground under their feet and jutting up through the walls here and there. It was black and grey and sparkled with unknown minerals in the torchlight.

"So weird," Jack said at one point, stomping on a block of bedrock with his flappy feet. His shoes were like no boots that Alex had ever seen before.

"What's weird?" Alex asked.

"How the bedrock is *different* from the rest of the world," Jack replied, reaching down and bending in a way that hurt Alex's brain to comprehend. He ran his tiny, smooth fingers along the floor.

"How do you reckon?" Liamfrey asked, pausing and looking over his shoulder as he was cutting out some more redstone. The ore glowed brightly and smoked with every strike of his iron pick axe.

"Well," the boy said, standing and pushing his glasses up his nose, "this might be hard for me to describe to you guys, but most of the world is a little ... *soft*. It's kind of *bouncy* to me. Trees, stone, dirt and grass, the houses of the village; *everything*. The only thing I've seen in this whole world so far that's not soft like that is *this bedrock*. Also the bedrock of the Divining Pool. It's as hard as ... um ... as hard as ... well ... *hard stuff* from my world. It's so hard that it scrapes my fingers."

"We can't break it," Alex said.

"Oh, I know," Jack said. "Nothing can break it unless you're in *creative mode*."

Alex had no idea what Jack meant by the world being 'bouncy', but that term threw her for a loop.

"What...?" she replied. "Creative mode??"

Jack smiled and shook his head. "Oh, never mind. Nothing."

Then, the kid stared in the distant darkness, held up his torch, and gasped.

Alex looked but saw nothing.

"What is it, Jack?" Liam said, lowering his pick axe and putting his other hand on the hilt of his sword.

The kid grinned and looked at both of them with bright eyes. "Diamonds!" Jack said. "I see some diamonds up ahead!"

Alex held her own torch up and looked. Down the tunnel of part-stone, part-bedrock, past the edge of their vision—in the darkness on the other side of the red glow of Liam harvesting redstone—was the pale blue glitter of something reflecting their light.

Jack was right.

"Hey, great!" Alex exclaimed. She had a precious handful of diamonds stored in her personal chest in her room back home. More were always welcome.

Steve always wanted to make armor out of the super-valuable resource, but that was too risky. What if they used several diamonds to make him the best suit of armor he could ever have, then he tripped underground somewhere and fell into lava? Diamonds were for pick axes and swords; not for armor. And ... did Jack mention something about using them to make an *enchanting table?*

"Just a tick," Liam said, hacking away at the redstone vein in front of him. "Those there diamonds can wait for a moment. Let's stick together. I'm almost finished here."

Once the Minecraftian was done harvesting the redstone vein, the three of them moved on toward the sparkle of the distant diamonds in the dark. Heading quietly down the corridor, listening to the hissing and groans of mobs in the walls around them, Alex raised her torch and looked up as the ceiling rose. She saw their tunnel open into a large, pitch-black cavern. The diamonds were in one wall up ahead.

Bats squeaked from somewhere over them in the darkness.

A chill rain up Alex's spine.

"Careful," she said a little too quietly. "We're in a big cave again..."

"I'm always careful, little lady," Liamfrey replied. His drawling voice echoed.

The three of them approached the diamonds in the wall, all holding their torches high and looking around. The cave was big. Alex couldn't even see the ceiling. She heard the hissing of spiders coming from somewhere above them, then the plodding of a single zombie down on the ground up ahead.

When the green undead mob appeared in their torchlight, dressed in ancient chainmail and wielding a glowing sword, they all paused to stare at it.

"What in tarnation?!" Liamfrey said, pulling out his red-glowing sword.

"Don't worry about it," Jack said. "They spawn that way sometimes."

The kid met the strange zombie without fear. He hacked at it and ignored the mob's attacks. Its glowing sword—obviously

458

enchanted—bounced off of Jack's soft body again and again harmlessly.

"You okay, Jack?" Alex said. She'd seen him fight several zombies now, but she just couldn't be okay with him charging into battle like that and getting beat up. She couldn't believe that he wasn't getting hurt; wasn't in danger. It wasn't long ago that Jack was hiding behind her in the woods while trying to get away from wolves.

"Yep!" he replied. "Chainmail isn't that great. Should just take one more..." He trailed off as he slashed his stone sword through the armored zombie, then the mob grunted out one last sound of pain and fell to the bedrock floor, disappearing in a puff of smoke.

The glowing experience orbs rolled toward Jack and melded with his feet with a tinkling sound.

It didn't drop anything else.

"Well, *that* was interesting," Liamfrey said, pulling out his iron pick axe and approaching the diamond ore.

"Aw, *man!*" Jack moaned. "I was hoping that it would drop that enchanted sword!"

Then, as Liam started picking away, there was a bizarre *zip* sound, and a monstrous black form twice Jack's height suddenly appeared in their midst among a burst of glowing, purple motes of light that drifted to the floor. The huge creature's arms and legs were impossibly long and its face was a terrifying mask of a wide, black mouth and glowing purple eyes...

Alex gasped. Jack gasped. It was right in front of them.

"An Enderman!" Jack exclaimed.

Liamfrey stopped and turned, then, there was a sudden sound that chilled Alex to the core; a growling that seemed to vibrate the inside of her head. It sounded like something about to explode; something so violent that Alex wanted to run away as fast as she could. The Enderman's purple eyes slanted into fierce, angry slits and it opened its mouth wider, revealing inky-black fangs. It looked like it could bite Alex's head off.

"Aw *shoot!*" Liam said above the murderous noise. "I looked at it!"

Jack looked terrified. His face was suddenly paler than normal and his eyes were wide. He bent his strange legs a little as if trying to make himself smaller. Alex saw his knees shaking.

The creature roared, filling the cave with such intense, savage energy that Alex thought she might just die from fright. She couldn't tell if the sound was in the cavern, in her head, or both. It raised its arms—black arms as long as she was—with its fierce face vibrating with fury and its purple eyes flaring...

Then it suddenly *vanished* with another *zip* sound.

Purple motes of light appeared in a line heading off into the darkness.

"There it goes!" Jack shouted. His voice shook with fear. "Look out! It'll come back!"

There was a second of silence. The mad roaring sound faded. Liamfrey dropped his iron pickaxe and pulled out his fiery sword.

Alex heard Jack breathing...

Then, it appeared again with a *zip* and a rush of fury. It was suddenly standing in front of Liam—towering over him—with its huge mouth open and its eyes full of violence. It raised its massive arms and swung down at him, smashing the Minecraftian on one shoulder. Liam's red scarf flew out as he buckled under the blow with a grunt.

Alex didn't think about it. She ran up with her iron sword ready and plunged it into the creature's back. Its cry of pain was something that would haunt her dreams.

Zip.

It disappeared again in a flash of purple bits of light.

"Liam!" she screamed. "Are you okay?!"

He was already back on his feet, holding his shoulder. He'd dropped his torch, but had his sword ready. They could hear the creature's terrifying, buzzing noises and cries flying all around the chamber as it was a ghost slipping through the walls.

"I'm okay!" Liamfrey replied. "Get ready! Give me some room!"

He switched his sword's grip just like he had that time he'd spun around and killed that skeleton. Alex knew that he was about to do that *special move* of his as soon as—

Zip.

Then Alex balked as the raging Enderman appeared looming over her like a nightmare. She looked up at its tall form—its menacing face, mouth, and purple eyes made her blood freeze—and it raised its arms.

She heard Jack letting out a small-voiced battle cry just before she was bashed so hard that she lost track of direction. Alex felt the mob's heavy fists smash into her torso, *clanging* loudly against what was left of her iron armor. She heard something break. Pieces of metal clattered to the ground. Another devastating strike followed, bashing her over the head, making Alex see stars. She fell back and raised her blade helplessly, hoping that she could stop another blow...

"Whirlwind *attack!*" Liam shouted suddenly. There was a flare of fire and the dark monster before her reared up in pain. Its eyes

461

seemed to spit purple flames. When it spun around—so fast!—she saw that its black back was *on fire*.

Jack and Liam were attacking it. The boy hacked at the Enderman again and again with his stone sword. Liamfrey recovered from his spinning move, flipped his sword's grip again, and *parried* one of the creature's falling fists. Then, he stabbed it through its perfectly-smooth, perfectly-black chest.

The fire spread over its body then it burned.

Zip.

It vanished again. A trail of purple motes of light and smoke from the Enderman's burning body streaked away into the darkness on the other side of the cavern. The entire cave was filled with the skin-scraping noise of its weird screams.

Alex was *so scared*.

Jack and Liam faced away from her. She bet that Jack was just as scared as she was. That thing was freaking terrifying!

"It'll be back!" Jack shouted.

Then it was. The monster appeared again, *zipping* back to stand between Liam and the diamond. Its whole body was on fire! It roared and shook Alex's skull, its howling mouth wreathed in flames as its purple eyes burned even brighter. The Minecraftian was quick though, and dodged backwards as the monster reared up and swung its mighty fists down again.

Liamfrey countered with his red-hot sword as it missed, slashing across the creature's burning torso. Jack also charged—more bravely than Alex could believe—and hacked at the creature's long legs with his stone sword. Alex found herself advancing—even though she was *flying* with freezing fear—and she stabbed at the monster with her iron blade.

That did it. The thing was on fire. It was surrounded. The sound of its dying scream hurt Alex's head and ears. The Enderman's tall form fell to one side under one last strike from Liamfrey, fire streaking from it as it toppled, then the whole, dark body vanished into a large cloud of grey smoke.

Experience orbs and a strange, green sphere appeared where the Enderman had disintegrated.

The three of them all stood still for a moment in the resulting silence.

Alex heard Jack breathing heavily. She looked at the boy and saw his chest heaving. His face still showed his fear.

Then, Liamfrey broke the quiet air.

"Alrighty then," he said, reaching down and picking up the odd orb. "Back to the diamonds."

"It never hit me!" Jack exclaimed. He looked partly relieved and part angry. "I still don't know what happens if an Enderman hits me!"

Alex finally relaxed. She hurt all over.

She felt so relieved that she actually laughed.

"That's something that you might not want to test out, Jack," she said.

They all laughed.

Liamfrey collected two diamonds from the stone wall. He turned to Alex and smirked, cocking his eyebrow. "One for me, one for you. I reckon that's fair, eh?"

Alex took the diamond he offered. She smiled back. "I reckon so," she replied. "What was that orb thing?"

Liam cracked open his grinning mouth to reply, but Jack beat him to it.

"An Ender pearl," the boy said.

"What's it do?" Alex asked.

"Well," Jack replied. "You can use it to teleport," he said. "You can also use it to make an *Ender Eye* to find a stronghold. Oh—you can also use it to make an Ender *chest*."

"Well I'll be," Liam said. "You sure know a lot about Ender pearls, kid."

"I know *a lot* about Vortexia," Jack replied. He looked proud now. The fear was gone.

Liamfrey tucked the diamond he kept away into his pack then rooted around inside. "I *suppose*," he finally said, "we should get a little more redstone, then I'll have enough for the *Thunderbird* for now. We'll head up in a short while to my airship. I've got furnaces and an anvil there. Your armor's pretty beat up there, little lady," he said, smirking and pointing at Alex's chest.

She looked down. Her chest plate was heavily damaged. It was cracked open. The majority of her right arm's plates had fallen off. Then, she felt the cool cavern air in her hair. Alex sheathed her sword and reached up to her helmet. It too, was so badly damaged that it probably wouldn't protect her anymore. Heck—it could hardly still sit on her head. She took it off and shook out her hair.

Dang.

Picking up the pieces of her armor on the ground, Alex put her helmet and what was too damaged to stay on her body into her pack.

She could probably fix it, but it would take a good bit of that iron they'd collected. She'd have to give some of that to Liam, too, since he'd helped them collect it. Dang—there were some pieces that she might not even be able to fix with iron and an anvil. She might have to craft whole new sections or armor to have a full suit again.

They continued around the bedrock level for a while, gathering more redstone. There were no more Enderman attacks and no more diamonds. Whenever zombies, skeletons, or spiders came at them, Jack took care of them for the most part. Whenever a creeper stalked out of the darkness, Liam killed it, or Alex filled it full of arrows. They collected a lot of mob parts and a good bit more of redstone.

On the way back up, when they reached the lava pool again, they took a nice break. Mobs didn't show up much around lava. It was too bright for them. That's what Steve always said, anyway.

Alex wondered what Steve was up to. Was he looking for them?

She'd have to leave him some sort of *message*.

When they continued, following the narrow path that Liam had carved for them along the side of the long, weaving lava pool, Alex was shocked to see two zombies walking their way from the other direction.

Without a moment's hesitation, the boy Jack stepped around Liam to kill them.

"Be careful, Jack!" Alex said.

The kid looked back with an over-confident smirk. Alex saw a flash of Steve in the expression.

"Don't worry," he said. "They can't hurt me."

"But that *lava* can," Liamfrey said. "Don't fall over or get pushed around now..."

Looking at the bubbling, blazing magma next to them all, Jack widened his eyes and swallowed. *That* seemed to smother his puffed-up attitude a bit. Then, the boy turned to face the incoming zombies, raised his sword, and waited…

S1E5 - Chapter 6 – Steve

"I'll save you, Steve!!"

Surrounded by zombies, terribly wounded, exhausted, and backed into a corner next to the glowing forge of the blacksmith's shop in a village full of undead, Steve stared at Alice the ninja as she dropped down from the roof.

She almost instantly killed two hostile mobs with her black, fiery *DevilScythe*.

Steve was beyond surprised. He was *shocked*.

He wouldn't have expected this in a million years! He thought that he was toast, yet here was the mysterious Minecraftian woman spawned from the Divining Pool, fighting before him like a swift and angry animal. As quickly as Alice dropped the first two zombies, she turned and cut through two more, spinning her blazing black weapon with a display of skill that Steve couldn't believe.

The zombie villager blacksmith that had emerged from inside the small shop was cut into two flaming pieces, then it collapsed in a puff of grey smoke.

Alice's pale blue eyes almost seemed to glow orange in the fiery light of her weapon and the small amount of lava in the forge next to them.

"Alice!" Steve exclaimed, finally finding his voice.

She met his gaze for just a moment. Her eyes were full of energy; she was focused like a laser. Her pale face was covered with a black mask. The woman's raven-black hair made her skin look as white as snow. Steve couldn't see her mouth on account of that mask, but he was certain that she was smiling with malicious *glee*.

"Get inside!" Alice shouted, whirling her black scythe around her body like a protective shield of fire and keen edges. "Take the gear! Eat the food!"

Steve obeyed. Alice had very quickly made an opening for him. He'd hardly seen the zombies fall under her lightning-fast attacks. There was more light now than there was a second ago because two nearby zombies—wounded but not destroyed—were *on fire*. A loud groaning and snarling filled the air all around them. Dozens more undead were pressing in from a horde approaching from the streets.

Dashing around the raised work area of the blacksmith's, Steve jumped over a falling body of another zombie villager that Alice killed, and rushed into the tiny abode where he knew a chest would be.

Moments ago, he'd hoped that there'd be a sword in there. Gripping his iron shovel, Steve was ready for another zombie to be hiding inside...

The inside of the shop was empty, save for the chest that Steve expected and a table with two oak booths in the corner.

Steve immediately ran to the chest and threw it open with a *creak*. He heard the constant sound of battle outside as he did. Zombies snarled. They grunted and hissed in pain. He heard the sound of them dying and burning. He didn't hear Alice making any noise, but occasionally, he heard the fiery fluttering of her weapon swinging through the air.

"What a woman!" Steve exclaimed to himself, looking into the wooden container with a grin.

Jackpot.

Inside the chest was a pile of loot that would help him quite a bit. Well—*mostly*. Steve picked up and quickly ate three red apples. Almost right away, he felt his body healing and energy flowing through him. He pulled out a brand-new iron chest plate and threw it on. Dang—it felt great to be wearing armor again! There was also a full suit of iron *horse* armor and a saddle, which Steve struggled to move aside, looking for more items below it. He found two blocks of obsidian—which he left—and an *iron pick axe*.

"Yes!" he exclaimed, picking up the high quality tool. If he managed to survive this, he'd have to give this pick axe to Alex to replace the one of hers he'd lost.

"Come on, Steve!" Alice called angrily from outside amidst the sea of zombie groans and snarls. "Let's get *outta here!*"

Steve considered the iron shovel in one hand and the iron pick axe in his other.

He wished that he'd found a sword, but one of these would have to do.

Stashing his shovel, Steve turned around—now renewed and armored with his new pick axe in his hands—and rushed out to help his savior.

He found Alice tumbling and running around through a crowd of dead-eyed, growling zombies. They reached for her and she evaded them easily, sometimes pausing to cut one down with her fiery *DevilScythe*. She'd left the deck of the blacksmith's structure and was now out in the street flitting around what looked like the base of some *stairs* that she'd hastily created on the side of a house with dirt blocks.

Wow. She made a way up to the roof while dodging and fighting countless undead?!

Steve then realized that he was standing at the entrance to the shop, grinning stupidly and watching Alice struggle to survive.

"Dummy," he muttered to himself then raised his pick axe and ran down to help, sinking the tool's metal tip into the back of a zombie in his way. "I'm here!" Steve shouted over the chaos. "You made those stairs?!"

He felt like a dummy again for saying that. *Of course* she made them.

"Let's go!" Alice said, flashing her pale eyes his way while ducking under the slowly swinging green fist of a zombie in pursuit. "Climb up! I'll cover you!"

Steve did. He felt weird about Alice ordering him around, but he knew that she was only trying to help him; to save their lives. Normally, Steve was the one taking charge in battles. He was always the one saving Alex. It was strange to be the one being rescued this time.

Leaping around the zombie he'd just struck in the back—it wasn't dead yet—Steve slammed his now-armored shoulder into another zombie in his way with a loud *clang* and knocked the mob backwards. As it recovered, he jumped up onto the first dirt block, swung down with his pick axe to knock away the strong hands of *another* zombie that was reaching for his legs, then he jumped up onto the next highest block.

"I'm up!" he called down to Alice, who flitted through the crowd of undead like a dark ghost, her face and eyes white surrounded by the black shapes of her hair, body, and twirling weapon. Her DevilScythe's wicked blade left a trail of fire as it whirled around and sometimes sliced through the mobs.

Steve wanted to wait for Alice to join him before climbing higher, but more zombies were already trying to climb the bottom block to chase him.

Then, Alice was suddenly there, spinning and cutting them down. She followed Steve up the improvised stairs, looking up at him with an intense glare.

"Go! Go on!" she shouted.

He did.

Steve reached the roof with Alice running up quickly behind him. After a moment of looking back down at the zombies pursuing them up the dirt blocks, Steve looked down at the iron pick axe in his hands, paused, then switched to his shovel again.

The moment Alice was on the roof next to him, Steve destroyed the highest two blocks, leaving the zombies following them nowhere to go. One of the mobs immediately fell back down into the street.

Both Minecraftians looked down at the many green faces staring back up at them with rotten teeth and dull, black eyes. The moaning and groaning grew louder. Some of them raised their arms and reached up, but Steve and Alice were *safe*.

Steve sighed.

They looked at each other and smiled.

Alice then pulled down her mask, letting Steve see her face. She was, indeed, smiling. She had a sharp, cruel face, but she seemed happy for the moment. Despite her ice-like hardness, she was actually rather pretty. There was a kind of crazy look in her eyes, but Steve also saw a warm softness in there ... deep, deep down in there.

He found himself grinning like a fool.

Steve opened his mouth to speak, but couldn't think of anything to say. He realized that he was standing very close to Alice. He could reach out and touch her, where before, she'd always stayed far away from him.

He felt awkward and shy for some reason.

Then, Alice stood bolt upright and turned away, looking out over the roofs of the dark village.

"You're *welcome*," she said.

Steve balked.

"Uh ... *thanks*," he replied. "Where ... where'd you come from?"

He walked to the middle of the roof. They were standing on top of one of the smaller houses. There wasn't very much room to move around. Looking across, Steve saw two spiders exploring the tops of the other buildings. One of them was just across the street on top of the blacksmith's canopy, and was scuttling their way. Its many red eyes glowed brightly in the very dark night.

"We need to keep moving," Alice said, scanning the town. She pointed with a black-gloved hand. "There. Let's head to the church. We can hole up there for the night. It's still dangerous here."

As if to accentuate her point, an arrow whistled by over Steve's head. He ducked.

"Dang!" he said, looking for the skeleton archer. It had shot at him from somewhere on the ground or in the dunes surrounding the village. They were close to the town's edge.

"Follow me!" Alice exclaimed, then took a running start and leapt from their roof to the roof of the house across another narrow, sandstone street. The ninja flew through the air and landed nimbly on the other roof with ease.

Steve huffed and puffed, shook the soreness out of his arms and legs, then ran to follow. He felt much heavier than Alice looked. His armored torso shook and jangled as he rushed to the roof's edge and *leapt* as hard as he could.

With a jolt of fear, Steve thought for a moment that he wouldn't make it. He looked down as he sailed through the air and saw many zombies looking up at him from the dark streets...

Then, he landed on the next roof.

They repeated the process a few times, leaping from roof to roof, heading for the other side of the village. The sky was pretty dark, but in the light of the moon, Steve could see the glass of the church's windows gleaming back at him. *That's* where she was leading them.

Once, Steve had to stop to fend off an attacking spider. Alice was already one building ahead of him when the mob pounced over the edge of the roof he was on, colliding with Steve with a *hiss* and a *clank* of his armor. It tried to bite him, but its fangs glanced harmlessly off of his iron chest plate.

Steve grimaced as he threw the eight-legged mob off of him. He spun on it and wound up his iron shovel with both hands. Then, when the hissing spider with its many glaring red eyes pounced at him again, Steve swung and *splatted* the thing with a loud *clang*. It fell off of the roof, either stunned or dead, and Steve ran on.

He met Alice on the last rooftop before jumping across to the church. She stood waiting, looking at a window leading into the church's second floor. If they were to jump across to the church like they had been across the many houses, they'd be able to leap right through the window ... *if* it was open.

"Now, *go!*" Alice ordered. "Jump through the window."

"But ... there's *glass!*" Steve replied. He felt pretty certain that he could make the jump, but it meant crashing through the glass and into the church. He couldn't do that. That would be just—

"Do it!" Alice said. Her pale eyes glittered with an energy that Steve didn't understand. "You go first. Your armor will protect you."

Two arrows whistled past them. One landed in the church's exterior wall with a *thunk*.

Steve looked at Alice, looked at the window across the street, narrowed his eyes, then sprinted.

He ran, leapt, covered his face with his armored arms, then *crashed* through the window, tumbling into the upper level of the church with a shower of tinkling, broken glass.

Alice sailed through the window after him without a sound, landing nimbly on her feet near him. Steve watched from the floor as she looked back through the window out into the night for a moment then turned to him with a wolfish grin.

She reached down to help him up with her slender, gloved hand.

Steve took it and pulled himself to his feet. Touching Alice's hand made him feel like cold water was rushing through his blood. His chest tingled.

"Good job," Alice said, meeting his gaze with a firm smile. "We're still alive."

Steve shook himself off. Glass tinkled to the floor.

"Uh ... thanks again."

The inside of the church was quiet. He could hear the muffled groans and snarls of the undead mobs outside. They must be down there in the streets, plodding along and slowly heading their way.

What a rush! Steve thought. He realized that he was smiling.

Then, a loud, clear growl came from the stairway down to the ground floor.

Alice immediately pulled out some dirt blocks and filled in the gap, sealing her and Steve off into the second level of the church. It wasn't a big building, but it was tall. There was another level above them, too—a ladder led to an open rooftop—hopefully zombie-free.

They were safe, for real this time.

They were also *alone*.

That made Steve feel nervous again.

He looked back at Alice and saw her looking at him hungrily.

"Where'd you come from, Alice?" he asked. "How'd you find me? I don't even know where I am."

Alice smiled, sighed, and looked around. Apparently satisfied, she slinked over to the ladder leading up and climbed it with an easy quickness.

"Come on," she said as she paused halfway to the roof.

Steve followed her up. The top of the church was taller than the rest of the village. They sat on the roof facing each other under the night sky with their backs to the railing that went all the way around. Steve felt curious and full of questions. This was the ... *third* time he'd run into Alice...? He wanted to know more about her. If she came from the Divining Pool, did she just *appear* that day and start living here? Or did she have a whole history of stuff that she'd been through before?

Why did she hate Alex?

And why did she *like* Steve...?

Mobs groaned and hissed and gurgled out of sight far below them in the streets. Steve felt an energy in his body that was *delightful*. What adventure! Fighting a zombie horde and leaping rooftop to rooftop, only to crash through a window?! What a great time!

Amazingly enough, the pitch-black sky was already shifting to a dark blue in what must have been the *east*. Morning was coming. Steve looked in the opposite direction of the lightening horizon and saw that the moon was low. He'd been running and fighting all night.

Alice watched Steve thinking with a small smile on her face, then, she pulled some cooked pork chops from her pack. Steve smelled the delicious meat and instantly felt hungry.

As if sensing his need, Alice handed some pieces of pork to him. Steve ate.

"Thanks," he mumbled between bites.

Jeez—he was full of nothing but *thank you's* and couldn't think of anything else to say. Alice wasn't really saying much at all. She still hadn't answered any of his questions. She just watched him. Her pale eyes played over him as he ate. She smiled as if amused.

Maybe *she* was afraid to talk to him as well...

"So, where are we?" Steve finally asked, suppressing a burp.

Alice looked off into the night and shrugged. "A zombie village," she said. "North of the temple."

North of the temple? Steve thought. He frowned. How the heck did he lose his way so badly?

"How'd you find me?"

476

Alice smirked. "I've been watching over you, dear Steve, while you ran through the desert at night like." She kicked her head back and laughed at the sky. "Like an *idiot!*"

Steve felt himself blush. He felt a stab of anger, but Alice's laughing face was hard to look away from.

"Since when?" he asked.

"Since home."

Steve swallowed.

Back when he ran away from the homestead to catch up to Alex, Jack, and Liamfrey, he'd *imagined* Alice being somewhere in the shadows of the forest, watching him. Was she actually there? Was *she* that dark shape that he'd thought might have been her?

"You're ... um ... a really good fighter," Steve said. "I've never seen someone fight as good as you."

That was the truth. Steve knew that he was a strong warrior himself, but he'd never seen the level of skill and speed that she'd displayed, fighting off those countless zombies and saving his butt down there.

"Thanks," Alice said. "You're pretty good yourself. And I'm not a *fighter*. I'm a ninja."

Her pale eyes spoke of many unsaid things. She looked back and forth between Steve's face, his armor, his hands, and the night around them. Alice seemed confident but also a little nervous. She smiled and looked away as Steve watched her.

"What's that weapon of yours?" Steve asked. "It's called the *DevilScythe*, right?"

That caught her attention. Alice met his gaze firmly and narrowed her pretty eyes.

"How'd you know that?!" she asked, suddenly angry. "What do you know about it?!"

"Um..."

Steve thought about the message from the Divining Pool. By now, he couldn't remember the whole thing, but he remembered the name of her weapon. It was a flaming scythe. It looked a lot like a black pick axe. It probably had some sort of *fire enchantment*, which was how it had set all of those zombies aflame. Looking at the unique weapon on Alice's back, Steve realized that he was starting to *see* a lot better. The sky was lightening in the east and now dark blue everywhere else. The sun would rise at any moment.

He didn't dare tell Alice about the Divining Pool. She seemed very ... *volatile*. Heck—the Divining Pool had said that she was evil. Steve remembered that much. What would Alice do if she knew that they'd known she was coming; if she knew that she was created by Alex's weird artifact?

Albert Einstein, Steve thought, thinking back. She's as intelligent as Albert Einstein. That was in the message, too.

"Who's ... um ... Albert Einstein?" Steve asked.

"Don't change the subject! Why aren't you telling me?!" Alice hissed. "Did Alex tell you its name? Did that *demon thing* tell her the name of my weapon after I attacked her?!"

Steve gasped.

"You ... *attacked her?!*" he said. "You attacked Alex?!"

"Yes, well," Alice stammered, instantly on the defensive and meek again. The anger vanished. "Dear Steve," she said with an alluring smile, "I had to ... um ... well..."

The sun peeked over the eastern horizon, sending shafts of bright, golden light streaking through the night sky. They both looked at the dawn for a moment. Steve looked back at Alice. She met his gaze with the breaking light in her pale eyes. She looked like she wanted something but was afraid to say it. She squirmed once, shifting her weight on the cobblestone rooftop.

"You can't do that, Alice," Steve said, meeting her gaze and feeling like he was pinning her down with his eyes. "Alex is my friend."

"She doesn't *deserve you*."

Steve scoffed. "She's my *best* friend. Look, Alice," he said with a sigh. "I don't ... um ..." He was going to say that he didn't know what she was after, but he remembered. She liked *him*. She was curious about Jack. She hated Alex. "Alice, you're such an amazing warrior—"

"I am a *ninja*," she countered. "There's a difference."

"You're an amazing ninja. Why don't you *join us*, and be our friend? It'd be *great* going on adventures with you. Think of what we can all do together with you on our team...?"

Alice's eyes flitted away. She frowned then looked back into Steve's eyes again.

"I ... I can't, my dear Steve," she replied. "I can't stand to be with Alex. I *hate her*. She just takes advantage of you; can't you see?! Why don't you just ... be with *me* and ... it'll be just you and me! We can go on all kinds of adventures and explore the world! We can—"

"I can't do that, Alice," Steve said. "Alex is my best friend. We've always been together. My friendship with her is the strongest part of me." Saying the words warmed Steve's heart. He meant it. He knew it now more than ever. "As long as Alex is in my life, we'll be together. She's with me. I can't let you hurt her."

Alice watched with wide eyes, digested what he'd said, then looked away.

She replied with her voice as cold as a knife's edge: "As long as she's in your life, huh?"

Steve felt a chill.

"Um ... I don't really like your *tone* there, Alice..."

With that, Alice smiled sweetly. She met Steve's gaze, and the desperate energy she'd been radiating a moment before was replaced with contentment. She pointed out into the desert.

"The temple is *directly* to the south, dear Steve," she said. "I'm sure you'll find your precious *Alex* and Jack *there*."

Steve looked at where she pointed. Quickly noting the position of the rising sun, he saw that she was, indeed pointing south. Now that the night was over, they should definitely head there and—

Looking back at Alice, Steve gasped.

She was gone.

Totally *gone*.

She'd vanished, no doubt leaping over the edge of the roof.

Steve stood like a shot and ran to the edge. He leaned over the railing and looked down into the village, but he didn't see any flitting, shadowy black shape running through the streets or on the shorter roofs. He didn't see any sign of Alice at all.

As the spreading daylight set all of the zombies and skeletons down below on fire, Steve looked around the village for any signs of her, but saw nothing but mobs.

When the last of the many undead were all burnt up into ashes by the light of morning, Steve prepared himself to climb back down to the streets. He had to go south to find Alex, Jack, and Liam.

Steve prepared to continue his journey to catch up to his friends, but a lump of dread grew in his belly...

Alice had been correct.

After making his way back down into the village streets—picking up several bits of zombie meat, bones, a few arrows, and even two potatoes from the destroyed undead on his way out of town—Steve walked south into the desert.

It was hot, and the sand was difficult to trudge through after a while, but he had a full stomach and felt a lot better than he did several hours ago.

Eventually, Steve saw the telltale shape and red markings of the desert temple in his path.

When he reached the ancient structure, he was glad to step into its interior and out of the sun for a while.

"Alex!" he shouted before pausing to listen for any mobs—husk zombies most likely—that might be lying in wait. "Alex? Jack? Are you guys here? Liam?"

The inside of the desert temple was silent, dry, and well-lit by many torches.

That's good, Steve thought. That would keep the zombies away.

Looking toward the center of the old, dusty place, Steve stared at the hole in the sandstone floor where he'd fallen through into the treasure chamber before. A chill ran up his spine. But heck—he'd died so many times that it was no big deal. It was fine. Dying wasn't a big deal. He always came back. They could always harvest more stuff and craft more items, right?

Just on the other side of the hole that used to be the blue block in the center of the main chamber was a crude wooden sign stuck into the floor on a thin pole.

"Hey, a sign!" Steve exclaimed, striding forward.

As he peered at the writing—that sign had *definitely* not been there before—Steve yelped when he almost stepped into the hole that was his doom before.

"Whoa!" he said, nearly slipping to his death. He stabilized at the edge of the pit.

Wow, Steve thought, looking down into the treasure chamber. The room full of chests that had been down there before was *gone*. In its place was a big hole that opened into a vast, dark ravine that went *way down*. He could see the glow of lava far away. Steve also saw a series of carefully placed dirt blocks leading down into the gaping opening then hooking around the unseen ravine ceiling; likely leading to the ravine wall.

"Probably still down there," he said to himself, letting out a nervous chuckle.

He'd almost died there again. If he'd fallen into that hole, he would have plunged to his death at the bottom of that deep, dark ravine. He would have lost his new iron armor chest plate and the new iron pick axe that he was going to give to Alex.

How embarrassing...

"Heh ... whatever," Steve said with a shrug. "I can always make new stuff."

He looked at the sign and read the words:

Steve, it said. *We are at Liam's airship to the east. – Alex.*

He smiled. So they were okay. They were with Liam at the *Thunderbird*.

"Okay," Steve said to himself, turning and facing the blinding light of the desert coming from the temple's front opening. "To the east!"

Steve left.

From the desert temple, he couldn't see the Thunderbird in the air, but he knew that it was there, lost in the haze beyond his vision.

After walking east for a while, Steve saw the magnificent airship again: a grey shadow in the distance, high above the ground and shaped like a sea vessel held up by four massive propellers that he couldn't hear yet from how far away he was.

Eventually, trudging on through the sands and grinning at the thought of seeing his friends again, Steve made it to the airship. He saw the ladder hanging down to the desert floor up ahead. Looking skyward, he heard the constant *whup whup whup* of the propellers.

"*Steve!* Hey, Steve!"

It was Alex's voice. Steve looked up and saw the silhouettes of her and Jack peering down over the edge of the ship. Alex waved.

"Hi, Alex!" he shouted back up, also waving.

Steve laughed. That airship was so cool! He was looking forward to going up there again. Maybe he'd be able to spot Alice somewhere in the distance with Liamfrey's big telescope! He was hungry. Alex probably had some *roasted chicken*. He had such a story to tell them!

He grabbed the lowest rung of the ladder and began to climb.

The warrior climbed and climbed, going higher and higher until he felt the desert wind blowing sideways against him and the *whup whup whup* of the propellers became a constant, loud drone. Steve heard Alex's voice—he didn't understand what she was saying, but he recognized the sound of it—up above. He heard Jack laugh in response.

Grinning from ear to ear, Steve hurried up the ladder, eager to see his friends.

Boy, did he have a tale to tell them!

Pulling himself up the final rungs onto the deck, Steve saw Alex wearing shining, new iron armor up top. The kid Jack sat on the wooden deck next to her. Liamfrey stood at the telescope up at the bow. They all turned to face him. Liam motioned for Steve to come closer.

Standing at the top of the long ladder, Steve grinned and shouted over the noise of the propellers and the gusty wind. He felt amazing.

"Man, am I glad to see *you guys!*" he shouted with a huge smile, waving with one hand. "Hey, there was a new message at the Divining Pool! Something about a trader in the village named *HelloDance-something-something!* Oh—and I fought off a billion zombies with nothing but *this shovel*, and—" A gust of wind made Steve slip a little, but he caught himself. He pulled out the shovel to show Alex, beaming at her. He wanted to tell them everything! "I found a *zombie village*, and Alice the ninja saved me, and I killed a spider by splatting it on the head like this!"

Steve swung his iron shovel. His friends' faces—all smiling and happy to see him—suddenly shifted into expressions of horror as the Minecraftian swung the tool, lost his balance in a gust of wind,

484

and *slipped off of the side of the ship*, tumbling over where the ladder met the deck...

The wind was suddenly roaring in Steve's ears and the pale desert sand rushed up to meet him...

You Died.

Steve woke up with his mind full of the *whup whup whup* sound of huge propellers and the heat of the desert wind.

He took a breath and gasped.

"What?!" he shouted then grimaced. "Oh, *come on!!*"

He died?!

He fell?!

He just ... *fell off of the airship?!*

Steve jumped to his feet, ready to shout out curses to the world. He'd have to cross the desert again! This was ridiculous! After all he'd been through last night, he just *fell* off of the side of the airship like a freaking *idiot?!* Come on!

Then, he paused.

Steve wasn't in his room.

His familiar space of oaken walls, empty armor stands, torches fixed randomly to the walls, and multiple dump chests was *gone*. He wasn't on his messy red bed.

He wasn't in *any* sort of bed.

Steve was standing in the middle of a dense, dark forest of tall pine trees and mossy boulders. Thick grasses waved in a cool, constant wind, and shadows stretched long from the many, thick trees.

He wasn't at home.

He'd spawned somewhere else.

"What the...?!" Steve mumbled, looking up at the blue sky and the towering trees around him.

Where the heck was he?!

Looking around, Steve had no idea where he'd appeared. He didn't recognize this forest. He didn't recognize *anything*.

"But ... *how?!*" he said to himself.

Why didn't he spawn in his bed? Unless ... something had *happened* to his bed?

Steve looked down. His chest was covered in nothing but a blue shirt. His armor was gone, of course, and so was everything else.

Dang.

Was his bed gone? Was something wrong with the homestead?

Steve sighed, suddenly afraid for Alex again. What was going on?

Looking up and around, trying to locate the sun, Steve tried to get his bearings. Then, he looked for some high ground and set off to try and figure out where the heck he was, if that was even possible.

If his bed was broken, then Steve could be *anywhere*.

He had to find his way home...

Season 1, Episode 6:
A Villager Returned Home
Season Finale!

Unwanted Guests
The Season ONE Finale!!

After falling to his death, Steve has respawned in a completely unknown forest, which is quite the surprise since he was supposed to appear back in his bed at home! Meanwhile, Jack the kid and Alex are with Liamfrey up on his airship, planning their next move and assuming that Steve is back at the homestead.

But, as Jack and his friends cross the desert again to rejoin the Minecraftian warrior, Steve is lost in the mountains where an Ender dragon dominates the land! And what they find when they return to the homestead turns out to be much worse—-and much deadlier—-than it seems. Will Steve make it back to his friends? And will Jack and Alex survive the terrible trap that awaits them?

S1E6 - Chapter 1 – Jack

Jack opened his eyes.

When he woke, he found himself under the clear blue sky, surrounded by the *whup whup whup* sound of massive propellers. His face was warm. In fact, he was warm all over. There was a gentle, mild breeze, and as he looked up at the sky and the blocky, semi-transparent clouds high overhead, he squinted his eyes in confusion.

He didn't remember falling asleep.

Jack remembered his little brother, Dex. They'd been home. Dex was watching Jack play Minecraft on his computer like usual, chatting constantly about all of the stuff he'd build and all of the zombies he'd kill when he finally got a computer of his *own* after his tenth birthday.

It had been an odd dream. Jack was playing a game where there was bedrock up on the surface. Alex was there, dressed in battered iron armor that was full of arrows and almost falling apart. Jack could both see the damaged armor with his eyes, but at the same time, he also saw her armor as shiny and pixelated and bright grey like it always was. He wouldn't be able to tell how damaged it *really* was until he looked at it in his inventory.

Yes, he had an inventory. When he'd been thirsty, playing at his computer with Dex watching over his shoulder and Alex sitting on his bed in the real world ... *the real world??* ... he'd opened his inventory and took out a can of Diet Coke.

Mom only kept Diet Coke in the house.

Now, back on the spongy floor of the airship with the propellers loud and repetitive around him, as he lay in the sun on the deck, Jack thought back to the real world...

He sat.

He looked at his hands; the curvy, fleshy hands of a real boy.

He was real.

Jack suddenly missed the real world. He missed Mom and Dad; Dex and his friends at school.

"What's happening back there?" he asked aloud. His mouth was dry.

The boy yawned, looking all around him at the hazy, bright vista of sand far below the *Thunderbird*; Liamfrey's unique airship bomber that probably didn't exist before the Divining Pool had mentioned it the other day.

Jack was still tired.

How long had he slept?

"Hey, Jack!" Alex called from the other side of the ship.

He looked over and saw Liam and Alex standing near the row of furnaces and other gear and chests near the opening to go down below decks. Liamfrey was helping her forge ingots of iron from all of the ore that they'd harvested from deep underground. Now, the airship pilot stood tall, squinting against the sun with his aviator goggles pushed up onto his leather helmet and putting his blocky fists on his hips. His red scarf fluttered in the wind. Alex— her smile and green eyes bright—smiled at him with an iron ingot in each hand. Her armor was off. She was dressed in a basic green shirt and brown trousers, just like she always had been in pictures and Minecraft posters. Both of the Damage Indicator bars hovering over their heads showed them at full health: 20/20.

Jack hadn't seen Alex out of her armor; not since he'd met her.

It was funny. She *was* Minecraft Alex. Steve was Steve. Where had they *come from?* Steve and Alex weren't around in normal games, right? They were just *characters*; the main characters of the game in advertisements and fan fiction. If this world of Vortexia really was the world that Jack had generated on his *Game Pendant* back in the real world, then why in the world were they *here*, anyway?

Then again, why were any of these characters here? Why was the Divining Pool here?

None of it made any sense.

Jack stood, standing shakily to his feet. His body was still numb and buzzing from his nap.

He wondered what Steve was up to. He hoped that the warrior would find their note...

"Hey, guys!" he called back, walking toward them across the wide, oak deck of the airship.

He yawned.

He needed more sleep.

"Welcome back!" Alex exclaimed as he approached. She smiled. Her orange-red hair blew in the wind. "How was your sleep?"

Jack rubbed his eyes then returned his glasses to his face. Mom was always getting on him about falling asleep with his glasses on. He'd broken glasses before by doing that. He'd still had his glasses on when he woke up just now. Mom would be mad f she knew.

"I ... I didn't mean to fall asleep," he said. "How long was I out?"

Alex smirked, put the iron ingots into her inventory, and looked up at the brilliant, square sun, high overhead.

"A few hours...?" she offered.

Jack sighed. He listened to his woozy head telling him to sleep some more and tried to ignore it. His body buzzed. He was exhausted. How long had he been awake *in real time?* Time was weird here. Sometimes, the days were passing in what felt like minutes—just like when normally playing the game—and other times it took *hours.*

He needed more sleep. Jack felt like he did that time he'd stayed up all night with Dex watching TV until the sunrise—even though Mom had told him to go to bed at 1:00AM—so, she made him and Dex stay up anyway, after just a few hours of sleep. That had been a hard day.

This was going to be a hard day. Heck—the day was already half-over!

"I think I need more sleep," he said to his Minecraftian friends.

Alex and Liam exchanged glances.

"Well," Alex said, "I'm almost done smelting all of this iron. We're about to fix up my armor and get going. Can you wait until we get home?"

Jack sighed. He looked up at the bright, blue sky then stared out into the desert that surrounded them.

"Yeah, I guess so," he said.

The first order of business when they got home: *Sleep.*

Jack decided to take a nice, long nap as soon as they returned home; to sleep until he didn't feel like sleeping anymore.

"Hey," Alex added. "We'll have enough iron left over to make you an iron sword. Want one?"

That perked Jack up.

Ever since he'd discovered that he was mostly *immune* to the attacks of zombies, skeletons, and spiders—he still didn't know about Endermen; that one deep underground had never hit him—he'd been doing a lot of the fighting. So far, Jack knew that he had to watch out for creepers and fire. That meant *lava*, too. He'd already broken a stone sword in their fights, so an iron sword would be *great* for him since he was bound to go through a lot of durability in—

Jack suddenly realized that his new stone sword was gone. Alex had made it for him underground when his last one had broken, and ... it was *gone*.

"Oh, duck feathers!" Jack exclaimed, looking around the deck of the airship frantically. "I lost my stone sword!"

He didn't remember falling asleep. If he'd just *dropped* it when he did, then it might have despawned while he was sleeping.

Dang.

"Oh, don't worry you worry about *that*," Liamfrey said with a smirk and a drawl.

"Yeah," Alex said. "We have plenty of wood and stone now. I can always make you another."

"I must have..." Jack muttered, shielding his eyes from the sun and looking back to the bow of the ship where he'd been sleeping next to the telescope. He reached into his collar behind his neck, hoping that it would still be hanging there in his shirt, but he already knew that it wasn't there. He would have felt its blocky edges uncomfortable against his back. "I guess I dropped it?"

"But who cares about that now?" Alex said with an excited look in her pixelated green eyes. "We have *iron*, Jack! We finally have iron again!" She smirked. "Hang on. I'll make you a *real* sword..."

Jack smiled and pushed his glasses up his nose, giving up on the wayward stone sword.

From now on, he thought, *put your stuff in a chest before going to sleep.*

"Well, heck yeah, I'd like an iron sword!" Jack said.

Alex smiled and nodded, reaching into the furnace near her and removing another ingot. Experience orbs tinkled and rang like little bells, absorbing into her body.

"So," Liamfrey said, raising his eyebrows and wandering a few steps toward what he called the 'port' side of the ship. He stared out over the desert. "I reckon that we should head down again and get some more redstone."

"More?" Jack asked, stepping up next to Alex and trying to access the interface of one of the several furnaces there lined up in a row. By reaching into it with his mind—intending to access the furnace and its fire—he could see a stack of ore burning inside, fueled by burning coal. "How much redstone do you need, Liam?"

Liamfrey laughed, facing the western desert.

"Well, Jack, *this here airship*—" He lovingly patted the wooden guardrail on the port side. "My good ole' *Thunderbird* eats a *heck* of a lot of redstone! I reckon I was gettin close to emergency levels before y'all came along. Now, thanks to yer help, I can keep her fires goin and keep her up in the air. It would be a terrible thing to ground her. But, if we have any hope of movin my Thunderbird out of the desert—like, say, to over yer home?—well, we'll need a *heck* of a lot more."

"How long will the new fuel last?" Alex asked.

"A few days, I reckon."

"Anybody seen Steve?" Jack asked. "While I was asleep?"

"Nah," Liamfrey said.

"No," Alex said, frowning and shaking her head.

"Think he'll get the note?" Jack asked. One piece of ore was finally transformed into an ingot as he watched the interface of one furnace. He reached in, pulled it out, and two glowing yellow orbs appeared at his feet. They rolled silently toward him until melding into Jack's shoes with a ringing sound.

So weird.

"I hope so," Alex said. "He's just so—"

"Hey!" Liamfrey said from the railing. "Speak of the devil!"

Jack and Alex looked toward the edge of the airship. Liam stood there with his red scarf whipping in the wind. He smiled, laughed, and pointed down at the desert to the west.

Alex and Jack both ran to the guardrail. Jack immediately felt a sense of fear jump up in him when he reached the edge. He didn't trust guardrails in this world. Everything he touched—with the exception of bedrock—was a little *squishy.*

There was a single figure down in the sand, heading their way.

Jack squinted his eyes to get a better look. He used one hand to shield the sun from his vision.

It was the shape of a Minecraftian ... carrying a *shovel.*

Huh.

"*Steve!*" Alex suddenly shouted above the noise of the propellers. She waved excitedly. "Hey, Steve!"

The figure stopped and looked up. He waved.

"Hi, Alex!" Steve shouted from far below.

It *was* Steve! He'd found the note. Well, it was a *sign* they'd left for him in the desert temple, but it was basically a note. There were no real, actual *notes* in this game.

"Quick!" Alex said, turning away from the railing as Steve headed toward the ship and its long, hanging rope ladder. "I wanna finish my armor!"

She ran to the anvil, pulled out her old armor, and Jack was shocked to see her either make new armor or fix up her old stuff within a matter of *seconds*. There were several loud *clangs* then she put it all back on in an instant, beaming with pride as her metal suit of iron shined in the sun, practically brand new.

"Awesome!" Jack said. "It looks so shiny!"

He wasn't lying. It did.

Liam laughed and leaned against the guardrail with his arms crossed over his chest. He watched her and Jack with a broad smile as his scarf fluttered in the wind.

"Hey, can you make my new sword, too?" Jack asked, walking up.

"Sure!" Alex replied with a grin. She looked very happy in her new armor.

They approached a crafting table together. Alex worked at the device as quickly as only a Minecraftian (or a player) could, then she pulled off a shining, blocky blade of iron. She handed it to Jack.

Upgrade, he thought with a smile. He took the weapon. The weird, blocky handle was just as strange and uncomfortable as on his previous stone swords. Jack wondered if he'd ever get used to it.

Then, he heard the sound of Steve grunting, shimmying up the ladder close to the deck. They all turned to watch their friend arrive. Liamfrey strolled up to the telescope at the bow.

There was a gust of wind that shook the floor beneath Jack's feet. Feeling a sudden fear of falling out of the sky, he sat down. Alex looked down at Jack to see if he was okay. He smiled up at her.

Steve appeared at the top of the ladder, unarmored, carrying nothing more than a shovel. He beamed and balanced on the wooden platform at the top of the ladder. He released the rope and waved exuberantly with one hand.

"Man, am I glad to see *you guys!*" Steve shouted as another strong gust of wind blew across the deck. The warrior seemed to lose his balance a little, righted himself, then opened his mouth to continue. Jack suddenly felt very afraid that he'd fall. "Hey, there was a new message at the Divining Pool! Something about a trader in the village named *HelloDance-something-something!* Oh—and I fought off about a *billion* zombies with nothing but *this shovel*, and—"

Another gust of wind blew through them, making Steve's balance falter again. Alex gasped. Liam took a step forward and reached out as if to catch him, but was too far away.

"Get away from the ladder, Steve!" Liam called from the bow.

Steve didn't seem to hear him. "I found a *zombie village!*" he shouted excitedly. "And Alice the ninja saved me, and I killed a spider by splatting it on the head like this!"

Much to everyone's surprise, Steve swung his shovel dramatically over his head ... and *fell!*

He disappeared.

One second, he was at the top of the ladder, shouting over the *whup whup whup* of the propellers and the roar of the gusting wind, then ... he'd vanished!

"Tarnation!" Liamfrey shouted, rushing toward the ladder.

"*Steve!!*" Alex screamed in horror.

Jack was speechless. He stared in shock for a second then jumped to his feet.

Did he really just *fall off the ship* by being careless?!

"Dang!" Jack finally exclaimed. "Still alive?!"

They all rushed to the edge, stopping at the guardrails around the precarious top of the ladder.

"Watch it, now!" Liam shouted over the wind. "Don't fall yourselves!"

Jack managed to get a good hold of the oak railing and peered over the blocky edge of the ship; enough to see below them. He heard Alex gasp and scoff, then saw that she was looking over, too...

Steve's sprawled form was below them, dressed in Minecraft blues, down in the sand far under the ship for just an *instant*, then, the warrior disappeared in a puff of grey smoke. Where his body lay a second before, there were now a handful of glowing yellowish-green orbs of light, some random junk like zombie flesh and blocks of sand, and a shovel.

"*Dang it*, Steve!" Alex roared, stepping backwards away from the edge.

She stormed back to the area of the furnaces, her green eyes wide and full of anger and upset.

"What in tarnation was he *thinkin?*" Liamfrey said, looking over the edge and shaking his head. He walked back to the furnace area, too. "Well," he added. "I reckon making redstone the priority just fell a few rungs *down the ladder...?*"

Alex scoffed. "Ugh," she said.

Was that supposed to be a joke?

"So, now," Jack said, shaking his head and walking back to his friends. He resisted a gust of wind that tried to push him over. "Steve's *home* again."

"*Again!*" Alex shouted.

"Did you hear him say something about a trader in the village?" Jack asked.

"I heard *HelloDance-something-something*," Liam said. "And I *do* still need more redstone. I'd be mighty appreciative of any help y'all—"

Alex sighed loudly enough to cut him off. She looked down at Jack. Jack could see her calming down already. Steve must die a lot.

"I like the idea of you moving your airship to be next to our house," Alex said to Liam. "Don't you have enough fuel to fly there? It's just *one day* across the desert."

"I'm afraid not, little lady," Liamfrey replied. "Another mining expedition should cover that, though, I reckon. However, I'm figurin that ... you don't want to do that just yet..."

"You wanna go back for Steve?" Jack asked.

Alex looked at the horizon, then, toward where he'd fallen off of the ladder.

"We should all get together again," she said.

It would be good to have Steve with them when they went underground for more redstone. That mine—the ravine directly under the desert temple's blown-up treasure room—was a great place to get resources. It was so open, and ... *heck* ... it even had an *abandoned mine shaft!* They hadn't even *set foot* in that place yet!

"So," Jack said, "let's head home, get Steve, then we go back to the temple for more redstone."

Alex sighed. "Oh, *Steve...*" she muttered.

"That's a fella who could definitely stand to be more careful," Liamfrey said.

"You have *no idea*," Alex replied. "Okay, Jack. Good plan."

"Y'all reckon we can be back within a few days?" Liam asked. "I don't wanna run outta *fuel*."

"Oh, yeah," Jack replied, looking up into the airship pilot's blue eyes. "Unless ... I dunno ... something *weird and crazy* happens."

Liamfrey frowned, groaned, crossed his arms over his chest, then sighed and smiled.

"It might be a good idea to take a gander at that village you mentioned," he said. "Either on the way there or on the way back. I have other supplies for the Thunderbird and my own personal gear to replace."

"Sure," Alex said. "We'll check out that *HelloDance* person." She stared out into the desert, kind of north-east. "Now, which way is home...?"

Liamfrey disappeared below deck. He was probably picking up some food for the journey.

Jack reached out to Alex, gripped her strange, blocky back, and turned her around.

"This way," he said, pointing her to the west. "*That's* west. The house and the village and the temple are to the west."

Alex signed and smiled down at the boy. "I have *no* sense of direction, Jack."

"That's okay," Jack said. "Hey—we should make you a compass! We have iron and redstone. Do you know how to make one? I know how if you don't."

Alex shook her head with a sheepish smile and shrugged.

"Don't bother," Liamfrey said, climbing the stairs from below again. "I've already got one. I made it while you were sleepin, Jack. I'm reckon I'll need a lot more compasses, too, if I expect to make a big map like I had before I lost my gear." He pulled out what Jack instantly recognized as a compass from his inventory and handed it to Alex. "Here," Liam said. "Just give it back later."

"Thanks," Alex said, looking over the device.

"The paper's gonna be the hardest thing to acquire," Liam added. "There's no dang *sugar cane* around here."

"You can probably buy some in the village," Jack said.

"I'm counting on it, boy," Liamfrey replied with a grin.

They gathered some more things—survival gear and food, mostly—then met at the top of the ladder.

Jack was thirsty. He was tired. He was hungry again, too. He'd have to eat whatever weird Minecraft food Alex had to give him whenever they took their first break. He hoped that she still had that bucket of water...

"Ah—tarnation!" Liam said, looking down over the edge. "Looks like we'll have to wait a little while."

"What's the problem?" Alex asked, cautiously stepping forward and looking over the edge too.

Jack looked down as well.

There was a large group of what had to be *husk zombies* milling around the bottom of the ladder. It looked like they'd been wandering through the sand until running into the bottom of the ladder—which was one block too high for them to climb—and seemed to be ... confused.

"Uh oh," Alex said.

Jack watched the zombies. They moved erratically, as if their programing was telling them to climb the ladder, but they couldn't. It looked like—from their movements—they might be there for a while.

He counted twelve of them.

"No problem, I guess," Jack said, looking up at his Minecraftian friends. He reached back and made sure that his new iron sword was still sheathed in the back of his shirt, secured by his collar. It was. "I'll just go down and take em out."

Liamfrey nodded after considering that for a moment. "I reckon that'd be okay. They likely can't hurt ya."

"That's what I figure," Jack said.

"Are you sure, Jack?" Alex asked. She looked concerned. "There's a lot of them."

Jack felt confident. It would be a great test for his new iron blade!

"Oh, sure," he said. "No creepers; no fire. I'll be fine. I'll try out this new sword!"

"Just ... be careful," Alex said.

"And don't *fall*," Liam added. "Take your time on the way down. I don't reckon you're immune to *falling*."

"I'm sure you're right," Jack said.

Then, swallowing his great fear of the gusty wind and being so high up, the boy got down onto his hands and knees and cautiously backed over the edge of the ship. He held his breath as he inched over the rim, moving his feet around desperately to find the first rope rung.

He was terrified of slipping and falling.

When Jack found the top rung, he made triple-sure that he was on it, then kept moving down and out until his hands were holding the sides of the ladder.

He started down.

"Be careful!" Alex repeated.

He looked up and saw both of them watching him intently.

"I will!" he shouted back over the *whup whup whup* of the propellers and the noise of the wind. The wind tried to pull him off of the ladder.

Looking down, Jack began his careful descent to the sandy desert floor, where a dozen husk zombies waited for him...

S1E6 - Chapter 2 – Alex

"*This is great!*" Jack the kid shouted, dashing around in the sand below the airship's ladder.

It was astounding to watch. Liamfrey had carefully designed his ladder to be high enough over the ground to keep mobs from mindlessly finding it and climbing their way up to the ship's deck, which also meant that Alex (and Jack) would need to put a block of dirt down onto the sand to be able to *reach* it. That also meant that when Jack recklessly dove down into the horde of husk zombies—waving his iron sword like a maniac—he had to drop down far enough that if he were to suddenly become overwhelmed by the zombies ... he'd have no way back *up* to safety...

However, the strange boy from another world didn't seem to care. He ran this way and that as the dozen sun-scorched zombies moaned and snarled and chased after him. He shouted words and phrases excitedly that Alex didn't understand, hacking into one after another with his new iron sword.

"Oh, Jack, be careful!" Alex shouted down.

"I know—" he yelled over the raspy moans and the vicious noises of the undead, "—that iron only does *one more point* of damage than stone, but the durability is like ... *twice* what it was on the stone sword! I can see ... *oh, duck feathers!*" He paused, falling down to the sand as one zombie knocked him off of his feet. Alex's heart leapt in her chest. Jack jumped back up and slew the zombie that had hit him. "I can see on the Damage Indicators that I'm doing a *little* more damage, but the sword *feels* better! I can't describe it! There's no reason why it should feel different in my hand. It's the same blocky shape, the same speed, just more DPS!"

DPS? Alex thought. *Damage Indicators?*

"What in tarnation is that little fella *talkin* about?!" Liamfrey asked.

Alex saw that Liam was standing next to her at the top of the ladder, also looking down over the edge. She shrugged at him and looked at the rail in front of them.

There's a guard rail! she thought angrily. *How the heck did Steve fall over it earlier?!*

Jack seemed to be doing just fine with the many zombies below. If anything, he was getting tired of running around. She couldn't hear the kid's heavy breaths from above because of the *whup whup whup* noise of the airship's huge propellers, but she knew that Jack was probably making all kinds of noises. Whenever they started fighting or running or climbing, the strange, soft creature always seemed to become *wet* and start making all kinds of odd, windy sounds.

Six zombies were already dead.

"Come on," Alex said to Liam. "Let's go down."

She carefully climbed over the edge of the Thunderbird and started descending the high, dangerous ladder. If she were to lose her grip and fall, she'd surely die on the desert floor, far below.

Jack kept hollering various things that Alex didn't understand about damage and durability as she and Liam climbed down the ladder. She paused a short distance over the ground as Jack faced off against the last two zombies. Liamfrey stopped above her.

They waited for the battle to die down.

When Jack finally plunged his iron blade through the dry and dusty skull of the last standing husk zombie, causing it to let out a rattling, raspy cry before collapsing into the sand, Alex climbed the rest of the way down and dropped to the ground.

Jack stood, bent over and heaving, grinning from ear to ear with his odd, curvy mouth, admiring his sword. Experience orbs glowed and tinkled, rolling though the sand until merging with the boy's feet with gentle, bell-like sounds.

As expected, Jack was gleaming-wet from exertion.

"Did you see me?" he asked, looking up at Alex and Liam with bright blue eyes partly-hidden by the mysterious 'glasses' that he wore perched on his little, curvy noise. "Did you guys see me kill all *twelve* of those husks?"

"We did," Alex replied with a smile. "Very good, Jack."

"I heard ya sayin that you couldn't *describe* all of that hullaballoo you were hollerin," Liam said with a laugh, "but you were *describin* it all as fast as you could!"

Jack laughed, leaning over onto his knees and breathing hard.

"Yeah, I guess I was," he said. He wiped some of the fluid from his shiny face and took a deep breath. The kid looked up at the sun and squinted. "Gosh—I sure am *thirsty* after that! I don't think I've drank anything since before my nap."

"Would you like the bucket?" Alex asked, looking into her pack.

"Heck yes!" Jack replied with a grin. "Thanks!" He awkwardly sheathed his sword within his odd, extremely-thin shirt on his back. Alex had no idea *how* he did that. She couldn't even comprehend how Jack's clothing moved like it did. Nothing physical about the boy made any sense; not to *this world*.

Alex handed Jack the bucket of water. As she did, she took another look at the enchanted golden apple in her pack. She'd picked it up from the place that Jack had called a 'spider spawner dungeon'. It seemed to be the most valuable thing in that chest, aside, perhaps, from the gold ingots.

As Jack awkwardly broke a hole into the sandy desert floor and filled it with water to drink, and Liam dropped down from the Thunderbird's ladder, Alex pulled the enchanted golden apple out to look over it again in the bright sunshine. The kid poured the water into the hole he made, then proceeded to drink from it strangely with his hands formed into a bowl-like shape.

The enchanted golden apple was beautiful.

Alex didn't want to eat it. She couldn't think of a reason to ever eat such a beautiful item. In fact, she figured that when they finally got home, she'd make a display frame for the lovely item and hang it on her bedroom wall. She loved display frames.

The apple looked like it was made of pure gold. It gleamed under the desert sun. On top of that, there was a subtle and gorgeous *glow* surrounding it of gentle, purple light.

It was enchanted, just like magical items and books were. She and Steve had hardly ever seen magical items before. There was one time when Steve had an enchanted sword for a while, but—just like always—he'd lost it when carelessly dying. That enchanted sword had been lost to the bottom of the sea where Steve had drowned at the time for staying too deep for too long. Alex had always wanted to make an enchantment table and learn more about magical items, but they'd never been able to build one.

Then, Jack the kid came along. She still remembered back on the first day she knew the boy: he told her about his knowledge of the world and that he could even make an enchanting table.

She was really looking forward to it.

508

"What are you plannin to do with that, little lady?" Liamfrey suddenly asked.

Alex looked away from the beautiful gleam of the enchanted golden apple.

She'd been lost in thought.

Jack was done drinking. He was collecting the water with the bucket again. Liam was watching Alex as she stared at the apple...

She met the pilot's blue-eyed gaze, smiled, and shrugged. Her armor *clanked*.

"I dunno," Alex said. "Just looking at it. Jack, what did you say that this was good for?"

Jack handed her the bucket full of water and wiped his little, soft mouth with part of his arm in a way that didn't make sense. He moved in such strange ways...

"Umm..." he said, looking up into the sky for a moment. He scratched his little, smooth chin. "An *enchanted* one does ... uh .... *gives* ... um ... Absorption IV, Regeneration II, Fire Resistance, and ... um ... well, *general* Resistance."

"What in tarnation does *that* mean?!" Liam asked with a smirk.

"Translation, Jack?" Alex added.

Jack smiled. "It ... uh ... makes you really, super tough, *heals* you, and makes you immune to fire for a while."

Alex looked at the apple again. She watched the purple glow swim over its gleaming golden surface for a moment, then returned it to her pack.

"Good for emergencies, looks like," she said.

"Yep," Jack said.

Liam looked up at the bottom of his airship, high and shadowy in the blue sky. He put his hands on his hips. "Well, I reckon we'd best get a move on! Fuel's a'*burnin*. Let's pick up Steve from yer house and check out that new trader in the village. I'm hopin I can get more *compasses*. Maybe some sugar cane or paper."

They started walking to the west.

"Why do you want so many compasses?" Alex asked.

"To make more maps," Jack said. "A compass and paper makes a new map."

"But ... you already *have* a compass," Alex said. "You showed us."

"That's true," Liam said. "But I require a *whole bunch* more."

"Why?" Alex asked.

"Why—to *make more maps*, of course," Liam replied with a smile.

"Why do you need lots of maps?"

"To make a *really big* map," Jack replied. "I guess if you travel around on an airship, you'd need a huge map to cover all of that distance, right?"

"Darn tootin," Liamfrey replied.

They walked. It wasn't long before the *whup whup whup* of the Thunderbird's mighty propellers faded into the distance behind them.

They walked and walked, keeping the sun ahead of them as the day went on. Eventually, the three passed the desert temple, drifting close enough to see whether or not Steve was there. He wasn't.

After a long time, when the sun's position was becoming dangerously close to sunset, Alex finally saw the glittering of sunlight on glass. They spotted the village in the distance. She hoped that it was *their* village, because honestly, Alex had no idea where the heck they were and couldn't tell if that distant desert village was one that she'd seen before or not.

"Hey, there's the village!" Jack exclaimed, pointing at the small collection of sandstone buildings.

From far away, Alex could see the dark forms of villagers rushing around in the pale streets tending to their mysterious business.

"Is that the village next to yer house?" Liamfrey asked, shielding the sunlight from his eyes with one gloved hand and squinting as he regarded the distance. "Where *is* yer house, anyway?"

Alex looked. She saw the edge of the desert past the little collection of sandstone homes. The grass continued in the same direction with occasional trees for a little while before climbing into what was either a ridge, a hill, or the beginning of some kind of mountain that disappeared into the haze.

"I ... I don't know," she replied.

It was the truth. Gosh—she was so bad with directions, and she really couldn't remember a thing when it came to navigating.

She wished that *Steve* was here...

"Yeah, that's the place alright," Jack said.

"You sure?" Alex asked.

"Definitely," the boy replied, pointing. "So, the village is at the edge of the desert. Then, there's an oak forest biome that rises to a steep ridge. Alex's house is just on the other side of that ridge ahead of us."

Liam stopped and put his hands on his hips. He considered the distant village then stared up, squinting, at the lowering sun.

"Well," he said with a low whistle. "I reckon, if that's true, that we should go to the village *first*, before we go and find Steve

511

at the house. If we go past the village to the house first, then the sun will go down, we won't have time to talk to the traders before nightfall."

Jack shrugged. "Good point. Alex?"

They were both looking at her.

She really wanted to find Steve. They'd been traveling for a while and he'd been gone for just as long. Who knows where the heck he was now? Was he at home? Or was he wandering through the desert trying to find *them* while they were trying to find *him?*

Maybe he was in the village...

"Alright," Alex said. "Real quick, okay? I don't want to get caught in the village at sundown either."

"Okie dokie," Liam said with a smile.

They continued. They hurried.

They quickly walked across the desert and the endless dunes of bright, hot sand until finally reaching the village. As they drew in closer, Alex could, in fact, tell that the rising forest beyond the desert's edge did look like some kind of ridge.

Was it the ridge next to the Homestead? She still couldn't tell...

When they stepped onto a solid sandstone street, suddenly surrounded by bustling villagers that *hurred* and *hummed* all around them, Alex suddenly felt a lot better. Even though she couldn't tell one way from another, the homes surrounding them did seem a little more familiar.

Walking through the streets, when she laid eyes upon one building that had evidently been damaged by an explosion then patched up with cobblestone, she then knew that they were in the right place.

"What's with the cobblestone?" Liamfrey asked suddenly, as if reading her mind.

"Oh, that was from a few days ago," Jack replied. "It was amazing! There was a freaking *wither!* It flew over the ridge and stopped over the village here, where it blew up three houses before continuing, flying away to the east."

"The *east?*" Liam replied. "As in ... where we just came from?"

"Yeah!" Jack said. "The wither flew off east and ... *who knows* where it is now?"

They walked through the streets. Liam stopped at a random villager and checked to see what the guy was selling. After turning away from the villager—who *harumphed* and went back to his business with a frown—Liam turned to Jack again.

"What in tarnation is a *'wither'*, anyway?!" he asked.

"A powerful, terrible monster from the Nether," Jack replied.

Liam didn't reply to that. Alex had no idea whether the airship pilot was familiar with the nether or not. She wasn't familiar with the other world, herself. Steve talked about it sometimes, but she knew that *his* knowledge only came from books they'd come across in village libraries.

They stopped whenever Liamfrey decided to talk to a villager. Alex figured that he was looking for compasses. Or paper. At one point, she saw the airship pilot smile and pocket a lot of sugar cane.

She watched for KittyPaws30, Steve's friend who'd come from the Divining Pool before Jack ever came along. She wanted to ask the always-cheerful Minecraftian whether or not she'd seen Steve. They never came across KittyPaws30.

Alex also kept her eyes peeled for someone *new*. Somewhere in this town was the 'HelloDance-*something-something*', who'd been brought forth from the Divining Pool ... at least, according to Steve before he died.

Then, they saw him.

A Minecraftian that Alex had never seen before suddenly appeared, walking with a villager next to him as they turned a corner. The man was talking to the villager as if he understood their language—gesturing with his hands as they strolled along—and paused when his bright, green eyes met Alex's. He was blonde, wore a red and green shirt, blue pants, and had some kind of blue-grey *winged* device on his back. Alex had never seen something like that before...

"Hey!" Jack exclaimed. "You!"

The kid was smiling.

The Minecraftian with the colorful clothing and the strange thing on his back excused himself from the villager—who glared at Jack with a furrowed brow and rushed off with his hands joined under his robe—then approached.

"Hi there!" the blonde man exclaimed with a wave, looking over the three of them. His green eyes were happy and almost sparkling in the afternoon sun. "And you are...?"

"I'm Jack!" the boy replied, returning the wave with his intricate little hand. "This is Alex, and Liamfrey, and you must be ... *HelloDance?* HelloDance the trader?"

"I am!" the Minecraftian replied with a broad smile. "I am HelloDance4436! Welcome to my village!"

"Oh, we've been to this village before!" Alex replied. "I guess it's more like we're welcoming *you* to *ours*. We live just over the—"

514

"*Your* village?" HelloDance4436 replied, a look of confusion sweeping over his otherwise sunny face. "What do you mean? I have not seen you before, ah ... *Alex*, is it? It's a pleasure to meet you, at any rate!"

"Didn't you just get here?" Jack asked, looking up at Alex and smirking. *He's crazy*, Jack seemed to say with his expression. "Hey, cool *Elytra*, man! Do you sell those?"

"I ... I don't understand what you mean," HelloDance4436 said. "I ... I've *always* been here! Would you like to see my wares?" The Minecraftian replaced his confused expression with a genuine smile again. "Yes, I *do* sell Elytras, *Jack* ... is it? Thank you for noticing mine! I don't have any in stock at the moment, but I do get them in from time to time."

Born of the Divining Pool, Alex thought.

Jack opened his mouth and took a breath, raising one little finger into the air. For a moment, Alex thought that the kid was going to argue with the trader, but then, he seemed to change his mind. Jack closed his mouth and smiled.

"Well, *I'd* sure like to look at your wares, fella!" Liamfrey said, piping up from behind Alex and Jack.

"Welcome, new customer!" HelloDance4436 replied with a broad smile. Then, he and Liam began going through his inventory.

Alex looked at Jack.

The kid was watching HelloDance4436. He looked back at her and shrugged.

"Remember Braydon?" Jack asked quietly.

The ranger who lives in the forest, Alex thought. *From the Divining Pool as well*. Braydon had saved her and Jack from the wolves.

"Yes," Alex said.

"He didn't know either," Jack said. "He thought he'd always been there, in the forest to the north of the Homestead."

Alex looked at Liamfrey, who was holding up another compass in the sunlight.

"Liam, too," Alex said. "He doesn't remember just appearing."

"Yeah," Jack said. Then, he turned to the airship pilot. "Hey, Liam, what's he got?"

Liamfrey turned back, pocketing a few compasses and handing over some sparkling emerald gemstones. The bright green stones gleamed in the sun.

"Some interesting things, little Jack," he replied. "Why, he's got—he *had*—several compasses, some empty books, *Ender* eyes, some magical fishing rods, and ... well, I don't truly... ah ... some *rare magical books*, I reckon."

"Rare, magical books?" Jack repeated. "*What* rare magical books?"

"Ah ... allow me!" HelloDance4436 interjected with a huge, bright smile. "Jack, right? What an interesting creature you are, Jack! Surely something as rare as *yourself* would be interested in such rare items as I have for sale!"

"What kind of books?" Jack repeated.

"Books of *enchantments*," HelloDance4436 replied. "One is an enchantment of *Butchering*; for dealing extra damage against animals. Another is an enchantment of *Clearskie's Favor*. Yet another book is for the enchantment of *Parry*, and another is *Disorienting Blade*."

"What are...?" Jack said, scrunching up his little, intricate eyebrows in confusion. He pushed his glasses up his nose.

"Where'd those *come from?* I don't have the *So Many Enchantments* mod on this server!"

Alex didn't understand part of what Jack had said, but she watched in interest the conversation between the new trader and the boy known as the *Weird Walker*. Strange things seemed to be happening all the time now on Vortexia...

"Why, my magical books and other items come from all over the world!" HelloDance4436 replied with a smile. "Far and wide! I carry unique items unlike any you've ever seen! Would you like one of these *most unique* books of enchantment? My prices are more than fair!"

Jack sighed and looked back at Alex. He shrugged.

"Well, I don't have any emeralds anyway," he said.

HelloDance4436's smile vanished for a moment. Then, he smiled softly again.

"When you do, small Jack, make sure to drop by and check my wares again."

"Actually," Liamfrey said, "I reckon I'll buy one more thing. Jack," he said, looking at the boy, "how about you take our little lady west, and you two start heading up toward that ridge. I'll catch up in a jiffy."

"Um ... okay," Jack said, sharing a concerned glance with Alex. He shrugged.

Alex looked up. The sun was getting low. They really did need to get home.

The two of them turned away from HelloDance4436. Alex had no idea which way she was facing, so she just followed Jack as he led her through the sandstone streets until they emerged into the open desert again at the edge of town.

She saw that Jack was leading her into the lowering sun, toward a distant ridge.

"Is that our ridge?" she asked.

"Yep," Jack said. "Home's on the other side."

A few minutes later, Liamfrey came running up behind them, his boots hissing in the sand. As he caught up, they stopped and turned around.

"What was *that* about?" Alex asked. "Why'd you send us away?"

Liam smirked, crossing his arms over his leather chest plate. Alex could imagine him standing the same way on the bow of his airship, looking into the wind, his red scarf whipping around in the gusts behind him.

"Well, I reckon that with how *helpful* you two have been to me and my *Thunderbird*, that I should get you a gift. It's not much, but *here*..."

He handed Alex a scroll of paper and a compass, then gave Jack a glowing book.

"A compass?" Alex said, looking down at the device and paper in her hand.

"Yep," Liam said. "You're always having such a hard time finding your way, little lady. This'll be a good help to ya. When we get to your house, I'll show you how to make a map with those two things, and yer house will always be right smack in the middle of it! And Jack?" he added, looking down at the boy, who admired the purple-glowing book in his little hands with a gleam in his eyes. His glasses reflected the magical light. "I reckon with your ... ah ... unique abilities and yer *limitations*, you might do well to have this here book. It's the *Parry* enchantment. You can—"

518

"I can imbue my sword with it when we get back to an anvil!" Jack exclaimed excitedly. "At least ... um ... I *think* I can. Thanks!" He beamed. He smiled up at Liam, then at Alex, then considered the book. "Um ... would you carry this, Alex? I can't."

"Sure," Alex replied, taking the book and putting it into her inventory. She did the same with the compass and paper, then turned to Liam again. "Thanks, Liamfrey. It's a nice gift."

He smirked, then turned toward the ridge to continue.

"We'd best hurry on now," Liam said. "The sun'll be down soon."

They climbed the ridge.

Alex didn't really recognize where they were. It was *possible* that she'd been here before, but she didn't really know...

When they crested the top, Alex looked down with the others onto a valley over the other side. Her heart leapt when she saw her farm, the animal pens, and ... the *homestead*.

"There's home!" she exclaimed, smiling, unable to hold back her excitement.

Gosh—she hoped that Steve was down there!

"Let's go!" Jack exclaimed, then, the boy began quickly lowering himself down the slope, block by block, obviously being careful to avoid losing his balance. That said, he was also moving very quickly, and was apparently just as excited to reach the house as she was.

The three of them hurried down the slope, leapt across the creek—Jack waded through it, taking the time to drink some more—then they rushed across the farm until—

Something was wrong.

Alex froze the moment she noticed it.

The first thing she saw was that the back door had been left *wide open*. That was annoying, but not *too* surprising. Steve forgot the doors open sometimes. But then, she noticed that the outside torches—the dozens of them that she'd painstakingly set up in a grid pattern around the farm and animal pens and along the exterior walls to keep the mobs away—were *gone*.

The sun was going down and shadows were stretching across the Homestead valley.

The familiar yellow glow of all of her torches wasn't there.

Then, she noticed that the inside of the house, through the windows ... was *also* dark.

Jack and Liam stopped, noticing Alex freeze in her tracks.

"What's wrong?" Jack finally said.

The house was open, all of the torches were gone, and the inside of her home was *dark*...

"The torches are gone!" Alex said. "*Steve...?*" she called into the lightless house.

The shadows stretched toward them...

S1E6 - Chapter 3 – Steve

Lost!

Steve grunted and huffed, climbing over rocks and ridges, scraping his hands and his unarmored chest against the rugged mountainside.

Pulling himself up another moss-covered boulder, the warrior strived to reach the top of the rocky outcropping, certain that from up there, he'd be able to figure out *where the heck he was.*

He was wrong.

As Steve clambered up onto the highest point he could see close to where he'd appeared in a chilly and dense pine forest after dying, he found that he could see a lot, but it didn't help him to figure out where he was in relation to *home.*

He was somewhere in the mountains. All around him were towering pine trees. The rocky ground rose and fell, creating sharp ridges and winding hills, some rising higher and higher eventually into snow-capped mountain peaks, some descending into green valleys or lowlands containing rivers and plateaus full of rock formations.

The sky was blue and clear, and the air was crisp.

He was somewhere high in elevation—higher than the Homestead—and ... he was really ... there had to be ... well, *dang.*

There was no telling where he was.

"I'm lost," Steve said to himself, putting his fists onto his hips and looking up at the sun.

He could tell direction by the big, bright sun gradually moving to the west, but, with no point of reference, there was no telling which way was home.

Which way should he go?

What the heck had happened?!

Where was his bed?!

When he'd died, falling off of the airship like a reckless *idiot*—Gosh, Alex must be so mad at him!—he'd been in the desert far to the east of the Homestead and their desert village where KittyPaws30 lived. But ... where...?

Steve scouted the horizons with angry eyes. He didn't see a desert. He didn't see the big ridge east of home. He didn't see *anything* familiar.

"What on Vortexia happened to my *bed?!*" he asked no one.

He should have appeared on his bed. Why did he regenerate out in the middle of the wilderness?! What had happened to his bed? The only reason he *shouldn't* be appearing on his bed was if something had happened to it.

What had happened?!

Steve sighed, looking out over the wild lands all around him.

The wind blew. It was a cold.

He shivered. He had no armor. No weapons. No tools.

Nothing.

"Dang it, Steve!" he said. "Why'd you have to go and fall off of the stupid airship?!"

He looked in all directions.

Yep. There was *no* way to tell which way to go...

Steve looked up at the sun again to orient himself.

Which way...? he wondered again.

With a deep sigh, he turned until the sun was on his left shoulder.

"North," he said. "We go *north*."

So, Steve began to walk.

He headed north.

The dry grasses of the mountains and the gravel of higher elevations crunched under his feet. Occasionally looking up at the sun to make sure that he was still going in the same direction, Steve hiked north, hoping to find something—anything—to help orient him to home, the village, or to the vast desert east of the Homestead.

Instead, he found mountains; endless taiga mountains and pine trees and moss-covered boulders and ridges that rose and fell.

After an hour or two of constant hiking through the woods, Steve found the trees thinning and noticed that he was climbing to higher ground. The mountains were becoming more visible all around him, and behind him were lower forests of dense, dark-green pines stretching as far as he could see.

He was going *up*.

Then, continuing along a rising mountain ridge, Steve began to see some really strange things...

As the mountains grew taller and more sparse of trees, he started seeing strange furrows dug through the ground. Here and there, deep and wide gouges ran through the mountainsides and ridgelines as if something big and powerful had dug great *trenches* through the land.

"What the heck...?" he said, staring up at a long scoop dug through the rising ridge of a tall mountain.

Steve stopped again when he saw daylight peeking through another such gouge poking through a mountainside. It was like a huge tunnel, boring through one side of the mountain from the air, then bursting out the side that was facing him.

He stopped to catch his breath.

What was making all of those weird tunnels through the mountains?

Checking the sun again, Steve figured that he had ... maybe four hours before dark? If he was stuck up here after sunset, maybe one of those weird cave-tunnel-trenches would be a good place to camp out for the night...

With that thought, Steve looked around and headed to the nearest pine tree.

He punched the tree until he had enough wood to make a crafting table, then, he made planks, sticks, and a wooden sword. He made a wooden pickaxe and continued walking, hoping to come across some surface coal so that he could make a handful of torches.

Stopping at another weird thing, Steve considered several pine trees that had been cleanly *cut in half* partway up their long trunks as if whatever had tunneled through the mountains had similarly passed right through them, snapping them off halfway up.

"Weird!" he said to himself.

Going on, higher and higher into the odd, gouged mountains, Steve stopped when he saw something strange moving in the sky up ahead.

There was a large, dark shape flying higher up in the mountains, sweeping around in the sky.

As Steve scrutinized the shape, squinting and shielding the mountain sunshine from his eyes, he gasped when he finally recognized the long, flowing body and tail and broad, black shapes *flapping* up and down at its sides...

"The *dragon!*" Steve said with wide eyes.

It was the Ender dragon; the same Ender dragon that had appeared over his house, fighting the wither several days ago.

"Holy smokes!" he added, instinctively crouching low and scrambling to hide behind a moss-covered boulder.

Steve watched the creature as it circled the skies in the distance.

Had the *dragon* carved those big tunnels through the mountains and the trees?

Wow!

It was definitely the dragon; most likely the same one that Steve had seen before. It *had* to be the same dragon, right? Dragons *never* appeared in the normal world. They only existed in *The End*, didn't they? That's what Steve had read in the past, anyway. Heck—the only reason that the Ender dragon and the wither had appeared on this world in the first place, fighting over the Homestead for a little while before going their separate ways, was because of that danged Divining Pool!

That dragon wasn't supposed to *be* here. *That's* why it was destroying the countryside, cutting holes in mountains and furrows through the earth; chopping trees in half as it swooped by over forests.

It wasn't *meant* to be here...

Steve watched the massive creature circle the sky in the distance, feeling a cold dread rise up in him.

He wondered how sharply a dragon could *see*. It could probably see pretty danged far...

"The dragon," Steve muttered to himself quietly, watching the terrifying creature flying around in the distance before him, "had gone *north*."

Steve thought about it. He tried hard to remember.

Yes.

After the brief fight between the dragon and the wither above the homestead, the dragon had gone *north*, while the wither flew east. That horrific skull creature had stopped to blow up the village a little, then continued east, far away into the desert...

If the dragon had gone *north*, then that meant that Steve was north of home, right?

He looked behind him.

He'd walked so far this way already. He'd gone the *wrong way*.

"Oh well," Steve said to himself. "At least I know the way now."

Hopefully, he added in his mind. He could be wrong. The dragon could have changed directions after going north, once it was out of sight. He could literally be *anywhere*. Heck—it could even be a different dragon, as unlikely as that would be.

"Still," Steve said. "It's something. I've got to try."

Turning, hoping that the dragon hadn't seen him and *wouldn't* see him, Steve oriented himself to the south and started hiking back down the mountains again.

He walked and walked as the sun grew lower in the sky.

He had time.

How far could the dragon have gone? Now, come to think of it, Steve recalled that north of the homestead were endless hills of pine forests, and if he was to follow the big ridge and the creek uphill in the same direction, he'd eventually reach some high mountains.

These mountains.

He knew where he was.

Eventually, back down in the dark woods again, Steve pulled his wooden sword and went on. He was determined to get as far as he could before the sun went down. If he needed to camp out somewhere, fine, but he *had* to get as close to home as he could.

Alex might need him.

He thought of the dragon again and shuddered.

That *thing* was north of their house. It might be far away—*he* might be far away, too—but there was a freaking *dragon* living in the mountains to the north of them!

And if that dragon was *here*, then what was the *wither* doing right now?

It had obviously gone farther east than the desert temple or Liamfrey's airship. But, was that nether monster living somewhere out in the desert causing who knows what kind of harm?

These were things that they'd have to take care of.

Steve felt a stab of dread—but also excitement—at the idea that one day, they'd have to head up north to go *dragon hunting*. That Divining Pool might mess up this world by putting a dragon and a wither into it. Steve and his friends would have to set things right; or, at least reverse the worst of the damages.

"Gotta get home..."

He picked up the pace.

Step after step, Steve headed south. He hiked up wooded hills, down gravelly slopes, around boulders and trees and through thick grasses and bushes, frequently pausing at high ground to check his orientation against the sun as it gradually made its way down the western sky.

He felt himself getting lower. Eventually, the gusts of wind blowing across his face weren't as cold as they had been when he'd first appeared in the wilderness.

At one point, he paused when he heard a *thump* somewhere off to his left.

Steve froze, standing close to a pine tree, ready to duck behind it if a skeleton appeared from a deep shadow to shoot him down with a bow and arrow.

He saw nothing.

Looking up at the sun again, as if to reaffirm his haste, Steve moved on.

Several steps more to the south, he stopped again when he heard quietest rustling in the bushes, again to his left.

"Who's there?!" he called out, stopping and half-hiding behind a boulder.

It was too early for mobs to start appearing. Any mobs that might come after him would be undead creatures that had somehow stayed safe in the shadows of trees all day, or...

Steve felt a little thrill of fear and turned to stare at where he'd heard the rustle again. It might be a *creeper*. Those didn't burn up in the sun. There was green and brown all over. If a creeper was slowly coming at him—creeping toward him—in taiga woods like these, he might not—

A patch of green and brown suddenly moved strangely over the background of the wilderness before him.

Steve made out a figure heading his way.

Adrenaline blasted through him.

"Gah!" he yelped. Then, he held up his flimsy wooden sword and stepped forth. Whatever it was, he was a warrior—a danged *good one*—and wanted to face his challenge head-on. "What the heck?!" he bellowed. "Creeper?!"

"Not a creeper," a clipped, low voice came back at him. "Hold your sword, Steve..."

Steve's narrowed eyes darted straight toward the voice. He held his weapon before him, considering the hill and shadowy woods full of greens and browns; tree trunks and patches of darkness and moss-covered boulders...

He made out a man standing there; a Minecraftian blending *perfectly* into the forest.

The more he saw, the more Steve could make out details: impeccably camouflaged clothing, a dark facemask that looked like tree bark, and the lines of a dark bow trained on him ... with two arrowheads glinting in the sunshine...

"Whoa!" Steve exclaimed, tempted to lower his sword but still unsure. "Nice camouflage! Holy cow!"

The figure didn't respond for a moment then eventually said: "Lower your sword."

"Why the heck should I?!" Steve replied. "Who are *you?*"

Steve was unarmored, and only had a wooden sword, a wooden pick axe, and some supplies, but he'd put up a heck of a fight if this guy was hostile. He *had* to. He had to get back to Alex.

"I'm here to help you, Steve," the concealed man replied. His bow and the two drawn arrows didn't waver.

"*Help* me?! You sure have a funny way of showing it..."

With a flicker of two dark eyes, the camouflaged Minecraftian eased up the tension on his bowstring and lowered his weapon. He stepped forward.

"My name is Braydon. You have entered my woods."

Braydon.

That name sounded familiar...

Steve gasped.

Braydon!! The forest scavenger that lives in the woods north of the homestead! He ... he came from the Divining Pool, didn't he? Alex and Jack had said that this guy helped them before.

"Braydon!" Steve exclaimed. "The dragon and the wither! You ... before!" He laughed and lowered his sword. *This* was the guy! "Hey—you helped Alex and Jack before the dragon appeared! *Hi!* I've never met you before!"

"Nor I, you," Braydon replied. He stepped forward. Dressed in brown and green clothing that was hardly more than rags, the Minecraftian ranger-sniper-survivor-type was almost completely covered in camouflage from the top of his head to the ends of his boots. The only parts of him that remotely looked like a man were his upper arms, which were naked, and what little bits of skin Steve could see around the man's dark eyes not completely hidden.

"Well, what are you doing here?" Steve asked.

"Like I said," Braydon replied. "These are *my woods*. I would ask the same of *you*. Why are *you* here?"

Oh yeah, Steve thought. *Duh.*

"Um ... I'm lost! Well, sort of. I figured out which way to go, but I wasted some time along the way. Hey—do you know that there's a freaking *Ender dragon* living in the mountains to the north?!"

"I do," Braydon replied, finally walking up close enough to have a normal conversation. Steve noticed that the guy's bow looked very nice, and he did indeed have *two* arrows nocked instead of one. He vaguely remembered the message in the Divining Pool saying something about that. "The dragon arrived a few days ago," Braydon said, "and now rules the northern peaks."

"It ... *rules?*"

"Yes," Braydon said. His voice was quick and clip, as if he was annoyed by speaking. "*Rules.* Some mobs in the area have been gathering there, following the creature. Endermen have also been showing up in great numbers to the north. They follow the dragon."

"Holy cow!" Steve said. "What's happening there?"

Braydon shrugged. "Steve, I once helped your friends find their way home from near here." He let out a small, cruel laugh. "I remember now. You tried to fight an entire pack of wolves with naught but a *stone sword.*"

Steve rolled his eyes. *Jerk.*

"Yeah. Don't remind me."

"Very well," Braydon said. He started walking. Steve followed. "I will now help you to find your way home before dark as well."

"I ... uh ... I don't need help. I'm just going to keep heading south until—"

"Until you reach the desert?" Braydon asked. "The 'house' you built upon the blessed wilderness—" He said 'house' as if he hated it. "—is to the southwest; *not* the south. You will be lost when the mobs come."

"Okay, wise guy," Steve said. "Lead on."

They walked.

Steve hurried to keep up with Braydon, who moved briskly through the forest, not slowed down in the slightest by their obstacles, the winding ridges and gullies, boulders and thickets, or anything else. He seemed meant to dwell here, even if Steve thought that it was ridiculous that this guy hated houses and villages so much. He seemed to recall that Braydon took what he needed from nature and would refuse to step indoors or into anything manmade. The Divining Pool had created him that way.

That's fine, Steve thought. *I need to hurry, anyway.*

So, quickly, almost too fast to keep up, Braydon led Steve through the woods until they very suddenly and surprisingly emerged from the trees into a vast, open vista showing the empty desert ahead as far as Steve could see. They were high up on a mountain at the tree line. Below and ahead, the slope led gently down until the trees vanished entirely and the grasses thinned to bare dirt. Then, there was sand. Endless sand.

The desert below and before him was golden in the dimming light of the late afternoon.

It only took Steve a moment to recognize KittyPaws30's village down in the desert ahead of them in the distance. The windows sparkled in the low sunlight. From there, he recognized the big ridge heading south and north, intersecting with the higher forest far to the west.

Steve understood that to get home from here, all he had to do was descend south into the desert, cross the sand for a ways, then turn west at the village. Or, he could head west along the tree line, then hook left onto the top of the big ridge, which he could follow until he saw the homestead appear on the other side in the setting sun.

He smiled and sighed, putting his hands onto his hips.

"Well, thanks, Braydon," Steve said. "I'm sure you saved me some time. I would have—"

"*Quiet*, Steve!" the ranger hissed, which surprised him.

Steve looked at Braydon, anger rising up in his gut, then saw the camouflaged man crouching low in the nearest bush. Braydon's dark eyes were laser-focused on something happening down in the sand down below of them.

Crouching himself, Steve looked down the slope into the desert to see whatever the heck Braydon was staring at...

He saw a group of slender, black figures down in the sand.

How did he not notice them before?!

There were six men, all as black as could be, as if coated in shadows. Steve and Braydon were pretty far away, but even from up next to the tree line, Steve could tell that they were a strange, shifting black color that just ... *didn't seem right*. Then, he noticed that they weren't men at all. They weren't Minecraftians, or even strange creatures like Jack.

They were *skeletons*; six skeletons, all carrying swords instead of bows.

And they were *tall*.

It was hard to tell from far away, but as the group of strange, black skeletons slowly walked west through the desert, Steve saw that they were taller than they should have been, compared to the cacti growing from the sand around them.

"What the heck...?!" Steve muttered.

He looked back at Braydon then scrambled to get into the bush next to him.

The ranger glared at him.

"Be *quiet*," he said.

They watched for a moment as the six too-tall shadowy skeletons made their way west through the sand. They skirted far north around the village, heading generally toward the western edge of the desert.

The creatures seemed aware of the village. They looked at it. One pointed with a long, skeletal arm. They might have been talking about it down there; discussing keeping their distance.

Steve immediately thought of the danger that such skeletons might pose to the villagers and Minecraftians living there. He thought of KittyPaws30. She was practically helpless. Then, he figured that if those skeletons crossed the ridge and went south ... why, then that'd bring them straight to the homestead!

What were they doing there?

Also, why in the world weren't they burning up in the sunlight? They were clearly skeletons. They were *undead*. Even though the sun was low, it was still daylight out. Any other zombies or skeletons would be burning up in the light. Those black skeletons were *not*.

"What are they?" Steve whispered to Braydon.

The ranger glared at him again with narrowed dark eyes— Jeez, he was so testy!—then pointed with one hand sporting fingerless camouflaged gloves.

"Wither skeletons," he said. "It's a squad of scouts."

Wither.

"They're from *the wither?!*" Steve asked a little too loudly. He gasped, covered his mouth, and watched the distant creatures. They didn't seem to notice his outburst.

"You are *too loud*, Steve!" Braydon hissed. Then, he calmed down and continued. "I am not familiar with 'the wither' that you mention. But those skeletons—wither skeletons—are creatures from the nether. I do not know *why* they are here, but this is the third squad I have seen exploring this direction from the east." He paused and met Steve's eyes. "I believe that they are part of a bigger *army*."

"An army of *those* things?!"

"Yes," Braydon said. "Two other squads of the same size of the same creatures have come this way already. Why? I do not know. But they are not natural to this world. I have slain the other two squads, but—"

"Wait," Steve said. "You have *slain* them? You killed the other two squads?!"

"Yes."

"By yourself?"

"Yes. And we must decimate this squad as well."

Steve looked down at the six black skeletons again. They were each armed with swords. None of them seemed to have any armor. With Braydon using his bow, it seemed ... plausible ... that Steve could fight them hand to hand...

"Now?" Steve asked.

Actually, come to think of it, he could handle a half-dozen unarmored skeletons without bows pretty easily...

"Before dark, yes," Braydon said. "Otherwise, we may lose them."

Steve pulled his wooden sword.

"Um ... do you have a better sword I can use? Can I borrow yours?"

"I have no need of a sword, Steve," Braydon said. "Now, listen. When you charge—"

"Charge...?"

Braydon suddenly whacked Steve on the side of his head with one end of his bow, drawing his sharp attention.

"Yes, *charge!*" the ranger replied. "I saw you battle the wolves. Maybe you have not battled wither skeletons before?! I have. They are fast, they are strong, they have good reach, and they inflict a terrible *but temporary* curse if they wound you. However, they are not much stronger than wolves. You are a strong warrior, Steve! Now *listen*: when you charge, I will flank left down the slope. I will destroy as many as I can with my bow, and I will cover you. If any try to get around at your back—and they will—I will take them down. *Are you ready?*"

The words flew over Steve like a storm.

Temporary curse...?!

He looked down at the little wooden sword in his hand.

Fine.

He could do it this way just fine.

Steve took a deep breath, sighed, then nodded.

"Yes," he said, narrowing his eyes. He looked down at the six wither skeletons. Their swords looked like stone swords. "I'm ready. Let's do this..."

S1E6 - Chapter 4 – Jack

"Steve!!"

Jack gripped his iron sword with both hands as Alex shouted their friend's name into the dark house from behind him. He looked through the open doorway into a house that had previously appeared so cheerful, bright, and colorful with torches all over the interior walls.

He couldn't believe how suddenly scared he felt, looking at the pixelated doorframe and the shadows full of simple textures leading inside, past the hall to the kitchen and into the main room...

The three of them stood before the open door leading into the back of the house.

Jack hadn't even noticed the lack of torches himself before Alex had mentioned it.

The sky was full of bright, colorful reds and oranges as the sun continued setting in the west on the other side of the house. Right now, they were standing in the house's shadow. The silvery light of the moon hadn't even appeared yet.

There had to be mobs inside...

Jack knew that he could handle zombies and skeletons—even spiders—without a problem, but ... what if there were *creepers...?*

He looked back at Alex. She and Liamfrey stood peering into the darkness. Alex looked afraid.

Jack had to lead the way. There might be creepers, but he was the best one to handle everything else...

"Steve?!" Jack shouted.

There was no reply.

Duck feathers...

Ignoring the fear buzzing through his arms and legs, Jack made himself climb the steps into the back of the house. He held his sword before him, slipping into the darkness. His feet made no noises on the spongy floor.

As soon as Jack was past the open doorway, he swung his blade to the right, facing the kitchen.

He realized that he was breathing heavy. His heart started pounding in his ears.

The small kitchen with its furnace, crafting table, and several chests holding foodstuffs was dark and empty. It was so dark that it was almost *black*. There was no window in that room.

"Do ... do you have any torches?" he said back to Alex and Liamfrey. "We should torch this place up as we go!"

"Yes!" Alex replied, her green eyes wide. She sheathed her iron sword and pulled out two. "Want one, Jack?"

He did. Oh, *gosh*, he did...

Holding his iron sword with his right hand, Jack reached back with his left and grasped the blocky torch that Alex handed him. In that moment, he was very thankful that he had installed a 'lighting' mod that let him light his way in the game by merely holding a torch in his hand instead of needing to mount it on a wall or on the ground like in the vanilla version of the game.

Jack faced the main room with his torch in one hand and sword in the other, both held before him. Shadows played out like crazy monsters, whooshing around the hall and the room waiting beyond...

There was a quiet moan.

Dang.

"I hear zombies!" Liamfrey said from behind. "Get on in there, Jack! Let's get out of this darned *hallway* so that we can all fight!"

Jack swallowed.

He listened for creeper feet. He didn't hear any.

"Okay," he said.

With his torch and sword before him, Jack crept forward through the short hall. Just before he stepped into the house's main room, he paused when he saw the glaring, golden light of the setting sun shining at him from up ahead.

What the heck?

Stepping into the big, main room, Jack saw that the entire front wall of the house was damaged. A good section of it had been blown apart, and the front door, both windows, and the wood around it all was now *gone*. Chunks of the floor and ceiling were missing, including the eaves of the roof where it had previously hung over the front porch.

"Oh, my gosh!" Alex breathed behind him, pushing into the room past Jack when he stopped. Her armor *clanked*. "What happened here?!"

It looked like the front of the house had suffered a huge explosion; maybe from a creeper.

"Steve!" Jack shouted. "Are you here, Steve?"

There was another moan. Jack turned to the hallway leading to the bedrooms and the Divining Pool room and saw a zombie stepping forth from the dark corridor. Its dark green skin and tattered blue shirt materialized from the shadows and the undead mob let out a sudden, loud *snarl* that made Jack jump! It was close enough that Jack could see its Damage Indicator window already:

Zombie. 20/20.

The creature raised its green claws, opened its rotten mouth, and started toward them. As soon as it stepped into the light of the setting sun—shining through the hole in the front wall—it *caught on fire!*

"Whoa Nelly!!" Liamfrey exclaimed, stepping into the room as the zombie burst into bright orange and yellow flames.

"Duck feathers!" Jack cried, raising his sword to fight it, but also taking a step back when he felt a wave of heat.

Flailing wildly on fire, the flaming zombie hissed and gurgled and growled, stomping and staggering their way in the golden light of the setting sun. It smashed into one wall, setting a small fire. It stumbled once, dropping to the floor for a moment, setting more flames on the carpet.

The zombie's damage indicator flashed repeatedly. Its hit points dropped one by one as it burned.

"Oh, gosh!" Alex cried. Her armor *clanked*. "Kill it! Put the fire out! It's gonna burn the house down!"

They all rushed forward in a panic, partly trying to avoid being hit by the creature and set on fire, partly trying to strike it with their swords. Jack saw the flash of Liam's red-hot *Inferno sword* and realized that any mobs that they encountered inside would be similarly set on fire if the airship captain hit them with his unique weapon.

The house would burn down to the ground. All that would be left would be the bedrock *Divining Pool*...

"Liam, don't use your sword!" Jack cried, ducking as he swiped at the flaming zombie with his iron blade. He felt one of the zombie's club-like arms swoosh over him, which wasn't really threatening by itself, but the crackling wave of heat from the *fire* sure scared him.

Jack fell back, afraid to be lit ablaze. He imagined his hair and shirt lighting on fire; his clothing and shoes melting onto his skin. It would be *terrible*.

Looking down, he saw a patch of the front room's carpet burning. He hit it with his sword.

Hiss.

The fire there went out.

The zombie coming after them while flailing around on fire was chaos. Alex managed to get a good hit in with her iron sword, wincing as she did because of the flames, but they all mostly tried to *keep away*. Liam sheathed his sword and dodged around behind the creature, putting out fires on the walls and floor until the sun went down enough that the shafts of daylight disappeared and they were left in the dark again, seeing by only the crazy light of the raging zombie.

"Torches!" Jack shouted.

Plunk.

Alex threw one torch up onto the wall in a random place, adding some light to the madness.

Just then, the flames on the zombie petered out. A scorched and blackened undead mob was left behind, still moving and—

"Gah! Tarnation!" Liamfrey shouted.

As soon as the fire went out, the zombie—even blackened and crispy as it was—spun on the airship captain with a fierce snarl and pounded him over one shoulder with a heavy, burned-up fist. Liam fell to the floor. The zombie smashed him again in the back.

Liam's Damage Indicator health bar dropped. Jack had grown accustomed to always seeing his friend's hit points whenever he was close to them. He'd come to ignore it for the most part. Now, as it dropped from 20 to 14, then again to 8, he couldn't help but notice.

Holy goose necks!

"Liam!" Alex shouted, throwing up another torch and charging in with her sword and fearful green eyes.

Jack, no longer afraid of the fire, dashed in himself, swinging his iron sword with both hands—he'd dropped his torch—cutting into the zombie's crispy back. He and Alex hacked into the creature. Jack knew that he had to save Liamfrey before the man was killed. There was no telling what would happen to Minecraftians spawned by the Divining Pool when they died.

As he attacked the burned-up zombie as fiercely as he could, he watched the creature's health drop from 7 to 2. After one last frantic strike from Alex—she thrust her sword through its back near one burnt-up shoulder—he watched the Damage Indicator, expecting to see zero before—

The creature swung out and smacked Jack on the side of the head.

It didn't really hurt much, and since the zombie wasn't on fire anymore, it wasn't much of a danger, but Jack staggered, tried to focus, then, he realized that he couldn't *see!*

Everything became a dark blur!

Gosh—he was blind!!

"Liam, are you okay?" Alex asked next to him.

Jack stumbled as his friends all jostled him; Alex trying to help Liamfrey up, who coughed, staggering to his feet. The boy stared at the blurry mess before his eyes. He heard more *thumping* coming from the storage room that was somewhere up in front of him. There was the heavy plodding of zombie feet. One of the undead snarled on the other side of the wall.

"I reckon I'll be alright!" Liam said from somewhere in the blur on Jack's right side. "I just need to *eat* somethin and take a load off for a minute!"

"No time!" Alex replied. Jack heard her armor *clank* as she reacted to the approaching zombies and other mobs that he couldn't *see*.

"I ... I can't see!" Jack cried. He felt dizzy. The room was dark, save for a strange, colorful glow on his left; probably from the sky after sunset. There was yellow flickering in places on his right. *Torches*. He saw the glimmering of Alex's new armor.

"What do you mean you *can't see?*" Alex replied.

Jack put his free hand to his face. At least he was still holding his sword with his right hand...

His glasses! His glasses were gone! He felt nothing but his face, nose, and some of his bangs plastered against his sweaty forehead.

"It's my glasses!" Jack replied, trying to keep from crying in a panic. He felt his chest choke up.

"Yer *what?!*" Liam replied from the dark blue blur. "Tarnation! More of 'em comin!"

There was a loud snarl; so loud and surprising that it made Jack fall backwards onto his butt.

His knees and elbows and chest seemed to freeze with fear; like ice-water had been poured into his body. He gasped. His heart was pounding.

How could he defend himself if he couldn't *see?!*

Jack tried to get up but tripped. Two zombies approached. Looking at the plodding sounds, Jack could see the blurry, white shape of their Damage Indicator windows above their heads. The zombies themselves were blending into the blurry darkness, but the white windows were easy to see. Heck—Jack could even see the little icon of their blocky, green heads next to what was probably the words *Zombie 20/20*; all too blurry to read.

"Look out, Jack!" Alex screamed.

There was movement. Jack felt a heavy hand whack him on the back between his shoulder blades, but it didn't hurt. He knew that one of the zombies was attacking him.

He had to find his *glasses!*

Keeping a hold of his sword in his right hand, Jack scrambled around the floor, feeling his way through the blurry darkness, searching with his hands. *Duck feathers*. If his glasses were stepped on or otherwise broken, he'd be stuck in Minecraft without the ability to freaking *see!*

Jack moved around the floor on his hands and knees, ignoring the many scuffling legs and bumps and battering all around him. The zombies snarled and gurgled loudly over him, and Alex and Liam struggled against them—grunting and attacking and parrying and dodging as they fought—but Jack ignored everything. He *had* to find—

The gentle sound of padded feet in front of Jack made him freeze in terror.

Those weren't the heavy, clumsy feet of zombies...

Jack squinted—still unable to see—and looked up at a dark green blur. The instant he did, he heard a *hissing* sound begin, like someone lighting the fuse on cartoon dynamite.

He gasped in total fear.

Creeper.

His friends were fighting the zombies and he was helpless, blind on the floor, facing a—

"Jack, get back!!" Alex screamed suddenly.

He did. Jack fought against all of the terror in his little body trying to keep him cemented to that spot; the part of his animal brain that made him want to just close his eyes and not pay attention and hope that all of the bad things would just *go away*. He made himself blindly scramble backwards across the room.

"*Creeper!*" Jack screamed. His voice sounded higher and more afraid than he'd expected. "Liam, *help!!*"

"My sword!" Liamfrey shouted back. "It'll set fire to—"

"Do it!" Alex shouted.

"I don't wanna die!" Jack cried, crawling blindly away from the sputtering *hiss* as fast as he could. He hit a wall with his shoulder and his head. If the wall wasn't made of Minecraft *spongy stuff*, it would have really hurt.

There was more commotion. The creeper's hissing filled Jack with terror. He could feel it about to explode. It sizzled and popped and made all of his hair stand up. The air felt heavy. Jack had never been more afraid in his whole life...

"*Whirlwind attack!!*" Liamfrey bellowed.

There was a *whoosh*, a tearing and crackling, a hollow, clattering sound, and a bright flare of yellow and red that filled Jack's blurry vision with fire.

It reminded him of lava.

He felt the heat in his face.

The violent *hissing* had stropped.

Then, there was more scuffling. Liam grunted. Jack heard a zombie gurgle, and the sound went *down*, as if the creature's voice was falling to the floor.

Jack held his breath. He had no idea what was going on.

There was crackling. Hissing. The blur of the house in front of him glowed and flickered with orange and red light. Jack felt heat in his face.

"Good job!" Alex exclaimed. Jack could hear a smile in her voice.

"Look out!" Liamfrey said. "More comin!"

"Guys?!" Jack cried. "What happened? Is the creeper dead? I can't see!"

"Help the boy," Liam said. "I'll have this fire out shortly!"

Alex's armor *clanked* several times. A shadow moved in front of Jack. He didn't even know which way he was facing. Wasn't his *bed* somewhere around here? What had happened to his bed, anyway?!

"Alex, is that you?" he asked. His heartbeat was quick, and his breaths panicked, but Jack felt like things were under control. His friends weren't freaking out.

"It's me!" she replied, right in front of him. "Liam killed the creeper. Are you okay, Jack?"

There was a louder *clank*, and Jack saw Alex crouching in front of him. He could see her armor gleaming in areas as bright lines against the otherwise dark blurry surroundings. He felt her blocky hand appear on his shoulder.

"My ... my glasses! That zombie knocked them off of my head. They're on the floor somewhere!"

Alex moved without a word—probably looking around—then she stood. "Oh, hang on a sec..."

She departed and returned a moment later, pushing something into Jack's free hand.

His glasses.

"You found them!"

"Here ya go, Jack," Alex said.

Without a moment to spare, Jack thrust them back onto his face and could *see* once again.

"Oh, thank goodness!" he exclaimed, taking in the sight around him. He had crawled to the far wall of the front room near the hall to the kitchen—kind of where his bed had been before— and the creeper was nowhere to be seen. Actually, there was a unit of gunpowder hovering over the floor a distance away, gently up and down, just above the carpet. Liamfrey was patting out fires in the carpet. Two more zombies were emerging from the storage room. Liam was still wounded. Alex was okay, according to her Damage Indicator. There were pieces of zombies on the floor. Four yellow experience orbs were rolling around, slowly following Liam as he put out flames.

Jack stood. His heart was still hammering in his chest, but he felt a heck of a lot better.

He found the torch that he'd dropped on the floor and picked it up. The moment it was in his hand, it flared to life, lighting up the room some more.

Two zombies' green faces, rotten teeth, and dead, black eyes were illuminated by the yellow glow. They plodded toward them with menacing moans from the storage room...

"Are you okay?" Alex asked him.

"I'm fine now! Thanks for killing that creeper, Liam!" Jack exclaimed.

Hefting his sword, the boy charged the first of the two zombies. When the brute whacked him on one shoulder, he ignored the attack and cut the creature down.

"I reckon he's just fine, now!" Liam exclaimed with a laugh.

"You guys stay behind me," Jack said. "I'm going into the storage room to kill whatever's there. If there's a creeper—"

"We'll step in!" Liamfrey said, finishing the thought.

"You're hurt, Liam," Alex said.

"I'll be fine, little lady! Let's finish this up and secure yer house!"

They pressed into the storage room. As they did, Jack cast a quick look back to where he'd placed his bed a few days ago. It was, indeed, gone.

Now surrounded by chests in the storage room, Jack ran into another zombie and a spider after dispatching the first two zombies. He fought them off casually, calling back to Alex as he did:

"Hey, my bed's gone! Did you notice?"

Alex looked back. "It *is* gone! You didn't break it?"

"Nope!" Jack shouted back as he dodged the fangs of the spider. He wasn't afraid of the creature—it couldn't hurt him at all—but he fought defensively out of habit anyway. There was an anvil in the main room next to the crafting tables. He was looking forward to applying that 'Parry' enchantment to his sword—if he could—after this fight. *That* would be interesting. "And my bed," he added, "it was too far to be blown up by the creeper that blew up the wall!"

He thought of Steve. An odd thought flashed through Jack's mind:

What if all of their beds were gone?

"Then where'd it go?" Alex replied, bouncing her sword in her hand, ready to jump in and help Jack with the spider if he needed it.

Jack skewered the arachnid between its many red-glowing eyes, ignoring the creture's frantic but harmless attacks as he did.

"What if Steve's bed is broken too?" Jack said. "Maybe that's why he's not here!"

Alex gasped.

The spider fell and died, leaving behind some string. The room turned quiet as no more mobs stepped forth.

Jack looked back at Alex and saw her standing still with her green eyes wide, seemingly staring through the walls at her own bedroom on the other side of this room and the hall.

"My bed!" she exclaimed. "I've got to check my bed!"

With that, she ran off.

Jack lowered his sword and sighed. He took a deep breath and met Liamfrey's curious gaze with a smile as the battle stopped. His heart was still pounding.

He heard Alex throw her bedroom door open and burst into her room.

The door immediately closed behind her.

Then, Alex *screamed*...

S1E6 - Chapter 5 – Alex

My bed! Alex thought frantically.

The idea of her bed being broken by some mysterious force filled her with amazing fear. She immediately thought of dying—for the first time in a long time—and respawning somewhere completely *random*. She imagined appearing many miles away from home, hopelessly lost and all alone. No Steve. No Jack. Heck—no *Liam*, even. Just Alex, all by herself, with no armor and no defenses, surrounded by hostile mobs in the night...

The idea was terror.

Without a second thought, Alex sprinted across the storage room, turned into the hall, rushed straight to her bedroom, threw open the door, and ran inside.

She held a torch up in front of her, because the inside of the room was *pitch black* aside from the faint, silvery moonlight coming in through the windows from outside.

It was dark.

Her bed ... was *gone*.

She rushed up, held her torch to see better, and felt stark panic rush through her as she confirmed that her most terrible worry—the fear that had consumed her back in the storage room—was true.

She was *vulnerable*.

Then, the door behind her closed with a *pop*.

There was a *plunk*.

Before Alex could react, she saw that her way out of the room was sealed, and in front of the door now stood a solid block of shiny, hard, black *obsidian*.

"Wha—?" Alex started.

She was surprised when the shadows suddenly *moved*, and something *smashed* Alex in the head, battering her nice, new helmet and sending her falling backwards farther into her room. The shape looked like a ghost—a *demon*—materializing out of the darkness full of claws and malice. Something *whooshed* down toward her—a huge claw or blade of some kind—and Alex felt heat. She barely dodged backwards enough to avoid the attack. A long, curving blade of darkness *thunked* into the wooden floor. It was coated in flickering, orange flames...

Alex yelped in surprised. She might have screamed in fear.

Then, everything suddenly came into view and made sense.

It wasn't some sort of clawed, toothed monster of blackness and fire that had emerged from the shadows right in front of her. No. It *was* a monster, but of a different sort:

The fiery black blade stuck in the floor was pulled free. Alex saw that it was attached to a long shaft, then, she saw in the light of her meager torch and the weapon's flames that *Alice* stood before her...

Alice the evil ninja.

The dark Minecraftian—born of the Divining Pool and designed to hate Alex—stood tall and proud and confident, dressed all in black with only part of her pale face showing from the darkness. Alex met her ice-blue, dagger-like eyes. Those eyes were brimming with hatred, cunning, and ... satisfaction. Excitement. Alice had been waiting for her and she radiated *giddiness*; the feeling of a plan perfectly executed, an end goal almost at hand...

It was a trap.

The trap was sprung.

Alex's eyes flashed over to the obsidian block holding the door to the rest of the house closed.

Obsidian. Alex wouldn't be able to break through that, even with her iron pick axe...

She was stuck with Alice, and the evil ninja seemed to have nothing nice in mind for the two of them to do together...

"Alex," Alice said, her voice cold and cutting and smug. She was already acting like she'd won. She probably *would* win. There was no way that Alex would be able to fight her off alone. "At last, Alex, we are *all alone...*"

"What do you want, Alice?!" Alex replied angrily, squaring off and raising her sword to protect herself. She *plunked* her torch onto one of the walls of her room, lighting up the space some more, and pulled out another to keep in her left hand. She didn't have a shield. Another torch would have to do. "Why don't you *leave us alone?!*"

Alice smiled like a predator through her black facemask. Alex could tell that she was smiling by the crinkling of her icy eyes.

"I'm afraid I can't do that, Alex," she said. Alice started moving toward her, pacing from side to side as if trying to determine the best course of attack. Alex stumbled backwards away from her. "You see, Alex, I *know* that Steve and I are meant to be *together.* You're in the way of that. You've *always* been in our way, and I'm going to make sure that you are *out of the picture* ... forever!"

"Why?!" Alex countered, raising her sword and making Alice pause. "You don't have any reason to hate me! I never did anything to you! And *if* Steve was interested in being with you—he wouldn't be, by the way, because you're a freaking *psycho*—I wouldn't stand in his way! Steve's my best friend!"

"That's not true," Alice replied coldly. "I *like* Steve. I hate you. And I'm ... *curious* about—"

"Curious about Jack!" Alex said. "I know! I read that line! And you keep your *DevilScythe* on your back! I know *all about you*, Alice!"

Alice glared. "How do you know my weapon's name?!" she spat.

"Because I was told that you'd be coming!" Alex said. "You don't have to *fight me*. You were designed by ... something I don't understand ... and you came from an artifact! I remember all of it! You're as sneaky as a fox. You're as smart as someone named *Albert Einstein*; whoever *that* is! I know all about you, because you came from an artifact and you're not real!"

The evil woman paused. She scoffed. Her eyes never left Alex's. They were frozen, like ice spires at midnight. She was terrifying.

"Nonsense!" Alice replied. "Of course I'm real! I don't know how you know that stuff, but—"

"You don't have to hate me, you know. You don't have to *envy* me, Alice!" Alex said. She remembered the original word from the Divining Pool. "I can *show* you the artifact. You don't have to be this way. We can be friends, or ... at least not *kill each other!*"

"What *artifact?!*"

"It's called the Divining Pool," Alex said, slightly lowering her sword. She hoped that the gesture would make Alice relax a little and lower her weapon, too. It didn't work. "It's in the room just across the hall. Alice, let's not fight. I'll show you. You don't have to be the way you were designed. We can be *friends*..."

Alice stared at the floor between them for a moment. Her DevilScythe lowered gradually, its black blade blazing with reddish-orange flames...

There were frantic knocks at the door.

"Alex!" Jack cried from the other side. "Alex, are you okay?!"

"Open up!" Liamfrey added from the hall.

Alice seemed to snap out of her thoughts. Her face and icy eyes became angry again and she glared at Alex, raising her weapon. The blade of the DevilScythe *flared* with terrifying red flames.

"*Lies!*" Alice hissed. "You're trying to *trick me!* It's not going to work! I'll kill you and Steve will be *mine!!*"

She attacked. Alice attacked like lightning; like a wicked-fast ninja would.

Alex raised her sword to block the attack, but the evil woman was just too powerful. Her dark, fiery blade pushed right through Alex's iron sword and *bashed* into her chest plate. Alex felt the flames burn her. She screamed again. She tried to push Alice off of her, who was now howling like a banshee, insane with rage!

They fought. Every time Alex raised her sword or try to thrust into the darkness of Alice's body, the ninja moved with amazing agility and evaded her with ease. Alice struck at Alex wildly with her terrible DevilScythe. Alex managed to block the evil blade once, twice, then missed her parry but was saved by her new armor once more.

Then, Alice made it through her iron defenses. Alex shrieked in pain as the DevilScythe sliced into her, then her scream doubled when she *burst into flames.*

Suddenly blinded and insane with pain, Alex staggered around her room trying to avoid Alice, smashing into the walls and tripping over her chests.

She was burning.

Oh gosh—she was burning again!

Then, seconds from passing out from the pain, as Alice laughed and cackled insanely over the crackling flames, Alex blindly reached into her pack...

She pulled out the enchanted golden apple and ate it as quickly as she could.

As suddenly as the flame had begun, the heat and burning and maddening pain was *gone!* Alex felt a warm, buzzing feeling flowing through her arms, legs, and body. Her muscles felt strong. She felt *invincible!*

Standing still as the fire raged around her armor, took the bucket of water out of her pack—the bucket she'd been using to help Jack drink—and dumped it onto herself, putting out the flames.

Alex felt amazing: better and stronger and more full of energy than she could *ever* remember feeling in her life!

Hefting her trusty iron sword, Alex composed herself and faced off against Alice.

The evil ninja blanched. Her excited pale eyes widened. The murderous intent inside those eyes transformed into blooming fear...

As Jack and Liam banged on the wooden door that was blocked by obsidian and Alice shrank into herself, realizing what her opponent had just done, Alex charged!

Her body moved effortlessly. She wasn't as fast as Alice, but she felt strong and unstoppable. Her armor moved around her weightlessly; normally heavy and cumbersome but worth the extra protection. Now, Alex fought as if wearing nothing but her clothes, and her iron sword went *snicker-snack* as if it was a quick stick in her mighty grip.

Alice was speedy and was able to evade her for a while. When the fight turned more desperate for the evil ninja, she tried to turn the tables by attacking relentlessly and viciously, but every time that wicked DevilScythe hit Alex, her armor or her fluid movement seemed to deflect it, and the fire *did not touch her.*

As Alex pressed her attack, Alice backed into a corner, screaming in rage as she tried everything she could to hurt her. Nothing worked. Alice couldn't touch her. Soon, the screams of the evil ninja changed from fury to panic to outright fear.

Finally, Alice slowed down her skillful defense and counter-attacks, and Alex managed to land a blow. The evil ninja cried out in pain. Then, Alex sliced her again, stabbed her good on one arm, then—as Alice glared at her with the hatred of a thousand suns in her pale, icy eyes—Alex ran the terrible woman through!

Alice the evil ninja let out a rattling scream at the ceiling and collapsed onto Alex's sword, dropping her DevilScythe to the floor ... and died.

Alex stood over her foe for a moment in victory, buzzing with the excitement of it all, her heart hammering. She glared down at the dead ninja before Alice suddenly burst into a puff of grey smoke and vanished.

All that remained was the black, fiery weapon, forgotten on the floor...

After staring for a moment with the blood pounding in her ears, reality seemed to come back into focus. Alex turned, hearing chopping sounds next to the door.

She gasped when she saw a stone axe blade penetrating the wall of her room next to the blocked door. When the hole in the wall opened up some more, she saw Liamfrey stick his head through. The torchlight gleamed on his aviator goggles up on his leather helmet. His red scarf hung inside.

"Alex!" Liam exclaimed. "Are you okay?!"

"What's going on?!" Jack cried from the hallway. "Alex! What's happening?!"

Liamfrey went back to hacking open the wall. He stopped when he'd cleared out enough space for Alex to get out.

"Hurry, Alex!" Jack said. "There are mobs coming in from all over!"

There was a sudden, clattering *explosion* from the front room. Both Jack and Liamfrey jumped in response. Jack moved to cover his head with his little hands. They both looked down the hall with wide eyes.

"Well, either you need to *come out*, little lady," Liamfrey added, turning back, "or *we* need to come *in* and wait out the night!" He looked around the hole in the wall at the obsidian block keeping the door shut. "What in tarnation is this block of *obsidian* doing here holdin the door?!"

"Obsidian?!" Jack echoed.

"Alice put it there," Alex replied, approaching the hole. She could see Jack trying to peer around Liamfrey to see inside.

Gosh—she felt amazing! That enchanted golden apple was really something!

"Alice?!" Jack repeated. "Alice the ninja is in there?!"

"Not anymore," Alex replied.

"Where is she?"

Alex allowed herself to smile.

"Alice is *dead*," she said.

S1E6 - Chapter 6 – Steve

"Wait! You fool!" Braydon shouted from far behind.

"Raaaauuggghhh!!" Steve shouted, charging down the hillside. His blood was rushing in his arms and leg, his heart felt lIke it was on fire, and he couldn't keep from smiling! He grinned from ear to ear as he charged the squad of six wither skeletons heading through the desert toward the western sun.

He was looking forward to a *battle*.

Braydon had told him to *charge*, after all...

It was fine. He could take them. None of them had armor. They weren't armed with bows. They clearly had nothing more than stone swords. Steve could already imagine their bones shattering under his wooden weapon. It would have been nicer to have a better blade, but maybe he could take one of *theirs*.

"I'm *charging!*" Steve shouted back to Braydon, who was now somewhere up the slope behind him.

The six skeletons all turned to look at Steve without expression. They held their stone swords high and faced the incoming Minecraftian warrior.

"But let me soften them up a little first!" Braydon shouted back from yet farther away.

It was *fine*.

Steve charged on, anticipating the moment he dove into combat. He visualized his sword plowing through the first blackened ribcage and extended it to his side, low, ready...

No problem. Skeletons were slow. He'd be able to run circles around—

The six dark skeletons suddenly burst into a surprising run. They charged at *him*. Their bones *clunked* from afar.

Steve balked.

Dang.

Not normal skeletons!

Two arrows streaked past him from Braydon. One hit one skeleton, then the other hit a second. The two struck wither skeletons stumbled with arrows in their ribs, but kept coming.

Gosh—they were fast! Just as fast as Steve was!

Then, they were on him. All of the wither skeletons moved to surround Steve, but he expected that. He was just sorry to see them all moving so *quickly*. He was supposed to dominate them with his speed. *Oh well*. He'd have to try something else.

Just before the nearest skeletons swung their swords, Steve ducked, rolled into them, then leapt, crashing through the enemy in front of him with his shoulder forward. The creature's bones *clattered* as he burst through the mob, continuing down the hill like a wrecking ball before stopping to turn. Bones were rolling down the hill all around him.

One down.

Steve was immediately shocked by how *tall* the wither skeletons were. They turned on him—just as quick as any Minecraftian—and reacted, spreading out to flank him. Two came straight at him, practically *sprinting*, raising their swords to attack...

Dodging to one side, Steve narrowly avoided being cut in two by a swinging stone sword as he parried another, counterattacking with his wimpy wooden sword and smashing his opponent on one black, sooty hip. Its bones *crunched*.

Two more arrows *thumped* and buzzed as they connected with the wither skeletons from behind. Steve caught sight of the white feather fletching of one of them vibrating from where its arrow was stuck into a big, black skull.

One wither skeleton peeled off from the group and started up the hill toward Braydon.

Now *four* for Steve to deal with...

The Minecraftian warrior tumbled to his left as he felt another sword blade coming in. He was almost hit. The wither skeletons were tall, had long arms, and enjoyed much more reach than he had.

Maybe I'm outmatched, Steve thought for a moment.

"Nah!" he replied to his own thought. "I'll kill you all!"

One of the black skeletons hissed as if in response, and three were on him. Steve blocked one blade, was *smacked* with the flat of another as he turned it aside but couldn't stop it completely, then, he jumped back as a third skeleton swung at him. Just the tip of the creature's stone blade streaked across his left arm.

Steve grunted in pain and counterattacked, swinging his sword at the skeleton he'd already hit, knocking its block off. The black skull fell to the ground as the bony body collapsed the other way, vanishing in a puff of smoke.

"Ha!" Steve exclaimed, roaring in laughter boiling up from the fire in his warrior's heart. He immediately reversed the movement of his sword and smashed the next skeleton in the center of its blackened sternum with its wooden pommel. The undead mob *crunched* and staggered.

Three left. Two of them wounded by arrows and—

Two more arrows *thunked* into his foes' backs. One of the wither skeletons collapsed with a clatter of bones that scattered down the hillside.

Okay, two left! Steve thought with a grin. *Plus, the one going after Braydon...*

One wither skeleton in front of him—still unharmed—hissed like a monster and swung its stone sword at him, attempting a vertical strike...

"Careless!" Steve exclaimed, raising his sword to block—

But his arm didn't obey. It was numb. His sword was heavy.

Steve got his sword up to parry barely in time to avoid being cut down in one blow, but his wooden sword was immediately batted aside by the force of the attack. The dark skeleton's blade continued down and struck Steve in the chest.

He cried out in pain.

The fire in his heart was suddenly gone.

He *knew* that he could outfight his foes. His sword skills were amazing! But ... his body was failing. Steve's muscles were suddenly weak and weary. His movements were—

Another arrow streaked past overhead, missing the melee. Yet another burst through one of the two remaining skeletons like a cannonball, making an explosion of bones as the wither skeleton staggered forward, dropping its sword.

Seeing his chance, Steve forced his cold, sluggish body to move. He swung his wooden sword up as hard as he could—it was like the sword was made of *lead!*—and plunged it into the wounded skeleton's chest.

He was so tired that he lost his blade in the creature's blackened body. The instant Steve released his wooden sword, he fell down to one side and the wounded wither skeleton fell the other way, dead.

The last wither skeleton fighting him approached with a black, bony face of no expressions—no desire, hatred, fear, or anything else—and *towered* over the fallen Minecraftian. Its long, dark shape reminded Steve of an Enderman. Heck—it was almost as tall as an Enderman!

Steve felt a jolt of fear.

He was hardly ever afraid.

I've got this! he thought as the wither skeleton raised its sword, a long shadow against the bright, blue sky. *It's fine!*

An instant before the wither skeleton struck to end Steve's life, the Minecraftian forced his numb, weak body to roll to his right. He reached out and grabbed the stone sword that the other wither skeleton had dropped, swung its heavy, heavy blade as hard as he could with muscles that felt like cold bread dough, and *smashed* the weapon's edge into the towering skeleton's lower legs!

The bones *crunched* and the wither skeleton fell in a clatter.

Steve jumped to his feet—he felt like he was moving in slow-motion—and, before the fallen wither skeleton could react, he raised the captured blade and *smashed* the mob in its black, bony chest! He smashed it a second time, then a third, then the creature let out a rattling hiss as it stopped moving. It vanished into a puff of smoke, leaving behind black bones and a piece of coal.

Steve smiled wearily.

What the heck was *wrong* with him?!

Why was he so tired?! He was just *withering away!*

Looking up the slope, he searched for Braydon. The five wither skeletons that were fighting him were all destroyed, but that sixth one might still be up there, going after the ranger...

He saw Braydon backpedaling along the slope, nocking two arrows into his impressive bow as the sixth wither skeleton ran after him, sword held high.

Steve ran to catch up and help. He had to help Braydon before ... *oh gosh* ... it was so hard to ... run ... uphill...

Collapsing onto his knees, Steve gasped and heaved. He looked at his free hand—it was numb—and flexed his fingers.

Looking up the slope again, he saw Braydon destroy the pursuing wither skeleton with two arrows to the ribcage, fired simultaneously.

That was impressive.

Steve tried to get up—he wanted to catch up, even as the last wither skeleton fell to the ground in a shower of black bones—but he was ... so *exhausted!*

He lay down on the hill, flipping over to look at the sky.

Steve breathed deeply, trying to ignore the weird, cold numbness crawling all over his body...

Several seconds later, the shadowy form of Braydon appeared looming over Steve, silhouetted by the sky. The strange Minecraftian ranger just looked down at him. He shook his head and lowered his bow to his side.

"Braydon..." Steve said weakly, gasping for breath. "Am ... am I ... *dying...?*"

The ranger's facemask kept Steve from seeing the smile that he heard in the man's voice. Braydon laughed. "You're not *dying*, Steve. At least, I don't think so."

"Why then...? Uh ... why am I so ... *numb?!*"

"It's the *wither effect*," Braydon replied. "You were hit by those things, I take it?"

"Yeah..." Steve gasped for breath. "Um ... *twice*..."

"You silly fool," Braydon said, shaking his head. It sounded like he was smiling still. "Withers are powerful opponents; more so than most creatures on the Overworld. You charged in before I could warn you! You should have waited for me to kill some with arrows first."

As Braydon spoke, Steve started to feel the life creep back into his arms and legs. He felt his breathing return to normal, and starting feeling a little better. Eventually, he found the strength to stand.

"It's like ... poison?" he asked, brushing himself off and feeling his wounds. They hurt.

"Kind of," the ranger replied. "You should definitely *eat*. Regain some energy. We need to run. The sun's going down."

Steve opened his pack.

Oh yeah.

He'd died. There was nothing useful.

"I don't have any food."

Braydon's dark eyes narrowed. "Are you serious?" he said. Then, he produced a cooked pork chop. "Here. Eat. Let's move."

Steve took the food, ate it, and almost immediately started feeling better again. Dang—there really was *nothing* that some good food couldn't make better!

He looked at the stone sword in his fist.

It was just a normal stone sword. There was nothing diabolical or otherworldly about it.

Braydon started walking down the slope into the desert without a word. Steve followed, letting the several experience orbs around him catch up and merge into his feet with a tinkling bell sound. Several steps down the hill toward the sand, he found the big, black skull of the wither skeleton he'd beheaded.

He reached down and picked it up.

It was cold.

"Huh," he said, looking into the frightening, blackened bony face. Empty dark eye sockets stared back at him.

Steve put the skull into his pack and continued.

They passed catty-corner around the village, heading straight for the big ridge. They climbed it easily. Up on top, Braydon stopped, leaning against a tree.

"There is your ... *home*," he said to Steve. The word 'home' was laced with bitterness.

"Uh, thanks," Steve said, stepping up next to the man. "Let's go!"

"I've led you here," Braydon replied. "Goodbye, Steve."

He turned to the north and began walking.

Steve paused, unsure of what to do.

"Hey, Braydon, why don't you come down with me?" he called after the ranger. "We'll give you some food! Come and hang out with us for a little bit. I'm sure that Alex and Jack'll be back at some point to find me!"

Braydon didn't respond. He moved briskly along the ridgeline then vanished into the shadowy woods as the sun dipped into the western horizon.

Steve watched him disappear then shook his head.

"What a weird guy," he said to himself then turned to look down at the homestead. The sun was setting, and the sky quickly turned orange and red and pink. Everything darkened quickly. "Good timing!" he added.

Steve descended the western side of the big ridge, leapt over the stream at the outskirts of their farm, then started through the wheat fields, hopping over the water trenches.

"Alex?" he called.

The back door was open.

Something was weird about the homestead, but he couldn't quite put his finger on—

Dark.

It was all dark. All of Alex's torches were gone. Well, *mostly.* The farmlands and animal pens were completely black—now in the shadow of the house with the sun setting on the other side— and the torches going along the exterior walls of their home were also gone. The inside of the house—through the open farm door and the windows on that side of the place—looked completely dark other than the flickering of maybe one or two torches somewhere in—

There was a scream.

It was Alex's scream.

Steve's blood ran cold.

He looked at Alex's bedroom windows and saw yellow and red light flashing and flickering around in there.

Alex is in trouble! he thought, immediately breaking into a run for the back door.

When Steve burst into the house, he found a zombie in the kitchen. Another zombie and a creeper were coming into the main room ahead of him through a huge hole blown in the front wall of the house.

Oh yeah!

He remembered that creeper blowing up in the front doorway. That was when he'd died before finding that zombie village, being rescued by Alice, and—

There was another scream. It was a woman, but ... *not* Alex?

Alex screamed again from her room as the zombie in the kitchen plodded toward Steve in a slow shuffle, groaning loudly...

"Alex!" Steve shouted.

The zombie was in his way. He ignored it when it bashed him on his right shoulder. Steve turned and cut the undead mob into pieces so that he could get to *Alex*. He had to save Alex...

Hisssssssss...

Now there was a creeper and another zombie in his way.

Steve growled and frowned, jabbing the sputtering green mob in its weird, crackly body as it shuddered and shook. The zombie paid the creeper no mind and pushed its way in at Steve, reaching for him with its rotten claws...

The creeper staggered once from being hit by Steve's stone sword. Its hissing was interrupted for a moment, then it came back, frowning with its big, black mouth and glaring with its deep, black eyes. The zombie trying to get to him was in the creeper's path. As the explosive mob *hissed* and sputtered and popped, bubbling and shaking with its violent attack brewing quickly in its guts, Steve realized that he wouldn't be able to hit it again. The zombie was in the way...

Steve dodged backwards and dove into the kitchen.

BOOM!!

The creeper blew up in the middle of the main room, no doubt taking out the zombie with it. Steve narrowly avoided the explosion by ducking into the kitchen just in time, and as he stepped out into the thick smoke, he saw that the floor and part of the roof was gone. Another wall was partly collapsing.

"Dang!" he cried. "Our house!"

Alex.

With fear for his best friend stirring him into action, Steve rushed into the main room once more. He leapt over the crater in the floor. There was raw dirt beneath it. There was another zombie heading into the hall, to the bedrooms. Everything was dark, save for a single torch randomly thrown up onto one wall that had somehow miraculously survived the explosion. Looking out of the big hole in the front of the house, Steve saw more mobs approaching in the night.

He rushed the zombie no doubt pursuing Alex into her room and attacked its back as savagely as he could. In two hits, Steve chopped it down to the ground.

Then, he saw Jack and Liamfrey in the hall!

"Guys!" Steve shouted.

They turned away from ... a hole in the wall next to Alex's door?

"Well, I'll be darned!!" Liamfrey exclaimed.

"Steve!" Jack shouted. The kid's face was wild and his strange, round eyes were wide. His shiny glasses had slipped down his nose. He shoved them back up. "You're here!"

"Where's Alex?" Steve demanded. He looked at what the two of them were doing. Liamfrey was holding a stone axe. They'd but a big hole in the wall.

"Steve...?" Alex exclaimed from inside her room. "I'm here!"

His heart jumped.

Liam and Jack stepped back as Alex pushed herself out through the hole. She was wearing nearly new armor, was wet from head to toe, and covered in soot. Despite looking like she'd just gone through a heck of a battle, Alex looked *great*. She almost glowed.

"Alex, are you okay?!" Steve asked, rushing up to his friends. "I heard you scream!"

"Behind ya, Steve!" Liamfrey exclaimed, pointing back out into the ruined main room with his axe.

Steve turned to see two zombies and a skeleton coming for him through the rubble of the floor.

Jack stepped forward. "I'll help!"

The four of them cleared the house. It wasn't long—killing one night mob after another—before Alex thought to pull out her large collection of dirt and start plugging up all of the damage, sealing up the outside of the house. They also patched a big hole from the second explosion that had opened the roof to the now-starry sky.

When things calmed down and the many zombie snarls and groans were contained to the *outside* where they belonged, Alex immediately set to torching up the place again.

As if making one final point on their wild battle to secure the house, after everything was sealed up and illuminated, Alex went to the back of the house and shut the farm door with a *pop*.

Everyone walked back to the partly-destroyed main room and took a breather.

Steve sighed.

Everyone sighed.

Steve looked around the front near the doorway to the storage room. At least their crafting chests, anvil, and furnaces hadn't been damaged. They'd lost the dump chests by the front doors, but—

"What the heck *happened?!*" Alex finally exclaimed.

"I was gonna ask you the same thing!" Steve replied, sheathing the stone sword that he'd taken from the wither skeleton. He was amazed that he hadn't really been hurt in the fight against all of the mobs in the house. Well, *mostly*. He'd been struck by that first zombie. "What happened to all of the torches? What happened with all of the mobs in here? What happened to—?!"

"*Alice* happened," Alex responded. "She came here and set a trap for me."

"Ohhhhh!" Jack exclaimed. "*That's* why all of the torches were gone!" the kid was sitting on a blocky piece of wooden rubble in a way that Steve's mind couldn't comprehend. Jack could sure move in weird ways. Heck—he was the *Weird Walker*, wasn't he? "You think she took down all of the torches to let the mobs in as a *diversion* so that she could ambush you in your room?!" he added.

"Exactly," Alex said.

She proceeded to tell Steve about what they'd been up to ever since he fell from the airship. Alex told him about HelloDance456 in the village and how Alice had attacked her in her room to kill her; to have Steve all to herself.

That made Steve feel ridiculously uncomfortable.

He recalled talking to Alice on top of the church in the zombie village. She'd called him her *Dear Steve*. He'd offered for her to join them but Alice had refused.

An ambush.

So *that's* what Alice had implied when she'd said to him: "As long as she's in your life, huh?"

Steve felt a chill run up his back.

Gosh. Alice had tried to *kill* Alex.

Again.

Well, he supposed that they'd never be able to trust her.

"I'm sorry," Steve said. "I guess ... I should have..."

He should have been there for Alex instead of falling off of the ship like a reckless buffoon. He *really* needed to start being more careful; to think things through a little better before just ... *charging* in.

Steve frowned.

"Don't worry about it," Alex said. "It's okay. There's nothing you could have done! It's just like the Divining Pool said, right?"

"Where *is* that Divining Pool, anyway?" Liamfrey asked. "That's the *artifact* y'all mentioned, right?"

"In a second, Liam," Alex said, looking at Steve again. "What happened to *you?* Your bed's gone, I take it? We haven't checked your room. Mine's gone. Jack's is gone."

"Alice must have broken them," Steve said. That made sense as part of her *trap*. "When I died, I appeared in the mountains far to the north where ... *oh Gosh*, you guys! It's where that Ender dragon is now!"

"The dragon?!" Jack repeated.

Steve proceeded to tell his friends *his* side of the story: appearing in the northern woods, watching and evading the dragon, the way that it had carved through the mountains. He told them about running into Braydon and fighting the squad of wither skeletons on the way back home.

"Well, that doesn't make sense!" Jack exclaimed. "Wither skeletons don't exist in the *overworld*. They only come from the nether."

"Braydon said that the squads were scouts for some sort of army," Steve said.

Alex gasped. "What if...?" she replied. "Listen—if that dragon is still up north in the mountains, what if the wither is still out there too, somewhere? What if that nasty thing is making an army of nether creatures?!"

"That would make sense," Jack said. "If the wither kept going to the east across the desert, maybe it opened a portal to the nether somehow and has been amassing an *army of darkness!*" The kid smiled. Steve was surprised by Jack's excitement about such a terrible concept.

"Braydon said that the dragon rules the north," Steve added. "The dragon's been collecting a following of mobs up there, too, apparently."

"Duck feathers..." Jack breathed, staring off into space.

"So ... Alice is *dead?!*" Steve asked Alex.

"Dead for now, at least," Alex replied with a solemn nod. She reached into her pack and, much to everyone's surprise, pulled out a large weapon of pure black metal shaped like some sort of *pick axe*. As soon as it was exposed to air, its curved, ebony blade burst into red-orange flames.

"The DevilScythe!" Steve exclaimed with a gasp. "She dropped it...?"

"When I killed her, yeah," Alex said. She smiled grimly. Steve suddenly felt very proud of his best friend.

"What are you gonna do with that?" Jack asked. The kid was wincing as if the heat of the nearby flames scared him.

"I reckon," Liamfrey said, "you should *keep it*." He cleared his throat and crossed his arms over his leather armor. "Looks like it might be a mighty fine *pick axe*."

575

Alex looked into the dark weapon for a moment. Its flames played in her green eyes.

She stood, brought it to one of their surviving crafting tables, and the glow disappeared. A moment later, Alex walked to the area where they crafted their weapons and armor and hung a display case onto the wall over the anvil.

The DevilScythe was mounted within.

They all watched it for a moment.

"You know what?" Liam suddenly said, breaking the silence. "With all of this talk of a *dragon army* in the north and a *wither army* in the east, ya know what I reckon y'all need?"

"What?" Alex asked.

The pilot smirked and put his hands on his hips. "An *airship!*" he said proudly. "I tell ya what. Let's get this place of yers fixed up, then we'll work together to gather up a *whole mess* of redstone. Then, we'll get my *Thunderbird*, and I'll take you on an airship trip to the east to see what we can see...?"

That sounded to Steve like an adventure.

He smiled.

"Sounds good to me," he said. "Alex?"

"Me too," she said. "What do you think, Jack?"

Jack shrugged, looking up at all of them. He looked a little glum. "Sure. Why not?"

"What's wrong, kid?" Steve asked.

Jack sighed. "I still don't know why I'm here. I've ... I've been here for a little while now, and I'm kind of wondering what's going on back home. I have a *family* and stuff, you know..."

"Maybe the Divining Pool will help us figure that out," Alex said. "And we'll help you find your way home, too, Jack, if we can."

"If that's what you want," Steve said. "Or ... you know ... you can just stay with us. You're ... *one of us*, you know?"

Jack smiled. His eyes were sparkling for a moment in the torchlight as if they were wet. Steve didn't understand what he saw, but he was glad to see the kid happy again.

"Thanks, guys," Jack said. "That'd be good. I'm glad." He sighed and looked around the ruined room. "Maybe in the morning we can rebuild this place and ... I guess I should build a bedroom of my own."

"Sure thing," Alex said.

"Now," Liamfrey said, clapping Steve on the shoulder with one hand and Alex on one armored shoulder with the other. Her iron shoulder pauldron *clanked*. "What say you three show me this *artifact?* I'd like to learn more about this *Divining Pool* doohickey!"

"Okay," Alex said, standing.

They all went to the Divining Pool room, which hadn't been affected at all by the crazy battle and the situation with Alice. In fact, strangely enough, when Alex opened the door and the light of the many torches mounted on the spruce interior walls poured out into the hall, everyone was surprised to see that the room wasn't dark.

All four of them filed in and stood around the pool.

Steve saw something small and shimmering deep within the blue waters...

"Hey!" he said. "Is that...? I think I see a message coming!"

"What timing!" Jack exclaimed, pulling himself up onto the bedrock to see more clearly. He held his glasses onto his nose with one hand to keep them from slipping off into the water.

They all squinted and peered into the Divining Pool's depths to read the coming message as soon as possible...

Alex read the words aloud:

"*Could you add a sorcerer that can shoot fireballs and summon lightning? He is a sorcerer of the light arts, so no summoning monsters. He also has amazing healing powers. He has a blue robe with enchantments Agility III and Protection II. He has a small crush on Alex, he is intrigued by Jack, and is slightly off-put by Steve. – Astro*"

The words slowly wavered and wobbled as they rose to the surface.

They all heard Alex read them, and Steve read them silently in his mind twice more before the message gradually dissipated and vanished altogether at the top of the pool.

All four of them were silent for a moment.

"What in tarnation?!" Liamfrey exclaimed suddenly. "What the heck was *that?!*"

"That was a message," Alex said. "That's how this thing works."

"Who's *Astro?*" Jack muttered, scratching his chin. He stared at the water, even though the message was gone.

"*Put off* by me?!" Steve finally said. "Why's he gotta be *put off* by me?"

"Hey," Alex replied, putting a hand on Steve's shoulder. "It's better than envying you and trying to *kill you*, right?"

Everyone laughed.

"Healing powers," Jack said. "That's cool."

Liamfrey stood, staring at the pool, shaking his head with a confused look on his face. "What in tarnation...?" he repeated quietly. "Where'd it *come from?*"

"None of us know," Alex replied. "But it brought us *Jack*..."

"The *Weird Walker*," the kid interjected. "My name is Jack Walker."

"And it brought *you*," Steve said, looking at Liam.

The airship pilot's blue eyes went wide for a moment then he shook his head again, as if in disbelief.

"Well," Liamfrey said. "I reckon I'm glad to be on *your side*, Steve, Alex, and Jack."

"We're glad you're here, too," Alex said.

"Heck yeah," Jack added. "You and your airship!"

They left the Divining Pool behind. With the house sealed up—still needing tons of repairs and looking pretty terrible—they all talked about getting some rest. First, Jack brought his iron sword and the enchanted book that Liam had given him to house's anvil. Steve watched as the kid struggled at the anvil for a minute—he supposed that Jack didn't know how to use it—then beamed when he finally figured out how to enchant the sword.

"I did it!" Jack exclaimed, smiling broadly, holding his purple-glowing sword before him. "Parry!"

Steve had never heard of a 'parry' enchantment before, but he figured that they'd experiment with it in the morning.

Jack made his way into Alex's room, where he fell asleep on the floor. Steve watched the kid for a moment, wondering what was going on in that strange, curvy head of his. The *Weird Walker* was so different than he and Alex were, but he was sure glad that Jack was his friend.

Alex then crafted something of her own: a brand new map with the homestead right smack in the middle of it. Now, she'd have something to help her find her way around, since she was so terrible with directions. Steve's best friend marveled at the map for a moment and thanked Liamfrey again for giving her its components.

For a little while, Steve, Alex, and Liam all stood in the main room, talking about how they could repair the home's damage. Alex mentioned their *mine* that was out front. The seemingly endless stone-carved stairs went all the way down to bedrock, which really drew Liam's interest. He needed a lot of redstone, after all.

Eventually, Alex said goodnight and went to her room. Liamfrey decided to relax in the main area. Morning wasn't too far away by that point.

Before heading to his own bedroom—he hadn't even checked it yet—Steve took one last look around the demolished front room.

His eyes landed on the frame hung on the wall above the anvil where Alex had decided to mount *DevilScythe*.

DevilScythe was gone.

Steve stared, doubting his eyes.

Yep. Alice's evil weapon was *gone*. Vanished. The frame was empty.

Steve felt his stomach drop. His eyes immediately flew to the back door. Rushing there, he threw open the door with a *pop*, revealing the night sky and the torchless farm.

For just an instant, he caught sight of Alice in the shadows of the trees. He saw her icy eyes staring back at him. He saw her *face*. It wasn't covered by a facemask.

The evil ninja smiled at him.

Then, she vanished into the shadows.

Steve felt a chill fly up his spine.

Staring out into the night with fear for Alex growing in his heart, Steve frowned. He looked down and shook his head.

He closed the door and went back inside.

Crazy things were coming. Dark armies were massing. Vortexia was getting weirder by the day. The Divining Pool would no doubt bring them new enemies, new friends, and other strange, unexpected things...

But they would deal with it ... *tomorrow*.

Wanna know what happens next??
Continue to the next book in Season 2!

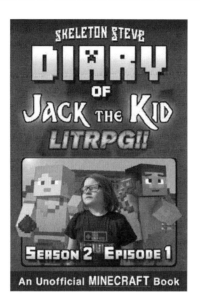

Love MINECRAFT? **Over 30,000 words of kid-friendly fun!**
This high-quality fan fiction fantasy diary book is for kids, teens,
and nerdy grown-ups who love to read epic stories about their
favorite game!

Flight of the Thunderbird

Their house is half-destroyed. A dragon, a wither, an evil ninja,
and who knows what else are after them. Jack the kid is starting
to miss his home and his family back in the real world, and the
mysterious Divining Pool brings something weird, new, and
sometimes dangerous to life every day! Despite all of it, Jack,
Steve, and Alex are happy, home, and safe for the moment.

After a crazy battle following a cunning trap set by Alice the evil ninja back at the homestead, Jack and his new friends (including Liamfrey, the pilot!) are working hard to repair the house and gather redstone to fuel the Thunderbird, Liam's beloved airship bomber. Will they be able to keep the Thunderbird from falling out of the sky so that they can set out east to scout out the dreaded wither and its growing army of darkness? And what wacky message will the Divining Pool hold for Jack and his friends today?!

... to find the NEXT BOOK!

Sign up for my Free Newsletter to get an *email* when the next book comes out!

Go to: www.SkeletonSteve.com/sub

Want More Jack the Kid?

1. Please go to where you bought this book and *leave a review!* It just takes a minute and it really helps!

2. Join my free *Skeleton Steve Club* and get an email when the next book comes out!

3. Look for your name under my *"Amazing Readers List"* at the end of the book, where I list my *all-star reviewers*. Heck—maybe I'll even use your name in a story if you want me to! (*Let me know in the review!*)

About the Author - Skeleton Steve

I am *Skeleton Steve*, author of *epic* unofficial Minecraft books. *Thanks for reading this book!*

My stories aren't your typical Minecraft junkfood for the brain. I work hard to design great plots and complex characters to take you for a roller coaster ride in their shoes! Er ... claws. Monster feet, maybe?

All of my stories written by (just) me are designed for all ages— kind of like the Harry Potter series—and they're twisting journeys of epic adventure! For something more light-hearted, check out my "Fan Series" books, which are collaborations between myself and my fans.

Smart kids will love these books! Teenagers and nerdy grown-ups will have a great time relating with the characters and the stories, getting swept up in the struggles of, say, a novice Enderman ninja (Elias), or the young and naïve creeper king (Cth'ka), and even a chicken who refuses to be a zombie knight's battle steed!

I've been *all over* the Minecraft world of Diamodia (and others). As an adventurer and a writer at heart, I *always* chronicle my journeys, and I ask all of the friends I meet along the way to do the same.

587

Make sure to keep up with my books whenever I publish something new! If you want to know when new books come out, sign up for my mailing list and the *Skeleton Steve Club*. **It's free!**

Here's my website: www.SkeletonSteve.com

You can also 'like' me on **Facebook**: Facebook.com/SkeletonSteveMinecraft

And 'follow' me on **Twitter**: Twitter.com/SkeletonSteveCo

And watch me on **Youtube**: (Check my website.)

"Subscribe" to my Mailing List and Get Free Updates!

I *love* bringing my Minecraft stories to readers like you, and I hope to one day put out over 100 stories! If you have a cool idea for a Minecraft story, please send me an email at *Steve@SkeletonSteve.com*, and I might make your idea into a real book. I promise I'll write back. :)

Other Books by Skeleton Steve

The "Noob Mob" Books

Books about individual mobs and their adventures becoming heroes of Diamodia.

   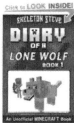 

    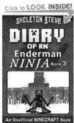

Diary of a Creeper King
Book 1
Book 2
Book 3
Book 4

Skeleton Steve – The Noob Years
Season 1, Episode 1 – *FREE!!*
Season 1, Episode 2
Season 1, Episode 3
Season 1, Episode 4
Season 1, Episode 5

Season 1, Episode 6
Season 2, Episode 1
Season 2, Episode 2
Season 2, Episode 3
Season 2, Episode 4
Season 2, Episode 5
Season 2, Episode 6
Season 2, Episode 6
Season 3, Episode 1
Season 3, Episode 2
Season 3, Episode 3
Season 3, Episode 4
Season 3, Episode 5
Season 3, Episode 6
Season 4, Episode 1
Season 4, Episode 2
Season 4, Episode 3
Season 4, Episode 4
Season 4, Episode 5
Season 4, Episode 6
Season 5, Episode 1
Season 5, Episode 2
Season 5, Episode 3
Season 5, Episode 4
Season 5, Episode 5
Season 5, Episode 6

Jack the Kid – Minecraft LitRPG
Season 1, Episode 1
Season 1, Episode 2
Season 1, Episode 3
Season 1, Episode 4
Season 1, Episode 5
Season 1, Episode 6

Diary of a Teenage Zombie Villager
Book 1 – ***FREE!!***
Book 2
Book 3
Book 4

Diary of a Chicken Battle Steed
Book 1
Book 2
Book 3
Book 4

Diary of a Lone Wolf
Book 1
Book 2
Book 3
Book 4

Diary of an Enderman Ninja
Book 1 – ***FREE!!***
Book 2
Book 3

Diary of a Separated Slime – Book 1
Diary of an Iron Golem Guardian – Book 1

The "Skull Kids" Books

A Continuing Diary about the Skull Kids, a group of world-hopping players

Diary of the Skull Kids
Book 1 – *FREE!!*
Book 2
Book 3

The "Fan Series" Books

Continuing Diary Series written by Skeleton Steve *and his fans!*
Which one is your favorite?

 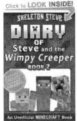 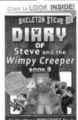 

Diary of a Warrior Villager
Book 1
Book 2
Book 3

Book 4

Book 5

Diary of Steve and the Wimpy Creeper

Book 1

Book 2

Book 3

Diary of Zombie Steve and Wimpy the Wolf

Book 1 *COMING SOON*

The "Tips and Tricks" Books

Handbooks for Serious Minecraft Players, revealing Secrets and Advice

Skeleton Steve's Secret Tricks and Tips

Skeleton Steve's Top 10 List of Rare Tips

Skeleton Steve's Guide to the
First 12 Things I Do in a New Game

Get these books as for FREE!

(Visit www.SkeletonSteve.com to *learn more*)

Series Collections and Box Sets

Bundles of Skeleton Steve books from the Minecraft Universe. Entire Series in ONE BOOK.

Great Values! Usually 3-4 Books (sometimes more) for almost the price of one!

Skeleton Steve – The Noob Years – Season 1
Skeleton Steve – The Noob Years – Season 2
Skeleton Steve – The Noob Years – Season 3
Skeleton Steve – The Noob Years – Season 4
Skeleton Steve – The Noob Years – Season 5

Jack the Kid – Minecraft LitRPG – Season 1

Diary of a Creeper King – Box Set 1
Diary of a Lone Wolf – Box Set 1
Diary of an Enderman NINJA – Box Set 1
Diary of the Skull Kids – Box Set 1
Steve and the Wimpy Creeper – Box Set 1
Diary of a Teenage Zombie Villager – Box Set 1
Diary of a Chicken Battle Steed – Box Set 1
Diary of a Warrior Village – Box Set 1

Sample Pack Bundles

Bundles of Skeleton Steve books from multiple series! New to Skeleton Steve? Check this out!

Great Values! Usually 3-4 Books (sometimes more) for almost the price of one!

Skeleton Steve and the Noob Mobs Sampler Bundle
Book 1 Collection
Book 2 Collection
Book 3 Collection
Book 4 Collection

Check out the website
www.SkeletonSteve.com
for more!

Enjoy this Excerpt from...
"Diary of a **Lone Wolf**" Book 1

About the book:

Dakota was a young wolf, happy with his life in a wolf pack in the taiga forest where he was born.

Almost fully-grown, Dakota was fast and loved to run. He had friends, loved his mother, respected his alpha, and had a crush on a young female pack-mate.

But his life was about to change forever when his pack was attacked by *the Glitch*, a mysterious and invincible horde of mobs that appeared and started killing everything in their path!

Now, he was a **lone wolf**. With the help of Skeleton Steve, would he ever belong to another pack again? Would they escape *the Glitch* and warn the rest of Diamodia?

Love Minecraft adventure??

Read on for an Excerpt for the book!

SKELETON STEVE

DIARY

OF A

LONE WOLF

BOOK 1

An Unofficial MINECRAFT Book

Day 1

So how does a *wolf* tell a story? What should I say, Skeleton Steve?

Oh? Where should I start?

Okay.

So, I guess, my name is *Dakota*. I'm a wolf.

Heh ... I already said that. I guess, technically, I'm a *dog* now. No? Doesn't matter?

Skeleton Steve is telling me that I'm a wolf. *Steve* calls me a dog. But I don't understand much about what *Steve* says.

Is this confusing? I'm sorry. Where was I?

Just from ... okay, right before.

Well, I guess I can start by telling you about my old pack. My family.

Just a few days before the attack, it was a day like any other.

I woke up in the forest and leapt to my feet! It was a *beautiful* morning. The forest was in shadows of the rising sun, a cool breeze was crisp on my face, and I could smell the woods come alive! Approaching a tall pine tree, I scratched my shoulders on its bark.

All of my pack was waking up around me.

What a great life!

I ran down to the creek, and drank some water. Splashed my face into it. *Cold!* And shook my fur, sending drops of cold mountain water all over before bounding back up the hill.

I guess it's a good time to introduce *the pack*.

My eyes went first to the alpha and his mate. Logan and Moon. Logan was a huge wolf, and he was really nice. He and Moon didn't talk with us very much, but he was a good leader. Logan mostly kept to himself, quiet and strong, and he led us through the mountains day by day whenever we moved.

Right now, we'd spent the last several days hanging out *here*. There were fields full of sheep nearby, and with this nice, flat area, a mountain creek down the hill a bit, and plenty of shade, it was a good clearing to stay in for a while. I was sure we'd move on soon. We always did.

My belly rumbled. We didn't eat yesterday. Today, I knew the alpha would probably send Archie and me to scout out another herd of sheep for the pack to hunt. I was so *fast*, one of the fastest wolves in the pack, and Archie was pretty fast too, so Logan usually sent us out to find the food.

I loved my job! It was great, roaming around with my best bud, running as fast as we could, exploring the mountains all around the clearing where the pack lived. It was only last year when I was finally old enough to be given a job to do. I loved being able to help my family so well.

Taking a big breath of fresh air, I looked around at the rest of the pack waking up and frolicking in the brisk morning.

Over at the edge of the forest were Colin and Arnou. They were the *warriors*, really. We all help each other, and we all have shared tasks given to us by the alpha, but the big and muscular brothers, Colin and Arnou, were really great at fighting, and they were always the first to defend the pack against any mobs that attacked us—the first aside from *Logan the alpha*, that is.

604

There was my mother, Minsi, one of the older female wolves. I loved my mother. She sat on her own this morning, watching the birds and chewing on a bone.

Running and playing together was the mated pair, Boris and Leloo. Leloo helped raise the cubs (all of the females did, really), and Boris, along with his brother Rolf, were very good at hunting and taking down our prey. The two hunter brothers were very skilled at circling a herd of sheep or other food, and making the animals run whichever way they wanted.

Sitting in the shadow of a couple of pine trees were Maya, and her daughter, Lupe.

Lupe was my age.

She was a beautiful wolf. And smart too. And funny.

I dunno. For some reason, I had a really hard time *talking* to her. Archie joked with me a lot that I should make her my mate, but whenever I walked up to her, whenever I tried to talk to her, my tongue became stupid, I forgot was I wanted to say, and I just embarrassed myself whenever I tried.

It was terrible! Yes, I guess, I really, really liked her. It should have been easy!

Easy just like with Logan and Moon. Logan has been alpha since before I was born, but my mother told me that before he was alpha, when he was younger, he just walked up to Moon one day and *decided* that they were going to be mates.

I don't really understand how that works. Maybe one day I will.

"Hey, dude!" said Archie, running up to see me.

"Oh, hey! Good morning!" I said, sitting in the dirt.

Archie was a year older than me, and my best friend. When we were growing up, we always did everything together.

605

And now that we were practically adult wolves (almost), we worked together whenever Logan gave us an assignment.

"You ready?" he said, wagging his tail.

"Ready for what?" I asked.

"Going to look for a herd, of course!" he replied.

"Well, yeah, but Logan hasn't told us to yet."

"I bet he will," Archie said.

Not an hour went by before the massive alpha called on us.

"Dakota! Archie!" he said, his deep voice clear above the rest of the pack, chatting in the morning. We ran up and sat before him.

"Yes, sir?" we said.

"You two explore down in the valley today, see if you can find another herd for us to hunt."

"Right away," I said. Archie acknowledged as well, and we departed our pack's temporary home, flying down the hill as quickly as our speedy wolf feet would take us. With the wind in my face, I dodged around trees, leapt over holes, exploded through the underbrush, and felt great!

When we emerged from the huge, pine forest, I felt the sun warm up my face, and I closed my eyes, lifting my snout up into the sky. Archie popped out of the woods next to me.

"Look at that," Archie said. "Have you ever seen anything so beautiful?"

The sunshine on our faces was very pleasant, and looking down, I could see a huge grassy field, full of red and yellow flowers. Little bunnies hopped around here and there, and in the distance was a group of sheep—mostly white, one grey, one black.

Beautiful. I thought of *Lupe*.

"Awesome," I said. "And hey—there's the sheep over there!"

We returned to the pack and led everyone through the forest back to the colorful and sunny meadow we found.

Soon, we were all working together to keep the sheep in a huddle while Logan, Boris, and Rolf, darted into the group of prey and eventually took them all down. After Logan and Moon had their fill, the rest of us were free to eat what we wanted.

I chomped down on the raw mutton and filled my belly. The sun was high, a gentle breeze blew through the meadow, and I felt warm and happy. Archie ate next to me, and I watched Lupe from afar, dreaming of a day when I would be brave enough to *decide* she was my mate.

Life was good.

Day 2

Today Archie and I went for a swim.

It wasn't necessary to go looking for more food yet, according to the alpha, so we were instructed to stay together, for the most part.

As a pack, we didn't eat every day. But sometimes, I got lucky and found a piece of rotten zombie flesh on the ground after the undead mobs burned up in the morning. Today wasn't one of those days, but it happened *sometimes*.

Anyway, it was fortunate that the mountain creek was just down the hill. Archie and I were able to run down and swim, while the rest of the pack sat around digesting all of the mutton we ate yesterday.

A section of the creek was nice and deep, so my friend and I splashed around and competed to see who could dog-paddle the longest. Archie won most of those times, but I know that I'm *faster* than him on the ground, ha ha.

There was a bit of a commotion around lunchtime when my mother happened upon a skeleton archer that was hiding in the shadows under a large pine tree. She gasped and back-pedaled as the undead creature raised his bow and started firing arrows into our midst.

Arnou was nearby, and responded immediately, with Colin close behind.

As the warrior wolves worked together to flank the skeleton, the mob did get *one* decent shot off, and Colin yelped as an arrow sank into his side. But the two strong wolves lashed out quickly, and were able to latch onto the skeleton's arms and legs, taking him down in no time. Only bones remained.

Colin and Arnou each took a bone, and went back to their business of lounging with the pack.

"Are you okay?" I said to my mother.

"Yes, thank you, Dakota," she said. "I'm glad you were out of the way."

"Oh come on, mom," I said. "I could have taken him."

"I know you could have, sweetie," she replied, and licked my face.

I don't know why the skeleton attacked. Sometimes the mobs attacked us. Sometimes not. Sometimes we (especially Colin and Arnou) attacked *them*. We did *love* zombie meat and skeleton bones, but I've never felt the urge to outright *attack* one of the undead to get it. I knew that if we were patient, we would always find more sheep and get plenty to eat.

Later that day, Archie caught me staring at Lupe, and decided to give me a hard time.

"You should go and *talk* to her, man!" he said, nudging me with his snout in her direction. Lupe noticed the movement, and looked over at us. I saw her beautiful, dark eyes for an instant, and then I turned away.

"Cut it out, man! Jeez!" I shoved him back with my body. "You made her look!"

"So what?" he said. "What's wrong with looking?" He laughed. "Maybe she *should* look. Then something will finally *happen*!"

I stole a glance back to her from the corner of my eye. She had looked away, and was laying in the grass again, looking at the

610

clouds as they rolled by. Usually she hung out around her mother, Leloo, but she was by herself for the moment.

Could I? Did I dare?

"Look, dude," Archie said. "She's by herself. *Go for it!*"

I gulped, and looked back at my friend. I looked around at all of the other pack members. They weren't paying any attention. Just going about their own things.

Padding silently through the grass, I approached. Quiet. Well, not *too* quiet. Didn't want to look like I was sneaking up on her! I just didn't want to look *loud*. Okay, I needed to be a *little* louder.

Snap. Crunch. I made some random noises on the ground as I approached.

Jeez, I thought. *I'm being a total weirdo! What am I doing?*

Lupe turned her head to my approach, and when I saw her face, my heart fluttered.

"Hi, Dakota!" she said.

She was happy. Good. I wanted to see her happy. Make her happy. Umm ... if she *wanted* to be happy. Then I'd help her be happy. *What?*

"Oh ... hi," I said. Gulped.

She watched. Smiled. Waited patiently. What would I say? I couldn't really think of anything.

"How's it going?" she asked.

"Good. *Great!*" I said. "*Really* great!"

"That's cool," she replied.

I looked back, and saw Archie watching. He nudged at me with his nose from far away. *Go on*, he said without words.

"Uh," I said, "How are you?"

Lupe smiled and looked back at the clouds.

"Oh, I'm fine, thanks." Her tail gave a little wag.

"So, uh," I said, trying to think of something to talk about. "Did you get plenty of mutton yesterday? Lots to eat? I hope you ate a lot! *I mean*—not that it looks like you eat a lot, or too much. I mean—you're not *fat* or anything; I didn't think you look fat—"

Her face contorted in confusion.

Holy heck! What was I doing?

"Um … I'm sorry! I'm not calling you fat I just … uh …"

Lupe laughed a nervous laugh.

"Ah … yeah," she said. "I got plenty to eat. Thanks to *you*."

"Um … me, and *Archie*. We found the sheep."

"Yeah, she said. "I know." She smiled, then watched the clouds.

"Yeah," I responded. I watched her, trying to think of something to say that wasn't completely *boneheaded*. After a few moments, she noticed me *staring*, and looked back at me. I looked up to the sky.

Her tail gave a small wag.

"Okay, well," I said, "I guess I'll go see how Archie is doing."

"Oh, really?" she asked. "Well, okay, I guess…"

"Okay," I said. "Well, bye."

"Bye," she said, gave me a smile, then looked back to the clouds she was watching.

I walked back to my friend feeling like an idiot, being careful not to walk like a weirdo.

Later that night, I laid in the grass, watching the stars. As the square moon moved across the sky, I looked at a thousand little pinpricks of light, shining and twinkling far, far away, drifting through space.

Most of the pack was already asleep. I could see Lupe sleeping next to her mom. Archie was sleeping near me, and the rest of the pack kept close together—my mother, the warriors and hunters, Leloo. The alphas slept away from us, a little ways up the hill.

The night was quiet, aside from the occasional zombie moan far in the distance, or the hissing of spiders climbing the trees. I was a little hungry, but tried to ignore my belly.

The stars all looked down at me from the vast, black sky, watching over all of us. So pretty.

Day 3

The morning started like all others.

We woke up and the pack was abuzz with hunger. It would be another scouting day for Archie and me. I ran down to the creek to splash cold water on my face, and found a piece of zombie flesh.

Even though I was hungry, I decided not to eat it. I took the delicious piece of meat in my mouth, careful not to sink my teeth into its sweet and smelly goodness, and brought it to my mom.

"Aw, *thanks*, honey!" she said. "Do you want to split it with me?"

"No, that's okay, mom. You have it," I said.

"But you're probably going to go looking for a herd with Archie today, right? You should take some and have the energy."

"That's alright, mom. I'll eat later."

"Okay, but I'll hang onto half of it in case you change your mind, okay?" She started to eat the zombie meat.

As we expected, Logan called on Archie and I to go out and find another herd of sheep. We happily complied, and ran through the forest for the better part of an hour, seeking out prey for the pack.

It was a warm day, and the breeze in my face felt great! My feet were fast, and the forest smelled good, and I ran like the wind. After a while, I caught the scent of mutton, and led Archie to a small herd of sheep wandering around in dense trees.

"There's our meal ticket!" Archie said. "Let's go back!"

"Let's *do it!*" I said, and we laughed as we sprinted through the woods back to the pack.

After dodging through the trees, leaping over boulders, and running silently through the straights like grey ghosts, we approached the forest clearing where the pack was living.

But something was *wrong*.

As we came down the hill, past enough trees to see the clearing, I smelled a weird smell. Something different that I hadn't smelled before. Something *alien*. And as we approached closer, I heard the sounds of battle!

Zombies moaned and growled. Skeletons clattered. Bows twanged, and arrows whistled through the air. I heard growls and scratches, thumps and crashes. Yelps and cries and raw wolf snarls!

"What the—?" Archie cried, as we ran down to the clearing.

Our pack was *fighting for their lives* against a group of zombies and skeletons!

I couldn't count how many of the undead were down there—the scene was confusing. For some reason, the battle was taking place in *broad daylight*, and the mobs weren't burning up in the sun!

In the chaos before us, I had a very hard time making out who was alive and who was already dead. The alpha was obviously still alive, running to and fro between the undead, striking with power and mainly pulling the attackers off of the other wolves. Moon, I think, was doing the same. Several wolves lay dead. My stomach suddenly turned cold...

**CHECK OUT
SKELETONSTEVE.COM**
... to CONTINUE READING!

Enjoy this Excerpt from...

"Diary of a **Teenage Zombie Villager**" Book 1

<u>About the book</u>:

Devdan wasn't your typical teenager.

He was a Minecraft villager.

And he was a *zombie*.

He spent his days and nights doing *zombie stuff*.

The zombie Devdan couldn't even remember his name anymore, that is, until he was visited by the pet cat he had when he was alive. Now, along with Skeleton Steve's help, Devdan sets out with his long-lost kitty to remember who he is and find his village home. But how will he find the way? And what will he do if he gets there? Will Devdan be destined to roam the Minecraft world as a *zombie villager* forever?

Love Minecraft adventure??

Read on for an Excerpt for the book!

Night 1

I don't know why, but I had this journal in my pack.

How is it that I can write? I don't remember how I *learned* to write, or how I'm reading what I'm writing. Am I reading?

Who am I?

There must have been a reason for this book to be in my pack. I suppose it was mine. So I may as well write.

Well …

There isn't much to write about right now.

When I came out from the shadows tonight, I was in a dark and cold place. The pine trees were dark and snowy, and the ground made frozen *crunching* sounds under my feet.

As the square moon moved across the sky above me, I walked through the mountain forest, watching the other mobs around me.

Mobs? Why did I call them that?

They must be called that. I don't remember how, but I guess I *knew*.

Looking down at my stubby arms, I could see that my skin was green.

There were others around me with green skin as well. They dotted the landscape, shadows of zombies standing and shuffling around through the snow all around me.

Zombies? What were zombies?

I guess I was a zombie.

I didn't remember much before the sun went down tonight. I just knew that I was *hungry*.

Hungry.

I walked with the other zombies for a while.

"Where are you going?" I asked one of them.

A zombie looked at me with a long, soft moan. His shirt was light blue, and partly pulled out of his pants. His eyes were black and dull, and his face empty. He regarded me for a moment, then stuck his arms out in front of him and continued plodding along the way he was going. *Crunch, crunch, crunch*, through the snow.

"Where are you going?" I asked again, in a *different* way.

The zombie looked back at me and stopped.

"We are going over *there*," he said. "There is a village that way, I think. Why were you speaking in *villager*?"

"Villager?" I asked.

"The language of the villager people!" the zombie replied.

Language? What was *language?* Oh yeah … I guess I had forgotten. Language is the way people speak to each other. I knew *two* different languages. Why in the world did I know the *villager* language?

"I don't know," I said.

"You *look* like them," the zombie said. "You were a villager before, I think..."

"I don't remember," I said.

The zombie turned and moved on.

There were many other zombies going in the same direction, across the snowy fields under the great mountain peaks. I walked with them until morning.

When the sun rose over the frozen horizon, we all suddenly burst into flames! The fire burned at my zombie body, burned at my clothes, but I didn't feel any pain.

Pain? What was pain? I didn't remember.

624

After a few wild seconds of wandering around *on fire*, the flames went out, and I was still alive, under a tree...

Other zombies around me were not so lucky. Some of them stayed in the fields, and burned until they were consumed, fell, and disappeared in a flash of ash and smoke. Only smoldering chunks of their bodies remained, sitting in the brilliant, white snow. Others made it into the shade, some on purpose, some on accident. Their burning bodies eventually calmed down, outside the deadly sunlight, and the flames snuffed out.

I was determined to stay under this pine tree until the sun went down again. It was obvious that the sunlight would kill us zombies! *Why I didn't realize that until just now?* I wondered.

I would try to remember.

Sunlight. Bad.

How long had I been a zombie? More than one night, I was sure.

Or was it?

In the shade of the pine tree, I watched as the sun crept up the horizon, filling the snowy, frozen mountainside with bright light and a trace of warmth...

Night 2

What's this *diary* in my pack?

The cover of the book had a single, scrawled sentence:

After reading through the diary, it looked like someone had written a single entry about a night of walking through the snowy mountains with a group of other zombies.

How about that? I didn't know I could *read*!

Was that just *last night?*

Did I write this?

I didn't remember. I guess I'll write some more later to see if the previous writer was *me*. If the handwriting looked the same, it had to be me, right??

I was still in the snowy mountains.

When the sun went down, I stepped out into a snowy field from under a pine tree.

Other zombies around me were moving as a group in one direction.

I followed.

My frozen, slow feet plodded along tirelessly, crunching through the snow.

I saw others in the darkness around me—more than just zombies! There were skeletons—their bones clattering as they wandered the darkness, bow in hand. Big, fat spiders could be seen as black shadows here and there, like blots of ink against the snow, easily visible because of their multiple red glowing eyes. They hissed and scuttled around the landscape, climbing trees and cliffs. And I saw silent, green sausage-shaped creatures on four tiny, stubby legs, quietly exploring in the darkness...

"What's *that?*" I said to the nearest zombie, speaking in the *mob* language he would understand. I pointed to one of the green creatures.

Mob language? What did *that* mean? Where did *that* come from?

I felt so confused!

"That ... *creeper*," the zombie replied, and shuffled off.

The 'creeper' was a strange-looking creature indeed. It stood and looked around as we walked by, turned and wandered silently through the snow, then, watched everything around it some more. Its face was dark and haunting, a gaping frown disapproving of the world around it.

I suddenly saw something *small* running across the snowy field toward the creeper I was watching, and the frowning green creature *fled* in the opposite direction!

The tiny mob that chased away the green creature did not pursue it. Small, black and white, the little animal sat in the snow for a moment, then, continued along its speedy path...

To me!

I stopped in the snow.

The nearest zombies around me paused when they noticed my change. They all looked at me for a moment with dull eyes, then, raised their arms again, moaned, and walked on.

The approaching small creature moved with *great speed*, faster than any other mobs around me—much faster than us zombies—and closed the distance in no time! I raised my zombie arms, ready to defend myself...

"Meow," it said.

Now that the little monster was closer, I could get a better look! Standing in the snow in front of me on four little legs, with a black and white tail swishing around in the cold air, the strange creature had bold, green eyes, and it tilted its cute, little head to one side as it regarded me from down below.

"Meow."

Kitty cat, my zombie brain said.

Kitty cat? What was a *kitty cat*?

Did I know what this creature was?

I couldn't remember...

But it was *very* interested in me.

"Meow," it repeated.

"What do you want, kitty cat?" I asked.

"Meow." It tilted its head the other way.

Where did this *cat* come from? Why was it up here in the snowy mountains? And why was it so interested in *me*?

The kitty cat approached closer, its tiny feet crunching in the snow, until it circled around my zombie legs, pushing and rubbing its cute little head up against my ankles through my tattered, brown leggings.

"Meow! *Purrrr purrrr...*" it said.

I reached down and touched the creature's soft, furry body; touched its black and white head with my clumsy zombie hands.

"Who *are* you?" I said.

"Meow," it replied.

"Do I know you?" I asked.

"Meow," the cat said.

If I *did* know this cat, I didn't remember it. I could see up ahead that the snowy mountain field descended into a green valley, where the trees eventually thinned out, until great, wide grassy plains stretched out for miles.

The zombies around me moaned and kept moving on, down toward the grasslands...

And in the distant valley, I could see the faint light of a torch!

A village??

I was definitely hungry for villagers to eat! That must be where all of these zombies around me were heading!

Is that village what I wanted? I couldn't remember.

Paying attention to the upcoming town, I continued walking, plodding through the snow, and forgot about the cat. When I remembered suddenly, I looked back again behind me...

"Meow," it said.

The cat was still with me, and was following me as I descended down into the valley.

The closer we zombies got to the village, the more I heard the sounds of battle. The living villagers screamed and squawked, fleeing from the zombies that were already in town, barricading themselves into their homes! They slammed their wooden doors, and screamed and cried as the zombies tried to break into their houses.

I heard wooden doors crash and break to pieces!

"Hold the door!" someone yelled, far below.

"Are we all that's left?" another villager shouted. "Don't let them inside!"

Zombies moaned and snarled and bashed on doors!

Even though I tried to get down to the village as fast as my slow zombie legs would carry me, I was afraid that the zombies who arrived before me would kill and eat *all of the villagers* before I could get there!

So hungry!

Crash!

I heard the splintering of another wooden door being broken apart.

"We're finished!" someone yelled. "Run! Get out! Get out!"

Screams. Sounds of battle.

When I arrived at the village and stepped onto the cobblestone street, I didn't hear the voices of any other villagers. I wandered through the skinny roads, past the town's well, and peered into each open doorway. Pieces of wooden doors and other debris were scattered all around!

No one. No villagers.

Other zombies milled about. There were even a few skeletons here and there, and a spider up on a roof.

But no villagers. They were all either killed before I arrived, or, whoever was left in the end just *ran away*...

Looking behind me, I saw the cat. He followed me, black-bodied, with white paws and a white chest. His green eyes watched me constantly.

His? I thought.

I shrugged. Did I remember this cat being a *he*?

Looking around the village, I let out a long, moaning sigh. There was nothing for me here...

I wandered away from the village into the grassy field nearby. When the sun was about to rise, I was near the tree-line. It was a good thing, too, because when the rays of the dazzling square of burning light pierced the night sky, and the day began, I *burst into flames!*

There was no pain, but I remembered from reading this journal and what I presumably wrote the night before, that my best chance to survive was to get under a tree!

I found a tall oak tree at the edge of the field. Once I stood in its shadow, the flames eventually died down, and I was safe again for the day.

"Meow," the kitty cat said. He crazily darted around me until the fire went out, then, cautiously approached my smoldering body. The cat sat down next to me in the grass.

I watched as random zombies and skeletons in the field burned to death. They fell, then were reduced to piles of ash...

Standing under the oak tree all day, I listened to the wind whistle across the open plains. The apples in the tree shook in the branches above me.

At one point, clouds rolled in, and it began to rain.

When the rain died down, the sun came out, and the world was clear and bright again!

My cat companion watched me most of the time, and alternated between sitting in the grass, wandering around by my feet, and climbing the rock and dirt blocks directly around us.

Reminder to self—stay out of the sunlight! Just in case I don't remember...

I looked at the cover of the diary.

Oh yeah, I thought. *I guess I already thought of that!*

Night 3

When I started paying attention again, I noticed the cat.

He was still with me.

Still with me? I had a memory of this black and white cat, the small creature down by my feet with the green eyes. And a memory of a village. *Last night maybe?*

It was hard to tell.

This journal I'm writing in right now had two previous entries. Was I the writer? I couldn't remember!

All I could recall was the cat. And a village...

Zombies attacking villagers.

According to this book's cover, I should stay out of the sunlight. It looks like at the end of these last two nights, I was having problems catching on fire whenever the morning came—at least on the last two nights I wrote about!

Was it last night? Whatever...

Sunlight bad. Good to know.

I supposed, since I was standing under an oak tree with apples in its branches, that I wrote the last entry the night before, where I left off. The diary mentioned standing under an oak tree with apples in its branches...

I really didn't remember!

In the distance, across the grassy field, I saw a village. A single torch cast a light from a lamp post in the center of town. Forms moved around among the streets and crop fields.

I was so hungry.

Well, if I were to believe this book in my hands, then it was likely that the villagers living there were all dead or gone. So, the folks I saw moving around over there were *probably* other zombies.

Easy enough to find out, I thought.

As I stepped out from under the oak tree into the open night sky, the cat followed.

"Meow," he said.

"What is it?" I replied.

The kitty cat ran up to my legs. "Meow, *purrrr...*"

I reached down and stroked his head with my clumsy zombie hand. "Let's go, cat," I said.

It was funny that I couldn't remember anything other than the cat and the village. Maybe if I investigated the village, I might remember more! I could read and re-read what the journal said, of course, and I *did* read it, but nothing helped me remember.

But—*if*—according to this book, I started each night not remembering *anything*, then why did I suddenly remember the *cat*?

So confusing...

The cat and I approached the village to find it empty, aside from the undead. The doors of most of the little homes were destroyed, the crops were ready to harvest but left unattended, and only *mobs* roamed the streets.

I approached the town's water supply and looked down into the well at the zombies climbing up from its depths...

"Hey," a male voice said from behind me. "It's *you!*"

I turned.

Standing in an open doorway of an abandoned house was a *skeleton*. He looked like all of the other skeletons I'd seen before, but had a pack on his back, and his *eyes* were different! Instead of the black, empty eye sockets of the random skeletons I saw out in the wild, *this* undead fellow had tiny, pin-point *dots of red light* in his otherwise dark eye cavities. The little red lights darted about as he looked around, but mostly focused on *me*. The skeleton's special eyes made him look more intelligent somehow...

"Who are *you?*" I asked.

He walked over, stepping around the mostly mindless undead. His bones *clunked.*

"You *zombies...*" he said with a smirk. "You forget *everything,* don't you?" He slung his bow around his shoulder and onto his back. "I'm Skeleton Steve. You know me!"

I pondered his bony face. The lively red lights in his eye sockets didn't seem familiar...

"I'm sorry, Skeleton Steve," I said. "I don't remember you."

"Doesn't surprise me," he said. "Lots of zombies have memory problems, it seems."

"My name is..." I paused. Thought about it. "My name—"

"Meow," the cat said, wandering around my legs. He looked up at us with brilliant, green eyes.

"Uh," I said, "I don't remember my name!"

Skeleton Steve put a bony hand on my shoulder. "Sorry, young zombie," he said. "That must be hard to deal with! I mean, if you *care*, that is..."

"I do!" I said. "I *do* care! This has been a strange ... few nights? It's hard to tell. I can't remember anything! But I think," I said, pulling out my journal, "I think that I *want* to..."

"Interesting," Skeleton Steve said, looking down at the cat, then, looking at the book in my hands.

"How do you know me, Skeleton Steve?"

"Well," he said, pointing at my journal. "I'm the one who gave you *that book!*"

... to CONTINUE READING!

Currently FREE!!

The Amazing Reader List

Thank you SO MUCH to these Readers and Reviewers! Your help in leaving reviews and spreading the word about my books is SO appreciated!

Awesome Reviewers:

MantisFang887 EpicDrago887

ScorpCraft SnailMMS WolfDFang

LegoWarrior70

Liam Burroughs

Ryan / Sean Gallagher

Habblie

Nirupam Bhagawati

Ethan MJC

Jacky6410 and Oscar

MasterMaker / Kale Aker

Cole

Kelly Nguyen

Ellesea & Ogmoe

K Mc / AlfieMcM

JenaLuv & Boogie

Han-Seon Choi

Danielle M

Oomab

So Cal Family

Daniel Geary Roberts

Jjtaup

Addidks / Creeperking987

D Guz / UltimateSword5

TJ

Xavier Edwards

DrTNT04

UltimateSword5

Mavslam

Ian / CKPA / BlazePlayz

Dana Hartley

Shaojing Li

Mitchell Adam Keith

Emmanuel Bellon

Melissa and Jacob Cross

Wyatt D and daughter

Jung Joo Lee

Dwduck and daughter

Yonael Yonas, the Creeper Tamer (Jesse)

Sarah Levy / shadowslayer1818

Pan

Phillip Wang / Jonathan55123

Ddudeboss

Hartley

Mitchell Adam Keith

L Stoltzman and sons

D4imond minc4rt

Bookworm_29

Tracie / Johnathan

Jeremyee49

Endra07 / Samuel Clemens

And, of course … Herobrine

(More are added all the time! Since this is a print version of this book, check the eBook version of the latest books—or the website—to see if your name is in there!)

Made in United States
Troutdale, OR
03/03/2025

29493293R00377